UNDERSTANDING LABOR AND EMPLOYMENT LAW IN CHINA

Continued economic prosperity in China and its international competitive advantage have been due in large part to the labor of workers in China, who for many years toiled in underregulated workplaces. Now, there are new labor law reforms raising the rights and standards of workers throughout China. These new laws have been praised for their progressive measures and, at the same time, blamed for placing too many economic burdens on companies, especially those operating on the margins, which in some cases have caused business failures. This, combined with the recent global downturn and the millions of displaced and unemployed Chinese migrant laborers, has created ongoing debate about the new labor laws. Meanwhile, the Chinese Union has organized Wal-Mart and many of the Global Fortune 500 companies, and a form of collective bargaining is occurring. Workers are pursuing their legal labor rights in increasing numbers.

This book provides a clear overview of the current labor and employment law environment in China and its legal requirements, as well as current practices under these laws used to deal with growing labor issues. Never has there been a time when understanding China's labor and employment laws was more important.

Ronald C. Brown is a professor of law at the University of Hawaii, where he has served as Associate Dean and as director of the University's Center for Chinese Studies. He has worked in China under the USIA's Professional-in-Residence Program, has served as a consultant with the World Bank, was a Distinguished Fulbright Scholar teaching at Peking and Tsinghua University Law Schools, and has lectured throughout Asia on comparative labor law topics.

Professor Brown currently serves as an active labor arbitrator. His teaching specialties include labor and employment law, employment discrimination law, arbitration, Chinese law, Asian International and Comparative Labor and Employment Law, and U.S.-China Labor and Employment Law. He has authored numerous articles and published a book, *Understanding Chinese Courts and Legal Process: Law with Chinese Characteristics.*

Understanding Labor and Employment Law in China

RONALD C. BROWN

School of Law, University of Hawaii

CAMBRIDGE
UNIVERSITY PRESS

CAMBRIDGE UNIVERSITY PRESS
Cambridge, New York, Melbourne, Madrid, Cape Town, Singapore,
São Paulo, Delhi, Dubai, Tokyo

Cambridge University Press
32 Avenue of the Americas, New York, NY 10013-2473, USA

www.cambridge.org
Information on this title: www.cambridge.org/9780521191487

© Ronald C. Brown 2010

First published 2010

Printed in the United States of America

A catalog record for this publication is available from the British Library.

Library of Congress Cataloging in Publication data

Brown, Ronald C.
Understanding labor and employment law in China / Ronald C. Brown. – 1st ed.
   p.   cm.
Includes bibliographical references and index.
ISBN 978-0-521-19148-7 (hardback)
1. Labor laws and legislation – China.   I. Title.
KNQ1270.B76   2009
344.5101 – dc22   2009011760

ISBN 978-0-521-19148-7 Hardback

Contents

Preface

China now has its legal system in place, and in recent years it has assembled substantive laws and regulations that govern the workplace, the employment relationship, and the contractual and statutory rights and benefits of its workers. As China moves ahead to raise the legal standards and levels of coverage and enforcement in these areas and its social security safety net, it also seeks to balance its very successful economic growth and competitive advantages especially as these relate to labor. Employers face increasing obligations and technical legal requirements, which in earlier years did not exist or at least were not consistently enforced. The current global economic downturn now puts added pressures on China to maintain advancement in labor and employment laws.

Although the Labor Law was issued in 1994 with its broad outlines and promises of regulation, the more substantive labor and employment laws were not issued and put into operation until the mid-2000s.

Suddenly, in the mid-2000s, Wal-Mart was unionized and the Chinese trade union, the All China Federation of Trade Unions (ACFTU), launched organization drives aimed especially at the Global Fortune 500 companies doing business in China. Early draft provisions of the new Labor Contract Law sent the American Chambers of Commerce reeling and arguing that the new labor laws and added regulations and costs would drive American companies out of the country. The discussion was so intense that the Chinese government raised issues about foreign interference in China's affairs.

By 2008, this law was operating and many related labor laws, the subject of this book, were dealt with by employers throughout China. Employees took their labor disputes to the government-provided labor arbitration in record numbers. Employers, as well as employees, became hungry for guidance on how to handle their labor and employment rights and obligations. Understanding human resource management and the laws regulating it became necessary, as the stakes for noncompliant employers became significant. Even the government-organized ACFTU began more aggressive efforts to organize and obtain contract protections for workers as they slowly, but perceptively, began increased separation from the employer in their daily functions.

This book is written for readers seeking to understand the current labor-related legal environment in China's workplaces. What laws and regulations exist? What is required? And how are the rights and benefits they bestow enforced? It is not written in such detail that legal practitioners will know where and how to file their legal documents, but those who are interested in business, human resource management, or worker rights, or just in knowing more about China's recent developments will have a well-based introduction to the laws and regulations in China's workplaces. Some readers will notice the areas of law still needing reform, and others will be surprised how well-developed and sophisticated many of the Chinese labor and employment laws are.

It is with the hope of adding insight and understanding into the area of Chinese labor and employment law and providing a benchmark of comprehensive examination of the area for future research and publications that this book is written.

Acknowledgments

The content of this book comes from off-and-on years of living and teaching in China, mostly in Beijing at Peking University Law School, but also at Tsinghua University Law School, both as a Distinguished Fulbright Scholar and also conducting training and exchange programs over the past two decades with Chinese government officials, including with the now Ministry of Human Resources and Social Security (MOHRSS).

One of my early mentors in the area of Chinese labor laws was Professor Jia Junling, labor law professor at Peking University Law School, who first allowed me to teach her students, continued to be my friend and teacher over several decades, and who has been intimately involved from the beginning in the creation of the labor laws now regulating China's workplaces. Her colleague at People's University Law School, Professor Guan Huai, whose credentials in labor law are unparalleled, also provided me counsel and insight over the years. Both were present, as was I, at the unveiling and implementation of the new Labor Law in 1994; and each continues to advise on and review new labor laws.

In more recent years, Professor Ye Jingyi at Peking University Law School assisted me in understanding Chinese labor laws and continues to provide opportunities to meet with and learn from the current leaders in the field. Jiang Junlu, now a lawyer at King and Wood, a leading law firm in Beijing, who also serves as Chair of the All China Lawyers Association Labor Law Committee, gives regular support to me in my ongoing understanding of the intricacies and practicalities of the current labor laws. Also, Earnest Zhou, Professor of Labor Law at Nanjing University Law School, has been helpful to me in understanding Chinese labor law. Both Professors Ye and Zhou were students of Professor Jia, as was attorney Jiang. My years as Director of Chinese Studies at the University of Hawaii and my stints as a consultant with the World Bank working with China's Ministry of Labor also contributed to my understanding of the Chinese and the Chinese legal system.

I also want to acknowledge the very significant technical assistance provided to me on this project by my research assistants at the University of Hawaii Law School, Wu Jing and Lan Na. Wu Jing ferreted out, collected, and analyzed untold tomes of laws and articles of possible relevance to my teaching a course on Chinese labor law here and in China and also used for this book. Lan Na, a third-year law student, more recently has assisted greatly in putting this book in proper form and providing the depth of her Chinese understanding to guide me in the appropriate contents of relevant legal comment. Wu Jing has now graduated and is working in China as a labor lawyer with the law firm of King and Wood.

Lastly, I wish to acknowledge my lovely wife, Mangmang, who has assisted and supported me in so many ways on this and all projects in life. Her keen mind, legal background, inherent understanding of "Chinese characteristics," and her endless encouragement are always assets to me as I move forward.

Understanding Labor and
Employment Law in China

PART I

UNDERSTANDING CHINA'S REGULATION OF THE WORKPLACE

1

Introduction

While settling into my seat at 35,000 feet as the second leg of my flight left Japan for China, a passenger next to me asked if this was my first trip there. I replied it wasn't and that I had been involved in China's legal developments over the years. He said he was going there to explore investing in China, but he had heard that the labor laws had come to undercut the advantages of operating in China and asked if that were true. That, I replied, depends on how well you understand China, its Chinese characteristics, and the variables affecting its workers. Some workplaces are sterile laboratories with highly trained and well-paid technicians, and others can be grimy, dangerous factories that use migrant labor and have no concern for labor standards: the significance of the labor laws depends on the size of these sectors in a country with more than 800,000,000 workers! Though I may have detected a faint glazing in his eyes, he said he needed to understand how the workplace is regulated and urged me to continue and to provide him with some insights and guidelines into China's new legal environment and approaches in regulating the workplace. So, I began.

Balancing Economic Development and Labor Reforms

The story of how labor and employment issues are dealt with on an everyday basis begins with an understanding of China and insight into its system of legal regulation. The Chinese workplace is a reflection of the diverse impacts of phenomenal economic development, tightening regulations, and an evolving safety net in the workplace. It is set in urban and rural areas; in manufacturing, construction, and heavy and light industries; and in white-collar jobs. In many sectors, there is a more stable and slowly evolving skilled workforce that has come to expect and demand better labor standards and protections. Add to this the ebb and flow of more than 150 million migrant workers into the urban areas and the absence of traditions of labor laws and law enforcement, and the image of China's workplaces comes into clearer focus. It is the story of how those workplaces accommodate to China's labor and employment laws and make them work.

Relatively low wages and labor standards for workers in China are usually initially credited for its continuing economic development and its sustained annual growth in the double digits. In recent years, with the transition to a market economy and privatization, these same low labor standards have evoked international and domestic pressures; in response, China's leaders have introduced labor reforms. These reforms attempt to meet worker needs while at the same time maintaining economic development and economic competitiveness. Since the issuance of the Labor Law in 1994, there has been a steady growth in labor legislation seeking to find that balance, provide a worker safety net, promote social and political stability, and address the often disparate effects of the economic miracle.

Labor reforms, like economic reforms, have had an uneven impact on China's 800 million workers. Rural workers too often fall outside the protection of the labor laws; and better wages and working conditions are more likely available in the urban areas that have benefitted from economic development, particularly the eastern coastal regions and cities. This concentration of workplace opportunities has worked like a magnet to attract the migration of nearly 150 million rural workers to urban areas. These migrant laborers are concentrated in manufacturing and construction and are often the victims of unpaid wages and substandard working conditions.

The great diversity of China's workplaces continues to hinder the focused application and enforcement of the newly emerging labor laws. State-owned enterprises (SOEs), former SOEs, private enterprises, foreign-invested enterprises (FIEs), and large and small enterprises all present varied challenges to local governments seeking to regulate the workplace. Employers are also mindful that they risk the loss of competitiveness if they comply with labor standards while their competitors do not.

1. Use of Laws to Regulate the Workplace

China's new legal system was developed since the *Four Modernizations* in the late 1970s. Centuries of traditions and China's more recent socialist and civil law heritage have blended together to create its present legal system, laden with Chinese characteristics. Although legislatures and government agencies serve as sources of law, as in the West, in China other legal institutions, such as the Supreme People's Court that issues interpretations guiding the courts in their application of the laws, serve that purpose as well.

China's recent explosion of new labor laws, implemented in 2008, ranging from the Labor Contract Law (LCL), the Employment Promotion Law (EPL), and the Labor Dispute Mediation and Arbitration Law (LMA), as well as laws dealing with related topics of mergers and acquisitions and bankruptcy, must be understood in the context of China's burgeoning economy and concern for social stability. Chinese legal regulations, based on legal traditions in civil law and of course with "Chinese characteristics," may appear somewhat similar to Western laws. However, under China's political-legal system, the lawmaking organs and the enforcement mechanisms often function differently from those in the West. The National People's Congress (NPC) and its Standing Committee enact legislation, the State Council issues regulations, and the Ministries formulate rules; their local government counterparts also issue laws and regulations. The legal system operates under a "rule-by-law" approach (with legislative supremacy), and the enforcement processes are distributed differently from Western law, involving numerous layers of government and legal institutions.[1]

How Chinese laws operate is surprising to many in the West. The relationship between central and local governments and their relative authority in legislation and enforcement form a practical reality that must be dealt with. Although China is a former socialist state, it generally has a decentralized government. Central government laws (such as the 1994 Labor Law) are often merely general guidelines that thereafter depend on consistent "local implementing regulations," legislated and enforced by appropriate local authorities. For that reason, it has taken some time to provide meaningful labor protections to its workers. Labor disputes are channeled through familiar routes of alternative dispute resolution machinery, though they play out somewhat differently than in the West.

Labor laws are generally administered by the various divisions of the local labor bureaus, which are under the central ministry but, in large part, are horizontally (locally) financed and staffed. Likewise, enforcement is generally handled at the local level. In recent years there has been a growth in the number of specialized administrative agencies that, with their local labor bureau counterparts, administer and supervise specific labor law programs. One of the constant criticisms of China's labor laws is the lack of consistent enforcement by the government. However, labor disputes in China are resolved mostly by individual workers through local governmental mediation

[1] *See* RANDALL PEERENBOOM, CHINA'S LONG MARCH TOWARD RULE OF LAW (2002).

and arbitration. The number of these cases has risen dramatically every year as new laws are passed and an increased awareness of labor rights takes hold in the workforce. In the heavy manufacturing area of Guangzhou in 2008 there was a more than 200 percent increase in the number of labor disputes after the new Labor Contract Law took effect.[2] Courts are available to enforce or review many of these labor arbitrations. Recently, the courts have been authorized to directly determine certain wage claims without the prior requirement of undergoing the labor arbitration process.

2. Disparate Economic Impacts in the Workplace

China's economic development began in earnest after Deng Xiaoping began his "Four Modernizations" in 1979. Since that time many economic and legal reforms have taken place. This economic development has been uneven, causing regional and urban/rural disparities that, in turn, have brought about an influx of millions of rural workers into the cities for better work opportunities, though not necessarily better treatment or working conditions. Many of the significant labor and employment laws are applied only in the urban areas, with some additional laws applying to certain aspects of employment in the rural areas.

With the transition from the "iron rice bowl system" to labor contracts, China has moved from a socialist planned economy using SOEs to a socialist market economy.[3] Privatization, layoffs, and new management strategies emphasizing profits and competition have produced both a "wage consciousness" and feelings of unfairness among workers because of regional wage disparities, occupational wage gaps, unequal job opportunities, and sagging labor and security safety nets.

Economic growth has produced a 100 to 150 million person "floating population" (predominantly underpaid migrant workers) seeking to earn their share of the pie. It also has produced national scandals in which employers refuse to pay the wages of migrant workers, presently an underclass in China. Coal miners are dying by the thousands each year because of unsafe working conditions. Consequently, the issue of better enforcement of the labor protections provided in the labor laws is part of the labor reform agenda.

China is at a crossroads. On the one hand, it has the necessary resources to make its labor law system work much better than it does. On the other

---

[2] Labor arbitration cases soaring, english.people.com.cn/90001/6551417.html.
[3] For a discussion of workers in SOEs, *see* WILLIAM HURST, THE CHINESE WORKER AFTER SOCIALISM (2009).

hand, labor relations have seemed to come second to the forces of economic development, and China seems unsure whether, if it makes the choice to better enforce its labor laws, it will be placed at a competitive disadvantage internationally. Employers who might otherwise follow the labor laws are in a quandary; why spend the money to follow these laws if they are not enforced?[4]

To understand the nuances of current employment relations in China, one must put them into the context of China's fast-moving economic transition. When the scope of economic transition broadened from policies establishing special economic development zones into policies transforming all of China's economy from a socialist planned economy to a socialist market economy, social and economic changes were both expected and indeed occurred. With a market economy came competition, the need for more flexible management, and the quest for profits – which required cutting costs. For China's labor-intensive industrial economy, this usually meant keeping labor costs low. Privatization and competitive measures brought layoffs (especially in the already overstaffed SOEs) and kept wages and benefits to bare minimums. With individual control waning, conditions fostered efforts to achieve workers' economic improvement through collective negotiations.

Wage concerns of workers came to have increasing importance as widening gaps occurred in the annual growth of real wages versus GNP, with great numbers of workers feeling left out. China's impressive economic growth in GNP for more than two decades was not matched by the real wage growth of workers, which has roughly kept pace with rates of inflation.[5] The lawful minimum wage in China varies by locales according to local economic factors, reflecting the national mandate under China's Regulations on Minimum Wage.[6] According to those regulations, China seeks to accommodate an international labor standard that sets local minimum wages within the range of

---

[4] Simon Clark, Chang-Hee Lee and Qi Li, *Collective Consultation and Industrial Relations in China*, British Journal of Industrial Relations, June 2004, at 248.

[5] The comparison of ILO official statistics (ILO LABORSTA database) to the rate of inflation shows that there was at least a relative wage decline among Chinese manufacturing workers. *See* Anita Chan, *A Race to the Bottom*, 46 CHINA PERSPECTIVES 41, 42 (2003). According to the ILO LABORSTA database, in 1993 the average wage at all economic enterprises was about 281 yuan/month and in 2006 it was 1750 yuan/month. Not surprisingly, the lowest average in 2006, 786 yuan/month, was in the agricultural services area, whereas the highest was in the financial sector (3273 yuan/month). In manufacturing, the average was 1497 yuan/month. See ILO LABORSTA, *Table 5A Wages, by Economic Activity*, available at http://laborsta.ilo.org/ (last visited Aug. 2, 2008).

[6] Zui di gong zi gui ding [Regulations on Minimum Wage] art. 6 (promulgated by Ministry of Labor and Social Security, Jan 20, 2004, effective Mar. 1, 2004), http://www.chinacourt.org/flwk/show1.php?file_id=91496 (last visited Aug. 2, 2008) [hereinafter Reg. Minim. Wage].

40 percent to 60 percent of the average wage standard in the locality.[7] One source states that in 1993 China's average minimum wages met or exceeded the 40 percent minimum, but by the late 1990s there had been a steady and consistent erosion below that minimum.[8] (The old interim measure to regulate FIE wages was abolished in 2004.)

Some Chinese citizens were able to realize Deng Xiaoping's famous slogan, "to get rich is glorious," much faster than others, and with economic reforms came great wage diversity between regions, between urban and rural areas, and between management and labor. In 2007, average income ranged from 3,432 yuan per month in Shanghai to 1,601 yuan per month in Chonqing.[9] Minimum wage variations between local governments ranged from 850 yuan per month in Nanjing to 730 yuan per month in Beijing.[10]

Observations by former World Bank President James Wolfensohn about China's wage gaps have raised alarms; he stated that their likely consequence is social unrest.[11] According to the World Bank, China in the past twenty years has achieved great progress in reducing the number of people in poverty (insufficient food and clothing) from 200 million people to 29 million, but

---

[7] Reg. Minim. Wage, Attachment Section 2. Calculations Methods of Minimum Wage Standard. The 40%–60% range is the international standard used when calculating the minimum wage.

[8] Chan, *supra*, note 4, at 42. In Beijing in 2000 the average wage was reported at 1,362.30 yuan/month and the minimum wage at 412 yuan/month. See Beijing Labor and Social Security Bureau, Guan yu tiao zheng 2000 nian Beijingshi zui di gong zi biao zhun de tong zhi [Notice on 2000 Beijing Minimum Wage Guideline] (June 27, 2000), http://www.bjld.gov.cn/tszl/zdshbz/t20010907_2142.htm (last visited Aug. 2, 2008). Beijing's minimum wage in July, 2008 was reported at 800 yuan/month. See Beijing Labor and Social Security Bureau, Guan yu tiao zheng 2008 nian Beijingshi zui di gong zi biao zhun de tong zhi [Notice on 2008 Beijing Minimum Wage Guideline] (June 30, 2008), http://www.bjld.gov.cn/zxzx/zxzc/t20080701_402248451.htm (last visited Aug. 2, 2008). The exact average wage of workers earning in China is difficult to ascertain, and it varies by political districts. According to a 2004 survey conducted by one research institute under the Development Research Center of the State Council (DRCSC), 70.8% of Chinese urban employees earned 800 to 2,500 yuan (US$96.74 to US$302.3) monthly. See *Chinese Urban Employees Earn More*, CHINA DAILY, May 31, 2004, http://www.chinadaily.com.cn/english/doc/2004-05/31/content_335250.htm (last visted Aug. 2, 2008).

[9] 2007 CHINA STATISTICAL YEARBOOK, *Table 5-23.*

[10] See Nanjing Labor and Social Security Bureau, Guan yu tiao zheng 2007 nian Nanjingshi zui di gong zi biao zhun de tong zhi [Notice on 2007 Nanjing Minimum Wage Guideline] (Oct. 10, 2007), http://www.njlss.gov.cn/pub/ldbz/xxgk/wjxx/zhgz/200710/t20071011_9925.htm; Beijing Labor and Social Security Bureau, Guan yu tiao zheng 2007 nian Beijingshi zui di gong zi biao zhun de tong zhi [Notice on 2007 Beijing Minimum Wage Guideline] (June 28, 2007), http://www.bjld.gov.cn/LDJAPP/search/fgdetail.jsp?no=10766 (last visited Aug. 2, 2008).

[11] David Murphy, *The Dangers of Too Much Success*, FAR EASTERN ECONOMIC REVIEW, June 10, 2004, at 29.

Wolfensohn pointed out that China still has 400 million people living on less than US$2/day. Incomes are rising, but the rate of increase in the urban areas is two times that in rural areas. President Wolfensohn estimated that the wage gap in ten years would be one of the highest in the world, and he noted that in 2003 ten million citizens engaged in protests, not only regarding labor issues (such as layoffs and wages) but also regarding rising rural taxes and forced relocation in urban areas.[12]

Another wage gap exists between workers and managers. A recent survey by the State Council found that 61 percent of managers of Chinese enterprises were paid salaries that were three to fifteen times higher than those of employees, whereas 21 percent were paid salaries that were fifteen to fifty times higher and 15 percent of the managers at FIEs were paid wages that were fifty times more.[13]

A large number of low-wage workers are not even paid. A December 2003 government survey in China found that 72 percent of China's millions of migrant workers were owed back pay. The Construction Ministry estimated that workers in 2003 were owed more than $12 billion in wages by their employers even though the law requires that wages be paid at least monthly; the unpaid debts to migrants were estimated to be one-third of the value of production in construction and real estate industries.[14] Those involved say most of the workers do not have formal labor contracts, as the law requires. The Beijing municipal government in the first six months of 2004 helped 110,000 migrant workers recover 290 million yuan (US$35 million) of unpaid wages, resulting in the first decline in labor disputes in Beijing since 2000.[15]

---

[12] *Id.* at 30. CCP's Outlook magazine reported that three million people staged 58,000 protests on labor issues across China in 2003. *See also Labor Activists Detect Change and China Repression*, REUTERS NEWS, Jan. 13, 2005, http://www.china-labour.org.hk/en/node/4090 (last visited Aug. 2, 2008).

[13] *Lao zong yuan gong shou ru cha ju zui da chao wu shi bei* [*Managers Earns Fifty Times More*], GUANGZHOU DAILY, (Apr. 25, 2004), A2 (citing Guo wu yuan fa zhan yan jiu guan li diao cha bao gao [Human Resource Report] (2004). News articles available at http://gzdaily.dayoo.com/gb/content/2004-04/25/content_1517025.htm (last visited Aug. 2, 2007). Comparatively, a 2003 U.S. report revealed that in private industry, the relative pay for white-collar occupations was 118; compared to 84 and 52 for blue-collar and service employees, respectively. Within the white-collar group, wages also varied considerably, with the relative pay of executive, administrative, and managerial workers (182) far surpassing the relative pay of sales workers (84) and administrative support workers (79). John E. Buckley, Relative Pay Rates among Major Industry and Occupational Groups, March 2003, http://www.bls.gov/opub/cwc/cm20030318ar01p1.htm. *See also*, Robert Z. Lawrence, Blue-Collar Blues: Is Trade to Blame for Rising U.S. Income Inequality? (2008).

[14] Anthony Kuhn, *A High Price to Pay for a Job*, FAR E. ECON. REV., Jan. 22, 2004, at 30-32.

[15] Li Jing, Beijing Government Urges Employers to Pay Up, CHINA DAILY, Sep. 14, 2004, at 3, http://www.chinadaily.com.cn/english/doc/2004-09/14/content_374270.htm (last visited

When adding up some of the negative side effects of economic reforms – slow-rising wages, widening wage gaps, and unpaid wages of migrant workers (who make up the "floating population" of 150 million Chinese citizens) – with each affected employee seeking to find his or her share of the new economic growth, one can understand why a top priority of the central government is to put a social security safety net in place with accompanying labor law protections. This effort brought into existence the 1994 Labor Law, which broadly outlined labor standards requirements. By 2004, many of the standards had been more formally enacted into specific laws and regulations, including those for minimum wage and hours. Notwithstanding the progress in legislation, employees have continued to demand that the laws be made to work, and some collective protests have demanded improved benefits.

Beginning in late 2008, after passage of the new labor laws and the onset of the global economic downturn, two effects were felt. First, some employers felt the burdens of the new laws, especially the *new Labor Contract Law*, impacted too heavily, causing some closures; second, the impact of the *global downturn*, with its declining demand for exports, caused layoffs and bankruptcies. Some employers evaded the requirements of the new labor reforms, which in turn caused many more labor arbitrations (now easier with new Labor Mediation and Arbitration Law) and even more worker protests.[16]

Meanwhile, declining global demand for China's textile and apparel products affects the employers of the 20 million workers in that industry, which in 2008 accounted for more than one-half of its $300 billion trade surplus[17]; wage

Aug. 2, 2008). See also Guo yu ji shu gong ren duan que de diao yan bao gao [Analyzing Labor Shortage and Skilled Labor Shortage], http://www.fsa.gov.cn/web_db/sdzg2005/map/CGL/glbg-082.htm.

[16] Sky Canaves, Closures Strain China's Labor Laws, WALL ST. J., Jan. 16, 2009, http://online.wsj.com/article/SB123215043508192065.html?mod=todays_us_page_one. Joanna Law, Employers, prepare for trouble, China Law & Practice, March, 2009, at 9-10, www.chinalawandpractice.com. Andrew Batson, China's Falling Exports Signal Shift, March 12, 2009, http://online.wsj.com/article/SB123674128193891921.html. On November 19, 2008, the government, attempted to counter the residual ill-effects on workers' wages and benefits caused by foreign employers who closed their factors and fled, by issuing *Working Guidelines on Cross-border Pursuit of Liability Initiation of Legal Action by Relevant Interested Parties in connection with Abnormal Withdrawal from China of Foreign Investors* (hereinafter, Working Guidelines) (Ministries of Commerce, Foreign Affairs, Public Security, and Justice); and *see* Susan Finder, Chasing the vanished foreign investor, China Law & Practice, February, 2009, at 20–21, www.chinalawandpractice.com.

[17] David Barboza, *Textile capital Shaoxing hobbled by a downturn gone global*, New York Times, February 28, 2009, www.nytimes.com/2009/02/28/business/worldbusiness/28textile.html?n=Top/Reference/Times%20Topics/People/B/Barboza,%20David.

defaults by employers continue[18]; and some reported that 23 million migrant laborers are unemployed.[19]

These impacts have also brought about some local legislative modifications, some of which lower the standards set by the recent labor law reforms.[20] Today, employers in China face choices: comply with the labor and employment laws, go bankrupt, or seek to evade the laws.[21] All these factors make understanding

[18] For example, in response to the economic downturn, the central government recently issued a series of employment-related policies: 1. The Notice as to Lighten Enterprises' Burden and Stabilize the Employment Situation (MOHRSS, Ministry of Finance, and the State Administration of Taxation (December 20, 2008) [postpone payment of social security fees for 6 months, lower rates for employees' medical, work-related injury, and child-birth insurance for a period of 12 months; use unemployment insurance funds to pay a social insurance subsidy if they minimize the number of layoffs]; 2. The Opinion on stabilizing Labor Relationship under Current Economic Situation (MOHRSS, ACFTU, and the China Enterprise Association (January 23, 2009) [promotes coordination of layoffs, cost-cutting measures, and use of collective consultation mechanisms]; 3. The Guidance to Improve Employment under Current Economic Situation State Council (February 3, 2009) [promotes creation of more employment opportunities, sets preferential policies of hiring unemployed workers new college graduates, and migrant workers, directs employers in layoffs of more than 20 employees or 10 percent of the workforce to seek consultation with the union 30 days in advance and then report the layoff plans to the labor bureau]; 4. The Circular about Extending Tax Incentives for Re-Employment of Laid-Off Workers (Ministry of Finance and State Administration of Taxation) [allows employers of qualifying employees, hired for additional positions, labor contracts longer than one year to receive tax preferences]. It was reported in Shenzhen in the last three months of 2008, there were 48 companies that closed without paying workers' wages; and overall in 2008, some 370 companies in Shenzhen defaulted on wage payments of 30 million yuan to 39,200 workers. Shenzhen has set up an employer-contributed fund to deal with wage defaults. Kelly Chan, *Wage defaults for fourth quarter hit 30 million yuan in Shenzhen*, South China Morning Post, February 24, 2009, http://www.scmp.com/portal/site/SCMP/menuitem. 2af62ecb329d3d7733492d9253a0a0a0/?vgnextoid=d1eadf53514af110VgnVCM100000360a0a0a RCRD.

[19] *China jobless migrants now at 23 million*, Reuters, March 25, 2009, english. siamdailynews.com/asia-news/eastern-asia-news/china-news/china-jobless-migrants-now-at-23-million.html. *See also* Tom Mitchell, *Daunting departure*, www.ft.com/cms/s/0/ b3990974-dcf1-11dd-a2a9-000077b07658.html.

[20] Modifications at the local levels include, for example, Shandong and Hubei provinces are reported to *mandate* government approval for layoffs of more than 40 workers (though the new Labor Contract Law (LCL) requires layoffs in excess of 20 only to be *reported* to the government; Guangdong has delayed implementation of the LCL's Implementing Regulations; and, Beijing has allowed employers to lower their contributions to worker social security programs and frozen minimum wage increases. *Legal Briefs*, China Law & Practice, December 2008/January 2009, at 3.

[21] According to one source, the Dagongzhe Migrant Workers Rights Center in Shenzhen, "pervasive tricks" used by employers to circumvent the new laws include "reduced overtime pay and using doctored contracts that were either blank, incomplete or written in English to confuse and limit possible legal liabilities." It reported that in a survey of 320 workers by

and successfully navigating China's new labor and employment laws even more necessary than before.

In sum, China's labor laws that regulate its diverse workplaces form a mosaic composed of many variables. Insight into these variables helps explain how and how well the labor laws work, and these insights then allow a clearer understanding of the substantive aspects of labor laws. It is with the intention to provide those insights that this book is written.

> Dagongzhe, nearly a quarter said factory bosses had hiked both food prices and penalties for minor mistakes on production lines. About 26 percent of workers never signed any contracts, especially in smaller factories, whereas 28 percent said they were paid less than the legal minimum wage. *Chinese labor laws buckle as economy darkens*, Reuters, January 29, 2009, www.reuters.com/article/lifestyleMolt/idUSTRE50R0D820090128.

2

Labor and Employment Laws and Administration

At the central government level under the State Council, the Ministry of uman Resources and Social Security (MOHRSS) administers labor and employment policies. In March 2008, this ministry took over the functions of the Ministry of Labor and Social Security (MOLSS) (see Table 2.1) and the Ministry of Personnel (MOP). It maintains vertical supervision at the local level through local labor bureaus, which are at the same time also greatly controlled by local governments through their funding and appointments power.

The MOHRSS is one of China's newly designated "super ministries." Since 1998 its predecessor, MOLSS, has been responsible for social security management and development of policies and legislation for urban, rural, and government workers. Before its 2008 reorganization, it was organized into the following departments: legal affairs, planning and finance, training and employment, labor and wages, pension insurance, unemployment insurance, medical insurance, work-related injury insurance, rural social insurance, social insurance fund supervision, international cooperation, and personnel and education. With the reorganization in 2008, it assumed the functions of the former MOP, with the exception of its civil service department, which is now part of the State Public Servants Bureau.

The reorganized ministry has twenty-three departments, including several new ones (see Table 2.2).[1]

---

[1] Ren li zi yuan he she hui bao zhang by zhu yao zhi ze nei she ji gou he ren yuan bian zhi gui ding [Notice on the Main Duties, Inner Structure, and Staffing of Ministry of Human Resources and Social Security (MOHRSS)] (issued by the State Council, July 12, 2008), http://www.mohrss.gov.cn/mohrss/Desktop.aspx?path=/mohrss/InfoView&gid=a0d4dfb0-c94b-48cb-ace2-444787468af9&tid=Cms_Info.

TABLE 2.1. *Administration of labor and employment policies*

劳动和社会保障部
Ministry of Labor and Social Security
省级劳动保障机构 (31个)
Labor and Social Security Bureaus in Provinces, Autonomous Regions, and Municipalities Directly under the Central Government
城市级劳动保障机构 (333个)
Prefectural (municipal) Labor and Social Security Bureaus
县级劳动保障机构 (2862个)
County Labor Bureaus
乡镇、街道劳动保障机构 (约16000个)
Labor and Social Security Offices in Towns, Neighborhoods
社区劳动保障平台 (约1000000个)
Ministry of Labor and Social Security

Source: MOLSS, 2007, http://www.molss.gov.cn.

1. Responsibilities and Functions of the MOHRSS

The MOHRSS, through its departments and subordinate institutions (unchanged from MOLSS, see Table 2.3), is responsible for formulating and implementing policies in the following areas. It drafts laws and regulations that promote employment and labor market development and exercises supervision and inspection functions over programs and local labor agencies. In vocational training, it drafts national standards for occupational classifications and skills, training, and certification. In labor relations, it formulates the principles for labor relations adjustment, enforcement of regulations and labor contracts, dispute settlement, and labor arbitration, and it works out policies on labor standards and protections. In wage regulation, it drafts macro-level policies and measures concerning wage guidelines and regulatory policies. The ministry formulates policies and standards on social insurance and manages the funding, implementation, supervision, and inspection of government programs on old age, unemployment, medical, work-related injury, and maternity benefits. The MOHRSS also is in charge of compiling and disseminating statistical information concerning national labor and social insurance and forecasting trends. It organizes and engages in scientific research in the fields of labor and social insurance. Lastly, it is responsible for international exchanges and cooperation, including participation in international organizations such as the International Labor Organization (ILO) and technical projects.

TABLE 2.2. *Departments of the Reorganized MOHRSS*

General Office
办公厅
Department of Policy & Research*
政策研究司
Department of Legal Affairs
法规司
Department of Planning and Finance
规划财务司
Department of Employment Promotion*
就业促进司
Department of Human Resource Market
人力资源市场司
Department of Job Placement for Demobilized Military Officers
军官转业安置司
Department of Professional Capacity-Building*
职业能力建设司
Department of Professional and Technical Personnel Management
专业技术人员管理司
Department of Personnel Management for Institutions
事业单位人事管理司
Department of Service for Migrant Workers*
农民工工作司
Department of Labor Relations*
劳动关系司
Department of Wage and Benefits*
工资福利司
Department of Pension Insurance
养老保险司
Department of Unemployment Insurance
失业保险司
Department of Medical Insurance
医疗保险司
Department of Work-Related Injury Insurance
工伤保险司
Department of Rural Social Insurance
农村社会保险司
Department of Social Insurance Fund Supervision
社会保险基金监督司
Department of Labor Dispute Mediation and Arbitration Management*
调节仲裁管理司
Department of Labor Inspection*
劳动监察司
Department of International Cooperation
国际合作司
Department of Personnel
人事司

* New or reorganized departments.

TABLE 2.3. *Major subordinate institutions*

机关服务中心
Ministry's Service Center
社会保险事业管理中心
Social Insurance Administration Center
信息中心
Information Center
中国劳动保险科学研究院
China Labor and Social Security Science Academy
中国就业培训技术指导中心
China Employment Training Technical Instruction Center
中国劳动保障报社
China Labor and Social Security News
中国劳动社会保障出版社
China Labor and Social Security Publishing House
教育培训中心
Education and Training Center
宣传中心
Publicity Center
国际交流服务中心
International Exchanges and Services Center
社会保障能力建设中心
Social Security Capacity Building Center

Source: MOLSS, 2007, http://www.molss.gov.cn.

2. Administration of Labor and Employment Laws

The primary labor law is the 1994 Labor Law, with many more recent labor and employment laws deriving from it. These laws cover hiring, working conditions and benefits (including social security, medical, work-related injuries, unemployment, and maternity insurance), discipline and termination, and even post-termination restrictive covenants. Often several agencies are involved in implementing these laws; for example, laws relating to occupational health labor and employment issues.[2] Laws passed in 2007 and implemented in 2008

[2] The Ministry of Health (MOH) is in charge of drafting occupational health statutes and regulations; setting up occupational health criteria; standardizing the prevention, health care, and oversight of the medical treatment of occupational diseases; and overseeing qualification certification for occupational health service agencies, occupational health assessment, and poisonous chemical assessments. The State Administration of Work Safety (SAWS), as a nonministry agency directly under the State Council, is in charge of the overall supervision and regulation of work safety, issuing occupational health and safety permits and investigating work accidents and relevant violations of work safety rules. *See* http://www.moh.gov.cn/publicfiles/business/htmlfiles/zwgkzt/pjggk/200804/621.htm (in Chinese). The MOHRSS is in charge of policy

include the Labor Contract Law (LCL), the Employment Promotion Law (EPL), and the Law on Labor Mediation and Arbitration (LMA).

3. Goals and Expectations

With China's workforce expected to reach 840 million by 2010 based on an annual projected 50 million new entrants, the MOHRSS plans to further strengthen its promotion and regulation of employment. As stated in its eleventh Five-Year Plan (2006–2010), its priorities include expanding and improving jobs, improving social security, creating a more effective inspection and law enforcement network, stabilizing labor relations, and improving legal education for employers and workers.

Those goals and expectations are built on its discernible progress made under the tenth Five-Year Plan (2001–2005). Employment increased in urban and rural areas by more than 40 million workers (including 21 million workers in small businesses).[3] Nearly 15 million workers were helped to find new jobs after being unemployed (the urban rate of unemployment was 4.2 percent at the end of 2005, with some 9 million people registered as unemployed).[4] Vocational training produced 500,000 new skilled technicians.[5] Social security funding and coverage were expanded. By the end of 2005, 175,000,000 people were covered for old-age insurance (an increase of 39 million from 2000), and 1,587.6 billion yuan were paid out to pensioners from 2000 to 2005 (an increase of 803 billion yuan since 2000).[6] Multiple financing sources were set up, with contributions from the employers and workers and subsidies from the government. The government also promoted enterprise annuity schemes, which some 24,000 enterprises established, covering 9 million workers.[7]

By the end of 2005, the financing and coverage of other government insurance schemes had expanded as well: unemployment (33.3 billion yuan; covering 107 million workers with 6.8 million receiving benefits), health insurance (138 billion yuan; covering 138 million workers), maternity insurance, (4.4 billion yuan; covering 54 million female workers with 620,000 receiving benefits), work injury insurance (9.3 billion yuan; covering 84.8 million with 650,000 receiving benefits), and social insurance in rural areas

research, work skill training, work safety insurance, and related dispute resolution, http://www.moh.gov.cn/publicfiles/business/htmlfiles/zwgkzt/pjggk/200804/621.htm (in Chinese). Further discussion on administration and enforcement is in Chapter 8.

[3] MOLSS, LABOR AND SOCIAL SECURITY IN CHINA, 2 (2007).

[4] *Id.* at 3.

[5] *Id.*

[6] *Id.* at 6.

[7] *Id.*

(2.1 billion yuan; covering 54.4 million farmers with 3 million participating farmers receiving pensions.[8]

Social security coverage continues to expand in urban areas. In the first half of 2008, the following increases were reported: urban pension coverage increased from 201.37 to 210.29 million people, with payouts up 33.9 percent to $54.52 billion; health insurance, from 223.11 million to 249.07 million people; unemployment insurance, from 116.45 to 120.1 million people; work injury insurance, from 8.52 million to 130.25 million workers; and maternity insurance, rose 6.77 million to 84.52 million workers.[9] The social security funds likewise continue to grow; by mid-2008, compared with same time the year before, the pension fund was up 30.5 percent to 440 billion yuan; basic medical insurance increased 34.2 percent to 129.6 billion yuan; the unemployment insurance fund increased 26 percent to 25.8 billion yuan; work security insurance rose 35.3 percent to 9.7 billion yuan; and the maternity insurance fund "soared" 44.4 percent to 5.1 billion yuan.[10]

In protecting the rights and interests of the labor force, the government reported that it had devoted increased efforts to labor enforcement and inspection. Between 2000 and 2005, several important laws and regulations on the coverage of occupational diseases, worker safety, and trade unions were passed and issued. These laws targeted the issue of delayed wage payments to migrant workers and promoted collective negotiations for collective contracts (more than 604,000 collective contracts covering 90 million workers by the end of 2005).[11] An increased focus on mediation and labor dispute arbitration produced an ever-increasing use of this process, culminating in 2008 with a new Labor Mediation and Arbitration Law, which has further fostered arbitration. More than 3,200 labor and social security inspection agencies in China in all levels of government, employing more than 50,000 inspectors, have corrected labor abuses and employer failures to pay contributions to social security.[12]

The MOHRSS reportedly has announced a new three-year agenda focusing on drafting a new law on social insurance; regulations on enterprise wages and employment contracts; issuing new rules on labor arbitration commissions' handling of cases and on implementing the Regulations on Paid Annual

---

[8] *Id.* at 7–8.
[9] *China Expands Its Social Security System*, Xinhua News Agency, July 31, 2008, http://www .chinadaily.com.cn/china/2008-07/31/content_6894100.htm.
[10] *Id.*
[11] *Id.* at 10.
[12] *Id.*

Leave for Employees; and considering revisions of regulations on work-related insurance, unemployment insurance, and the labor protection of female staff and workers.[13]

---

[13] Andreas Lauffs & Jeffery Wilson, *Newly Merged Employment Ministry Announces 3-Year Agenda for Labor Rule Revisions*, INT. LABOR & EMPLOYMENT L. COMM. NEWSLETTER (May 2008), http://www.abanet.org/labor/intlcomm/newsletter/2008/05/may-china02.shtml.

PART II

EMPLOYMENT RELATIONSHIPS

3

Employment Relationships

1. Introduction

a. Workforce Profile

Labor force demographics show dramatic distinctions among workers in China based on many factors, including location (urban/rural and region), occupation and skills, and employers (domestic/foreign/SOEs; see Table 3.1).[1]

b. Employment Relationships

In China, defining "employer" and "employee" and their employment relationship for the purposes of delineating legal rights and duties has become more important in recent years. The 1994 Labor Law sought inclusive language for "employees/workers," but workplace realities produced many categories, including "dispatch" workers; independent contractors; managers and supervisors; and migrant, temporary, part-time, and de facto workers. An issue facing China's drafters of new labor laws was how each subsequent labor law would be applied (or *not* applied) to these categories. Likewise, employer designations under the labor laws produced some uncertainties, as they too came in a variety of forms.

Defining the employment relationship for purposes of coverage under China's legal system often requires a two-step examination of the national and local laws to determine the proper "operating law" at the level of application. This is due to China's decentralized system, in which the central government passes broad, general legislation and leaves to the local governments the

---

[1] There is some discussion of workforce profile by age and gender in Qinwen Xu and Farooq Pasha, People's Republic of China, Statistical Profile No. 5 (November, 2008), agingandwork.bc.edu/documents/CP05_Workforce_China_2008-11-13.pdf.

TABLE 3.1. *Employment profile, 2007*

Economically active population	786,450,000
Total number of employed persons	769,900,000
Primary industry	314,440,000–40.8%
Secondary industry	206,290,000–26.8%
Tertiary industry	249,170,000–32.4%
Urban employed persons	293,500,000
State-owned units	64,240,000
Urban collective-owned units	7,180,000
Cooperative units	1,700,000
Joint ownership units	430,000
Limited liability corporations	20,750,000
Shareholding corporations	7,880,000
Private enterprises	45,810,000
Units with funds from Hong Kong, Macao, and Taiwan	6,800,000
Foreign funded units	9,030,000
Self-employed individuals	33,100,000
Rural employed persons	476,400,000
Township and village enterprises	150,900,000
Private enterprises	26,720,000
Self-employed individuals	21,870,000
Number of staff and workers	114,270,000
State-owned units	61,480,000
Urban collective-owned units	6,840,000
Units of other types of ownership	45,950,000
Number of registered unemployed persons in urban areas	8,300,000
Registered unemployment rate in urban areas	4.0%

Source: *China Statistical Yearbook, 2008.*

responsibility of promulgating "detailed implementing regulations" to apply the national laws. Coverage by the labor laws may also be determined on a geographical basis rather than by the employment relationship. That is, the distinction between urban and rural may be determinative. Additionally, until recent legislative clarification, the large number of migrant workers raised interesting questions of coverage.

China's continuing economic and social transition has transformed state workers, staff, and cadres of the "iron rice bowl era" to modern-day employees under individual and collective labor contracts. These employment relationships are regulated by new labor laws and regulations largely originating from the 1994 Labor Law.

Article 2 of the Labor Law specifies that the law is applied to laborers who form a "labor/employment relationship" or have a "labor contract." Many interpretations over the years have attempted to clarify this language. The latest attempt came in 2008 with the Labor Contract Law, which confirmed the relationship and again required a written contract.[2]

Yet, even without a written contract, a de facto employment relationship can arise.[3] In addition to illegal employment relationships, the usual (though not the only) situation giving rise to a de facto employment relationship occurs when a previous labor contract expires, the employee continues to work, and the employer does not object.[4] In 1996, early guidance on the application of the 1994 Labor Law provided that within the territory of the People's Republic of China (PRC), as long as the employment relationship (including de facto) exists, the Labor Law applies. The key elements are that the worker (1) provides physical or mental labor for compensation and (2) becomes a member of the enterprise or entity.[5] Even without a contract, a worker is a de facto employee if he or she is a member and is paid for labor.[6] This de facto employment relationship also provides the right to access arbitration, litigation, and worker's compensation.[7]

2. The Employer

Under the 1994 Labor Law, the "employing unit" is called by a variety of terms, such as enterprises; individual economic organizations, and state organs, institutions, and public organizations. The Chinese terms for "employer" also require explanation.

"Enterprise"(*qi-ye*), although not precisely defined, has acquired a common meaning to include employing units that are engaged in production, distribution, and servicing and are under all kinds of ownership, such as

---

[2] Lao dong he tong fa [Labor Contract Law] (promulgated by the 28th Standing Comm. of the Tenth Nat'l People's Cong., June 29, 2007, effective Jan. 1, 2008), art. 10, 11, (PRC) [hereinafter LCL]. Implementing regulations were issued by the State Council on September 18, 2008.

[3] *Id.* art. 11, 82.

[4] Guan yu shi xing lao dong he tong zhi du ruo gan wen ti de tong zhi [Notice on Labor Contract Issues] (promulgated by Ministry of Labor, 1996), art. 14, http://law.chinalawinfo.com/newlaw2002/slc/slc.asp?db=chl&gid=17563.

[5] Laodongbu guan yu guan che zhi xing Zhonghua Renmin Gongheguo lao dong fa de ruo gan wen ti de yi jian [Opinion on Several Issues of Implementing PRC Labor Law by Ministry of Labor] (promulgated by Ministry of Labor, Aug. 4, 1995), art. 2 [hereinafter 1995 Labor Law Implementing Opinion], http://www.chinacourt.org/flwk/show1.php?file_id=23218.

[6] *Id.* art. 1.

[7] Zuigao Renmin Fayuan guan yu lao dong zheng yi an jian shi yong fa lv ruo gan wen ti de jie shi [Interpretations of the Supreme People's Court Concerning Several Issues Regarding the Application of Law to the Trial of Labor Dispute Cases] (April 16, 2001, effective April 30, 2001), art. 1, http://www.dffy.com/faguixiazai/msf/200502/20050221112552.htm; Gong shang bao xian tiao li [Regulations on Work-related Injury] (promulgated by State Council, April 27, 2003, effective Jan. 1, 2004), art. 18, http://www.law-lib.com/law/law_view.asp?id=74508.

factories, farms, corporations, etc. That is, it refers to any profit-making under-taking in any kind of organizational form.[8]

The term "individual economic organization" is defined as an individual industrial and commercial business that employs fewer than seven employees but has undergone the industrial and commercial registration process.[9] Because the private economy was not the norm until the late 1990s, this term as used in early laws seemed to have a connotation of business activities in the private economy.

The term "state organs" refers to governments and government agencies at all levels. "Institutions" refers to nonprofit organizations that are normally initiated and financed by the government, such as schools and hospitals. However, as China has made the transition to a socialist market economy, government finances and controls are changing, with some institutions still reflecting the traditional model, whereas others are becoming enterprises and may be referred to as "private institutions." Moreover, private institutions, such as schools and hospitals, because they are not typical enterprises, are called "private nonenterprise units" or "nonenterprise private units."

The term "public organizations" covers nonprofit societies acting on behalf of certain groups of people, usually organized and financed by the government. For example, the All China Federation of Trade Unions (ACFTU) and the All China Women's Federation (ACWF) are typical public organizations.

More recent legislation uses a variety of these terms in defining what is an employer:

- Minimum Wage (2004): "enterprises, nonenterprise private units"; "individual and industrial commercial households with employees"; and "state organs, public undertaking units and social organizations"[10]
- Work-Related Injuries (2004): "enterprises and individual industrial and commercial households hiring employees"[11]
- Work Safety (2002): "units that engage in production and operation"[12]

---

[8] Laodongbu guan yu Zhonghua Renmin Gongheguo lao dong fa ruo gan tiao wen de shuo ming [Explanations on the Articles of PRC Labor Law] (promulgated by Ministry of Labor, Sep. 5, 1994), art. 2, http://law.chinalawinfo.com/newlaw2002/slc/slc.asp?db=chl&gid=27173.
[9] 1995 Labor Law Implementing Opinion, art. 1.
[10] Zui di gong zi gui ding [Regulations on Minimum Wage] (promulgated by Ministry of Labor and Social Security, Jan. 20, 2004, effective Mar. 3, 2004), art. 2.
[11] Gong shang bao xian tiao li [Regulation on Work-Related Injury Insurance] (promulgated by State Council, April 27, 2003, effective Jan. 1, 2004), art. 2.
[12] Zhonghua Renmin Gongheguo an quan sheng chan fa [Law of the PRC on Work Safety] (promulgated by the Standing Comm. of the Nat'l People's Cong., June 29, 2002, effective Nov. 1, 2002), art. 2.

- Unemployment Insurance (1999): "urban enterprises," including SOEs, collectively owned FIEs, privately owned within urban area, and other enterprises within urban areas[13]
- Collective Contract (2004): "enterprises," "public institutions," and "state organs"[14]
- Labor Contract Law (2007): "enterprises," "individual economic organizations," "private nonenterprise entities," or "other organizations"[15]

Therefore, although there has been an attempt to use broad, inclusive definitions of the term "employer," still each labor law must be examined to determine whether coverage exists for traditional and newly emerging economic, nonprofit, and other employment relations. During China's transition to a market economy, questions continue to arise involving new applications. For example, unregistered enterprises; branch or representative offices; enterprises formed after mergers, acquisitions, or bankruptcy; and enterprises using dispatch workers all require legal answers to coverage issues.

Illegal employers – because of the failure to meet required registration or obtain a license or those who have been deregistered or have lost their license – typically remain an employer under labor laws. For example, an employee disabled at work is still entitled to compensation from the illegal employer under the Work-Related Injury Insurance program.[16]

Other practical variations test the employer designation and the question of which employer is the responsible employer in the employment relationship. In China, these issues are raised by the usual processes of enterprise restructuring, including mergers, successors, and failed enterprises, as well as by use of dispatch employees. For example, for employers of merged enterprises, the law holds the surviving entity liable for existing labor contracts,[17] and new modifications or replacements of these contracts will be treated as amendments to existing labor contracts, thus not triggering the severance provisions

---

[13] Shi ye bao xian tiao li [Regulations on Unemployment Insurance] (promulgated by State Council, Jan. 20, 1999), art. 2.

[14] Ji ti he tong gui ding [Regulations on Collective Contract] (promulgated by Ministry of Labor and Social Security, May 1, 2004), art. 3. Some definitions of "state organ, institution, and public organizations" are discussed in an analysis of the LCL at http://www.laodonghetong.org/540a.html.

[15] LCL, art. 2.

[16] Fei fa yong gong dan wei shang wang ren yuan yi ci xing pei chang ban fa [Measures for Compensation in A Lump Sum to the Disabled or Deceased Employees of An Illegal Employing Unit] (promulgated by MOLSS, Sep. 18, 2003, effective Jan. 1, 2004).

[17] LCL, art. 34, but see discussion *infra* on LCL, art. 41 re: impacts on labor contracts justifying reduction of workforce.

under the LCL.[18] This differs from an asset transfer in which severance pay would be required.[19]

Employers' use of dispatch or temporary workers sent from a placement agency, sometimes referred to as "in-sourcing," raises the issue of who is the employer. In the United States, some employers use contracted employees to exclude themselves from liabilities under the labor laws while substituting the supplying entity as the statutory "employer," which is liable under the labor laws because the employees are still on its payroll. Thus, the employer, using the contracted employees, may not be responsible as the "employer" under the labor laws because the workers were not its "employees." However, in the United States, often the employing unit that controls the worker is found to be responsible through the "joint liability" doctrine.[20]

In China, the 2008 LCL addressed this issue by in effect making the supplier of the contracted employees (dispatch workers) the employer and limiting the liability of the entity using the supplied employees, although this can be modified contractually.[21] Under the law, the supplier-employer must hire its dispatch workers for regular full-time employment for at least two years, with wages no lower than the minimum wage level and at the same level as those of the other employees.[22] The entity using the dispatched workers may not use these workers to displace its regular workforce and is limited to using dispatched workers for temporary positions.[23] It likewise must make contractual arrangements with the supplying employer regarding labor law obligations.[24]

Employers acting as "representative offices" of foreign companies raise an emerging issue. Although FIEs can hire employees and are clearly subject to China's labor laws, presently a foreign representative office is not by itself allowed to hire PRC citizens as employees because it is not permitted to be registered as a foreign-invested employer engaged in direct business activities.[25] Foreign representative offices must hire employees through a local

---

[18] 1995 Labor Law Implementing Opinion, art. 13, 37. Under article 34 and article 35 of the LCL, the modification or replacement of the labor contracts must be based on mutual agreement between employers and employees.

[19] ANDREAS LAUFFS, EMPLOYMENT LAW & PRACTICE IN CHINA, 81–94 (2008).

[20] 73 A.L.R. Fed. 609 (1985).

[21] LCL, art. 58, 92.

[22] LCL, art. 58, 63.

[23] LCL, art. 66 ("The worker dispatch services shall normally be used for temporary, auxiliary, or substituting positions").

[24] LCL, art. 59.

[25] Zhong wai he zi zhong wai he zuo zhi ye jie shao ji gou she li guan li zan xing gun ding [Interim Provisions on the Administration of the Establishment of Sino-foreign Equity Joint and Sino-Foreign Cooperative Job Intermediary Institutions] (promulgated by MOLSS and

labor service agency under labor service contracts; however, even so, the 2008 LCL appears to cover this arrangement and obligates the employer to follow its relevant provisions on using staffing firms.[26] Foreign employees, complying with formal requirements, may also be employed in China by Chinese employers and FIEs (including representative offices).[27] WTO conditions call for the legalization of "branch offices" of foreign companies, but as of yet they are not allowed and issues still remain.

3. The Employee

Employees/workers were not explicitly defined in the 1994 Labor Law. "Employees" were subsequently referenced in the 2001 amendments to the Trade Union Law as "individuals who perform physical or mental work in enterprises, institutions and government authorities within the Chinese territory and who earn their living primarily from wages or salaries."[28] Under China's transition to a market economy, iron rice bowl terms, such as worker, staff, and cadre, seem to have given way to the newer terms of employee and even to such designations as blue collar, white collar, and "golden" collar (young professionals in high demand).

Under the 1994 Labor Law, "employment relationship" is intended as an inclusive term in covering employees/workers. The 2003 Work-Related Injury Insurance Regulation defines it as "laborers who keep a labor relation with the

State Administration for Industry & Commerce, Oct. 9, 2001) [hereinafter 2001 Prov. on Adm. of Est. of Sino-foreign Job Intermediary Inst.], art. 6, http://law.chinalawinfo.com/newlaw2002/slc/slc.asp?db=chl&gid=37522; Guan yu wai guo qi ye chang zhu dai biao ji gou deng ji guan li ban fa [Administrative Measures for the Registration of Resident Representative Offices of Foreign Enterprise] (promulgated by State Administration for Industry & Commerce, Mar. 15, 1983), art. 3, http://www.law-lib.com/law/law_view.asp?id=193; Zhonghua Renmin Gongheguo Guowuyuan guan yu guan li wai guo qi ye chang zhu dai biao ji gou de zan xing gun ding [Interim Provisions of the PRC on the Administration of Resident Representative Offices of Foreign Enterprises] (promulgated by State Council, Oct. 30, 1980), art. 11, http://www.law-lib.com/law/law_view.asp?id=2161.

[26] LCL, art. 57–67; ANDREAS LAUFFS, EMPLOYMENT LAW & PRACTICE IN CHINA, 12–16 (2008).

[27] Wai guo ren zai Zhongguo jiu ye guan li gui ding [Regulations for the Administration of the Employment of Foreigners in China] (promulgated by Ministry of Labor, Ministry of Public Security, Ministry of Foreign Affairs, and Ministry of Foreign Trade and Economic Cooperation, Jan. 22, 1996) [hereinafter 1996 Reg. for the Administration of the Employment of Foreigners], http://www.people.com.cn/zixun/flfgk/item/dwjjf/falv/2/2-1-51.html. Likewise, it is reported the State Council in 2008 issued new enforcement regulations to require Chinese contractors sending workers overseas to work to provide labor contracts and ensure employers meet host country standards. *New Rule to Keep Firms within Law on Foreign Contracts*, Xinhua News Agency July 29, 2008, www.Unpan_ap@sass.org.cn.

[28] Zhonghua Renmin Gongheguo gong hui fa [Trade Union Law of PRC] (promulgated by the 24th session of the Standing Comm. of the Ninth Nat'l People's Cong., Oct. 27, 2001), art. 3.

employing entity in all forms of employment and within all forms of employment period."[29] Documented foreign employees legally working in China generally are covered under the Labor Law.[30]

Whether "contingent" workers are employees covered by the labor laws was resolved in 1996 by the then-Ministry of Labor. It formally abolished any legal distinction between contingent or temporary workers and formal employees; and they are to enjoy the same rights, unless provided otherwise.[31]

Under most labor service contracts (*laowu hetong*), independent contractors lack a legal "employment relationship" with the "employer" in question. Typically, therefore, the daily performance by these workers is not under the direct control of the employer and there is no right of control. This distinction is significant in that many employer duties under the labor laws apply only to employees rather than to independent contractors, whose breaches are dealt with under the Contract Law,[32] not the LCL and LMA. These workers may have labor protections with their employing entity that has contracted to provide the services.

Part-time workers, as defined in the 2008 LCL, are limited to work an average of not more than four hours per day or twenty-four hours per week for the same employer.[33] They must be paid at least the local minimum wage, are terminable at will, and have no rights to a written contract or severance pay.[34] These regulations replace the earlier MOLSS interpretations that had defined part-time as working no more than thirty hours per week, five hours per day, and had provided more employee rights.[35]

Migrant workers, under new laws and regulations, have the right to labor contracts, to participate in worker's compensation, and to have medical insurance. The 2008 Employment Promotion Law (EPL) clearly states, "[R]ural workers who go to cities in search of employment shall enjoy labor rights equal to those of urban workers. It is prohibited to set discriminatory

---

[29] Regulation on Work-Related Injury Insurance, art. 61.

[30] 2001 Prov. on Adm. of Est. of Sino-foreign Job Intermediary Inst., art. 6; *see* 1996 Reg. for the Administration of the Employment of Foreigners.

[31] Laodongbu Bangongting dui guan yu lin shi gong deng wen ti de qing shi de fu han [Rely to Questions re Contingent Workers etc.] (issued by Ministry of Labor, 1996), http://www.molss.gov.cn/gb/ywzn/2006-02/15/content_106797.htm.

[32] Zhonghua Renmin Gongheguo he tong fa [PRC Contract Law] (promulgated by the 2nd session of the Ninth Nat'l People's Cong., Mar. 15, 1999, effective Oct. 1, 1999). This is similar in approach to the U.S. labor laws exclusion of independent contractors.

[33] LCL, art. 68.

[34] LCL, art. 71.

[35] Guan yu fei quan ri zhi yong gong ruo gan wen ti de yi jian [Opinions on Several Issues regarding Part-time Workers] (promulgated by MOLSS, Mar. 30, 2003), http://www.law-lib.com/law/law_view.asp?id=78005.

restrictions against rural workers seeking employment in cities."[36] Prior to
this law, there were some limited protections for migrant workers, including prohibiting discrimination based on workers' residence (*hu kou*), prohibiting delays in payment of wages, and paying workplace injury insurance
benefits.[37] Some local governments had implemented migrant worker rights
through local regulations, although some had questionable restrictions (e.g.,
part-time migrant workers were excluded, in a possible contradiction with the
MOLSS 2003 Interpretations on Part-Time Workers.[38]

Foreign employees employed in China, with proper documentation, may
work in China for Chinese employers or FIEs (including representative
offices).[39]

4. Exclusions

Exclusions from applicable legal obligations developed as the laws sought a
balance between promoting economic development and labor protections.
Exclusions are found explicitly and implicitly under definitions of "employer"
and "employee," as well as in specific provisions excluding and exempting
employee categories, such as independent contractors (not employees), civil
servants (excluded), and managers (exempted from overtime).

Examples of explicit exclusions can be found in local regulations such
as in Shanghai, which expressly exclude "non-urban enterprises or rural

---

[36] Jiu ye cu jin fa [Employment Promotion Law] (promulgated by the 29th Standing Comm. of
the Tenth Nat'l People's Cong., Aug. 30, 2007, effective Jan. 1, 2008), art. 31.

[37] Guan yu nong min gong can jian gong shang bao xian you guan wen ti de tong zhi
[Notice on migrant workers' rights of participating in workers' compensation insurance
system] (promulgated by MOLSS, June 1, 2004), http://www.molss.gov.cn/gb/ywzn/2004–
06/01/content_213986.htm.

[38] Beijingshi Lao dong he she hui bao zhang ju guan yu yin fa "Beijingshi wai di nong min gong
can jia gong shang bao xian zan xing ban fa" he "Beijingshi wai di nong min gong can jia ji ben yi
liao bao xian zan xing ban fa" de tong zhi [Notice on Temporary Measures for Migrant Workers
in Beijing to Participate in Work Injury Insurance and Basic Medical Insurance] (issued by
Beijing Labor and Social Security Bureau, July 28, 2004, effective Sep. 1, 2004) [hereinafter 2004
Beijing Temp. Measures for Migrant Workers], http://www.51labour.com/lawcenter/lawshow-
40933.html.

[39] 1996 Reg. for the Administration of the Employment of Foreigners; 2001 Prov. on Adm.
of Est. of Sino-foreign Job Intermediary Inst. "A dispute between an employer and a foreigner shall be dealt with in accordance with Labor Law of PRC and Enterprise Labor
Dispute Treatment Regulation of PRC." Wai guo ren jiu ye guan li ban fa [Measures for
Administrating Foreigner Employment in China] (promulgated by Ministry of Labor, Ministry of Public Security, Ministry of Foreign Affairs, and Ministry of Foreign Trade and
Economic Cooperation, Jan. 22, 1996, effective May 1, 1996), art. 26, http://www.people.
com.cn/zixun/flfgk/item/dwjjf/falv/2/2-1-51.html.

enterprises."[40] Likewise, in 2004, Beijing excluded certain migrant and domestic workers and migrant farmers from receiving some forms of social insurance.[41]

Implicit exclusions can arise from omissions under the labor laws. For example, the 1999 Regulations on Unemployment Insurance cover only "urban" enterprises (SOEs, collective owned, FIEs, privately owned, and other enterprises in the area), thus implicitly excluding rural enterprises.[42] In addition, implicitly excluded (unless affirmatively included) are nonprofit social institutions, privately owned nonenterprises, and urban individual economic entities, for which local governments are authorized to expand coverage to include them, if so desired.[43]

Subsequent interpretation of an omission may clarify coverage issues. For example, in 1995, the MOLSS interpreted the 1994 Labor Law as inapplicable to civil servants.[44] Although excluded civil servants are covered by other regulations, non–civil-service workers employed by "state organs, institutions, and public organizations" who form labor contract relations are covered by the 1994 Labor Law and the various labor laws.[45]

Interpretations of "outsourced" individual subcontractors or their workers may determine they are not "employees" and are therefore excluded, or they may be explicitly excluded from coverage, as for example, in the Interpretation of the Shanghai Wage Regulation that expressly excludes independent contractors.[46] It identifies independent contractors as including those who have entered into a general service agreement, a lease agreement for equipment, or a construction service agreement.

[40] Shanghaishi shi ye bao xian ban fa [Procedures of Shanghai Municipality on Unemployment Insurance] (Feb. 5, 1999) [hereinafter 1999 Shanghai Unemployment Insurance Procedures], art. 2, http://www.shanghai.gov.cn/shanghai/node2314/node2316/node2330/node2493/userobject6ai429.html.

[41] 2004 Beijing Temp. Measures for Migrant Workers.

[42] Unemployment Insurance Regulations, art. 2.

[43] Unemployment Insurance Regulations, art. 32.

[44] 1995 Labor Law Implementing Opinion, art. 4. Likewise, the LCL is inapplicable to civil servants. See analyses of LCL, http://www.laodonghetong.org/540a.html.

[45] Zhonghua Renmin Gongheguo lao dong fa [Labor Law of PRC] (promulgated by 8th session of Standing Comm. of the Eighth Nat'l People's Cong., July 5, 1994, effective Jan. 1, 1995), art. 2; Guo jia gong wu yuan zan xing tiao li [Civil Servant Interim Regulations] (promulgated by State Council, Aug. 14, 1993, effective Oct. 1, 1993); Gong shang bao xian tiao li [Regulations on Work-related Injury Insurance] (promulgated by State Council, April 27, 2003, effective Jan. 1, 2004) (setting up a separate coverage program for civil servants).

[46] Guan yu "Shanghaishi qi ye zhi gong zui di gong zi gui ding you guan tiao wen de jie shi" [Interpretation on the Articles of "Regulations on Minimum Wage of Shanghai Enterprise Employees"] (promulgated by Shanghai Labor Bureau, Feb. 20, 1995), art. 2, http://www.legalcare.cn/zhuanti/newsd.asp?id=7888.

Chinese workers who work outside China are subject to special regulations. If a foreign employer recruits Chinese workers through an intermediary agency to work overseas, the intermediary agency shall be governed by the Regulations on Overseas Employment Agency (MOLLSS, 2002).[47] These agencies must meet licensing requirements of the government,[48] and they have an affirmative duty to instruct employees to sign a labor contract with the employer. They must also verify that the labor contract covers hours, wages, condition protections, room and board, liquidated damages, terminations, and other important items.[49] The actual implementation of these labor contracts is left to the parties and does not appear to be subject to China's labor laws, as they involve Chinese citizens working outside China for a foreign employer. It appears there is no guarantor provision in the regulations.

5. Exemptions

Outside China, executive, administrative, and professional employees are often partially exempted from specific labor law obligations such as overtime pay. Employer classification of these employees determines the applicability or exemption of labor law obligations, such as overtime pay. It can also lead to illegal misclassifications in an effort to save labor costs. When the salary of these exempt workers is lower than the total costs of wages and overtime pay for nonexempt employees, employers are not limited in scheduling them to work long hours, saving employers added costs. This incentive causes many employees who are actually entitled to overtime pay, to be incorrectly classified as managers and supervisors to fit into exempt categories of employees. In 2008 in Japan, a McDonald's store was found to have misclassified its employee as a manager even though he appeared to have much authority over many employees, causing the employer to be liable for years of overdue overtime pay.[50] The implications of this widespread employment practice did not go unnoticed by other employers throughout Japan, and very quickly Seven-Eleven and other large enterprises changed many of their classifications to conform to the law's application. In China, lawyers immediately began advising employers about

---

[47] Jing wai jiu ye zhong jie guan li gui ding [Regulations on the Administration of Foreign Employment Intermediary Agencies] (promulgated by State Council, MOLSS, Ministry of Public Security, and State Administration of Industry & Commerce, May 14, 2002, effective July 1, 2002), art. 2, http://law.chinalawinfo.com/newlaw2002/slc/slc.asp?db=chl&gid=40264.

[48] *Id.* art. 3.

[49] *Id.* art. 10(2).

[50] Martin Fackler, *Standing Up for Workers' Rights in Japan*, N.Y. TIMES, June 11, 2008, http://www.nytimes.com/2008/06/11/business/worldbusiness/11suits.html?pagewanted=print.

this Japanese case, as it also had been a common practice in China to classify employees as managers and avoid overtime pay, usually without too much concern about enforcement.[51]

In China, managers are not explicitly exempted in legislation from overtime obligations. However, certain categories such as "senior managers of the enterprise, field staff, sales personnel, guards and other employees" appear to be exempted from overtime payment requirements, as they fall under the "irregular working time arrangement" because "their work cannot be measured according to normal hours of work."[52] The irregular working time arrangements are available to employees as follows: (1) senior managers of the enterprise, field staff, sales personnel, guards, and other employees whose work cannot be measured according to normal hours of work; (2) transport personnel of the enterprise, taxi drivers, loaders, stevedores, warehouse workers, and other employees whose job requires great flexibility; and (3) other employees who are more suited for variable hours of work because of the nature of their production activity, work, or function.[53] However, some argue there is a question of whether they are entitled to time off in lieu of overtime pay.[54]

There is an application process for companies to obtain approval for certain categories of employees to qualify for the irregular working hour system, which is the closest thing to "exempt" that the PRC has.[55] Approval requirements vary depending on the jurisdiction and district. In some districts the application form may require approval of the labor union or Workers Congress. Some local regulations require exceptions for work performed on national holidays. Which employees are "senior managers" – only the general manager or line manager – also varies by locality.[56]

---

[51] Guan yu qi ye shi xing bu ding shi gong zuo zhi he zong he ji suan gong shi gong zuo zhi de shen pi ban fa [Regulations on the Approval of Variable Hours of Work and Consolidated Hours of Work in Enterprises] (promulgated by Ministry of Labor, Dec. 14, 1994, effective Jan.1, 1995), art. 3–4, http://www.ilo.org/dyn/natlex/docs/SERIAL/44577/63616/F1419578998/CHN44577.PDF. In a rare case, a hotel manager in Qingdao won his case against his employer for overtime payment and was awarded more than 30,000 RMB. *See* http://news.sina.com.cn/s/2005-12-12/09507686140s.shtml.

[52] *Id.* art. 3.

[53] *Id.* art. 4.

[54] Zeng Xiangquan, Lu Liang, and Sa'ad Umar Idris, *Working Time in Transition: The Dual Task of Standardization and Flexibilization in China*, Conditions of Work and Employment Series No. 11, International Labor Organization, at 19, http://www.ilo.org/public/english/protection/condtrav/pdf/11cws.pdf.

[55] *Supra*, note 50.

[56] *See* Ben shi qi ye shi xing bu ding shi gong zuo zhi he zong he ji suan gong shi gong zuo zhi de shen pi ban fa [Shanghai Municipal Regulations on the Approval of Variable Hours of Work and Consolidated Hours of Work in Enterprises] (promulgated by Shanghai Labor and Social Security Bureau, Nov. 10, 2006, effective Jan. 1, 2007), http://www.shanghai.

Students, as employees, make up another category for which employers can obtain exemption from overtime obligations. A student older than sixteen years of age may be employed, but "exempted" from otherwise applicable, overtime regulations, if he or she works in a work/study program and meets certain requirements.[57] For example, in Beijing and Jiangsu, regulations authorize such an "exemption" where the student is an intern or a participant in a work/study program in a college (excluding vocational colleges) pursuant to an agreement between the enterprise and the college.[58] Hours of work are limited to thirty per week or six hours per day.[59] For work/study students, working hours should not exceed four hours per day, and compensation should not be below the local minimum wage standard.[60] There are also child protection and child labor laws protecting children.[61]

gov.cn/shanghai/node2314/node2319/node12344/userobject26ai9087.html; Beijingshi qi ye shi xing bu ding shi gong zuo zhi he zong he ji suan gong shi gong zuo zhi de ban fa [Beijing Municipal Regulations on the Approval of Variable Hours of Work and Consolidated Hours of Work in Enterprises] (promulgated by Beijing Labor and Social Security Bureau, Dec. 9, 2003, effective Jan. 1, 2004), http://www.bjld.gov.cn/LDJAPP/search/fgdetail.jsp?no=1673.

[57] 1995 Labor Law Implementing Opinion, art. 12.

[58] Guan yu gui fan qi ye jie na zai xiao xue sheng shi xi he qin gong zhu xue huo dong de tong zhi [Notice on Regulating Enterprises Accepting Student Interns and Work Study Program] (promulgated by Jiangsu Labor & Social Security Bureau and Bureau of Education, Aug. 9, 2006), art. 4, http://www.jiangning.gov.cn/art/2006/08/09/art_803_1688.html.

[59] *Id.*, art. 3.

[60] *Id.*, art. 5.

[61] Zhonghua Renmin Gongheguo wei cheng nian ren bao hu fa [Law of PRC for Protection of Children] (promulgated by 25th session of Standing Comm. of the Tenth Nat'l People's Cong., Dec. 29, 2006, effective June 1, 2007); Wei cheng nian gong te shu bao hu gui ding [Regulations for the Special Protection of Under-age Employees] (promulgated by Ministry of Labor, Dec. 9, 1994, effective Jan. 1, 1995); Jin zhi shi yong tong gong de gui ding [Regulations on Prohibiting the Use of Child Labor] (promulgated by State Council, Oct. 17, 2002, effective Dec. 1, 2002).

4

Individual Labor Contracts

Formation and Content

The passage of the Labor Contract Law (LCL) in 2007 was preceded by much public comment and hue and cry from foreign employers.[1] Although some employers argued that the law would increase costs, others countered, saying that the law was aimed only at preventing illegal conduct. Before the law took effect on January 1, 2008, some employers tried to avoid its effects by prompting the resignations of employees and then rehiring many of the same employees, thereby avoiding the new law's grant of "open-ended" labor contracts for employees working for an employer for a consecutive period of not fewer than ten years.[2] The Huawei Technologies of Shenzhen offered redundancy packages of $134 million to its employees, 7,000 of whom resigned but were subsequently rehired so as to "restart" the counting of their years of service. However, because of the public outcry and pressure from the press and the ACFTU, Huawei suspended its program. This "loophole" arguably was inapplicable, as many of the employees reportedly never lost a day of work, resigning one day and working the next under a new contract.[3] Employees seem to be embracing the rights provided in the Labor Contract Law, as there are reports of sharp increases in labor dispute cases.[4] The number of labor disputes heard by the courts in 2008 rose 94 percent in 2007, with the number nearly tripling in some coastal cities. Figures from the 2009 Supreme

---

[1] Ronald C. Brown, *China's New Labor Contract Law*, 3 CHINA LAW REPORTER 4 (2007); Brandon Kirk, *Putting China's Labor Contract Law into Practice*, CHINA LAW & PRACTICE 15–18 (March 2008).

[2] LCL, art. 14(1).

[3] Thousands of Huawei staff "quit," CHINA DAILY, November 3, 2007, http://www.chinadaily .com.cn/bizchina/2007-11/03/content_6228248.htm.

[4] Cases soar as workers seek redress, CHINA DAILY, April 22, 2009, english.people .com.cn/90001/90776/90882/6642282.html; Fiona Tam, Caseloads Surge as Laborers Air Gripes, SOUTH CHINA MORNING POST (July 9, 2008). Highlights of Work Report on China's Supreme Court, www.npc.cn/englishnpc/news/Events/2009_03/10/content_1488815.html.

People's Court Work Report showed a 59 percent increase during the prior year for the first 3 months. The types of disputes have expanded to include back pay for social insurance and pensions and the processes related to signing or terminating labor contracts.

1. Contract Formation

Individual labor contracts have become more comprehensive and formal following the 2008 implementation of the LCL. Employers' refusals to provide contracts to workers, particularly to members of vulnerable groups, such as migrant workers, have been addressed and labor rights strengthened. The new law uses a tripartite mechanism, at the county level and above, to study and resolve major issues arising from employment relationships.[5]

Many statutory provisions existing before the new law remain in force, but clarifications and strengthened sanctions have been added. For example, all employment contracts, except for part-timers, must be written,[6] and if not concluded and signed within thirty days, the employer must pay double wages for the period of the violation. The law established shorter probationary time limits, depending on the length of the contract, with maximum periods of one month for contracts between three months and one year; two months for contracts of one to three years; and six months for contracts of three years or longer or open-ended contracts.[7] When first hired, a new employee must be informed of the working and safety conditions.[8]

Three types of contract are prescribed – fixed term, open-ended term, and project contracts.[9] Workers employed for longer than ten years may be entitled to an open-ended contract[10]; workers whose second consecutive term expires will be entitled to have an open-ended contract, if they so demand,[11] as will workers without a written contract after one year.[12] An illustrative court case under the LCL upheld a labor arbitration award that an employee was entitled to an open-ended labor contract where the facts evidenced she had worked the requisite number of years.[13] A minimum-term-of-service-contract may be

---

[5] LCL, art. 5.
[6] LCL, art. 10.
[7] LCL, art. 19
[8] LCL, art. 8.
[9] LCL, arts. 12–15.
[10] LCL, art. 14(1).
[11] LCL, art. 14(3).
[12] LCL, art. 14.
[13] "Employee Wins First Reported Employment Contract," Baker & McKenzie Employment Newsletter, Beijing, Quarter 1, Feb. 2008, at 5.

used for employees who are provided with professional technical training under a special training fund; in those situations, a liquidated damage provision is permitted, to be paid by the breaching employee.[14]

The law highlights and prohibits many forms of employer misconduct in the formation of employment contracts. There is a long list of "don'ts." Article 26 invalidates an employment contract secured by a contractual party's deception, coercion, and taking advantage of the other's difficulties, and an employer cannot refuse to give a written contract.[15] Furthermore, an employer cannot keep a worker's ID card or require a security payment by a worker;[16] employment agencies cannot require a fee to be paid by the worker;[17] the employer cannot "disguise" overtime;[18] and most worker-liquidated damage provisions are prohibited.[19] Also prohibited are acts of violence, threats, or unlawful restriction of personal freedom to compel a worker to work.[20]

2. Content of Contracts

a. Formalities, Application, and Required Content

Formalities and required substantive terms, in the tradition of civil law legal systems, are provided in the law and generally replicate the content requirements of the 1994 Labor Law, though additional information is required in the labor contract.[21] It must specify duration, job descriptions, working hours, leaves and benefits, labor protections, and the like. Provisions of the law deal with performance, termination, severance pay, collective contracts, and dispute resolution. Additionally, some attention is given to dispatch workers, part-time labor, inspections, and remedies and damages for violations.

The LCL authorizes protection of confidential information, trade secrets, and intellectual property, and a competition restriction may also be included in the contract, though limited to certain senior management and technical personnel.[22] The limit on competition requires postemployment compensation, paid in monthly installments, and is limited to two years. Liquidated damage provisions are permitted for violations by those personnel,[23] but for

---

[14] LCL, art. 22.
[15] LCL, art. 11.
[16] LCL, art. 9.
[17] LCL, art. 60.
[18] LCL, art. 31.
[19] LCL, art. 25.
[20] LCL, art. 38.
[21] LCL, art. 17; Labor Law, art. 19. Illustrative if not model contracts are provided in Chapter 16.
[22] LCL, art. 23.
[23] LCL, arts. 23–24.

no other reason[24] except to recoup certain professional technical training costs.[25]

The LCL adds several categories of labor contract coverage. For example, early drafts dealing with the dispatch worker issue were very controversial. The new law, which appears to reduce employers' wide use of "agency" workers from staffing firms, reached accommodation on the controversial issues as follows: Staffing firms now must be established under the Company Law, are liable as an "employer," must have fixed term contracts of not fewer than two years with their workers, and must pay minimum wage compensation when there is no work assignment for the worker.[26] The placement must be based on "actual" requirements of the job position, and the parties may not conclude several short-term placement agreements to cover a continuous term of labor use.[27] Therefore, these temporary assignments should be limited to temporary, auxiliary, or substitute openings, and wages paid must be equal to those of the regular workers at the accepting unit.[28] Additionally, the staffing firm is prohibited from "pocketing" any of the compensation paid by the accepting unit for the workers or from charging fees to the workers placed.[29] Finally, these temporary workers are accorded the right to join or organize a labor union of either the staffing firm or the accepting unit.[30]

Obligations of the accepting unit also include implementing government labor standards, working conditions, and labor protection; paying overtime and performance bonuses, as well as normal wage adjustments; and providing training necessary for the job position.[31] Termination is to be done by the staffing firm,[32] and accepting units are prohibited from setting up their own staffing firms.[33]

Part-time workers are limited to an "average" of not more than four hours per day or twenty-four hours per week for the "same" employer,[34] but if there is a second employer, the subsequently concluded contract cannot prejudice the performance of the first.[35] Wages are usually paid on an hourly basis and must meet local minimum wage standards.[36] The contract may be oral

---

[24] LCL, art. 25.
[25] LCL, art. 22.
[26] LCL, arts. 57–58.
[27] LCL, art. 59.
[28] LCL, art. 63.
[29] LCL, art. 60.
[30] LCL, art. 64.
[31] LCL, art. 62.
[32] LCL, art. 65.
[33] LCL, art. 67.
[34] LCL, art. 68.
[35] LCL, art. 69.
[36] LCL, art. 72.

and terminated "at will," there is no severance pay, and there cannot be a probationary period.[37]

Some questions have arisen regarding employment of students not as "regular" workers, but as interns or participants in work/study programs. Pursuant to an MOLSS interpretation, this relationship falls outside the 1994 Labor Law, and subminimal compensation is often paid, as confirmed in the recent cases in China involving McDonald's and KFC.[38]

b. Performance

Performance requirements are located in six provisions in LCL; some are old and some new. Article 30 reiterates the employer's obligation to pay wages on time and in full, with possible further damages if there is a failure to do so.[39] Interestingly, Article 30 allows the unpaid worker, "in accordance with the law," to apply to the court for an order to pay; presumably, this "labor dispute" would still need to be preceded by labor arbitration except in exceptional circumstances.[40] Article 31 provides that an employer may not compel overtime; this is a clearer mandate than the prior law's right to negotiate same. Again, if enforced, this worker's "right" could provide an obstacle to termination under Article 39 for its exercise. Finally, without breaching their employment contracts, workers may withhold their services rather than perform certain dangerous operations.[41]

Mergers and acquisitions, a growing phenomenon in China and covered by new legislation, are addressed by Articles 33 and 34, respectively, which clarify the continuing validity of incumbent workers' employment contracts, absent a proper termination or amendment of their employment contracts.

c. Termination

Termination and ending employment contracts, discussed later in Part VI, are covered in fifteen provisions of Chapter 4 of the LCL and its implementing

---

[37] LCL, arts. 69–71.

[38] *McDonald's and KFC Seeking to Resolve Chinese Minimum Wage Issue*, April 5, 2007, http://www.iht.com/articles/2007/04/05/news/labor.php (last visited Sept. 5, 2008); Olivia Chung, *China's Part-Time McDonald Workers Exploited*, April 20, 2007, http://www.atimes.com/atimes/China_Business/ID20Cb02.html (last visited Sept. 7, 2008).

[39] LCL, art. 85.

[40] Discussed *infra* in Part V; for example, in one recent case, an employee did recover past due wages in a claim directly with the court. *China Employment Law Update*, Baker & McKenzie, April 2008, at 3.

[41] LCL, art. 32.

regulations, which clarify and create some new rights and obligations. Severance pay (with caps) may be required on expiration of a nonrenewed fixed-term labor contract and termination in a variety of circumstances.[42]

d. Legal Liabilities

Other aspects of the LCL involve monitoring, inspections, and enhanced legal liabilities. The administration and monitoring provisions add few, if any, changes, but may trigger liabilities. The law emphasizes the authority of the inspectors by stating that they have the authority to review employment contracts and conduct on-the-spot inspections of the work premises.[43] Workers whose rights are infringed have the right to "request" government action or to apply for arbitration or sue in court, as may be permitted by law.[44] Labor unions are permitted to complain about violations, file for arbitration,[45] and assist workers if they arbitrate or go to court.[46]

Remedies and damages for violations of the aforesaid legal liabilities are contained in fifteen articles of Chapter 7. For example, failure to provide a written employment contract in the first year requires the employer to pay twice the wages for the period in violation[47]; failure to pay owed compensation can render the employer liable for damages at 50 to 100 percent of the amount owed[48]; and if an employer unlawfully terminates or ends a contract, it must pay damages to the worker at twice the rate of severance pay due.[49] In April 2008, a labor arbitration decision held that the employer failed to provide a labor contract to a worker, as required by the LCL, and ordered the employer to pay double the wages from one month after the effective date of the LCL.[50] Other miscellaneous provisions include employer liability for (1) "raiding" another worker who is still employed[51] and (2) violation of the employment contract law by an "individual" who is an employer's "contractor" (jointly and severally liable[52]). Lastly, there is a provision for sanctions (including damages) against

---

[42] LCL, art. 46–47. Implementing regulations were issued on September 18, 2008, linked in Manfred Elfstrom, *Implementing Guidelines for China's Labor Contract Released*, http://laborrightsblog.typepad.com/international_labor_right/2008/09/implementing-gu.html.

[43] LCL, art. 75.

[44] LCL, art. 77.

[45] LCL, art. 56.

[46] LCL, art. 78.

[47] LCL, art. 82.

[48] LCL, art. 85.

[49] LCL, art. 87.

[50] *China Employment Law Update*, Baker & McKenzie, June 2008, at 5.

[51] LCL, art. 91.

[52] LCL, art. 94.

the government as labor-contract enforcers (including the labor agency, other offices, or "a member of its working personnel") that act negligently or fail to perform their duties and cause harm to a worker or the employer.[53] Transitions from employment contracts existing at the time of the LCL's implementation are dealt with in Article 97, with an employee's existing contract continuing, but with its renewal counted as a first renewal of a fixed-term contract under Article 14.

e. Collective Negotiations

The LCL also brings changes and new emphasis to collective negotiations (bargaining) and the role of unions.[54] It expands the concept that collective bargaining can occur at the county level or below across an industrial or regional sector in industries such as construction, mining, and catering services.[55] The law confirms and enhances the role of the labor union by providing it the authority to consult on employer rules, bargain collectively, and provide opinions on mass reductions in force and terminations.[56] These provisions come a year after the Company Law was amended to require greater participation by employee representatives (often the union) to serve on the supervising boards of companies.[57]

f. Employer Rules and Codes of Conduct

Other possible employer liabilities may arise from contractual obligations found in at least two sources: employer rules and regulations and employer codes of conduct. Article 4 of the LCL allows the employer to establish work rules (including conduct) that, if violated, can provide a basis for discipline or termination.[58] Under the LCL, consultation with the employees (or their representative congress) must precede the implementation of enumerated workplace issues.[59] These rules, as long as they are legal,[60] are incorporated into the labor contract and are part of the enforceable obligations; however,

[53] LCL, art. 95.
[54] Collective contracts and collective negotiations are discussed in Chapter 5.
[55] LCL, art. 53.
[56] LCL, arts. 4, 51, 41, 43.
[57] Gong si fa [Company Law] (promulgated by the 18th session of the Standing Comm. of the Tenth NPC, Jan. 1, 2006), art. 118 (PRC).
[58] Discussed *infra* in section 12.
[59] *Id.*
[60] LCL, art. 80.

unlike other labor contract provisions, they can be changed unilaterally (after consultation).[61]

By contrast, *external* corporate codes of conduct come in many varieties, often from industry standards and are separate from the labor contract.[62] Rights provided to employees, if any, to enforce these labor code standards are typically dealt with through internal procedures (not the labor arbitration process), with the employer being the ultimate decision maker. Although these external standards could be expressly or implicitly incorporated by reference into existing labor contracts, thus becoming the subject of a labor dispute for labor arbitration, most employers would likely be disinclined to expressly incorporate these standards. Because employees are not parties to the codes, any civil contract enforcement would be difficult, at best.

---

[61] LCL, art. 35 (The law requires written agreement to amend the labor contract).

[62] Robert J. Liubicic, *Corporate Codes of Conduct and Product Labeling Schemes: The Limits and Possibilities of Promoting International Labor Rights through Private Initiatives*, 30 LAW & POL'Y INT'L BUS. 111, 125, 128 (1998). Robert J. Liubicic, *New Labour Standards Compliance Strategies: Corporate Codes of Conduct and Social Labeling Programs* (March 7, 2008), http://www.hrsdc.gc.ca/en/labour/employment_standards/fls/research/research21/page07.shtml.

5

Collective Labor Contracts and Collective Negotiations

1. Trade Unions in China

The trade union in China is the All China Federation of Trade Unions (ACFTU), and all unions must be affiliated with it.[1] It is regulated by law, as is the process of negotiating collective contracts.[2] It is a quasi-governmental social organization with multiple functions, one of which is to further government goals. Its policies are designed to promote economic development and enterprise interests as well as labor protections. In recent times, these policies appear to be changing, certainly from its original approaches, to be more aligned with employee interests.

Establishing a local labor union in China is a relatively straightforward process: 25 employees join the union and, with the approval of a higher-level union, initiate its establishment by making a formal request of the employer.[3] The Trade Union Law allows an employee, in some circumstances, to retain union membership even after the original employment relationship has ended.[4]

---

[1] Trade Union Law, art. 11.

[2] Ji ti he tong gui ding [Provisions on Collective Contracts] (promulgated by Ministry of Labor and Social Security, Jan. 20, 2004, effective May 1, 2005).

[3] Qi ye gong hui gong zuo tiao li (Shi xing) [Provisions on the Work of Enterprise Trade Unions (for Trial Implementation)] (promulgated by All China Federation of Trade Unions, July 6, 2006), art. 10 ("An enterprise with 25 or more trade union members shall establish a trade union committee. And an enterprise with less than 25 trade union members may separately establish a trade union committee, or may jointly establish a grass-roots trade union committee with such similar enterprises according to the region or industry"); Trade Union Law, art. 11.

[4] Trade Union Law, art. 12 ("Any organization and individual shall not annul or merge trade unions randomly. When an enterprise ceases to exist and when an institution or organ is abolished, the grassroots trade union organization of that enterprise, institution, or organ shall be annulled accordingly, and the annulment shall be reported to the next higher trade union. The membership of members to trade unions that are annulled according to provisions of

As it seeks to find a balance between economic development and labor protection, the ACFTU has unionized foreign-owned companies, such as Wal-Mart, McDonald's, and KFC, and it continues to seek expansion of the union's presence, including in the Fortune Global 500 companies.[5] Even American unions are seeking to cooperate with China's union; in addition to meetings of international union delegations from the United States with Chinese unions, the Los Angeles County Federation of Labor, AFL-CIO, on July 5, 2007, signed an agreement with the Shanghai Trade Union Council (an affiliate of ACFTU) to provide mutual assistance, especially in organizing and bargaining with multinational companies in Shanghai.[6] In an attempt to expand its membership, the ACFTU recently amended its Labor Union Charter to allow membership by migrant workers.[7]

The trade union's role is still evolving. The path was clearer in the early days of the People's Republic of China, when "within the state socialist system, the interests of both management and the trade union were supposed to be identical and their identification was reinforced by the subordination of both to the Party-state."[8] Although the Chinese Communist Party (CCP) in recent years has stepped back somewhat from seeking to directly influence management's micro-market decisions, it continues to maintain a close policy relationship with the ACFTU. Even though the union is set up as an independent and autonomous body, as is the All China Women's Federation, it is maintained as a quasi-governmental entity.[9]

the preceding Paragraph may be reserved and the specific administrative measures shall be formulated by ACFTU").

5 David Barboza, *Foreign companies Pushed to Allow Chinese Unions*, INTERNATIONAL HERALD TRIBUNE, www.iht.com/articles/2008/09/11/business/yuan.php; *McDonald's, KFC Allow Unions in China*, April 10, 2007, http://www.msnbc.msn.com/id/18035954/; *The Chinese Trade Union's Big Rush to Set Up Unions in Fortune 500 Companies*, China Labor News Translations at www.clntranslations.org/file_download/59; *Focus–China Trade Union Moves against Foreign Firms Driven by Politics, Money*, http://www.forbes.com/afxnewslimited/feeds/afx/2007/04/11/afx3601009.html. By the end of September, 2008 the ACFTU claimed it had reached its target of establishing unions in 80 percent of the branches and subsidiaries of the Fortune Global 500 companies in China. Liang Caiheng, Zai hua shi jie 500 qiang, 82% jian gong hui [Fortune Global 500 Companies in China, 82% Unionized], PEOPLE'S DAILY, Oct. 13, 2008, http://mnc.people.com.cn/GB/8162041.html.

6 *U.S. and Mainland Labor Unions in Historic Alliance*, SOUTH CHINA MORNING Post, July 7, 2007.

7 The ACFTU passed these amendments during its national congress in October 2008. Society – Weekly Watch, BEIJING REVIEW, Oct. 30, 2008, http://www.bjreview.com.cn/print/txt/2008–10/28/content_159386.htm.

8 Simon Clarke, Chang-Hee Lee and Qi Li, *Collective Consultation and Industrial Relations in China*, BRITISH J. INDUSTRIAL RELATIONS 241 (June 2004).

9 Trade Union Law, art. 4.

During China's dramatic economic development in the past three decades, the ACFTU has emerged as an organization that under law plays "a dual role in the transition towards a market economy."[10] In that dual role of promoting both employee interests and economic reforms and social stability, there has been some internal discussion, if not struggles, between those in the union who want the ACFTU to be more active in the advocacy and representation of the employees' interests and those in the CCP who want the union to be more responsive to the needs of society for social stability.[11] In practice, some observers feel the ACFTU's current predominant role in the workplace is to fulfill a management function.

Existing alongside labor unions are Worker's Congresses, which originally were established in SOEs to provide workers with democratic management; they are not particularly common in private enterprises. When present, they can be one more player in the complex negotiations relating to the welfare of the employees and the enterprises. According to regulations promulgated in 1986,[12] each Worker's Congress is supposed to meet at least once a year, with its executive body, usually the trade union, implementing its functions.

These functions include review and approval or disapproval of management's plans, appointments, and decisions. However, the Worker's Congress's efficacy in practical terms is suspect, and post-1979 history and rapidly changing governance structures in China seem to have reduced its usefulness. For example, the current Corporation Law has greatly weakened the power and role of Worker's Congresses, reducing them to merely exercising "democratic management"[13] and "democratic supervision."[14] The former "legal" functions of the Worker's Congress to appraise and supervise the cadres and elect the director of the enterprise have now been assumed by a corporate board of directors and supervisory committee.[15] Whether this will be a *fatal blow* to the Worker's Congresses, at least in SOEs, remains to be seen, as China seems determined to keep the entity alive and in 2008 released new draft regulations concerning them.[16] In addition, its role (and possibly the role of the union,

---

[10] Clarke, *supra* note 8.

[11] Bill Taylor, Chang Kai, and Li Qi, Industrial Relations in China 115 (2003).

[12] Quan min suo you zhi gong ye qi ye zhi gong dai biao da hui tiao li [Regulation on State-Owned Enterprise Workers' Congress] arts. 1–6 (1986), http://law.chinalawinfo .com/newlaw2002/SLC/SLC.asp?Db=chl&Gid=2977 (last visited Sept. 13, 2008).

[13] Gong si fa [Company Law] (promulgated by the 18th session of the Standing Comm. of the Tenth NPC, Jan. 1, 2006), art. 16 (PRC).

[14] *Id.* art. 16, 55.

[15] Taylor et al., *supra* note 11.

[16] Draft regulations on Employee Representative Congresses (ERCs) were released by the ACFTU on September 10, 2008, which will be sent to the State Council for consideration

which is often connected closely to the Worker's Congress) was enhanced by the Company Law, which authorized participation by employee representatives on supervisory boards.[17] The 2008 Labor Contract Law empowers an "employee representative congress" *and* a labor union in the company to deal with the employer on employee interests, such as the formulation of employer rules.[18]

The process and results of collective negotiation vary widely. In 2006, the ACFTU reported it had negotiated more than 862,000 collective agreements covering 112.5 million workers.[19] Because of policy changes in recent years, some collective contracts embody more than the usual statutory protections and include wage increases and contractual rights and benefits. Therefore, dealing with the union is an individual endeavor for which any but general patterns are difficult to describe.

Collective contract obligations and procedures under new laws follow the 1994 Labor Law, the 2004 MOLSS Provisions on Collective Negotiations, and the 2006 ACFTU's trial implementation of the Provisions on the Work of Enterprise Trade Unions, which call for "consultation.[20] The 2008 Labor Contract Law[21] and 2008 Law on Labor Mediation and Arbitration[22] have also brought changes, confirming and enhancing the role of the union in negotiation of collective contracts and particularly in the dispute resolution mechanisms. Of particular interest to employers is LCL Article 51, which states that, where there is no union, the employer shall conclude a collective

---

and possible passage in 2009. Xiao Yao, Quan guo zong gong hui: Qi ye min zhu guan li tiao li ming nian huo li fa [ACFTU: Draft Regulations on Employee Representative Congresses In Legislation Next Year], LEGAL DAILY, http://news.sohu.com/20081023/n260204447.shtml. *See also, China's State Enterprises*, http://reddiarypk.wordpress.com/2008/08/22/chinas-state-enterprises/.

[17] Company Law, art. 52.

[18] LCL, art. 4.

[19] Guan Xiaofeng, *Workers to Get Power to Negotiate, Union Says*, CHINA DAILY, May 25, 2007, http://www.chinadaily.com.cn/china/2007-05/25/content_880121.htm. This is reported to include about 50,000 foreign employers with collective contracts. David Barboza, *Foreign Companies Pushed to Allow Chinese Unions*, INTERNATIONAL HERALD TRIBUNE, www.iht.com/articles/2008/09/11/business/yuan.php;

[20] Qi ye gong hui gong zuo tiao li [Provisions on the Work of Enterprise Trade Unions (for Trial Implementation)] (promulgated by All China Federation of Trade Unions, July 6, 2006); for full discussion *see*, Ronald C. Brown, *China's Collective Contract Provisions: Can Collective Negotiations Embody Collective Bargaining?* 16 DUKE J. COMP. & INT'L LAW 35 (2006).

[21] LCL, arts. 51–56. Implementing regulations were issued on Septmber 18, 2008, linked in Manfred Elfstrom, *Implementing Guidelines for China's Labor Contract Released*, http://laborrightsblog.typepad.com/international_labor_right/2008/09/implementing-gu.html.

[22] Lao dong zheng yi tiao jie zhong cai fa [The Law on Labor Dispute Mediation and Arbitration] (promulgated by the 31st session of the Standing Comm. of the Tenth NPC, Dec. 29, 2007, effective May 1, 2008), arts. 4 8, 10,19 (PRC).

contract with an employee representative under the guidance of higher-level unions.

A newly developed feature is the shifting emphasis from enterprise-level negotiations to *industry-wide* or *area collective contracts* in industries such as construction, mining, catering services, etc., within areas below the county level (LCL, Art. 53). Article 54 stipulates that these contracts are binding on employers and workers in the industry or in the area in the locality concerned; this provision could allow collective contracts to cover competing employers in the same industry located in the same area. Reportedly, the ACFTU is allowing companies with branch offices to establish head office unions, with the power to represent all employees in the company – in effect creating a nationwide union for that company.[23]

The 2008 Labor Contract Law arguably has enhanced the union's dominant status as the representative of the workers in collective negotiations, in arbitration, and in the policing and enforcing of this new law. However, some observe there is nothing new in this rhetoric and that this law brings little change to labor relations, arguing, for example, that Wal-Mart and others took little risk when they embraced the labor union. Others argue there are signs that unions at Wal-Mart and in China may be more than hollow shells and may be having a real effect in the workplace.[24]

a. Role of the Union

In fact, Chinese labor law requires the ACFTU to serve two masters. In addition to representing "the legitimate rights and interests of the workers,"[25] it must also assist the government and the CCP in "upholding the overall rights and

---

[23] *China Employment Law Update*, Baker & McKenzie, June 2008, at 1; *see* ACFTU News, http://www.china.com.cn/gonghui/2008-06/16/content_15826764.htm.

[24] *The Emergence of Real Trade Unionism in Wal-Mart Stores*, China Labor News Translations, http://www.cintranslations.org/article/30/draft; Kelly Chan, Unions Force Wal-Mart to back down over reshuffle SOUTH MORNING CHINA POST, April 21, 2009; but see Wal-Mart China management destructuring hits snag, Portland Tribune, April 22, 2009, www.congoo.com/news/2009April21/wal-mart.reshuffle-plan-china; Ying Ge, *What Do Unions Do in China*, papers.ssrn.com/sol3/papers.cfm?abstract_id=1031084; Chen Feng, *Legal Mobilization by Trade Unions*, 52 CHINA J. 27–45 (July 2004); *Wal-Mart China Branches Sign Collective Contracts with Trade Unions*, China CSR, http://www.chinacsr.com/en/2008/08/04/2690-wal-mart-china-branches-sign-collective-contracts-with-trade-unions/. The new collective contracts emerging appear to broadly encompass many employee rights and interests; *see* model collective contract in Chapter 16(2) *infra*, and a model proposed by the Shenzhen Labor Bureau (in Chinese) and said to be followed by some large local employers, http://www.sz12333.gov .cn/main/Web/Article/2005/10/24/1113507702C18328.aspx (last visited Nov. 7, 2008).

[25] Trade Union Law, art. 2.

interests of the whole nation."[26] LCL Article 56 explicitly states that the union may take a labor dispute to arbitration or the court and otherwise act as an advocate in termination cases (LCL, Art. 43) and other disputes.

As to the union's advocacy role on behalf of the employees, the ACFTU is to provide guidance and assistance to workers on obtaining individual labor and collective contracts and to advance workers' interests by securing employers' compliance with a variety of health, safety, and labor laws.[27] In the event of a work stoppage or slowdown, the ACFTU's responsibility is both to represent the employees' interests and to assist the employer in properly dealing with the matter to restore the normal order of production; thus, in effect, mediating solutions to the dispute.[28] The union maintains this bifurcated loyalty by serving on intra-enterprise mediation committees and the tripartite Labor Arbitration Commissions, both of which seek to resolve disputes over employees' labor rights.[29] While conducting its work "independently," the ACFTU is admonished to "concentrate on the focus of economic construction, adhere to the socialist road,"[30] and, as its basic responsibility, "safeguard the rights and interests of workers."[31] Additionally, Article 7 of the Trade Union Law requires that "trade unions should mobilize and organize employees to participate in the economic construction positively, to complete production duties and working duties with great efforts. Trade unions shall educate employees... to build disciplined employee groups."[32]

2. Historic Obstacles to Collective Negotiations

As China moves forward in implementing labor reforms, including engaging in collective contract negotiations, it also carries with it the Chinese characteristics of the past. This section focuses on the period before the passage of the 2004 Collective Contract MOLSS Provisions. A study conducted by Clarke and colleagues of the collective negotiation process in SOEs, private enterprises, and FIEs pointed out some of its more persistent deficiencies, some of which have been addressed by the 2004 Provisions. First, with regard to process, the Clarke study observed that, although the system of collective consultation is a means for the state to intervene in enterprises, it does not

---

[26] *Id.* art. 6; Provisions on the Work of Enterprise Trade Unions (for Trial Implementation), art. 18(1–10).
[27] Trade Union Law, arts. 20–25;
[28] *Id.* art. 27.
[29] Labor Law, arts. 80–81; Law on Labor Dispute Mediation and Arbitration, arts. 10, 19.
[30] Trade Union Law, art. 4.
[31] *Id.* art. 6.
[32] *Id.* art. 7.

provide the framework for a new industrial relations system. It continues to be essentially an "anachronistic system of 'workers' participation in management' and a (rather ineffective) adjunct to the juridical regulation of labor relations, providing a means to remind employers and trade union officers of their legal obligations . . . "[33]

With regard to content of the collective contracts, the Clarke study concluded,

> [e]mployers remain reluctant to incorporate any substantive detail in the collective contract, so that the contract adds little or nothing to the existing legal regulation of the terms and conditions of employment. At best, the collective contract provides a means of reminding employers of their legal obligations and monitoring the implementation of labor legislation in the workplace.[34]

Typically, there are three categories of clauses in collective contracts in SOEs: The first deals with principles and formalities, such as who are the parties, the second includes the clauses to be implemented by the parties, and the third category deals with commitments of the parties and their duration.[35] One study showed that the second category of clauses took up an average of about 70 percent of the total number of clauses, with more than 60 percent of these clauses defined by the Labor Law (usually a duplication), 20 to 30 percent made in reference to that law (e.g., time schedule for implementing certain required female medical examinations), and about 10 percent dealing with subjects relating to improvement of employee benefits.[36]

Lastly, the role of the trade union in China has drawn much attention. The Clarke study argues that it does not serve as a real advocate for employee interests, noting that "the predominant functions of the trade union at the workplace still tend to be management functions."[37] Clarke's study describes its function as follows:

> [To] "take economic development as its central task," encouraging workers to increase productivity, enforcing labor discipline and conducting extensive propaganda on behalf of management. "Protecting the rights and interests of employees" is at best interpreted as monitoring managerial practice to ensure that it conforms to all the relevant laws and regulations, and implementing the social and welfare policy of the enterprise – visiting sick workers, dealing with personal problems, distributing benefits, organizing picnics and arranging celebrations.[38]

---

[33] Clarke, *supra* note 8, at 251.
[34] *Id.* at 250.
[35] TAYLOR, *supra* note 11, at 193–4.
[36] *Id.*
[37] Clarke, *supra* note 8, at 242.
[38] *Id.*

Part of the explanation why trade unions serve management funtions is provided by who typically serves as a trade union official:

> Trade union officers are drawn largely from the ranks of management. A full-time trade union president is paid by the employer and normally enjoys the status (and salary) of a deputy general director of the company; the personal careers of union leaders revolve around the positions of party cadre, union leader and enterprise manager; they are usually members of the Board of Directors and/or the Supervisory Board of the company; and they (rightly) regard themselves as members of the senior management team. Whether or not there is a formal election of the trade union chair, the latter was normally appointed by management [until new limitations were issued by the ACFTU in 2008].[39]

In prior years, the CCP would have played a more direct and active role in ensuring that the employer and union worked "harmoniously," but in recent years the CCP has been working more indirectly, usually through the trade union. In that respect, the Clarke study shows that "at least five of the 12 trade union presidents also held the post of party secretary or deputy party secretary."[40]

This ambiguity of who is the employer and who is the union (though not necessarily who is the boss) is further complicated by China's legacy of SOEs being units of larger, integrated bureaucracies in the planned economy, the periodic use of Worker's Congresses, and the absence of unions in many enterprises across China. The traditional SOEs used "employers" and trade unions as agents for controlling bureaucratic entities of an economic plan. With economic reforms and new laws, legal responsibility is increasingly fixed on the "employing unit" – the employer. However, at the enterprise level, there is little meaningful influence to prevent the union and the employer from wearing each other's hats and in the process basically becoming the same voice.

Another emerging feature of collective negotiations is the introduction and, since the 2008 LCL, the institutionalization of industrial unions. The many small to medium-sized FIEs, privately owned enterprises (POEs), and town and village enterprises (TVEs) in the new socialist market economy employ a large number of workers coming from rural or less industrialized areas of China, and as is well documented, their labor rights are exploited all too often.[41] The unionization rate in these enterprises is very low, and there is

---

[39] *Id.* at 242–3. The ACFTU issed measures in 2008 limiting human resource managers, other senior management officials, foreign nationals, and close relatives from being union president; candidates must be approved by the upper level labor union, which can also nominate a nonemployee candidate. The Trial Measures for Election of Enterprise Labor Union Chairman (ACFTU August 1, 2008).

[40] *Id.* at 243.

[41] *Id.* at 248.

little expectation of labor law enforcement, let alone negotiation of collective contracts. It has been suggested that these largely overseas-funded enterprises do not necessarily resist collective negotiations; rather, they see unions and negotiations as irrelevant and the government and the CCP as either reluctant or impotent to induce the enterprises to sign labor agreements.[42] The ACFTU has taken notice of this perception, and as early as 1996 in a document issued jointly by the then-Ministry of Labor, the ACFTU, the SETC, and the China Enterprise Confederation, approval was given for the use of "professional or industrial unions" of the primary trade union to negotiate collective contracts on behalf of the employees at these various enterprises.[43] This was further confirmed in the LCL, Article 53.

Pursuant to this policy of using industrial unions, the ACFTU has reportedly established these types of local trade union organizations in twenty-five provinces since 1996.[44] The agreements made by these industrial unions cover all of the private enterprises in one district or industrial sector. The union signs the agreements with the "employers' associations" at the same levels. These associations are described as "established under the relevant government departments rather than genuine employers' organizations."[45] Clarke's study, written before the 2004 Provisions, indicates that in at least one area, Chengdu (where there were some thirty agreements), there has been an increase in union membership following the agreements.[46] An added bonus for workers in Chengdu is that the city-level ACFTU had "successfully been taking cases to the City Arbitration Committee when the employers had failed to abide by the agreement."[47] A downside noted was that this effort worked because of government intervention (as employers' associations were local government

---

[42] *Id.* The new LCL and the strengthened labor arbitration system will likely have employers paying closer attention to legal requirements, as the penalties for violation have certainly become meaningful.

[43] TAYLOR, *supra* note 11, at 196. The Trade Union law states, "[E]nterprises of some industries or industries of similar nature may set up national or regional industrial unions as circumstances require." Trade Union Law, art. 10.

[44] Clarke, *supra* note 8, at 249. The ACFTU reports that the sector-wide contract covers some 12,000 textile workers at 116 enterprises. *See Putting Up Pay Rates through Bargaining,* at http://english.acftu.org/template/10002/file.jsp?cid=57&aid=407. A union in Hangzhou reportedly had recent guarantees of 800 yuan per month through collective contracts. Interestingly, a comment by Fu Nanbao, president of the trade union in Xinhe, said that with the help of the trade union and the new wage negotiating system, "the relationship between employers and workers has gone from being 'adversarial' to 'cooperative.'" Shao Xiaoyi, *Negotiated Salary System Saves Industry,* CHINA DAILY, Feb. 24, 2005, at 5, http://www.chinadaily.com.cn/english/doc/2005-02/24/content_418852.htm (last visited Sept. 13, 2008).

[45] Clarke, *supra* note 8, at 249.

[46] *Id.*

[47] *Id.*

authorities supervising local private enterprises) rather than because of voluntary regulation of collective negotiations by private employers.[48]

Some positive aspects were observed in the pre-2004 collective negotiation
process. The "existing system provides an effective method of soliciting the
reactions of employees to management proposals"; however, because of the
great amount of discretion a union has, the ability of employees to have an
effective channel to articulate their own aspirations was more limited.[49] In
some cases involving large FIEs who wished to be "good citizens," such as
Beijing Jeep Ltd., Babcock & Wilcox Company, and Shanghai Volkswagen
Automotive Company Ltd., comprehensive collective contracts were negotiated, though they were not necessarily prompted by the laws.[50] Willing unions
also demonstrated their abilities "to design sophisticated negotiation strategies
involving high, medium and bottom lines for their wage negotiation."[51]

The 2001 Trade Union Law protects the union and the employees against
improper interference with the rights granted under this law, including the
rights of employees and trade unions to engage in lawful union activity.[52] It
also provides remedies for certain violations, discussed in the law on the fair
treatment of employees.[53] The 1994 Labor Law obligates the trade unions at
various levels to "safeguard the legitimate rights and interests of the workers
and exercise supervision over the employers with regard to the implementation
of labor discipline and the laws and regulations."[54] The 2006 Trial Regulation
on the Work of Enterprise Trade Unions reiterates the grant of collective
negotiation rights to the union, and this grant, combined with the procedural
rights and duties for negotiation outlined in the 2004 regulations in the next
section and the express permission to engage in industry-wide negotiations
provide in the 2008 Labor Contract Law, strongly defines the intended future
role of the ACFTU.[55]

3. Current Law on Collective Negotiations

The fifty-seven new provisions of the 2004 Collective Contract MOLSS Provisions, as divided into eight chapters and building on the 1994 Labor Law,

---

[48] *Id.*
[49] *Id.* at 245.
[50] TAYLOR, *supra* note 11, at 202–3.
[51] *Id.* at 203.
[52] Trade Union Law, art. 3.
[53] *Id.* arts. 50–3.
[54] Labor Law, art. 88.
[55] Provisions on the Work of Enterprise Trade Unions (for Trial Implementation), art. 31; LCL, arts. 51, 56, 78.

and as confirmed in the 2008 LCL in articles 51–56, provide the current legal framework on the growing development of collective negotiations[56]:

a. Coverage and Purposes

The Provisions are enacted in accordance with the Labor Law and the Trade Union Law. Article 56 emphasizes the union's authority by subjecting employers to the relevant laws and regulations if they refuse to engage in collective negotiation requirements.[57] These requirements include "regulating the behavior of collective negotiation," "signing of the collective contract," and "protecting legal rights and interests of laborers and employing units."[58] All "enterprises and public institutions that practice commercialized management within the P.R.C" are covered by the Provisions.[59] This broad coverage parallels the coverage of employers and employees under China's individual labor contract system, but the collective contract supersedes the individual contract if inconsistencies arise.[60]

b. Negotiating Representatives

There shall be legal negotiating representatives of equal numbers (at least three) on each side and each with one chief representative.[61] The representative in the "employee party" shall be selected by the trade union of the unit (or, if none, then by democratic recommendations as agreed on by one-half of the staff in that unit).[62] The chief representative is the chair of the trade union unless that chair by written delegation selects an alternative (or, if a union does not exist, the chief representative shall be elected from the negotiating representatives through democratic means).[63]

In a significant change from past practice, Article 24 of the 2004 Provisions stipulates that "negotiation representatives of the employing unit and those of

---

[56] Ji ti he tong gui ding [Provisions on Collective Contract] (promulgated by Ministry of Labor and Social Security, Jan. 20, 2004, effective May 1, 2004), art. 1.

[57] *See id.* art. 56.

[58] *Id.* art. 1.

[59] *Id.* art. 2.

[60] Labor Law, arts. 2, 16–32; LCL, art. 2. Regarding inconsistencies, *see* Labor Law, art. 35; LCL, art. 55.

[61] Provisions on Collective Contract, art. 19.

[62] *Id.* art. 20. The original text says that the representative shall be appointed by the existing union of the unit. It does not appear that the appointed representative has to pass the simple majority vote. The employer has a duty to recognize the existence of such a bargaining unit by making an affirmative response to any negotiation request. Id. art. 32. *See also* Trade Union Law, art. 10.

[63] Provisions on Collective Contract, art. 20.

the staff shall not act as each other's representatives."[64] This would appear to foreclose an employer designating a trade union official as a negotiating representative of an employer, even where that official is a managerial employee of the employer, a scenario all too familiar under earlier practices. The employer otherwise is free to select its own negotiating representatives.[65]

An interesting provision, Article 23, permits both sides to select "professional personnel" (*Zhuanye Renyuan*) to act as the negotiation representative.[66] However, the number of such professional personnel may not exceed one-third of each side's representatives, and no person outside one's own unit can act as chief representative.[67]

Certain traditional responsibilities and functions, such as participation and sharing information, are assigned to the negotiating representatives.[68] Additionally, they are called on to "safeguard the normal order of work and production and shall not adopt any action of threatening, buying popular support and deception."[69]

Employee representatives' terms of service are determined by the represented party,[70] and their employment tenure is protected during that term against the employer's retaliation by terminating the representative's labor contract.[71] If the representative's labor contract were to expire during the representative's tenure, Article 28 automatically extends the contract up to the completion of his or her representative obligation.[72] Exceptions exist where the representative seriously violates employer rules or other employment-related duties or has been investigated for criminal violations.

c. Scope of Negotiable Subjects

References to the delineated subjects for negotiation are found in Article 33 of the Labor Law and Articles 3 and 8 to 18 of the 2004 Provisions. Article 3 of the Provisions describes the content of the collective contract as follows:

> [W]ritten agreement signed through collective negotiation . . . concerning labor remuneration, working time, rest and holiday, labor, security and sanitation, professional training, and insurance and welfare in accordance with the stipulation of

---

[64] *See id.* art. 24.
[65] *Id.* art. 21.
[66] *Id.* art. 23.
[67] *Id.* LCL, art. 51.
[68] *Id.* art. 25.
[69] *Id.* art. 26.
[70] *Id.* art. 22.
[71] Provisions on Collective Contract, art. 28.
[72] *Id.*

laws, regulations and rules; the special collective contract as set forth refers to the special written agreement signed between the employing unit and employees of that unit, in accordance with laws, regulations and rules, concerning the content of collective negotiation.[73]

Article 8 includes the scope of negotiable subjects that can be covered in the collective contract, listing some fifteen *categories* relating to employment.[74] Articles 9 to 18 then list examples under each category.[75]

d. Labor Bureau Supervision of Collective Negotiations

General provisions in Chapter 1 provide the principles and supervision for the conduct of negotiations. Article 4 states that negotiation shall mainly adopt the form of a consultation "conference."[76] Conduct during negotiations shall observe the following principles: act legally, respectfully, honestly, and fairly; consult, cooperate, and collaborate equally and in consideration of legal rights; and finally, "no drastic behavior is allowed."[77]

Responsibility for supervising the collective negotiation process and the "signing, reviewing and performing" of the signed collective contracts or special collective contracts shall be with the Labor Bureaus above the county level.[78] Under the 2008 LCL, Article 54, a completed contract should be submitted to the Labor Bureau and, unless it is objected to within fifteen days, it shall become effective. For any unresolved disputes that occur during the collective negotiations but prior to the contract signing, either or both parties may submit a written application to the Labor Bureau requesting resolution.[79] The Labor Bureau may also initiate resolution procedures, such as mediation, on its own as necessary. The procedures in most cases should be ended within thirty days of acceptance of the case by the Labor

---

[73] *Id.* art. 3 (emphasis added). A "special agreement" usually refers to a wage agreement or other agreement on a specific topic. LCL, art. 52 stipulates the topics can include "work safety and hygiene, protection of the rights and interests of female employees, the wage adjustments mechanism, etc." Article 4 again distinguishes between signing the "collective contract or special contract," and Article 6 states both are legally binding on the employer and employees. Id. arts. 4, 6.

[74] Provisions on Collective Contract, art. 8. LCL, art. 51 lists "labor compensation, working hours, rest, leave, work safety and hygiene, insurance, benefits, etc." as the subjects for collective negotiations.

[75] *Id.* arts. 9–18. LCL, art. 51.

[76] *Id.* art. 4.

[77] Provisions on Collective Contract, art. 5.

[78] *Id.* art. 7; *see also id.* arts. 42–8.

[79] *Id.* art. 49.

Bureau.[80] The Labor Bureau, at the conclusion of its process, formulates an Agreement on Dispute Resolution.[81] Thereafter, the Labor Bureau and the parties must sign, indicating their agreement to be bound by that document before it is effective.[82] Items in the agreement for which there was no unanimous resolution shall be carried on with continuous consultation.

Separate dispute resolution provisions protect the rights of individual employees who are also negotiating representatives against improper termination[83] and modification of their normal work status.[84] Such disputes are to be resolved by the local labor arbitration commission.[85] The same forum is used to resolve any *rights* disputes that arise out of the performance of the concluded collective contract.[86]

e. Collective Negotiation Procedures

Within the general rules of convening a conference, wherein the meetings take place following prescribed rules of conduct conducive to negotiation, the Provisions specify certain other procedures. To initiate the process, Article 32 states that a party to the collective negotiation may make written request of the other party, and a written response must be given within twenty days; this request to negotiate may not be refused without proper reason.[87] The "preparation phrase" then calls on parties to familiarize themselves with the laws and regulations concerning collective negotiations and with collective recommendations from the employer and employees and to identify topics for discussion during negotiation.[88] After a location, time, and recorder are chosen, the parties are prepared to begin.[89]

The collective negotiation process begins with each chief representative in turn addressing the agenda and procedures of the meeting. Thereafter, each puts forward concrete proposals to which the other side responds, and discussion ensues regarding the proposals.[90] During the negotiations, the chief representatives shall make summaries of the recommendations. Those unanimously

---

[80] *Id.* art. 52.
[81] *Id.* art. 53.
[82] *Id.* art. 54. Thus, the Dispute Resolution Agreement appears to remain entirely voluntary.
[83] *Id.* art. 28.
[84] *Id.* art. 27.
[85] *Id.* art. 29.
[86] *Id.* art. 55.
[87] *See* Provisions on Collective Contract, art. 32.
[88] *Id.* art. 33.
[89] *Id.*
[90] *Id.* art. 34.

agreed on shall be incorporated into the collective contract or special collective contract and signed by the chief representatives of both parties.[91] In case there is no agreement on issues, the negotiation may be suspended, and the parties shall negotiate the next meeting place and content.[92]

To conclude the collective contract, the agreed-on draft is presented to the employees for discussion. Thereafter, a two-thirds quorum must be present, and the draft must be approved by a majority of the Worker's Congress representatives or a majority of all the employees (if a Worker's Congress has not been established).[93] Thereafter, the chief representatives of each side sign the contract, which is usually of one to three years in duration but can be extended by request and agreement of the parties.[94] The contract, though binding on the parties, may be modified by the parties or altered or terminated by certain conditions that cause an inability to perform, such as bankruptcy, *force majeure*, or conditions in the agreement.[95]

The final step is to submit (register) the concluded collective contract to the Labor Bureau for review and examination.[96] It is examined to ensure compliance with legal requirements.[97] If there is an objection by the Labor Bureau, the parties are notified and the contract is referred back to them; then they can renegotiate or re-sign it, absent those portions.[98] In practice, there seems to be little or no referral back to the parties.[99] In the case of no objection by the Labor Bureau, the contract is effective within fifteen days of receipt of the document.[100] The law requires the contract to be promulgated "by the negotiation representative" to all employees on the day it becomes effective.[101]

f. Duties of Proper Conduct for Collective Negotiations

The regulatory framework of collective negotiations is set up to be monitored by a government agency – the Labor Bureau and its division – with responsibility

---

[91] *Id.* art. 34(4).

[92] *Id.* art. 35.

[93] *Id.* art. 36.

[94] Provisions on Collective Contract, arts. 37–8.

[95] *Id.* arts. 39–41.

[96] *Id.* art. 42.

[97] *Id.* art. 44.

[98] *Id.* art. 46.

[99] Clarke, supra note 8, at 246.

[100] Provisions on Collective Contract, art. 47.

[101] *Id.* art. 48.

to supervise and to resolve disputes.[102] The principles of conduct can be organized into three categories.

1. *Fair and consultative representation*: The negotiating representatives must "participate" in the negotiations[103] after having consulted with employees regarding negotiating topics[104] and must accept inquires from their constituency, publicize the status of negotiations, collect employees' opinions,[105] and provide information concerning collective negotiations.[106]
2. *Negotiating duty*: The negotiating representative must be legally authorized[107] to conduct negotiations on behalf of the represented party's interests, must "not refuse" to respond to requests to engage in collective negotiations,[108] and must "participate."[109] He or she must also provide "information" concerning collective negotiations[110] and determine the time and place for negotiations.[111] The employer is prohibited from refusing to abide by the collective negotiations requirements without "proper reason,"[112] and a violation of said provision is expressly subject to the Trade Union Law, which confirms in Article 53(4) that "[r]ejecting consultation on an equal footing without justifiable reasons" is a violation.[113] Subjective measures of the conduct during negotiating include "honesty," "keeping promises," "fair collaboration," and "consideration of legal rights and interests for cooperation."[114]

The Provisions are based on and incorporate those parts of the Labor Law and the Trade Union Law that also set forth standards on negotiating conduct as well as the fair treatment of employees.[115] Furthermore, Article 25(6) of the Provisions obligates the negotiating representatives to those other obligations stipulated by laws, regulations, and rules.[116]

---

[102] *Id.* art. 7.
[103] *Id.* art. 25(1).
[104] *Id.* art. 33(2).
[105] Provisions on Collective Contract, art. 25(2).
[106] *Id.* art. 25(3).
[107] *Id.* art. 19.
[108] *Id.* art. 32.
[109] *Id.* art. 25(1).
[110] *Id.* art. 25(3).
[111] *Id.* art. 33(4).
[112] *Id.* art. 56.
[113] Trade Union Law, art. 53(4).
[114] Provisions on Collective Contract, art. 5.
[115] *Id.* art. 1.
[116] *Id.* art. 25(6).

3. *Fair treatment of employees*: Although the 2004 Provisions do not directly regulate the fair treatment of employees, said Provisions do incorporate the Trade Union Law stipulations on the subject, including employees' right to organize and join a union. Article 3 of the 2001 Trade Union Law provides in pertinent part the following basic guarantee:

> [Employees] who rely on wages...regardless of their nationality, race, sex, occupation, religious beliefs or educational background, have the right to organize and join trade unions according to law. No organizations or individuals shall obstruct or restrict them.[117]

Article 11 provides,

> [T]rade union organizations at higher levels may dispatch their members to assist and guide the workers and staff members of enterprises to set up their trade unions, no units or individuals may obstruct their effort.[118]

Article 50 instructs that if anyone violates Article 3 or 11 by obstructing employees in joining trade union organizations or obstructing higher level trade unions in assisting and guiding employees in preparation for establishing trade unions, then the violation shall be ordered to be corrected by the "administrative department for labor" (Labor Bureau), with appeals to appropriate government offices.[119] There is also possible criminal violation if there is violence or intimidation.[120]

Article 51 prohibits anyone from retaliating against any staff member of a trade union by modifying that employee's job.[121] Said provision also prohibits insults, slander, or personal injury to any staff member of a trade union who performs his or her duties "according to law." Punishment for violations includes criminal prosecution or administrative sanctions by the public security (the police).[122] Article 52 provides that any employee or staff member of the union who has his or her labor contract cancelled because of joining the trade union is entitled to reinstatement with retroactive pay or an order by the Labor Bureau to pay "two times the amount of his annual income."[123]

Article 53 prohibits obstructing the trade union in performing its work to organize employees to exert "(1) democratic rights through the congress of the workers and staff members and other forms"; (2) unlawfully "dissolving

---

[117] Trade Union Law, art. 3.
[118] *Id.* art. 11.
[119] *Id.* art. 50.
[120] *Id.*
[121] *Id.* art. 51.
[122] Trade Union Law, art. 51.
[123] *Id.* art. 52.

or merging trade union organizations"; and "(3) preventing a trade union from participating in the investigation into and solution of an accident causing job-related injuries or death to workers or staff members or other infringements upon the legitimate rights and interests of the workers and staff members."[124]

Employees who are negotiating representatives are protected by the 2004 Provisions from retaliation.[125] For example, an employee who is a negotiating representative cannot have his or her labor contract terminated when it expires during the performance of representative obligations; instead, it must be automatically extended up to the completion of those representative obligations.[126] Such employee can only be terminated on a sufficient showing by the employer of the serious violation of duty or employer rules.[127] Similarly, an employer shall not adjust or remove an employee's working position without proper reason,[128] and the employee shall be regarded as performing normal work when participating in collective negotiations.[129] Moreover, provisions of the Trade Union Law likewise provide protections for trade union funds and proscribe improper conduct by trade union staff members against employees or the trade union.[130]

The negotiating representative also has two affirmative obligations under Article 26 of the Provisions. The representative has a duty to "safeguard the normal order of work and production and shall not adopt any action of threatening, buying popular support and deception."[131] The first part appears to obligate the union representative to act affirmatively to avoid or end any employee disruption of services, whereas the second part seems to place an obligation of proper conduct on both employee and employer representatives as leaders in negotiations. The second affirmative obligation is to maintain secrecy of any commercial secrets of the employer acquired during the collective negotiations.[132]

Disputes relating to "proper conduct" regarding the objective and subjective aspects of the negotiations, including disagreements or impasses on proposals, are to be resolved by the Labor Bureau.[133] Other disputes

---

[124] *Id.* art. 53.
[125] Regulation on State-Owned Enterprise Worker's Congress, art. 14.
[126] Provisions on Collective Contract, art. 28.
[127] *Id.*
[128] *Id.*
[129] *Id.* art. 27.
[130] Trade Union Law, arts. 54–5.
[131] Provisions on Collective Contract, art. 26.
[132] *Id.*
[133] *Id.* art. 49. This is for "any disputes" that occur during the collective negotiation process.

that relate to retaliation against an employee representative's *rights*, as well as those under Articles 27 and 28, are to be resolved by the local labor arbitration commission.[134]

Collective contract regulations are also issued at the local levels. For example, Shanghai issued new regulations in August 2007 that require employers to bargain whenever establishing or changing any "aspects directly related to the personal interests of employees," including salaries, etc.[135] It is well established that all laws and regulations require that employees cannot be paid less than the legal rates or the standards set forth in the collective contract.[136]

Strikes are not outlawed and do occur.[137] The union by law is directed to assist in the resolution of labor disputes resulting in a work stoppage.[138] In addition, a safety law does permit workers to stop work where there is imminent danger of harm.[139] A new regulation in Shenzhen provides for a "cooling off" period of thirty days for workers in certain public sectors to avoid work stoppages.[140]

---

[134] Provisions on Collective Contract, art. 29; LCL, art. 56.

[135] Shanghai ji ti he tong tiao li [Shanghai Collective Contract Regulations] (promulgated by Standing Comm. of Shanghai Municipal People's Cong., effective Jan. 1, 2008), art. 25, http://www.shanghai.gov.cn/shanghai/node2314/node3124/node3125/node3130/userobject6ai11845.html; *see* The US-China Business Council, at 8 (2007).

[136] Labor Law, art. 35; LCL, art. 55.

[137] A strike by Shenzhen bus drivers over wages and working conditions recently occurred after the employer failed to implement arbitration decisions. Fiona Tam, *Shenzhen Strike Strands Thousands*, SOUTH CHINA MORNING POST, August 30, 2008, p. 7, http://www6.lexisnexis.com/publisher/EndUser?Action=UserDisplayFullDocument&orgId=1746&topicId=100410004&docId=l:843943078&start=20. *Trade Union Official Says China Is Just One Step Away from the Right to Strike*, http://www.clb.org.hk/en/node/100263.

[138] Trade Union Law, art. 27.

[139] An quan sheng chan fa [Work Safety Law] (promulgated by the Standing Comm. of the Nat'l People's Cong., June 29, 2002, effective Nov. 1, 2002), art. 47 (PRC).

[140] Shenzhen jing ji te qu he xie lao dong guan xi cu jin tiao li [Regulations for the Promotion of Harmonious Labor Relations in the Shenzhen Special Economic Zone] (promulgated by Standing Comm. of Shenzhen Municipal People's Cong., Oct. 6, 2008, effective Nov. 1, 2008), art. 53, http://www.npc.gov.cn/npc/xinwen/dfrd/guangdong/2008-10/08/content_1452415.htm. Article 53 provides, in the event that a collective work stoppage, go-slow, or lockout due to labor dispute in an employing unit in the water, electricity and gas utilities, and public transport sectors has resulted in or could result in consequences of the serious impairment of public interest, such as endangering public security and upsetting normal socioeconomic order and people's everyday life, the city and SEZ governments may issue an order demanding the employing unit or workers to stop the action and restore normal order. The period within thirty days of the issuance of this order is called the "cooling off period," during which time the employing unit and workers may not take actions to aggravate the situation.

PART III

HIRING AND EMPLOYMENT PRACTICES

6

Hiring and Employment Practices and the Law

1. Employment Promotion and Labor Market Management

Because of China's huge and growing population, the labor force is expanding faster than jobs can be created. The government has initiated education and training programs to upgrade the skills of workers and has an active plan of employment promotion under the 2008 *Employment Promotion Law*. This law seeks to protect workers by creating employment opportunities and prohibiting job discrimination. It promotes employment in specified industries and enterprises by providing assistance to employers. It also establishes public employment service organizations to assist workers in securing job opportunities, both in rural and urban areas. However, some view this law as merely a policy statement, as it provides few penalties and enforcement mechanisms.

The Employment Promotion Law (EPL), effective January 1, 2008, puts into place broad "proactive labor policies" to promote employment in the private sector, ease burdens on the unemployed, and promote equal employment in the workplace. It is guided by the "principles of workers selecting their own jobs, the market regulating employment and the government promoting employment, and increasing employment through multiple avenues."[1] Responsibility is placed on the governments at the county level and above to "create employment conditions and expand employment through development of the economy and through such measures as adjusting the industrial structure, regulating the human resource market, improving employment services, strengthening vocational education and training, providing employment assistance, etc."[2]

---

[1] Zhonghua renmin gongheguo jiu ye cu jin fa [Employment Promotion Law of the PRC] (promulgated by the 29th session of the Standing Comm. of the Tenth NPC, Aug. 20, 2007, effective Jan. 1, 2008), art. 2 [hereinafter EPL].

[2] EPL, art. 5. Local governments have enacted local implementing regulations; for example, *see*, Guangxi province: http://gx.people.com.cn/GB/channel3/200901/09/1359532.html; Jiangsu

The law's nine chapters create policies and rights covering employment and fair treatment through the use and regulation of government employment services and assistance, private employment agencies, and vocational education and training. Responsibility for supervision and inspection of mandated employment funds is placed with auditing organizations and public finance departments, whereas the labor administration authorities oversee implementation of the law through reporting systems.[3]

Under the law, the State Council establishes, with the MOHRSS, a coordinating mechanism for promoting employment.[4] Policies are promoted through a variety of channels, including labor-intensive businesses, the service sector, small and medium-sized enterprises, construction projects, and an enhanced unemployment system.[5] Governments above the county level are to establish exclusive, dedicated funds for employment promotion,[6] provide preferential tax treatment for enterprises that hire laid-off or disabled employees,[7] and increase loans to small and medium-sized enterprises.[8]

Part of the focus of employment promotion is on rural workers who have moved to the urban sector – and have become "the main constituent part of the industrial workforce."[9] The government is faced with the pressing need to create more employment opportunities and at the same time upgrade its skilled workforce. In that quest, some concern has been raised regarding whether too much emphasis on job creation may diminish attention to job quality (including labor standards and job protections, security, and benefits).[10]

While the EPL sought to promote employment, earlier regulations dealt specifically with labor markets. In 2000, the Ministry of Labor and Social Security (MOLSS) sought to regularize and bring more order to labor market management by issuing Regulations on Labor Market Management (hereinafter Labor Market Regulations).[11] These regulations' stated purpose is to protect the legal interests of employees and employers, to develop and standardize the

province: http://www.xinhuanet.com/chinanews/2009-01/07/content_15385599.htm; Tianjin: http://news.sohu.com/20090109/n261655083.shtml.

[3] EPL, art. 7.

[4] EPL, art. 6.

[5] EPL, arts. 12–16.

[6] EPL, art. 15.

[7] EPL, art. 17.

[8] EPL, art. 19.

[9] Fang Lee Cooke, HRM, WORK AND EMPLOYMENT IN CHINA, 197 (2005).

[10] *Id.* 196–7.

[11] Lao dong li shi chang guan li gui ding [Regulations on Labor Market Management] (promulgated by the Ministry of Labor and Social Security, Dec. 8, 2000, effective Dec. 8, 2000) (PRC), http://www.chinacourt.org/flwk/show1.php?file_id=36355 [hereinafter Regulations on Labor Market Management].

labor market, and to promote employment.[12] The Labor Market Regulations apply to the employee's job application and work, the employer's recruiting process, and to the "career introduction activities" of job centers.[13] They are administered by the Labor Bureaus above the county level.[14]

The regulations relating to recruitment[15] provide for "public and fair competition"[16] and state that employers can acquire employees in numerous ways, including through the use of job centers and advertising in the mass media.[17] Interestingly, Article 9 requires employers who place ads for vacancies in the mass media to first obtain the approval of the local labor security administrative authorities.[18] The regulations also prohibit a number of well-documented employer abuses, including charging the hired person a deposit fee or holding worker documents, such as identity papers.[19] The 2008 LCL, Article 9, also provides that an employer, when hiring an employee, may not retain the employee's residence ID card or other papers or require him or her to provide security or property under some other guise.

The most significant provision in the Labor Market Regulations is Article 11, which bans employment discrimination in recruitment. It reads, "[W]hile hiring a person, the employer shall not refuse to hire or enhance the hiring standard on the basis of gender, nationality, race, or religion, except those provided by state laws concerning unsuitable types of work or positions."[20]

The Labor Market Regulations also cover "career recommendation organs," or employment services and agencies, both nonprofit and for-profit.[21] Article 21 is of significance, as it prohibits career recommendation agencies from certain activities including "recommending jobs prevented by laws and regulations."[22] This provision would seem to ban recommendation of a job advertised by an employer as "for men only" where there is no legal basis for a sex-specific limitation.[23]

---

[12] *Id.* art. 1.

[13] *Id.* art. 2.

[14] *Id.* art. 4. The hired person also must register with the Labor Bureau within thirty days of being hired.

[15] *Id.* arts. 7–14.

[16] *Id.* art. 7.

[17] *Id.* art. 8. These ways include (1) using a job center, (2) participating in labor exchange activities, (3) publishing advertisements for employers in mass media, (4) recruiting on the Internet, and (5) other means stipulated by laws and regulations. *Id.*

[18] *Id.* art. 9.

[19] *Id.* art. 10(4)–(5).

[20] *Id.* art. 11.

[21] *Id.* arts. 15–25.

[22] *Id.* art. 21. This is further codified in EPL, art. 26 and arts. 39–41.

[23] *See* Zhonghua renmin gongheguo guang gao fa [Advertisements Law] art. 7(7) (promulgated by the Standing Comm. of the Nat'l People's Cong., Oct. 27, 1994, effective Feb. 1, 1995),

Sanctions for violations of these regulations provide for general fines of 1,000 yuan (for violations of Article 10 or 14) and fines ranging from 10,000 yuan to 30,000 yuan for a violation of several enumerated articles, including Article 21.[24] Penalties may also include revocation of the employer's business license.[25] Of greatest significance, however, is the absence of sanctions for violations of Article 11 prohibitions on employment discrimination.

In 2001, the Ministry of Personnel and the State Administration for Industry and Commerce issued the Rules on the Administration of Human Resources Markets (hereinafter Rules on HRM).[26] These rules apply to the administration of labor agency services, including the general hiring activities of employers and the treatment of individual job applications.[27] Article 3 mandates that "human resource market activities must abide by the laws, regulations, and policies of this country, persist in the principles of openness, equality, competition, and selection of the best.[28] Employment agencies are required to have the "capacity to independently bear civil liabilities, and sanctions are provided for violations, ranging from 10,000 yuan to 30,000 yuan.[29] Of greatest significance is Article 39, which provides,

> Any employing unit that, in violation of these Rules, refuses to recruit talents or heightens the qualifications for these talents by such reason as *nationality, sex, and religion* or recruits personnel who should not be recruited . . . shall be ordered to make corrections by the administrative department in charge of personnel of the people's government. . . . If the circumstances are serious, there shall be imposed a fine of less than ¥10,000.[30]

The 2008 Employment Promotion Law further underscores the requirements for fair treatment of employess in the implementation of its quest to expand and improve the labor market and employment opportunities. Chapter 8 addresses the requirements of employment agencies to be licensed and operate properly in accordance with the law. In the case of the employer, it

---

1994 Quanguo renmin daibiao dahui changwu weiyuanhui gong bao [Standing Comm. Nat'l People's Cong. Gaz.] (PRC), http://www.chinacourt.org/flwk/show1.php?file_id= 20976 (banning discriminatory advertising by stipulating the ad shall not contain any racial, ethnic, gender, or religious discrimination language).

[24] Regulations on Labor Market Management, *supra* note 21, at arts. 34–8. Article 10 prohibits false information etc., and article 14 requires registration of employees. *Id.* arts. 10, 14.

[25] *Id.* art. 37.

[26] Ren cai shi chang guan li gui ding [Rules on the Administration of Human Resources Market] (promulgated by the Ministry of Personnel, Sept. 11, 2001, effective Oct. 1, 2001, revised Mar. 22, 2005) (PRC), http://www.chinacourt.org/flwk/show1.php?file_id=101542.

[27] *Id.* art. 2.

[28] *Id.* art. 3.

[29] *Id.* arts. 6(4) and 35.

[30] *Id.* art. 39 (emphasis added).

specifically prohibits providing false employment information, retaining resident ID cards or similar documentation of workers, charging workers a deposit, or failing to properly allocate or appropriate employee education funds. Civil and criminal liabilities are provided for violations.

In sum, the Chinese government is seeking to regularize and standardize HRM practices in China through labor market regulation. Nonetheless, the government continues to struggle to respond to persistent claims of inequality and inadequate legislative remedies.

2. Recruitment, Selection, and HRM

Since the mid-1980s, limitations on employers' recruitment and selection activities have eased, and beginning in the 1990s, HRM became of interest in the universities, with materials and curriculum developed and taught. At the same time, employers began taking more serious interest in using principles of HRM more systematically in their employment policies to meet the challenges of recruitment and retention of skilled and technical employees, as well as of migrant workers who tend to migrate en masse during holiday periods.[31] With enterprise autonomy ever increasing, there has come to be an increasing use of HRM practices by some Chinese firms, ranging from planning, recruitment, training, and promotion to discipline and dismissal.[32] Challenges to the HRM systems in China are the need to professionalize and establish professional networks and to adapt HRM principles to Chinese characteristics.[33]

The current hiring route is multifaceted and usually involves advertising for positions (rather than earlier practices of having labor supplied through Labor Bureaus), word of mouth, use of labor supply brokers (including Labor Bureaus and employment agencies), and posting notices on walls and the Internet. Recruitment practices do not usually require testing, with the exception of civil service jobs and those needing certain proficiencies.[34] Employment and

---

[31] Cooke, *supra* note 9, at 172–93, 201, 204.

[32] *Id.* at 174.

[33] *Id.* at 204–8. *See* HUMAN RESOURCE MANAGEMENT 'WITH CHINESE CHARACTERISTICS': FACING THE CHALLENGES OF GLOBALIZATION (Malcolm Warner ed., 2008).

[34] Ronald C. Brown, *China's Employment Discrimination Laws during Economic Transition*, 19 COLUM. J. ASIAN L. 361, 399 (2006). *See* Zhonghua renmin gongheguo gong wu yuan fa [Civil Service Law] arts. 21–32 (promulgated by the Standing Comm. of the Nat'l People's Cong., Apr. 27, 2005, effective Jan. 1, 2006) (PRC), http://www.chinacourt.org/flwk/show1.php?file_id=101410. *See* Robert Taylor, *China's Human Resource Management Strategies: The Role of Enterprise and Government*, 4 ASIAN BUS. & MGMT. 5, 11–18 (2005). Commercial services are offered in China for pre-employment screening. *See e.g.*, *Inquest Pre Employment Screening Service*, http://www.inquestscreening.com/international_asia.asp (last visited Feb. 28, 2006).

working conditions are mostly governed by the employer and its rules, with the employer authorized to make evaluative decisions.[35] Both recruitment and conditions, however, are limited somewhat by labor laws, labor contracts, and collective contracts.[36] Dismissals and other labor disputes are regulated by statutes and generally are resolved within the enterprise by mediation or by resort to government labor arbitration commissions and tribunals, with review provided by the courts.[37]

The U.S.-China Business Council reports that, for multinational corporations (MNCs) and Chinese companies, "acquiring talented employees is more than ever, one of their greatest challenges in China."[38] The turnover rate from 2001 to 2005 rose from 9 to 14 percent; the salary rates increased by nearly double digits; and of the estimated 15.7 million college graduates, "only 1.2 million are suitable for employment in the large MNCs because they lack the necessary mix of skills and experience."[39] With such conditions, it is foreseeable that some employers may seek to hire employees who are already employed by another employer. That practice of corporate raiding,[40] sometimes referred to as "poaching," is proscribed by the LCL, Article 91, which provides that, if an employer hires an employee whose contract is not yet terminated or ended, which causes damage, it is jointly and severally liable with the employee for damages.[41] It is especially important for employers to understand the recruitment provisions of the LCL, which place limits and penalties on the employer for unilateral termination and for severance pay requirements. Likewise, limits on poaching are important in cases involving trade secrets and other types of confidential information that could be carried away by the recruited employee.

Employers are understandably focused on how and where to find the appropriately qualified candidates to hire. Workers and recent college graduates, however, report that they must surmount many hurdles to find a job. Currently, they may have to respond to newspaper ads, employment agencies, job fairs, hiring contractors, posted notices, and word of mouth opportunities to gain

---

[35] Lao dong he tong fa [Labor Contract Law] (promulgated by the 28th Standing Comm. of the Tenth Nat'l People's Cong., June 29, 2007, effective Jan. 1, 2008), art. 4 (PRC), [hereinafter LCL].

[36] LCL, Art. 80.

[37] *See* Zhonghua renmin gongheguo lao dong zheng yi tiao jie zhong cai fa [Law on Labor Dispute Mediation and Arbitration of the PRC] (promulgated by the 31st session of the Standing Comm. of the Tenth NPC, Dec. 29, 2007, effective May 1, 2008); LCL.

[38] *Best Practices: Human Resources: Strategies for Recruitment, Retention, and Compensation,* The U.S.-China Business Council, Oct. 2006, at http://www.uschina.org/info/chops/2006/hr-best-practices.html.

[39] *Id.*

[40] Labor Law, art. 99.

[41] LCL, Art. 50 requires employers to provide proof of termination.

employment.[42] Sophisticated hiring and screening processes, involving testing, structured interviews, or even background checks, are relatively rare except in a few industries and occupations.[43] However, many employers require physical exams, and there seems to be some evidence suggesting use of at least initial interviews.[44]

The hiring of *dispatched* employees from secondary employers (also called "staffing firms") is regulated under the LCL,[45] which places an "employer's obligation" on the staffing firm, requiring adherence to the labor laws.[46] In 2003, new provisions were issued regulating the management of intermediary employment agencies that service FIEs.[47] These provisions require any FIE using intermediary services to conduct its "activities through a specialized job intermediary agency jointly established with a Chinese company, enterprise or other economic organization for offering job intermediary services."[48] These agencies are authorized to collect data about the employment market; provide job recommendations; conduct recruitment activities, job testing, and appraising of applicants; and provide training courses.[49] They must abide by "the principles of voluntary participation, equity and good faith."[50] Enterprises needing temporary employees (also called "accepting or host firms") often contract their needs to an employment or staffing agency. For example, in July 2007, Humanpool Human Resources Co. Ltd., reportedly one of the largest labor suppliers, supplied 6,000 workers per month to more than 200 companies in the Yantze River Delta, a manufacturing area. Pay for the services was about 80 yuan per month per employee. Many of those employees were reported to have been subsequently hired by the employing enterprise.[51]

---

[42] Still, many feel their rejection based on lack of experience is discriminatory. Lin Lin, *College Graduates Find Job Market Discriminatory*, CHINA DAILY (North American ed., October 3, 2006).

[43] Brown, *supra* note 34, at 361, 399. However, testing may be used by international companies in the recruitment of Chinese tradespeople; *see* Resourcenet International Group at http://www. chinalabour.com/index.html.

[44] *See* Cooke, *supra* note 9, at 158.

[45] LCL, arts. 57–67.

[46] LCL, arts. 58, 62.

[47] Zhong wai he zi ren cai zhong jie ji gou guan li zan xing gui ding [Interim Provisions Concerning the Management of Chinese-Foreign Joint Job Intermediary Agencies] (promulgated by the Ministry of Personnel, the Ministry of Commerce, and State Administration for Industry & Commerce, Sept. 4, 2003, effective Nov. 11, 2003) (PRC), http://www.chinacourt.org/flwk/show1.php?file_id=89004.

[48] *Id.* art. 3. Wholly foreign-owned job intermediary agencies are prohibited. *Id.*

[49] *Id.* art. 11.

[50] *Id.* art. 12.

[51] *Humanpool Sources Blue-Collar Workers for Companies in the Yangtze River Delta*, CHINA BUSINESS WEEKLY, June 4–10, 2007.

Hiring *foreign workers* also requires meeting certain legal procedures and receiving proper government permissions.[52] These requirements apply to FIEs[53] and Representative offices as well. Individuals hired from Taiwan, Hong Kong, and Macau are subject to separate regulations,[54] although all employees, Chinese and foreign, who work in China are covered by the labor laws, except as stipulated by law.[55]

3. Privacy and Defamation Limits

There are few limits placed on employers in the recruitment and hiring stages. Not many employers use sophisticated screening devices, but occasionally there are applicant background investigations and the use of medical records, which can raise issues of *privacy* and *defamation*. Occasionally, work rules or corporate codes of conduct exist that may in some way address these employee rights, but usually they lack meaningful enforcement provisions.[56]

For many years, personnel files for cadres and "floating" personnel have been kept exclusively by the government and the CCP, even when these employees moved between jobs.[57] However, the files of regular employees working at enterprises are kept with their employers.[58] Certain privacy rights

---

[52] Wai guo ren zai Zhongguo jiu ye guan li gui ding [Regulations for the Administration of the Employment of Foreigners in China] (promulgated by the Ministry of Labor, Ministry of Public Security, Ministry of Foreign Affairs, and Ministry of Foreign Trade and Economic Cooperation, Jan. 22, 1996).

[53] These include China-foreign joint equity ventures, China-foreign cooperative ventures, wholly foreign-owned enterprises, and China-foreign joint-stock limited companies. *2008 Update to Guide to Establishing a Subsidiary in China (Company Overview)*, Mondaq Business Briefing, Jan 11, 2008, goliath.ecnext.com/coms2/summary_0199-7575323_ITM.

[54] Taiwan Xianggang Aomen ju min zai nei di jiu ye guan li gui ding [Regulations for the Administration of the Employment in Mainland China of Taiwan, Hong Kong, and Macau Residents] (promulgated by the Ministry of Labor and Social Security, June 14, 2005, effective Oct. 1, 2005).

[55] E.g., LCL, arts. 2 and 57–67. An issue may exist whether certain foreign seconded employees have the requisite employment relationship for LCL coverage or are engaged in a labor service contract. By stipulating in their contract to use home-country law, they may be subject to the LCL or PRC Contract Law and foreign laws. A highly publicized case was the *Microsoft v. Google* lawsuit in the United States, which raised the issue of whether Microsoft's employee breached the no-compete provision by accepting work in China for Google. *See Gates' Microsoft and Google Settle Employee Row*, www.forbes.com/2005/12/23/gates-microsoft-google-ex_cn_1223autofacescan02.html.

[56] Marisa Anne Pagnattaro and Ellen R. Pierce, *Between a Rock and a Hard Place: The Conflict between U.S. Corporate Codes of Conduct and European Privacy and Work Laws*, 28 BERKELEY J. EMP. & LAB. L. 375 (2007).

[57] LCL, art. 50.

[58] Qi ye zhi gong dang an guan li gong zuo gui ding [Regulations Concerning the Administration of Personnel Files of Enterprise Workers] (promulgated by the Ministry of Labor and State Archives Administration, June 9, 1992), art. 5; Wais hang tou zi qi ye dang an guan li zan xing

of employees were codified in 2007 when new regulations required employers to keep employees' personal information confidential.[59] These regulations require the employee's consent to disclose personal information or to use technology or intellectual achievements of employees,[60] and they impose monetary fines for requiring an employee to take certain medical tests (e.g., hepatitis B).[61] However, there are no penalties for employers who fail to obtain the employee's consent.[62]

Interestingly, and perhaps paradoxically, there are legal protections prohibiting third parties from listening to telephone calls without the employee's consent.[63] E-mail and Internet use by employees also have some, but less, protection because other laws more closely regulate them, as they may affect China's "security" interests.[64] However, employers often adopt policies and rules providing disclosure and obtain "consent" of their employees to monitor e-mail, Internet, and telephone use.

In 2003, 5,596 defamation cases were heard in court.[65] Most of these cases involved suing the media rather than employment disputes.[66] The law of defamation emanates from the 1987 General Principles of the Civil Law, which protect the reputation and personal dignity of individuals and authorize redress, including compensation.[67] In 1998, an Interpretation of the Supreme People's Court added that release of information regarding certain health

gui ding [Interim Regulations on the Archive Management of the Foreign-Funded Enterprises] (promulgated by the Ministry of Foreign Trade and Economic Cooperation, State Economy and Trade Committee, and State Archive Administration, Dec. 29, 1994), arts. 6(4), 7, http://www.ccda.gov.cn/ccda/PubTemplet/prite.asp?infoid=375&style=prite.

[59] Jiu ye fu wu yu jiu ye guan li gui ding [Provisions on Employment Services and Employment Management] (promulgated by the Ministry of Labor and Social Security, Oct. 30, 2007, effective Jan. 1, 2008).

[60] *Id.* art. 13. ("An employer shall keep confidential the personal materials of workers; and shall first obtain the worker's written consent before publicizing the personal materials or information of a worker or using his technology or intellectual property.")

[61] *Id.* arts. 19, 68.

[62] *Id.* arts. 68–75.

[63] Exceptions include government agencies. Zhonghua renmin gongheguo dian xin tiao li [Regulation on Telecommunications of the PRC] (promulgated by the State Council, Sept. 25, 2000).

[64] Ji suan ji xin xi wang luo guo ji lian wang an quan bao hu guan li ban fa [Measures for the Administration of the Protection of the Security of International Networking of Computer Information Networks] (promulgated by the Ministry of Public Security, Dec. 30, 1997); Hu lian wang dian zi you jian fu wu guan li ban fa [Measures for the Administration of Internet E-mail Services] (promulgated by the Ministry of Information Industry, Feb. 20, 2006, effective Mar. 20, 2006).

[65] *2004 China Law Yearbook*, at 123.

[66] Benjamin L. Liebman, *Innovation through Intimidation: An Empirical Account of Defamation Litigation in China*, 47 HARD. INT'L LAW J. 33 (2006).

[67] Zhonghua renmin gongheguo min fa tong ze [General Principles of the Civil Law of the PRC] (promulgated by the NPC, April 12, 1986, effective Jan. 1, 1987), arts. 101, 120.

conditions (e.g., gonorrhea, syphilis, leprosy, AIDS, etc.) can be the basis of a claim of defamation.[68]

Defamation cases in employment are not easily identified, but illustrative cases have arisen. In an employment dispute against Yahoo, a former employee alleged that misinformation about the employee (that he engaged in "unethical business practices") circulated by the employer, constituted defamation.[69] In 1998 in Guangzhou, an employee sued his employer, Proctor & Gamble, for defamation and invasion of privacy, claiming that it disclosed private and personal information when it publicized the contents of his computer after taking it into possession on the employee's announcement that he was leaving to take another job.[70]

---

[68] Zuigao renmin fayuan guan yu shen li ming yu an jian ruo gan wen ti de jie shi [Interpretation of SPC Regarding Some Questions in the Adjudication of Cases involving the Right of Reputation], art. 2 (Sept. 15, 1998).

[69] Liu Baijia, *Former Yahoo! China Boss Sues for Defamation*, CHINA DAILY (Aug. 18, 2006), http://www.chinadaily.com.cn/bizchina/2006-08/18/content_667898.htm.

[70] Zhan, *Local Employee Sues P&G in Privacy Case*, CHINA DAILY (June 11, 1998).

7

Employment Antidiscrimination Laws

1. Protected Status and Hiring Practices

In China, there are a number of protected classes against which employment discrimination is prohibited. There also are some statuses that are largely unprotected, such as age and height and some that lack meaningful enforcement provisions, such as disability. Maternity and child labor and sexual harassment have special protections.

In China, hiring procedures often openly discriminate on the basis of gender, social origin, and age. It is not uncommon to see or hear the following solicitation in a recruitment ad: "[S]eeking an office clerk. Female, decent height and appearance. All five facial organs must be in the right place (*wu guan duan zheng*)."[1] Today in China, job advertisements with those facial requirements are widely seen. Such ads, of course, are but an explicit articulation of what many employers around the world take implicit note of in the employment hiring process. In practice, other factors in considering applicants and employees in China include sex, ethnicity, social origin, health, disability, age, or migrant status, but some of which are prohibited by Chinese labor laws.[2]

---

[1] Though the Chinese disagree on which organs constitute the "five sense organs," they have been defined as "ears, eyes, lips, nose, and tongue" and mean "regular features; pleasant-looking face with the five organs in normal shape and position." THE ABC ENGLISH-CHINESE COMPREHENSIVE DICTIONARY 1004 (John DeFrancis et al., eds., 2003).

[2] *See* Jing Tao, *Gender Discrimination in the Chinese Labor Market Is Severe* (Apr. 12, 2005) (unpublished manuscript, on file with author); Jiu dian zhao gong ting kou yin, wei pin yong zhi yin fangyan bu di dao [*Hotel Rejected Job Applicant for Speaking Tongue-Tied Dialect*], BEIJING YOUTH DAILY, Feb. 11, 2004, at 6, http://edu.sina.com.cn/l/2004-02-12/60863.html [hereinafter *Tongue-Tied Dialect*]; Shangshui, jiu ye qi si an li ju jiao [Shang Shui, *Cases on Employment Discrimination*], PEOPLE'S DAILY, June 15, 2005, at 15, http://legal.people.com.cn/GB/42731/3469925.html [hereinafter Shang Shui]; Chao diao bai

The 1994 Labor Law's antidiscrimination provisions covered only employees and not *applicants*. The EPL extends this coverage to include applicants.[3]

Of course, inequality and discrimination against different categories of employees occur in every society. China is interesting both because of the diversity of workers reportedly facing obstacles to equal employment opportunities and because of the sheer size of its labor force. That size makes the number of workers within each category economically significant both because of the possibility of an enormous explosion of arbitration and litigation and the potential waste of capable and employable human resources.

Since the 1994 passage of the Labor Law, protected statuses include "ethnic groups, race, sex, or religious belief."[4] However, Article 14 exempts from protection "people of minority ethnic groups," along with the disabled and demobilized army men where "special stipulations in laws, rules and regulations" apply.[5] In fact, other laws protect members of ethnic minority groups and the disabled in addition to gender and religion, disability/health conditions, and migrant worker status.[6] The Regulations on Labor Market Management also prohibit discrimination in recruitment or employment based on race, gender, religion, and ethnicity.[7]

The 2008 EPL both expands the categories of protection (ethnicity, communicable diseases not directly transmittable, and rural residences [migrant workers]) and reiterates protections to those in a protected status.[8] The means of enforcement of the EPL is through litigation initiated by the employee;

ming yi gan huan zhe re jiu fen [*Dispute Arises When Employer Fired Hundreds of Hepatitis B Carriers*], INFO. CHRON., Apr. 1, 2004, at D03 [hereinafter *Dispute Arises*].

[3] Jiu ye cu jin fa [Employment Promotion Law] (promulgated by the 29th session of the Standing Comm. of the Tenth NPC, Aug. 20, 2007, effective Jan. 1, 2008), art. 3 (PRC) [hereinafter EPL]. Likewise, since 1992 women applicants have had protections by law (e.g., "refusing to employ women by reason of sex" is prohibited in the Women's Rights and Interests Law, art. 23).

[4] Lao dong fa [Labor Law] (promulgated by the Stand. Comm. of the Nat'l People's Cong., July 5, 1994, effective Jan. 1, 1995), art. 12 (PRC).

[5] *Id.* art. 14.

[6] For example, any public official interfering with the exercise of protected religious activities will face criminal penalties. Xing fa [Criminal Law] (promulgated by the Standing Comm. of the Nat'l People's Cong., Mar. 14, 1997, effective Oct. 1, 1997, revised Feb. 28, 2005) art. 251 (PRC). *See also* Guo wu yuan ban gong ting guan yu jin yi bu zuo hao gai shan nong min jin cheng jiu ye huan jing de tong zhi [Notice from the State Council on Further Improving Working Conditions for Migrant Workers] (Dec, 27, 2004), http://www.gov.cn/zwgk/2005-08/15/content_23262.htm [hereinafter Notice on Improving Working Conditions for Migrant Workers].

[7] Lao dong li shi chang guan li gui ding [Regulations on Labor Market Management] (promulgated by the Ministry of Labor and Social Security, Dec. 8, 2000, effective Dec. 8, 2000) (PRC), art. 11, http://www.chinacourt.org/flwk/show1.php?file_id=36355 [hereinafter Regulations on Labor Market Management].

[8] EPL, arts 3, 26, 28, 30–1.

however, as there are no monetary damages provided in the law, claimants may be more inclined to use labor arbitration as applicable.[9] The 2008 LCL also prohibits discrimination against employees within certain categories of occupational diseases and those, in certain circumstances, with not less than fifteen continuous years of working for the employer.[10]

a. Gender

Gender is a protected status under Article 12 of the Labor Law and several other laws, including the 2008 EPL (Art. 27). Women are also covered by Article 13 of the Labor Law, which provides,

> [W]omen shall enjoy the equal employment right with men. With exception of the special types of work or posts unsuitable to women as prescribed by the State [Labor Law, Articles 59–63], no unit may, in employing staff and workers, refuse to employ women by reason of sex or raise the employment standards for women.[11]

The "unsuitable work" exceptions apply to work in mine pits[12]; work on high ground, in low temperatures, or in cold water; in Grade III physical labor during a woman's menstrual cycle[13]; and work during pregnancy,[14] and they provide entitlement to maternity Leave for childbirth.[15] The exceptions further limit work during periods of breast-feeding for children younger than one year old.[16]

China's Constitution guarantees women equal rights with men, protects the rights and interests of women, and provides that there shall be equal pay for equal work.[17] However, it is non–self-executing; in other words, it is aspirational

---

9 EPL, art. 62; for workers hurt by job intermediary agencies, only refunds are available, arts. 63, 66.

10 LCL, art. 42, which refers to arts. 40 and 41 dealing with termination and reductions in force, respectively. This could, in a given case, limit discrimination based on age.

11 *See* Labor Law, art. 13.

12 *Id.* art. 59.

13 *Id.* art. 60.

14 *Id.* art. 61; Fu nv quan yi bao zhang fa [Law on the Protection of Women's Rights and Interests] (promulgated by the Stand. Comm. of the Nat'l People's Cong., revised Aug. 28, 2005, effective Oct. 1, 1992) (PRC) [hereinafter Women's Rights Law]; Nv zhi gong lao dong bao hu gui ding [Regulations on Labor Protection of Female Workers] (promulgated by the State Council, Sept. 1, 1988).

15 Labor Law, art. 62.

16 *Id.* art. 63.

17 XIAN FA [CONST.] art. 48 (2004) (PRC); *see also* Christine M. Bulger, Note, *Fighting Gender Discrimination in the Chinese Workplace*, 20 B.C. THIRD WORLD L.J. 345, 352 (2000).

and cannot by itself be enforced in Chinese courts. Instead, constitutional doctrines must be incorporated into laws promulgated by the government.[18]

China's Law on the Protection of Women's Rights and Interests (hereinafter Women's Rights Law) provides legal prohibitions against employment discrimination based on gender.[19] Under this law, women and men enjoy equal employment rights.[20] The law also prohibits any *hiring* discrimination against women, and, unless the job position is unsuitable for women, the hiring standard for men and women must be the same.[21] For promotions as well, under the equality principle, men and women are to be treated equally.[22] Likewise, women and men must be paid the same rate when they are working on the same job,[23] and the employer may not terminate any female employee on the grounds of marriage, pregnancy, maternity leave, or nursing.[24] For violations, there are administrative remedies, arbitration, or a lawsuit.[25]

Currently in China, the law fixes different retirement ages for men and women.[26] As a result, women receive substantially smaller pensions than men do, even though other employee benefits are equal. Correspondingly, men are discriminated against by not having the same early retirement age as women. Though this difference is based on gender and is thus perhaps in conflict with China's Constitution, it does not appear to violate any employment discrimination laws and is in fact authorized by law. On the other hand, a gender discrimination case was recently reported in Jinjiang District Court in Chengdu, Sichuan, in which the court held that an employer illegally discriminated against women workers when it did not provide them the same retirement options as men.[27]

---

[18] Xian Fa [Const.] arts. 58, 62(2), 89(1) (2004) (PRC).

[19] Women's Rights Law, *supra* note 14, arts. 23–6.

[20] *Id.* art. 22. It appears, therefore, that in most situations, the ban on gender discrimination is equally available to male victims.

[21] *Id.* art. 23; *see* EPL, art. 27 ("Higher Standards").

[22] *Id.* art. 25.

[23] *Id.* art. 24.

[24] *Id.* art. 27.

[25] Women's Rights Law, art. 52.

[26] The retirement age is 60 for men, 50 for female workers, and 55 for women cadres. *See* Guan yu qi ye zhi gong "fa ding tui xiu nian ling" han yi de fu han [Reply by the Ministry of Labor and Social Security on the Meaning of "Legal Retirement Age" of the Workers in State-Owned Enterprises] (promulgated by the Ministry of Labor and Social Security, May 11, 2001), http://www.chinacourt.org/flwk/show1.php?file_id=37327 [hereinafter Reply on Legal Retirement Age]. *See also* Bulger, *supra* note 17, at 358. *See generally* the Ninth Women's National Congress, http://www.cctv.com/lm/124/41/90118.html (last visited Sept. 18, 2008).

[27] Huang Zhiling, *Women Win Sexual Discrimination Case*, China Daily, June 20, 2005, at 3, http://www.chinadaily.com.cn/english/doc/2005-06/20/content_452706.htm. The seven women plaintiffs' case had been denied by the Chengdu Municipal Labor Arbitration

Despite the Constitution, inequality between the sexes continues in the workplace, notwithstanding Mao Zedong's admonition in 1955 to end it:

> Enable every woman who can work to take her place on the labor front under the principle of equal pay for equal work. This should be done as soon as possible.[28]

In 1990, China ratified the International Labor Organization (ILO) Convention on Equal Remuneration for Equal Work[29] and, with subsequent legislation and government policies discussed in this section, has sought to curb gender discrimination in many areas of society, including education, political office, and economic opportunity.[30] Nonetheless, wage disparities between men and women remain, with urban women earning about seventy cents for

Committee before they brought the suit to the court. The legal basis of the claim is gender, but it is unclear whether the court's finding was based on the Labor Law, the Women's Rights Law, the Constitution, or some other basis. Article 27 of the new amendments to the Women's Rights Law states, "(a)ny unit shall not discriminate against women by reason of gender when implementing the national retirement system." This amendment became effective December 1, 2005. *See* Women's Rights Law, *supra* note 14, art. 27.

[28] John DeFrancis, ANNOTATED QUOTATIONS FROM CHAIRMAN MAO 136 (1975); *and see Equality Called for Women*, CHINA DAILY, July 2, 2004, http://www.china.org.cn/english/China/100112.htm.

[29] International Labor Organization, *Convention Concerning Equal Remuneration for Men and Women Workers for Work of Equal Value*, 165 U.N.T.S. 32 (1951). For ratification status, *see* http://www.ilo.org/ilolex/cgi-lex/ratifce.pl?C100.

[30] UN Committee on the Elimination of Discrimination against Women, 20th Sess., *Third and Fourth Periodic Reports of States Parties*, 2–9, U.N. Doc. CEDAW/C/CHN/3–4 (1997). The United Nations Committee on Economic, Social and Cultural Rights recently reviewed China's report on its implementation of Articles 16 and 17 of the International Covenant on Economic, Social and Cultural Rights, G.A. Res. 2200, U.N. GAOR, 21st Sess., Suppl. No. 16, at 64, U.N. Doc. A/6316 (1966). The committee, in its Concluding Observations, included as one of its "Principles of Concerns" "the persistence of gender inequalities in practice in the State party, particularly with regard to employment and participation in decision-making." Article 16 of the Covenant requires State Parties of the Convention to submit periodical reports to the Secretary-General of the United Nation on the measures that they have adopted and the progress made in achieving observance of the rights recognized under the Convention. Article 17 further requires that reports may indicate factors and difficulties affecting the degree of fulfillment of rights recognized under the Convention, and reports shall have a precise reference of information. International Covenant on Economic, Social and Cultural Rights, arts. 16–7, G.A. Res. 2200, U.N. GAOR, 21st Sess., Suppl. No. 16, at 64, U.N. Doc. A/6316 (1966). "The Committee regrets that it has not received sufficient information from the State party regarding affirmative action to promote gender equality and measures to prevent sexual harassment in the workplace." U.N. Committee on Economic, Social and Cultural Rights, 34th Sess., *Concluding Observations of the Committee on Economic, Social and Cultural Rights People's Republic of China*, at 3, U.N. Doc. E/C.12/1/Add.107 (2005) [Hereinafter *UN Concluding Observations*]. It recommends "the State party to undertake effective measures to ensure the equal right of men and women to enjoy economic, social and cultural rights as provided for in Article 3 of the Covenant, including through implementing the principle of equal pay for work of equal value, the elimination of wage gaps between men and women, and providing equal opportunities for both men and women." *Id.* at 7.

every dollar earned by men for similar work and rural women earning less than sixty cents per dollar earned by their male peers.[31] An MOLSS investigation of sixty-two selected cities "clearly shows that 67% of the work units set gender limits and expressly stipulate in writing that females must not become pregnant or bear children during the term of their employment."[32]

The All China Federation of Trade Unions (ACFTU) has publicized some of the stark conditions women face in the workplace.[33] It compiled information gathered between 1978 and 2002, which found that reforms and transition to a market economy were less kind to female than to male workers. Specifically, women were laid off at a significantly higher rate than men.[34] In addition, after being laid off, only 39 percent of women versus 63.9 percent of men were able to find new work.[35] One positive finding was that between 1990 and 2000 – the early years of market transition – the wage gap between female and male workers dropped from 77.5 percent to 70.1 percent.[36] Yet, still in 2002, "there were twice as many women [as men] in jobs below the 500 yuan (approximately US$60) monthly income level, with 1.5 times as many men holding 2,000 yuan (approximately US$240) jobs as women." In addition, women were said to hold only 1.3 percent of management posts in all organizations during 2002.[37] The ACFTU Report concluded that "problems faced by female employees result from the influence of [a] market economy and society."[38] Of course, there are in fact many factors that cause inequality in society, including education level, experience, qualifications, and an employer's intention to discriminate.

Another indication of gender inequality is the frustration experienced by recent female college graduates who are looking for jobs. It is said to be "an open secret in China that female college graduates suffer discrimination from employers when applying for jobs, with the inequality known to almost all college students, including graduate students."[39] Some graduates have even

---

[31] State Dept. Rpt.

[32] Tao, *supra* note 2.

[33] *Equality Called for Women*, CHINA DAILY, July 2, 2004, http://www.china.org .cn/english/China/100112.htm. The report, cited in CHINA DAILY, was compiled after studying information gathered between 1978 and 2002, on the working lives of female workers in Shanghai, Chongqing, and provinces such as Liaoning, Jiangsu, Zhejiang, Guangdong, and Gansu. It found that as reforms have been implemented in the transition to a market economy, industries such as the textile sector and some other female-dominated areas have sustained large-scale layoffs. Not surprisingly, a disproportionate number of women were laid off.

[34] *Id.*

[35] *Id.* The All China Federation of Women (ACFW) confirmed these findings in its own report, *cited in Equality Called for Women, supra* note 28.

[36] *Id.*

[37] *Id.*

[38] *Id.*

[39] Xing Zhigang, *Job Hunt a Battle for Female Grads*, CHINA DAILY, Apr. 3, 2004, http://www.chinadaily.com.cn/english/doc/2004-04/02/content_320244.htm.

opted to include revealing photos – of them wearing bikinis or short skirts – on their resumes.[40]

The ACFTU report also showed that many employers, in clear violation of labor laws, refused to issue labor contracts to women workers, especially younger women. Instead, these employers required them to work long overtime hours, ranging from seventy-six to ninety hours per week, and assigned female workers to hazardous jobs in violation of labor laws.[41] The report described in detail these violations:

> Non-SOEs very rarely provide maternity benefits, nor do they accommodate the special needs of women during menstrual periods, pregnancy, or after the birth of a child. Some female employees still work high above the ground or in low temperatures, or carry out hard physical labor while menstruating. Reports also circulate that women, some who are seven months pregnant, are scheduled to work night shifts in some factories.[42]

The ACFTU report concluded, "Sex discrimination is the norm in today's workplace. Progress made in the early decades of the PRC has in many cases been abandoned in the years since economic reform began."[43]

b. Sexual Harassment

For the first time, a 2005 amendment to the Women's Rights Law protected against sexual harassment in the workplace.[44] Though as of yet there is no clear

[40] *Id.* Xiaqqo Yu, a female undergraduate at Beijing Normal University, reports that her job searches at job fairs and elsewhere were often met with "[I]f only you were a boy." Reportedly, it is not uncommon for employers to openly state their requirement or preference for male applicants, and this attitude is enhanced by the usual age of a female college graduate, which, at 22, is thought by some employers to be entering their time for marriage and family. A personnel manager at a Beijing electronics firm reportedly stated his view that "employing more women will push up our production cost because female workers have to be given pregnancy and maternity benefits in line with labour laws." *Id.*

[41] Wang Zhiyong, *Women in the Workplace: A Great Leap Backward*, (Mar. 22, 2004), http://www.china.org.cn/english/2004/Mar/90950.htm. This source, China Internet Information, is under the auspices of the China International Publishing Group and the State Council Information Office.

[42] *Id.*

[43] *Id.*

[44] Women's Rights Law, Art. 40. Zhongpeng Zhao, *Legislative Recommendation by the All China Women's Federation Puts Forth Concept of "Sexual Harassment" for the First Time*, BEIJING MORNING DAILY, Mar. 4, 2005, http://www.chinalawdigest.com/article.php?aid=123 (accessible by free registration).

"[T]he changes proposed by the ACWF include stopping discrimination against women in the workplace. For the first time in China, the very concept of sexual harassment will enter the national legal system. The proposed amendment requires all employers to try to stop harassment at work. And there will also be new clauses that insist on gender equality in retirement terms. Once the ACWF's definition is accepted by the NPC, sexual harassment is likely to be

legal definition of this right, the concept is based on gender discrimination and is still being pursued in court litigation (though, arguably, such a right would fall under either or both the Labor Law and the Women's Rights Law).[45] The All China Women's Federation (ACWF) also had originally recommended a ban on sexual harassment and a requirement that employers take measures to prevent it, but the NPC Standing Committee only passed the former.

In 2007, Shanghai aimed at implementing the national law by passing a law specifying acts that may constitute sexual harassment.[46] These acts include speech, words, images, electronic information, and physical contact. Unlike the national law, it mandates the employer to investigate and take measures to prevent sexual harassment, though no specific measures are included. There are no penalty provisions, but the woman is given the right to file a civil suit in court; a similar regulation was issued in Shaanxi in 2007.[47]

A recent survey in China, in which about 80 percent of women identified themselves as "victims of sexual harassment," has brought about an increasing interest in sexual harassment cases.[48] A recent sexual harassment case provides

made a criminal offence." *The Yin and Yang of a Harmonious Society*, CHINA DAILY, Mar. 8, 2005, http://english.people.com.cn/200503/08/eng20050308_176060.html.

The NPC Standing Committee declined to include the clauses imposing mandatory duties on employers to prevent sexual harassment in workplaces on the grounds that it could not formulate a national standard of such duty and such duty would rather limit the anti-harassment effort to narrowly defined workplace settings. Xin fu nv quan yi bao zhang fa: wo guo fa lv shou ci dui xing sao rao shuo bu [*A New Law on Protection of Women's Rights and Interests: Law Says No to Sexual Harassment for the First Time*], XINHUA NEWS AGENCY, Aug. 28, 2005, http://news.xinhuanet.com/legal/2005-08/28/content_3414548.htm; *see also* Quanguo renda changwei guan yu xiu gai "fu nv quan yi bao zhang fa" de jue ding [Decision of the Standing Committee of the National People's Congress about Amending the Law on Protection of Women's Rights and Interests] (promulgated by the Standing Comm. of the Nat'l People's Cong., Aug. 28, 2005, effective Dec. 1, 2005) (PRC), http://www.legaldaily.com.cn/misc/2005-11/08/content_216846.htm.

45 Women's Rights Law, arts. 40, 58; Labor Law, arts. 12, 13. Likewise, cases have also been brought under the General Principles of the Civil Law for infringement of reputation. Min fa tong ze [General Principles of the Civil Law] (promulgated by the Nat'l People's Cong., April 12, 1986, effective Jan. 1, 1987), art. 120 (PRC).

46 Shanghai shi shi "fu nv quan yi bao zhang fa" ban fa [Measures of Shanghai Municipality for Implementation of the Law on Protection of Women's Rights and Interests] (promulgated by the Shanghai Municipal People's Cong., April 26, 2007), http://www.shlaw.com.cn/ReadNews.asp?NewsID=2811.

47 Shaanxi shi shi "fu nv quan yi bao zhang fa" ban fa [Measures of Shaanxi Municipality for Implementation of the Law on Protection of Women's Rights and Interests] (promulgated by the Shaanxi Municipal People's Cong., April 26, 2007), http://www.sxzffz.gov.cn/News_View.asp?NewsID=674.

48 Jane Macartney, *China Jails Liu Lun, Its First Office Sex Pest*, http://www.timesonline.co.uk/tol/news/world/asia/article4346994.ece?print=yes&randnum=1222467799853; Wang Ying, *Women to Get Protection from Harassment*, CHINA DAILY, Mar. 5, 2005, http://www.chinadaily.com.cn/english/doc/2005-03/05/content_421943.htm.

a useful guide to lawsuits in court without prior labor arbitration, at least where a criminal assault is involved.[49]

c. Race/Ethnicity

Race does not appear to be a much-used category in employment discrimination, except to the degree that it is intertwined with ethnicity or with one of its indirect manifestations, such as language, dress, or custom. In China, it is difficult to discuss race (except as to "foreigners") apart from ethnicity. The question concerning ethnicity is whether it is exempted by Article 14 of the Labor Law (discussed later), thereby leaving race as a protected status vacant of use, except perhaps as it overlaps with ethnicity and as it is applied to either foreigners or Chinese citizens of non-Chinese descent.[50]

Pursuant to international conventions, China has agreed to treat the issues of welfare and employment discrimination against ethnic groups under the category of "race."[51] Therefore, there appears to be a dual legislative avenue of relief – either race or ethnic minority status – under the Labor Law for those claiming employment discrimination based on ethnic minority status.

As to the possible Article 14 exemption of "people of minority ethnic groups," some laws provide general protection for the national ethnic minorities,[52] but

[49] Tania Branigan, *Chinese Man Jailed in First Sexual Harassment Case under New Law*, THE GUARDIAN, July 17, 2008, http://www.guardian.co.uk/world/2008/jul/17/china.gender (last visited Sept. 19, 2008); Li Xinran, *Man Jailed for Sexually Harassing Colleague*, http://www.shanghaidaily.com/sp/article/2008/200807/20080715/article_366896.htm.

[50] A person can obtain Chinese citizenship by blood or by birth. The law says, "When the parents, who have no nationality or whose nationality is uncertain, reside in China, and the child was born in China, then the child automatically obtains Chinese citizenship." Guo ji fa [Nationality Law] (promulgated by the Standing Comm. of the Nat'l People's Cong., Sept. 10, 1980, effective Sept. 10, 1980), art. 6 (PRC), http://www.chinacourt.org/flwk/show1.php?file_id=1543. This was a dead provision for years because it was extremely difficult to get permanent residence in China. However, China now allows a foreigner and his or her spouse to become permanent residents, if, among other conditions, the foreigner invests at least US$500,000. Wai guo ren zai zhongguo yong jiu ju liu shen pi guan li ban fa [Provisions for the Administration of Examination and Approval of Foreigners' Permanent Residence in China], art. 7 (promulgated by the State Council, Ministry of Foreign Affairs, and Ministry of Pub. Sec., Aug. 15, 2004, effective Aug. 15, 2004) (PRC), http://www.bjqb.gov.cn/data/news/fgtl/2004830113528.htm. Other ways to obtain Chinese permanent residence include employment and teaching. *Id.* art. 8.

[51] International Convention on the Elimination of All Forms of Racial Discrimination, art. 14, opened for signature Dec. 21, 1965, 660 U.N.T.S. 195 (entered into force Jan. 4, 1969), http://www2.ohchr.org/english/law/cerd.htm [hereinafter ICERD].

[52] For example, the Law on Regional National Autonomy prohibits discrimination against minority ethnic groups. Min zu qu yu zi zhi fa [Law on Regional National Autonomy]

the first specific prohibition on employment discrimination against "ethnic groups" did not appear until the 2008 EPL, though with limited remedies; thus, one could argue, apparently perfecting the exemption by removing the status from the 1994 Labor Law and moving protections under the EPL.[53]

China has a relatively homogeneous population, as 92 percent of its people are of the Han ethnicity; the remaining 8 percent includes more than 106 million Chinese of fifty-five different ethnic minorities.[54] Defining race can be a complex undertaking. For example, the U.S. Supreme Court defined "race" under an 1800s civil rights law as being "genetically part of an ethnically and physiognomically distinctive sub grouping of homo sapiens."[55] In a report under the International Convention on the Elimination of All Forms of Racial Discrimination (ICERD) (agreed to since 1981), "race" is defined as "race, colour, descent, or national or ethnic origin."[56]

According to the ICERD committee's comments, this report urges China to

> consider giving full effect to the provisions in the Convention in its domestic legal order and that it ensure the penalization of racial discrimination; and also, that it ensure access to effective protection and remedies through the competent national tribunals or other state institutions, against all acts of racial discrimination. It should be noted that the structural inadequacies in respect of anti-discrimination laws are in violation of Article 4 of ICERD.[57]

(promulgated by the Standing Comm. of the Nat'l People's Cong., May 31, 1984, effective Oct. 1, 1984, revised Feb. 28, 2001), art. 9, (PRC), http://www.chinacourt.org/flwk/show1.php?file_id=36850 [hereinafter Law on Regional National Autonomy]; Gong hui fa [Trade Union Law], art. 3 (promulgated by the Standing Comm. of the Nat'l People's Cong., Apr. 3, 1992, effective Apr. 3, 1992, revised Oct. 27, 2001) (PRC), http://people.com.cn/GB/shizheng/8198/29614/29642/2071559.html (prohibiting racial discrimination on union benefits). *See also* the Law on Regional National Autonomy, art. 23 (requiring enterprises in national autonomous areas to give priority to minority groups when recruiting personnel).

53 EPL, art. 6; *See* Labor Law, art. 14.

54 UN Committee on the Elimination of Racial Discrimination, 59th Sess., *Ninth Periodic Reports Submitted by States Parties*, at 3, U.N. Doc. CERD/C/357 Add. 4 (Part I) (2001).

55 St. Francis College v. Al-Khazraji, 481 U.S. 604, 613 (1987). Justice Brennan, in a concurring opinion, noted, "I write separately only to point out the line between discrimination based on 'ancestry or ethnic characteristics' and discrimination based on 'place of origin' is not a bright one." Often, the two are identical as a factual matter." *Id.* at 614. National origin discrimination then can include "place of origin, physical, culture or linguistic characteristics of that group." *Id.*

56 ICERD art. 1; *see also* summary in *Ninth Periodic Reports Submitted by States Parties, supra* note 54, at 5–7.

57 UN Committee on the Elimination of Racial Discrimination, 59th Sess., 1648th & 1649th mtg. at 3–5, U.N. Doc. CERD.C.59.Misc.16.Rev.3 (2001) [emphasis added].

This report clearly calls for prohibitions on all acts of racial discrimination. It therefore promotes the elimination of any discrimination based on ethnicity, including that of national ethnic minorities.

Although China must be credited with great success for the economic progress of regions with substantial racial minority populations, the ICERD report makes the point "that economic development in minority regions does not ipso facto entail the equal enjoyment of economic, social, and cultural rights in accordance with Article 5(e) of the Convention."[58] Anecdotal information about hiring practices in China suggests that some employers continue to show racial prejudice against "outsiders" (those not of the local area), migrants, ethnic minorities, those speaking a different language, and those "looking different."[59] The extent of these purported instances of racial discrimination in employment in China is unknown, and as in the United States, laws alone do not eradicate racial discrimination.[60]

Ethnicity is another category of worker status and can be closely associated with race, as discussed earlier.[61] In China, the population of ethnic national minorities exceeds 106 million (about 8.4 percent of the population), and job discrimination at the hands of the majority Han, particularly in border areas near the minority-dominated autonomous regions, is reported to occur.[62]

---

[58] *See Report of the Committee on the Elimination of Racial Discrimination*, U.N. GAOR, 59th Sess., Supp. No. 18, at 48, U.N. Doc. A/56/18 (2001); *see also* Information Office of the State Council of the People's Republic of China (Beijing), Regional Autonomy for Ethnic Minorities in China, http://www.china.org.cn/e-white/20050301 (last visited Sept. 18, 2008).

[59] In a reported case, a Hangzhou-based hotel refused to hire a job applicant simply because the applicant spoke in a nonlocal dialect. *See Tongue-Tied Dialect, supra* note 2.

[60] Harold S. Lewis, Jr. & Elizabeth J. Norman, LEWIS AND NORMAN'S HORNBOOK ON EMPLOYMENT DISCRIMINATION LAW AND PRACTICE 215–25 (2d ed. 2004) [Hereinafter Lewis & Norman]. During fiscal year 2004, the U.S. Equal Employment Opportunity Commission (EEOC) received 27,696 charges of race discrimination. The EEOC has observed an increasing number of color/race discrimination charges. Color/race bias filings have increased by 125% since the mid-1990s. U.S. Equal Employment Opportunity Commission, RACE/COLOR DISCRIMINATION, http://www.eeoc.gov/types/race.html (last visited Sept. 18, 2008).

[61] *Merriam-Webster's Collegiate Dictionary* defines ethnicity as a particular affiliation of "large groups of people classed according to common racial, national, tribal, religious, linguistic, or cultural origin or background." MERRIAM-WEBSTER'S COLLEGIATE DICTIONARY 326 (11th ed. 2003). The U.S. Supreme Court defined "race" as being "genetically part of an ethnically and physiognomically distinctive subgrouping of homo sapiens." *St. Francis College v. Al-Khazraji*, 481 U.S. 604, 607 (1987).

[62] U.S. Dept. of State, Country Reports on Human Rights Practices (2004), http://www.state.gov/g/drl/rls/hrrpt/2004/41640.htm (last visited Sept. 18, 2008) [hereinafter State Dept. Rpt.]. The concluding observations of a recent report by the UN Committee on Economic, Social and Cultural Rights reviewing China's report on its implementation of Articles 16 and 17 of the International Covenant on Economic, Social and Cultural Rights stated as one of its "Principles of Concern" that "the reports regarding the discrimination of ethnic minorities in the State party, in particular in the field of employment, adequate standard

For example, there have been anecdotal reports of preference for Hans over minorities for new construction jobs in Xinjiang, Inner Mongolia, and Tibet.[63] In the mid-1990s, some foreign advocates claimed discriminatory treatment was occurring in Tibet: Tibetans were receiving lower wages, and there was a preference for proficiency in Mandarin, the national language, over the local language of Tibetan.[64] It has been reported that in Hangzhou, the capital of Zhejiang Province, bus drivers and attendants must speak standard Mandarin (*Putonghua*) during working hours and face employer-imposed fines if caught speaking local dialects.[65]

In the United States, employment discrimination based on "physical, cultural, or linguistic characteristics of a national group" is prohibited by law where it is not shown to be a "bona fide occupational qualification" or "business necessity."[66] Discrimination based on language has been categorized as both "race" and "national origin" discrimination, as there is often a clear connection between ethnicity and language.[67] Speak-English-only employer policies still generate legal controversy.[68]

d. Migrant Workers

The 2008 EPL provides that migrant workers (Art. 31) are entitled to equal labor rights, and it prohibits discrimination against them. The 2008 Labor Contract Law further indirectly affirms protection for migrant workers.[69]

of living, health, education and culture." UN Committee on Economic, Social and Cultural Rights, 34th Sess., Concluding Observations of the Committee on Economic, Social and Cultural Rights People's Republic of China, at 5, U.N. Doc. E/C.12/1/Add.107 (2005) [hereinafter U.N. Concluding Observations].

[63] State Dept. Rpt., *supra* note 62.

[64] It is reported that a minimum wage has been introduced everywhere in China except for the Tibet Autonomous Region. Tibetan Centre for Human Rights and Democracy, *1997 Annual Report: Human Rights Violations in Tibet* (on file with author). *See also* Osman Chuah, *Muslims in China: The Social and Economic Situation of the Hui Chinese*, 24 J. Muslim Minority Aff. 155 (Apr. 2004).

[65] *Bus Personnel Must Speak Putonghua or Else*, China Daily, June 4, 2005, http://www.chinadaily.com.cn/english/doc/2005-06/04/content_448499.htm.

[66] *See* 29 C.F.R. § 1606.1 (2005); 42 U.S.C. § 2000e–2(e)(i) (2005); 42 U.S.C. §§ 2000e–2(k)(1)(A)(i) (2005).

[67] *Hernandez v. N.Y.*, 500 U.S. 352, 364 (1991) (in the context of a community with a substantial foreign-speaking ethnic population, classification based on language can be purposeful discrimination against ethnicity).

[68] *See Garcia v. Spun Steak Co.*, 998 F.2d 1480 (9th Cir. 1993), *cert. denied*, 512 U.S. 1228 (1994); for general discussion, see American Civil Liberties Union of North California, Language Rights, http://www.aclunc.org/language/lang-report.html (last visited Sept. 18, 2008).

[69] E.g. LCL, art. 11, confirms employer obligations even without a labor contract. This addresses the problem faced by many migrant workers who were not provided employment contracts.

Discrimination based on "social origin," as would seem to be the proper classification of biases against Chinese migrant workers, is recognized by the United Nations Universal Declaration of Human Rights and the International Covenant on Civil and Political Rights (ICCPR), both of which China has ratified.[70] Additionally, ILO Convention 111, which China has not ratified, eliminates all forms of discrimination, including "social origin."[71] However, because Convention 111 is a "core labor standard," nations are thought to be bound to the principle of providing equal employment opportunity, including the prevention of discrimination caused by "social origin."[72]

Impediments to equal employment opportunities for migrant workers exist in China's historic use of the *hukou* system, which restricts the ability of migrating workers to obtain residential status, as well as social insurance and social benefits in geographic areas other than that of their original

[70] Universal Declaration of Human Rights, art. 2, G.A. Res. 217A (III), U.N. Doc A/810 at 71 (1948), International Covenant on Civil and Political Rights, art. 2, G.A. Res. 2200A (XXI), 21 U.N. GAOR Supp. (No. 16) at 52, U.N. Doc. A/6316 (1966), 999 U.N.T.S. 171, entered into force Mar. 23, 1976. China ratified ICCPR on Oct. 5, 1998. *See also* Constance Thomas & Yuki Horii, Fundamental Rights at Work and International Labour Standards 62 (2003) ("Social origin" is frequently used in major international human rights treaties without a precise definition in the treaties themselves). The ILO in its Convention No. 111 uses "social origin" as a status protected against employment discrimination. International Labour Organization Convention (No. 111) Concerning Discrimination in Respect of Employment and Occupation, June 25, 1958, 362 U.N.T.S. 31. "This criterion refers to situations in which an individual's membership of a class, socio-occupational category or caste determines his or her occupational future, either because he or she is denied access to certain jobs or activities, or because he or she is only assigned certain jobs. Even in societies with considerable social mobility, a number of obstacles continue to prevent perfect equality of opportunity for the various social categories." *Id.* at art. 1.

[71] International Labour Organization Convention (No. 111) Concerning Discrimination in Respect of Employment and Occupation, June 25, 1958, 362 U.N.T.S. 31. In a document prepared by an ILO Committee of Experts, "[c]ertain principles relating to the application of the Conventions, which are not explicitly set out in the instruments" but have been "developed in the comments of the Committee of Experts." *See* Thomas & Horii, *supra* note 71 ("Social origin" is frequently used in major international human rights treaties without a precise definition in the treaties themselves). Regarding "social origin," the Experts commented, "[p]rejudices and preferences based on social origin may persist when a rigid division of society into classes determines an individual's opportunities in employment and occupation, or when certain 'castes' are considered to be inferior and are therefore confined to the most menial jobs." *Id.* at 73. Moreover, a U.S. Department of Labor report on international labor standards noted that "in response to concerns that *internal* migrant workers in China are not covered by Convention 111, an ILO official noted that they are considered to be covered by the prohibition on discrimination on the basis of social origin." U.S. Dept. of Labor, International Labor Standards: Discrimination and Equality, http://www.dol.gov/ ilab/webmils/intllaborstandards/discrimination.html (last visited Sept. 19, 2008) [hereinafter International Labor Standards].

[72] Harry Arthurs, *Reinventing Labor Law for the Global Economy*, 22 Berkeley J. Emp. & Lab. L. 271, 294 n.46 (2001).

employment.[73] Notwithstanding these residential restrictions, some changes, both legal and de facto, are taking place. For example, in response to widespread reports of labor exploitation, discrimination, and abuse by employers,[74] China's central government has issued new regulations to protect the labor rights of migrant workers. In December 2004, the State Council issued its Notice on Migrant Workers' Employment.[75] It holds that migrant workers enjoy all of the rights provided by the Labor Law[76] and that for hiring purposes they must be treated equally with urban residents.[77] The State

[73] For a detailed description of the history, development, functions, impact, and operational mechanisms of China's hukou system, *see generally* Fei-Ling Wang, ORGANIZING THROUGH DIVISION AND EXCLUSION: CHINA'S HUKOU SYSTEM (2005). For a brief summary, *see* Canada Immigration and Refugee Board, CHINA: REFORMS OF THE HOUSEHOLD REGISTRATION SYSTEM (HUKOU) (1998–2004), http://www.irb-cisr.gc.ca/en/research/publications/index_e.htm?docid=279&cid=50 (last visited Sept. 19, 2008); *People on the Move, Old Residence Registration System in Being Unified*, BEIJING REV., Jan. 1, 2004, at 32.

[74] *Let's Protect Migrant Workers*, CHINA DAILY, Apr. 4, 2005, http://news.xinhuanet.com/english/2005-04/04/content_2783301.htm; *Ensure Equal Payment*, CHINA DAILY, Mar. 29, 2005, http://www.chinadaily.com.cn/english/doc/2005-03/29/content_428901.htm; *City Job Hurdles Cleared for Migrants*, CHINA DAILY, Feb. 21, 2005, http://www.chinadaily.com.cn/english/doc/2005-02/21/content_417890.htm. John Knight & Linda Yueh, *Job Mobility of Residents and Migrants in Urban China*, 32(4) J. COMP. ECON. 637, 642 (2004).

A legal *notice* provides that migrant workers have equal rights to participate in worker's compensation. *See* Guan yu nong min gong can jia gong shang bao xian you guan de tong zhi [Notice on Migrant Workers' Right to Work-related Social Insurance] (promulgated by the Ministry of Labor & Soc. Sec., June 1, 2004) (PRC), http://news.xinhuanet.com/zhengfu/2004-06/18/content_1533078.htm. In 2003, the State Council issued a legal opinion on migrant labor that added that the government shall eliminate all the discriminatory, restrictive regulations aimed at migrant labor. *See* Guan yu zuo hao nong min jin cheng wu gong jiu ye guan li he fu wu gong zuo de tong zhi [Notice on Managing and Servicing Migrant Workers] (promulgated by the General Office of the State Council, Jan. 5, 2003, effective Jan. 5, 2003) (PRC), http://www.molss.gov.cn/correlate/gbf200301.htm. The Agriculture Law standardizes procedures for recruiting rural laborers. This law provides additional assistance to migrant workers, though not necessarily protecting against job discrimination. *See* Non ye fa [Agriculture Law] art. 82 (promulgated by the Standing Comm. of the Nat'l People's Cong., July 2, 1993, effective July 2, 1993, revised Mar. 1, 2003) (PRC), http://www.chinacourt.org/flwk/show1.php?file_id=81931.

[75] The Notice on Improving Working Conditions for Migrant Workers provides that "in every field of industry, migrant workers shall enjoy the equal treatment of job qualification requirement with fellow urban resident workers." Guan yu jin yi bu zuo hao gai shan nong min jin cheng jiu ye huan jing gong zuo de tong zhi [Notice from the State Council on Further Improving Working Conditions for Migrant Workers] (Dec, 27, 2004), art. 1, http://www.gov.cn/zwgk/2005-08/15/content_23262.htm [hereinafter Notice on Improving Working Conditions for Migrant Workers]. Local government shall "vigorously [enforce] the law to crack down on over-time, default payment, child labor and other violations of migrant workers' legal rights." *Id.* art. 2(2). Local government shall "support and encourage labor unions' activities under the Labor Union Law and protect migrant workers' legal rights." *Id.* art. 2(4).

[76] Notice on Managing and Servicing Migrant Workers, *supra* note 74, art. 3.

[77] *Id.* art. 2

Council also sought to stop local governments' use of administrative detention against migrant workers, declaring that they shall not restrict migrant workers' employment opportunities by such methods.[78]

The 2008 EPL gives further government impetus for the meaningful enforcement of the labor rights of migrants. The Labor Mediation and Arbitration Law likewise supports the ability of migrant workers to more easily gain access to labor arbitration.[79]

Yet migrant workers continue to be stigmatized, as seen in the following comment:

> Appear[ing] to urbanites as aimless and ominous as errant waters, China's sojourning peasant transients in the cities are outsiders, out of place. In their millions, they seem to city folk and their supervisors to be streaming in, as if incessantly, out of control. In the minds of their metropolitan detractors, they are aptly labeled: they are unrooted noncitizens, wanderers; they are the elements of the "floating population."[80]

The number of migrant workers flowing between the rural and urban locations of China is estimated to be at least 130 million,[81] and some project that this number will reach 300 million by 2010.[82] The 2000 census figures reported that 65 percent of the flow was intra-province, with young and middle-aged people between fifteen and thirty-five years of age constituting more than 70 percent of all migrant workers.[83] Much of the movement is a result of China's transition to a market economy and its relaxation of the household registration (*hukou*) system that prior to the reforms had restricted mobility.[84]

Migrant workers eager for better wages travel to urban areas to find jobs better than those available near home. Urban centers have many such jobs, and the

---

[78] *Id.* art. 2. This notice also requires employers in certain construction projects to provide decent living conditions whenever the job requires migrant workers to live on the project premises. *Id.* art. 4.

[79] For example, large impediments to accessing arbitration included fees and the short filing deadlines for seeking redress, which were removed and improved, respectively, by LMA, arts. 53 and 27.

[80] Dorothy J. Solinger, Contesting Citizenship in Urban China: Peasant Migrants, the State and the Logic of the Market 1 (1999).

[81] *Reforms of China's Household Registration System Underway*, http://www.china.org .cn/baodao/english/newsandreport/2002sep1/18-4.htm (last visited Sept. 19, 2008). *See also China's Floating Population Exceeded 10% of Total Population, supra* note 9. Other estimates put the figure at 140 million in 2003, rising from 70 million in 1993. *Id.*

[82] David Lague, *The Human Tide Sweeps into Cities*, 166 Far E. Econ. Rev. 24, 25 (2003).

[83] *Id.*

[84] For discussion of the *hukou* system, *see* Fei-Ling Wang, *supra* note 74. For more information on the early uses of *hukou* and its ties to employment, housing, education, and social security, *see Reform of China's Household Registration System Underway, supra* note 81.

labor of migrant workers has contributed to China's economic development and its transition to a market economy. Despite this economic contribution, migrant workers are often taken advantage of in the workplace: they are often given dirty, difficult, and dangerous jobs; made to work under substandard working conditions; and sometimes are not paid for months at a time.[85]

Many hardships exist for such workers who are far from home and in need of money.[86] Certainly, migrant workers' lack of awareness of their legal rights, combined with urban employers' HRM methods, illegal practices of withholding wages, refusing to give overtime pay, and long working hour requirements, contribute to workplace discrimination against migrant workers. This migrant status can arguably be associated with one's "social origin," a topic covered in international covenants, as described earlier.[87]

Gender descrimination also often blends with migrant worker discrimination in the workplace, as female migrant workers (*dagong mei*) are often given preference for certain factory jobs,[88] as described in the following:

> More than 10 million migrant laborers work in Guangdong Province according to China's 2000 national census, and the Guangdong Statistical Bureau estimates that more than 60% of these are women. Migrant workers tend to staff wholly-foreign-owned enterprises, joint ventures, township and village enterprises, and private enterprises that produce toys, clothing, footwear, electronics, and other consumer goods. Female workers usually come to Guangdong from poorer provinces along the Yangzi River such as Hubei, Hunan, Jiangsu, Jiangxi, and Sichuan. They find jobs in Guangdong factories through labor bureaus, from relatives and friends, or by word of month. Guangdong's economy has grown more than 14% per year on average during the last decade, and the province has accounted for about half of the country's total GDP growth. Guangdong alone generates more than 40% of China's foreign trade in terms of value. While both

[85] See Zhiqiang Liu, *Institution and Inequality: The Hukou System in China*, 33 J. COMP. ECON. 133, 137 (2005). Vice-Premier Zeng Peiyan revealed in a 2004 national conference that more than ¥360 billion (US$43 billion) in unpaid wages remain owed to migrant workers at thousands of real estate projects. *See Zeng: Pay All Owned Wages to Migrants*, CHINA DAILY, Aug. 24, 2004, 2004 WLNR 11949200; *see also* Am. Ctr. for Int'l Labor Solidarity, JUSTICE FOR ALL: THE STRUGGLE FOR WORKER RIGHTS IN CHINA 39–40 (2004).

[86] *See* Pun Ngai, *Women Workers and Precarious Employment in Shenzhen Special Economic Zone, China*, 12 GENDER & DEV. 29, 30 (July 2004).

[87] It is argued that the use of "social origin" in ILO Convention No. 111 covers China's internal migrant workers. U.S. Dept. of Labor, *International Labor Standards: Discrimination and Equality*, http://www.dol.gov/ilab/webmils/intllaborstandards/discrimination.html (last visited Feb. 27, 2006) [hereinafter *International Labor Standards*].

[88] Zhang Ye et al., *Hope for China's Migrant Women Workers*, CHINA BUS. REV., May/June 2002, at 30, 31; *see also* Xiao-Yuan Dong et al., *Gender Segmentation at Work in China's Privatized Rural Industry: Some Evidence from Shandong and Jiangsu*, 32 WORLD DEV. 979, (2004). Pun Ngai, *supra* note 86, at 29.

the central and local governments have recognized the indispensable contribution of migrant labor, so far government policy [as of 2002] has provided migrant laborers few protections.[89]

This situation is confirmed by other sources:

> In 2003, some 70% of the 5.5 million migrant workers in the Shenzhen special economic zone were women. In Shenzhen's industrial district of Nanshan, 80% of the half-million workers were women; their average age was 23.[90]

The cheap cost of labor provided by migrant workers has made a significant contribution to China's economic development during its economic transition. Yet it was not until the 2008 EPL that migrant status was explicitly designated as a protected class similar to gender.[91] The continuing presence and growth of this "floating population" of migrant workers will certainly have a significant impact on China's legal system in the areas of coverage and enforcement of labor and social security laws, labor contracts, worker injuries, and unemployment.[92]

e. Religious Belief

Religious belief is another protected status insulated against employment discrimination under the Labor Law.[93] As in many countries, religious beliefs are often intertwined with other protected statuses, such as ethnic background

---

[89] Ye et al., *supra* note 88, at 31. New protections under the labor laws were issued by the central government in 2003 and 2004.

[90] Am. Ctr. for Int'l Labor Solidarity, *supra* note 85, at 39. *See also* Yuchao Zhu, *Workers, Unions and the State: Migrant Workers in China's Labour-Intensive Foreign Enterprises*, 35 Dev. & Change 1011 (Nov. 2004).

[91] EPL, art. 31.

[92] Ingrid Nielsen, Russell Smyth, & Mingqiong Zhang, *Unemployment within China's Floating Population: Empirical Evidence from Jiangsu Survey Data*, 39 Chinese Econ. 41–56 (2006). In a recent report by the UN Committee on Economic, Social and Cultural Rights reviewing China's report on its implementation of Articles 16 and 17 of the International Covenant on Economic, Social and Cultural Rights, the committee, in its Concluding Observations, stated as one of its "Principles of Concern" "the de facto discrimination against internal migrants in the fields of employment, social security, health service, housing and education that indirectly result, *inter alia*, from the restrictive national household registration system (*hukou*) which continues to be in place despite official announcements regarding reforms"; further, the Committee is "deeply concerned about the insufficient implementation of existing labour legislation in the State party that has resulted in generally poor conditions of work, including excessive working hours, lack of sufficient rest breaks and hazardous working conditions." U.N. *Concluding Observations, supra* note 62.

[93] Labor Law, art. 12.

and race.[94] The Labor Law prohibits workplace discrimination for religious belief,[95] but other laws and regulations relating to religious activities do not cover employment discrimination in the workplace.[96] There seems to be little anecdotal evidence that employment discrimination based on religious belief occurs, except as where it might be combined with discrimination based on race or ethnic minority status. In one case involving a Muslim member of the *Hui* nationality, a job as a cook was first offered but then later withdrawn when the employer discovered the Muslim's religious beliefs would not allow him to cook pork for the customers of the employer.[97] The case was taken to the labor arbitration committee, which decided in favor of the employer.[98]

f. Disability/Health

Article 14 provides an "exemption" for the disabled where "special stipulations" otherwise provide protection. This exemption for the disabled, however, appears meaningless because disability was not covered by Article 12 in the first instance.[99] In 2008, the EPL specifically prohibited employment discrimination against the disabled and some health conditions.[100] Prior to that, there were a number of laws addressing the disabled.

---

[94] Under U.S. discrimination law, discrimination against language, accents, and customs can be categorized as race, religion, or national origin. *See* Lewis & Norman, *supra* note 60, at 45–8.

[95] Labor Law, art. 12.

[96] For a discussion of religious freedom in China, *see generally* White Paper – Freedom of Religious Belief in China, PRC & Embassy, www.china-embassy.org/eng/zt/zjxy/t36492.htm. Arguably, criminal prosecution could be used in an employment context against violators. *See* Criminal Law, art. 251 (imposing a two-year prison sentence for violation of religious rights committed by public officials). Local governments have the obligation to protect religious freedom in ethnic minority regions. Law on Regional National Autonomy, art. 11.

[97] Lao dong fa xin lei xing an li jing xi [Discussions on the New Types of Labor Law Cases] 123–4 (Zhang Buhong & Zhang Luhaoeds., People's Court Press) (1997) [hereinafter Discussions on the New Types of Labor Law Cases]. *See also* Lao dong fa xin shi yu li jie [New Annotated Labor Law and Cases] 58–9 (Huang Chengjian ed., Tongxin Press) (2001).

[98] Discussions on the New Types of Labor Law Cases, *supra* note 97, at 124.

[99] "[S]pecial stipulations in laws, rules and regulations" do exist for the "disabled" and therefore, at any rate, those laws control discrimination against disabled workers. The 1990 Law on the Protection of Disabled Persons prohibits discrimination, in society generally, against the disabled. Law on Protection of Disabled Persons, *supra* note 102, at art. 3. It also specifically bans discrimination in job "recruitment, employment, obtainment of permanent status, promotion" and other areas discussed more fully in a subsequent section. *Id.* art. 34. *See also* Anhui sheng an bi li an pai can ji ren jiu ye ban fa [Regulations of Anhui Province on Arranging Employment for the Disabled Persons According to Employment Quota], art. 7 (promulgated by the People's Government of Anhui Province, May 30, 2004, effective July 1, 2004) (PRC), http://www.chinacourt.org/flwk/show1.php?file_id=95143.

[100] EPL, arts. 29, 30.

Neither descrimination based on disability nor on health status is expressly prohibited by the Labor Law.[101] However, the Disability Law of 1990 prohibits some employment discrimination against disabled persons.[102] Specifically, it prohibits "discrimination against, insult of and infringement upon disabled persons" and provides "equal rights with other citizens in political, economic, cultural and social fields, in family life and other aspects."[103] It describes a disabled person as one with "visual, hearing, speech or physical disabilities, mental retardation, mental disorder, multiple disabilities and/or other disabilities."[104] Another clause provides that a "disabled person refers to one who suffers from abnormalities or loss of a certain organ or function, psychologically or physiologically, or in an anatomical structure and has lost wholly or in part the ability to perform an activity in the way considered normal."[105]

Chapter IV of the Disability Law deals with employment, and Section 30 protects the "disabled person's right to work," combining this right with "guiding principles" to promote and establish preferential hiring by state organs, nongovernmental organizations, enterprises, institutions, and urban and rural collective economic organizations.[106] Section 38 clarifies that "no discrimination shall be practiced against disabled persons in recruitment, employment, obtainment of permanent status, promotion, determining technical or professional titles, payment, welfare, labor insurance or in other aspects."[107] Although arguably this law aims to promote and protect the rights of disabled persons working in "protected industries or jobs" and does not refer specifically to private employers, the language may clearly be read as broadly prohibiting employment discrimination based on disability by all employers throughout China.[108]

[101] Labor Law, art. 12.

[102] Can ji ren bao zhang fa [Law on the Protection of Disabled Persons] (promulgated by the Standing Comm. of the Nat'l People's Cong., Dec. 28, 1990, effective May 15, 1991, amended April 24, 2008) (PRC), http://www.gov.cn/jrzg/2008-04/24/content_953439.htm [hereinafter Law on Protection of Disabled Persons]; *see also* International Disability Rights Monitor, PEOPLE'S REPUBLIC OF CHINA: RIGHTS OF PEOPLE WITH DISABILITIES, http://www.cirnetwork.org/idrm/reports/compendium/china.cfm (last visited Sept. 19, 2008).

[103] Law on the Protection of Disabled Persons, art. 3.

[104] *Id.* art. 2.

[105] *Id.*

[106] *Id.* arts. 30–40.

[107] *Id.* art. 38.

[108] In 2003, a case of employment discrimination based on disability was decided in favor of the victims. Three long-term employees, who were handicapped, were terminated but prevailed in arbitration and subsequent court processes based on the Law on the Protection of Disabled Persons. Though they did not have labor contracts, the Beijing Intermediate Level People's Court determined they had de facto contracts and were entitled to a remedy. *See* Legal Aid

The Disability Law, which predated the 1994 Labor Law, thus targets the needs of the sixty million disabled persons in China.[109] It would seem to fit under the Labor Law's Article 14 exemption, thereby removing it from the Labor Law.[110] If that is the case, then an administrative enforcement mechanism is built into the law at the national level.[111] Therefore, when such mechanisms are absent at the local level, local regulators could resort to the national enforcement mechanism and to the usual dispute resolution processes in resolving actual labor disputes.[112]

Because definitions of disability include many health-related qualifications,[113] there would seem to be an overlapping relationship between disability and health status and perhaps additional protections provided to health discrimination under the disability laws. The Disability Law defines disability as including physical disabilities, physiological disabilities, or other disabilities.[114] Thus, an employer's use of medical examinations to ascertain an employee's health information, such as whether he or she has hepatitis B or HIV/AIDS, might run afoul of protections where the information pertains to an enumerated physical disability or to some "other disabilities."[115] If so, there seems to be legislation addressing employment discrimination based on those diseases, as discussed in this section.[116]

Center of Beijing Municipality, *The Eighth of Ten Typical Legal Aid Cases in Beijing – Legal Aid Helped Disabled Workers*, Sept. 9, 2004, http://www.china.com.cn/ chinese/2004/Sep/655932.htm (last visited Sept. 19, 2008).

[109] National Bureau of Statistics of China, 2004 [2004 Stat. Y.B. China] § 23–41, http://www .stats.gov.cn/tjsj/ndsj/yb2004-c/indexch.htm (last visited Sept. 19, 2008) [hereinafter 2004 Stat. Y.B. China].

[110] Law on the Protection of Disabled Persons, arts. 3, 34; Labor Law, art. 14.

[111] Where the lawful rights and interests of disabled persons are violated, victims or their relatives "shall have the right to appeal to the competent authorities for disposition, or institute lawsuits at people's courts in accordance with the law." Law on the Protection of Disabled Persons, *supra* note 103, art. 49. In other words, victims can either petition the relevant local government agency to obtain an administrative decision or file a civil action in the court for injunctive remedies.

[112] In addition to the remedy of labor arbitration, victims of discrimination may be able to directly bring the suit to People's Court. *Id.* art. 49.

[113] *See* Can ji ren shi yong ping ding biao zhun (shi yong) [Interim Rules on the Qualification for Disability], http://www.qingdao.gov.cn/n172/n1191/n975769/n981846/130265.html.

[114] *Id.* art. 2.

[115] *Id.*

[116] The Civil Service Law also covers health/disability issues in public employment. Gong wu yuan fa [Civil Service Law] (promulgated by the Standing Comm. of the Nat'l People's Cong., Apr. 27, 2005, effective Jan. 1, 2006), arts. 11–29 (PRC), http://news.xinhuanet. com/lianzheng/2005-08/10/content_3333496.htm. For example, qualification is defined in Art. 11(5), mandatory disqualification is defined in Art. 24, and the standards for physical exams are governed by the relevant rules from the Ministry of Health. *Id.* art. 29.

The broadest health law, which regulates the entire public health system, is the Contagious Disease Law, which was passed in 2004 in the wake of the SARS epidemic.[117] Under Article 16 of this law, any person suspected of being a carrier of a contagious disease, including HIV/AIDS or hepatitis B, must be allowed to work *unless* there is a statutory provision explicitly prohibiting persons with those conditions from working.[118] It should be noted, however, that the law itself does not seem to contain any penalties or remedies for victims of such discrimination.[119]

In addition, the Ministry of Health has issued new regulations clarifying which types of medical conditions, including certain types of hepatitis B and HIV/AIDS, disqualify applicants from being hired in the public service.[120] However, these regulations apply only to civil servant positions and not to positions in other sectors[121] and seem to be limited just to the hiring process.[122] Incumbent government employees are not directly covered by these regulations but perhaps will benefit indirectly from them because they are otherwise protected by the Contagious Disease Law.[123]

[117] Chuan ran bing fang zhi fa [Law on Prevention and Treatment of Contagious Disease] (promulgated by the Standing Comm. of the Nat'l People's Cong., Feb. 21, 1989, effective Sept. 1, 1989, amended Aug. 28, 2004) (PRC), http://www.chinacourt.org/flwk/show1.php?file_id=96086 [hereinafter Contagious Disease Law].

[118] *Id.* art. 16. The law provides that any person who has a contagious disease, carries a contagious disease, or is suspected of being a carrier of a contagious disease shall not be allowed to work in positions that are susceptible to their spreading, as prohibited by the law, administrative rulings, or regulations from the State Council. Contagious disease is defined by Article 3. *Id.* art. 3.

[119] *Id.* art. 16. The new laws are being tested; it is reported that a case was brought in a Beijing court by an applicant denied a job with Shenzhen Airlines because he had suffered hepatitis B in the past. *Hep B Discrimination Case Hits Court*, CHINA DAILY, July 8, 2005, at 5.

[120] Gong wu yuan lu yong ti jian tong yong biao zhun (shi xing) [Health Qualifications for Hiring Civil Servants (provisional)] (promulgated by the Ministries of Health and the Ministry of Personnel, Jan. 17, 2005) (PRC), http://www.dffy.com/faguixiazai/xzf/200501/20050123163654.htm [hereinafter Health Qualifications for Hiring Civil Servants].

[121] *Id.* art. 2.

[122] *Id.*

[123] However, the new Health Qualifications for Hiring Public Servants, although banning some forms of employment discrimination, address and disqualify applicants who may have a number of health risks, including serious heart disease and other heart conditions (*Id.* art. 1), elevated blood pressure (*Id.* art. 2), TB positive status (*Id.* art. 4), hepatitis A, B, C positive status (*Id.* art. 7), kidney disease (*Id.* art. 9), STDs and HIV-positive status (*Id.* art. 8), diabetes (*Id.* art. 10), severe vision/hearing impairment (*Id.* arts. 19–20), and other medical conditions that effect satisfactory job performance (*Id.* art. 21). Further detailed analysis of numbers of legal issues (such as privacy) related to health discrimination can be found in Ye Jingyi & Wei Qian, *Legal Problems Concerning Health Discrimination in Employment*, http://www.humanrights.cn/zt/magazine/200402004921170301.htm (last visited Sept. 19, 2008); *and see* Civil Service Law, *supra* note 18, arts. 24 and 29, which appear to extend the coverage to all applicants in civil service who are required to take a physical exam.

The EPL, in Article 30, states this prohibition on job discrimination:

> When hiring personnel, an employer may not refuse to employ someone on the grounds that he or she is a carrier of an infectious disease. However, a certified carrier of an infectious disease may not, until he or she has recovered or the suspicion of infectiousness has been eliminated, engage in work that he or she is prohibited by laws, administrative regulations or the State Council's health authority from engaging in due to the fact that it would facilitate the spread of the disease.

In a recent reported case of hepatitis B discrimination, a court-mediated settlement awarded damages to an employee who was rejected for employment after failing a pre-employment test showing him to be a carrier of hepatitis B virus.[124]

The term "disability" potentially includes many areas, including a person's physical or mental limitations (such as blindness, deafness, etc.) or health status (such as having SARS, hepatitis B, or HIV/AIDS or being an injured worker).[125] Protecting against disability discrimination in the workplace is usually balanced against an employer's desire to have a qualified worker. As mentioned earlier, China has an estimated sixty million disabled people (about 5 percent of the population), with about 80 percent residing in rural areas.[126] In 2000 it was estimated that 75 percent of China's disabled people had some type of employment.[127]

How widespread disability-based employment discrimination is in the Chinese workplace depends somewhat on the legal interpretation of disability. The number of Chinese workers screened out from equal employment opportunities by appearance requirements ("five facial organs in the right place"), mental or physical conditions, or health considerations is unknown.[128]

---

[124] *Shanghai HBV Discrimination Case Reaches "Satisfactory" Conclusion* in CLB, April 24, 2008, http://www.clb.org.hk/en/node/100245; for other cases, see *Responding to Hepatitis B Discrimination in the Workplace*, http://www.clb.org.hk/en/node/46945.

[125] BLACK'S LAW DICTIONARY 474 (8th ed. 2004).

[126] Center for International Rehabilitation, People's Republic of China Rights of People with Disabilities, http://www.cirnetwork.org/idrm/reports/compendium/china.cfm (last visited Sept. 19, 2008). In May, 2005 it was reported that of "China's 25 million disabled *job seekers* . . . 1 million live in urban areas with Beijing home to over half their number, according to China's Disabled Persons Federation (CDPF). The employment rate of the disabled in Beijing, those of working age and capable of employment, is around 85%." The CDPF reported though many have jobs, "their general employment situation remains grave and they are facing increasing pressure and difficulty in finding a job." Liu Li & Wu Chong, *Nation to Create More Jobs for Disabled*, CHINA DAILY, May 16, 2005, at 2, http://www.chinadaily.com.cn/english/doc/2005-05/16/content_442328.htm.

[127] Center for International Rehabilitation, *supra* note 126.

[128] Examples of anecdotal incidents of disability discrimination reported in newspaper accounts include disfigurement on a hand, "ugly appearance," and being too short by 5 millimeters. *See* Shang Shui, *supra* note 2.

In addition, Chinese employers have broad discretion in the selection of employees and often screen out those whom they feel may pose a problem, including those with certain health ailments such as hepatitis B and HIV/AIDS. About 120 million Chinese citizens (approximately 10 percent of the population) are affected by hepatitis B and about 840,000 people by HIV/AIDS.[129]

A survey conducted in China by Britain's Synovate Healthcare reported that 52 percent of 425 hepatitis patients lost a job or educational opportunity because of their disease; furthermore, about 47 percent were concerned that employers would terminate them if their disease were discovered.[130] One Guangdong machinery and electronics company compelled 107 hepatitis B carriers to quit because of their condition.[131]

In April 2003, a university student in his senior year applied for a government position in Zhejiang Province and passed both the examination and the interview. However, he was rejected once the employer discovered he was a hepatitis B carrier. Distressed, the student, Zhou Yichao, retaliated by stabbing two officials, killing one. Zhou was later tried and sentenced to death.[132] His case aroused public attention and stirred national pressure for protective legislation to protect those with hepatitis B.[133]

Another student who also was rejected for a government job after testing positive for hepatitis B chose to file a lawsuit against the government, challenging the rejection.[134] The People's Court in Xinwu District of Wuhu City in Anhui Province accepted the case, China's first hepatitis B discrimination case. In April 2004 the court ruled in the student's favor, finding improper discrimination.[135] However, the court did not order the government to provide a job for the student.[136]

Some local governments, including the government of Hunan Province in central China, have reportedly dropped bans on hiring hepatitis B carriers,

---

[129] Statistics Released by Ministry of Health (May 1, 2005) (on file with author); Ye & Wei, *supra* note 123; *see also* Liang Chao, *Law Drafted to Fight Hep B Discrimination*, CHINA DAILY, Aug. 11, 2004, http://www.china.org.cn/english/government/103598.htm.

[130] *Hep B Carriers Allowed to Join Public Service*, CHINA DAILY, Jan. 21, 2005, http://www.chinadaily.com.cn/english/doc/2005-01/21/content_411013.htm.

[131] *Dispute Arises, supra* note 2.

[132] *See* Liang Chao, *supra* note 129.

[133] Cao Lin, *See the Cost of Discrimination against HBV Carriers from the Zhou Yichao Murder Case*, CHINA NEWS WK., Sep. 15, 2003, at 8, http://www.chinanewsweek.com.cn/2003-09-22/1/2262.html; *See also* Ye & Wei, *supra* note 123.

[134] *See* Liang Chao, *supra* note 132.

[135] *Court Confirms Right of Hepatitis B Carrier*, CHINA DAILY, Apr. 3, 2004, http://www.chinadaily.com.cn/english/doc/2004-04/02/content_320351.htm; *Government Loses Hep. B Discrimination Case*, SHENZHEN DAILY, June 1, 2004, at 4.

[136] Liang Chao, *supra* note 129.

perhaps in anticipation of new legislation regulating disability and health qualifications for jobs in government service.[137] However, as late as 2004, health/disability requirements for government jobs still persisted. For example, in Guangdong, any applicant who manifested certain diseases or physiologic deficiencies was deemed to be unqualified for a position in the Guangdong public service. A partial list of disqualifying positions included an obvious squint (*xie shi*), cleft lip, torticollis (wry neck), pigmentation moles, curvature of the spine, certain incomplete fingers, poor performance on vision tests, hearing deficiencies, stuttering, a history of enuresis (bed-wetting), signs of heart disease, hypertension, bronchiectasis, diabetes, hepatitis, too many fillings in their teeth, and lower jaw arthritis.[138] Tests were available to allow an applicant to show that his or her past history of disease was fully under control.[139] This list may need to be revisited in light of China's recent laws and regulations.[140]

In sum, China has legal protections against health and disability discrimination, including the specific diseases of HIV/AIDS and hepatitis B; despite some limitations, the protection from discrimination itself is rather significant.[141] The Contagious Disease Law prohibits HIV/AIDS or hepatitis from serving as a basis for denying employment except where statutes so require.[142] Article 16 indirectly functions as a protection against employment discrimination by public and private sector employers (except for civil servant applicants) where no statutory exceptions exist.[143] Since January 1, 2008, the EPL prohibits discrimination against applicants who, as carriers, test positive for many infectious diseases, but where that disease does not affect their ability to work. However, discrimination is not prohibited where carriers are banned by law

---

[137] *Hep B Carriers Allowed to Join Public Service, supra* note 129.

[138] Guangdong sheng guo jia gong wu yuan lu yong ti jian shi shi xi ze (shi xing) [Regulations of Guangdong Province for Physical Examination on Hiring Public Servants (provisional)] art. 11 (Apr. 29, 2002), http://www.rsj.sz.gov.cn/gzdt/200511/t8107.htm [hereinafter Guangdong Regulations].

[139] *Id.* art. 12.

[140] EPL, *supra* note 3; Contagious Disease Law, *supra* note 117; Health Qualifications for Hiring Civil Servants, *supra* note 120.

[141] At least one successful lawsuit against discrimination based on hepatitis B occurred in 2004. *See* Liang Chao, *supra* note 10.

[142] Contagious Disease Law, *supra* note 118, at art. 16. The original text reads, "Infectious disease patients, pathogen carriers and suspected infectious disease patients shall, before they are cured or cleared of suspicion, be barred from jobs which the health administration department under the State Council prohibits them from doing because of the likelihood of causing the spread of infectious diseases." *Id.*

[143] With the addition of China's 2005 Civil Service Law, which also addresses health issues, discussed earlier, that statutory prohibition appears limited to contagious "carriers" of hepatitis B, etc. Civil Service Law, art. 29.

or regulations, until they are recovered beyond suspicion of infectiousness.[144] This means that some 130 million Chinese thought to have hepatitis B will have increased job opportunity and protection.

2. Unprotected Status Categories

a. Age

Age discrimination is not prohibited in the workplace. In fact, it is embedded in the legal retirement ages, in the requirements of some government positions, and in practice by many employers.[145] However, the 2008 LCL indirectly protects against "age"-based discrimination in some circumstances by limiting the employer's ability to terminate an employee with more than fifteen years of service.[146]

In China, there are many job advertisements requiring applicants to be, for example, "below 35 years old."[147] Though old age is generally revered in China, such ads reflect the attitudes of many employers who hold stereotypes about the abilities of older people to work. But as the average age in China rises and as labor shortages appear from time to time, some employers have turned to employing older workers with satisfactory results.[148]

For some years, the age of retirement in China has been set at fifty for female workers, fifty-five for female cadres, and sixty for male workers and cadres.[149] Such policies may need to be adjusted in view of the increasing age of the population and the demands placed on pensions during long years of retirement.[150] It seems the government must choose between eliminating

---

[144] EPL., art. 30.

[145] *See* discussion in Cai Shangyao, *Age Discrimination's High Cost to Society*, SHANGHAI STAR, Dec. 16, 2004, at 4, http://www.shanghai-star.com.cn/2004/1216/v02-1.html.

[146] LCL, arts 42(5), 40, and 41.

[147] Bai Tianliang, *Discrimination Exists in Hiring Process; Equality to Be Achieved through Law*, PEOPLES' DAILY, Feb 11, 2003, at E1, http://past.people.com.cn/GB/shenghuo/78/116/20030211/920873.html.

[148] Dali L. Yang, *China's Looming Labor Shortage*, 168 FAR E. ECON. REV. 19, 20 (2005).

[149] *See* Reply on Legal Retirement Age, *supra* note 26; certain female teachers, doctors, and scientific and technical personnel can retire at age sixty, but men in the same positions may work until age sixty-five. Christine M. Bulger, Note, *Fighting Gender Discrimination in the Chinese Workplace*, 20 B.C. THIRD WORLD L.J. 345, 358 (2000). The Labor Law states that employees can enjoy social security benefits only after legal retirement. Labor Law, art. 73(1).

[150] This issue will continue to grow with the rapidly aging population in China of persons aged sixty-five and over; that group grew from 100 to 200 million from 2000 to 2007, constituting 14 percent of China's total population and increasing by more than 14 million people per year. Fu Jing, *Huge Sum to Be Put Into Social Security*, CHINA DAILY, Sep. 18, 2004, http://www.chinadaily.com.cn/english/doc/2004-09/18/content_375540.htm.

this form of employment discrimination or paying enormous amounts in unemployment and pension insurance.

b. Height

Though the Constitutions of both the United States and China provide that all citizens are equal,[151] neither country's antidiscrimination labor legislation explicitly identifies height as a protected status in the same way it does other characteristics such as race and gender. Interestingly, history teaches that short people can become great leaders of countries as well as of companies.[152]

In the United States, however, the antidiscrimination laws protect height indirectly through other protected statuses, such as gender or national origin.[153] For example, an employer's use of non–job-related height requirements for job applicants (e.g., prison guards) that disproportionately disqualified large numbers of potential women and applicants of Asian descent was held to be in violation of the law.[154] Despite finding no discriminatory intent in the policy, the court ruled that its indirect effect ("disparate impact") of denying jobs to many qualified persons violated antidiscrimination protections.

Although height requirements are often spelled out in government job qualifications in China,[155] they are less likely to be found in the job requirements of private employers. For example, in the Physical Examination Regulations for Hiring Public Servants in Guangdong Province, Clause 11 of Article 12 states, "[M]en must be above 1.6 meters [five feet, three inches] and forty-eight kilograms [105.8 pounds]; females must be above 1.5 meters [four feet, eleven inches] and forty-two kilograms [92.59 pounds]"; Article 14 says, "Police must be taller and have better eyesight."[156] Such height restrictions may well eliminate women and certain ethnic groups from the applicant pool without consideration of their merits.

---

[151] U.S. Const. amend. XIV, § 1; XIAN FA [Const.] art. 33 (2004) (PRC).

[152] For example, Deng Xiaoping's height was 4 feet 11 inches, and the shortest U.S. president, James Madison, was 5 feet 4 inches. *See* Dan Harbord, *Famous People Height List*, http://members.shaw.ca/harbord/heights3.html (last visited Sept. 19, 2008). For an essay on being short, *see* Jonathan Rauch, *Short Guys Finish Last*, ECONOMIST, Dec. 23, 1995, at 19.

[153] 16B AM. JUR. 2D *Constitutional Law* §§ 808-17; *and see* statutory interpretation of Title VII dealing with height in *Dothard v. Rawlinson* 433 U.S. 321 (1977).

[154] *Dothard v. Rawlinson*, 433 U.S. 321 (1977).

[155] Guangdong Regulations, *supra* note 141. *See also* Joseph Kahn, *Chinese People's Republic Is Unfair to Its Short People*, N. Y. TIMES, May 21, 2004, at A13.

[156] Guangdong Regulations, *supra* note 138.

Height discrimination has been litigated in at least one case.[157] Part of the claim was based on the Constitution, which states that "all citizens of the People's Republic of China are equal before the law."[158] In December 2001, Jing Tao brought a lawsuit in Wuhou District Court after the Chengdu Branch of the People's Bank of China denied him a job because of his height.[159] The advertisement for the job, among other qualifications, required male applicants to be taller than 168 centimeters, which was estimated to exclude 40 percent of the men in Sichuan. His case was first accepted, but later dismissed as nonjusticiable because during the interim the bank had dropped the height requirement and because such personnel decisions were determined to be exempt from the Administrative Litigation Law. [160]

3. Enforcement

New laws in China reiterate the legal requirements of job discrimination, but as in any society, the culture and attitudes must become more enlightened before the laws can be really effective. During that transition period, the antidiscrimination laws do provide avenues for redress. Human resource managers can increasingly avoid liabilities and lost efficiencies by meeting those legal requirements.

Most labor disputes under the Labor Law are resolved through enterprise mediation processes and government labor arbitration procedures. Where discrimination is involved and prohibited, as in the case of gender, there may be other legal avenues of redress. The EPL, like the Women's Rights Law,[161] specifically authorizes an employee to file a lawsuit in court against an employer.[162] There may be some question of whether, in the cases of labor disputes, labor arbitration must first be exhausted, as discussed later[163]; this

---

[157] See Michael C. Dorf, *What a Chinese Height Discrimination Case Says about Chinese and American Constitutional Law*, FINDLAW, May 26, 2004, http://writ.news.findlaw.com/scripts/printer_friendly.pl?page=/dorf/20040526.html.

[158] XIAN FA [Const.] art. 33 (2004) (PRC).

[159] Plaintiff argued that the local limitations were in conflict with China's Constitution, See XIAN FA [Const.] art. 100 (2004) (PRC); Li fa fa [Legislation Law] (promulgated by the Standing Comm. of the Nat'l People's Cong., Mar. 15, 2000, effective July 1, 2000), arts. 62–3, 2000, STANDING COMM. NAT'L PEOPLE'S CONG. GAZ. 112 (PRC), http://www.chinacourt.org/flwk/show1.php?file_id=34719 [hereinafter Legislation Law]; Kahn, *supra* note 155 at A13.; *see also* Dorf, *supra* note 157.

[160] Dorf, *supra* note 159.

[161] Women's Rights Law, art. 52.

[162] EPL, art. 62.

[163] Ronald C. Brown, *China's Employment Discrimination Laws during Economic Transition*, 19 COLUM. J. ASIAN L. 361, 423–4 (2006); LMA, art. 2.

arguably differs from the wording in the provisions in the LCL that gives specific authorization to bypass arbitration and proceed directly to court on a limited number of claims, such as agreed-on wage debts.[164] On the other hand, there is a right to access the court and to receive civil damages when proven, and in the case of sexual harassment involving public security, specific authorization is given to use either administrative punishments or initiate an action in court.[165]

[164] LCL, art. 30.
[165] Women's Rights Law, arts. 52–9.

PART IV

WORKING CONDITIONS, WAGES, AND HOURS

8

Safety and Health Protection

1. Workplace Environment

a. Safety

Protecting workplace safety and health by laws and labor standards that seek to prevent accidents, deaths, and occupational diseases is an increasing priority as the number of workplace-related deaths and accidents continues to remain unacceptably high. The State Administration of Work Safety (SAWS) reported that there were 88,923 work-related fatalities and 457,000 accidents in the first eleven months of 2007.[1] More than 60 percent of fatal and severe accidents in the chemical industries are reported to be associated with unsafe work practices and the lack of safety awareness.[2]

The government, in further implementing the 1994 Labor Law, passed the *Law on Prevention and Treatment of Occupational Disease* in 2001, which requires certain preventive medical procedures and replacement of dangerous technology and materials.[3] In 2002 the *Work Safety Law* was added, which requires worker education and training before beginning a job for which proper protective equipment is provided. Special legislative mandates deal with safety

---

[1] Hu Yinan, *Fewer Accidents and Deaths but Work Safety Still a Worry*, CHINA DAILY, Dec. 24, 2007, http://www2.chinadaily.com.cn/china/2007-12/24/content_6342344.htm; more recent data can be found at *Chinese Safety Watchdog Issues Work Safety Regulations*, Jan. 11, 2008, http://www.chinamining.org/Policies/2008-01-11/1200012456d8605.html; Li Fengchao, *More Time Needed to Improve Work Safety*, CHINA DAILY, Dec. 22, 2006, http://www.chinadaily.com.cn/china/2006-12/22/content_765070.htm.

[2] Youxin Liang, Quanyong Xiang, *Occupational Health Services in PR China*, 198 TOXICOLOGY 45, 49 (2004). The LCL addresses this by requiring employers to inform employees at the time of hire of hazards and safety conditions. Art. 8.

[3] Zhi ye bing fang zhi fa [Law on Prevention and Treatment of Occupational Disease] (promulgated by the Stand. Comm. of the Nat'l People's Cong., Oct. 27, 2001, effective May 1, 2002) (PRC), http://www.chinacdc.net.cn/n272442/n272530/n272907/n272922/3310.html.

in the mining and construction industries and with the safety and health of female workers who are pregnant, nursing, or menstruating. Employees and the union have a role in their enforcement.[4] In 2008, State Council's Decree No. 516 repealed several administrative laws, a number of which had governed labor and work safety, in order to further clairfy and streamline legal obligations.[5]

China has been called the "world's factory floor," as its continually expanding economy sends its products throughout the world, securing huge percentages of the world markets and, often, trade surpluses.[6] But there is a cost in human terms. In 2007, 101,480 workers died in workplace accidents (10% fewer than in 2006).[7] Government sources estimate that the cost of occupational illnesses and work-related injuries is between $12 to $25 billion annually.[8] In particular, predominant causation is attributed to small and medium-sized enterprises that take few or no preventive measures to protect their workers; and the high number of migrant workers who are concentrated in hazardous industries, such as mining, construction, and manufacturing, are especially lacking in protection.[9]

The coal industry is particularly dangerous. In China, the death toll for every million of tons is 2.041, which is more than fifty times that of the United States, the number-two coal producer in the world after China.[10] In 2004

---

[4] An quan sheng chan fa [Law on Work Safety] (promulgated by the Stand. Comm. of the Nat'l People's Cong., June 29, 2002, effective Nov. 1, 2002) [hereinafter Work Safety Law].

[5] E.g., Code of Factory Safety and Health, Technical Code for Construction and Installation Project Safety, Measures for Preventing Asphalt Poisoning, Provisions on Production Safety in Enterprises, Measures for Prevention Management of Silicon Dust, Interim Regulations on Worker's Congresses in State-Owned Enterprises, Interim Regulations on Factory Directors Work in State-Owned Factories, Regulations on Safety for Mining Construction Projects, Regulations on the Safety Supervision of Mining Construction Projects, Regulations on Rewards and Punishment for Enterprise Employees, and Regulations on Recruitment of Employees under the Rural-Resident Contract System in Enterprises Owned by the Whole People. The regulations are considered repealed effective as of the date of the decree's promulgation; *see Old Labor and Safety Regulations Repealed*, Jan. 25, 2008, http://www.csrlaws.com/news-26. html.

[6] *China: The World's Factory Floor*, Nov. 11, 2002, http://news.bbc.co.uk/1/hi/business/ 2415241.stm; *On the Factory Floor: Inside China's Engine Room*, April 20, 2006, http://www. independent.co.uk/news/world/asia/on-the-factory-floor-inside-chinas-engine-room-474836. html.

[7] *Chinese Coal Mine Fatalities Down 20% in 2007*, Jan. 12, 2008, http://www2.chinadaily. com.cn/china/2008-01/12/content_6389679.htm.

[8] *Occupational Illnesses and Injuries Cost China 100 Billion Yuan Each Year, Official Warns*, http://www.china-labour.org.hk/en/node/38698.

[9] *Id.*

[10] Duan Kun, *Time for Zero Tolerance of Workplace Accidents*, China Daily, May 25, 2007, http://www.chinaelections.net/newsinfo.asp?newsid=5782.

it was reported that, of the total deaths in coal mine accidents worldwide, 80 percent occurred in China.[11] Since 2000, China's coal consumption has increased more than 10 percent annually.[12] More than half of the 5.5 million coal miners are migrant laborers.[13] Small private mines produce about one-quarter of China's coal but two-thirds of its mining accidents.[14] In recent years, there appears to be some improvement in worker safety, with the number of coal mine accidents declining.[15]

In general, the International Labor Organization estimates that China's 2001 workplace fatality rate was 11.1 per 100,000 workers, compared with a rate of 4.4 per 100,000 workers in the United States. Industrial accidents rose 27 percent between 2000 and 2001, whereas occupational diseases rose by 13 percent in the same period, according to government statistics.[16]

Although the extent of duties imposed and who bears the costs have not been resolved, there is at the same time an increased demand, particularly from the foreign firms, for the purchase of personal protection equipment in China in response to the safety laws and increased worker awareness.[17] The Chinese government reported that across all industries it spends more than US$3.6 billion annually on safety equipment and services in its effort to reduce workplace accidents and occupational diseases.[18]

b. Health

Although China has made considerable progress in improving health standards and the quality of work life over the past several decades, it was not

---

[11] Tu Jianjun, *Safety Chanllenges in China's Coal Mining Industry*, May 15, 2006, http://www.asianresearch.org/articles/2997.html (citing CHINA DAILY, Nov. 13, 2004).

[12] *Id.*

[13] Calum MacLeod, *China Seeks to Improve Workplace Safety*, Jan. 30, 2008, http://www.usatoday.com/news/world/2008-01-30-chinasafety_N.htm.

[14] *Id.*

[15] *Chinese Coal Mines' Safety Record Improves in 1H 2008*, XINHUA NEWS AGENCY, July, 9, 2008, http://www.chinadaily.com.cn/china/2008-07/09/content_6829784.htm.

[16] Garrett D. Brown & Dara O'Rourke, *The Race to China and Implications for Global Labor Standards*, 9 INT. J. OCCUP. ENVIRON. HEALTH 300 (2003); U.S. figures are also in the National Census of Fatal Occupational Injuries in 2001, http://stats.bls.gov/iif/oshcfoi1.htm; Wing-yue & Trini Leung, *What Can be Done for the Largest but Deadliest Manufacturing Center in the World*, CHINA LABOR BULLETIN, November 2, 2002, also http://www.cecc.gov/pages/roundtables/110702/leung.php.

[17] *Analysis: Demand for PPE in China Escalates*, April 27, 2008, http://www.ohsonline.com/articles/61288/.

[18] *China Spends US$3.6bn on Safety Equipment*, May 22, 2006, http://www.ferret.com.au/c/3rd-China-International-Occupational-Health-Safety/China-spends-US-3-6bn-on-safety-equipment-n682933.

until 2001 that it initiated comprehensive protective legislation with the aim of preventing occupational diseases, as had been promised in the 1994 Labor Law.[19] Chinese government statistics show that migrant workers are at the greatest risk of contracting occupational diseases, with more than 90 percent of those suffering from diseases relating to the workplace being migrant workers.[20] In China, the leading cause of occupational disease is pneumoconiosis, a lung disease prevalent among workers in industries where there is silica dust, such as mining and construction. It has been estimated that more than 12 million workers have been exposed, resulting in 10,000 to 15,000 new cases annually,[21] which is about 75 percent of the total reported cases of occupational diseases.[22] In 2002, 52.7 percent of these cases occurred in the coal mining industry.[23] That same year, 2,343 workers died from pneumoconiosis, representing 82.6 percent of all deaths from occupational diseases.[24] Other occupational diseases include poisonings, caused most often by toxic and asphyxiating atmospheres (carbon monoxide, hydrogen sulfide, and ammonia) in confined workspaces.[25]

The size and ownership of enterprises affect working conditions. Larger employers typically have more resources to establish and maintain decent workplace safety and health. Many state-owned enterprises (SOEs) certainly have had the resources and staff to do the job, but some have yielded to the pressures of a market economy to keep low costs to remain competitive. Those enterprises are often characterized by a failure to implement health and safety measures, negligence, and violations, as well as the reluctance to properly compensate victims according to the law.[26] Too often, health and safety conditions in the workplace reflect the level of government inspection and enforcement. In 2002, the Chinese government reported

---

[19] Liang & Xiang, *supra* note 2; Labor Law, arts. 52–4.

[20] Cao Desheng, *Diseases at Work Haunt Migrant Workers*, CHINA DAILY, Feb. 17, 2006, http://www.chinadaily.com.cn/english/doc/2006-02/17/content_521301.htm.

[21] Zhong Y, Li D. *Potential Years of Life Lost and Work Tenure Lost When Silicosis is Compared with Other Pneumoconioses*, 21 SCAND. J. WORK ENVIRON. HEALTH (Suppl. 2) 91 (1995); Xiaorong Wang & David C. Christiani, *Occupational Lung Disease in China*, 9 INT. J. OCCUP. ENVIRON. HEALTH 320 (2003).

[22] Liang & Xiang, *supra* note, at 46.

[23] *Id.*

[24] *Id.* at 47. In 2007, the Ministry of Health reported 10,963 cases of pneumoconiosis among the 14,296 cases of occupational diseases. *Reported in China Records 14,296 Cases of Occupational Illness*, XINHUA NEWS AGENCY, May 20, 2008, http://www.chinadaily.com.cn/china/2008-05/02/content_6657365.htm.

[25] *Id.* at 48.

[26] Garrett D. Brown, *China's Factory Floors: An Industrial Hygienist's View*, 9 INT. J. OCCUP. ENVIRON. HEALTH 326, 328 (2003).

that 60 percent of the 20 million TVEs had "minimal industrial safety measures."[27]

2. Legal Regulation

As described earlier, the 1994 Labor Law's original requirements and its promise of improved regulation of worker safety and control of occupational diseases were implemented in 2002 in two major laws. The first, the Work Safety Law,[28] requires employers to meet safety standards and to undertake safety management through (1) appointing personnel committees charged with the task, (2) providing education and training, (3) establishing safety rules, and (4) following reporting requirements.[29] Regulations cover a variety of workplace health and safety concerns, including women workers, coal safety, chemicals, radioisotopes, and pneumoconiosis.[30] In addition, the Labor Contract Law requires that provisions on work safety and the measures taken to prevent occupational hazards be included in the labor contract.[31] It also requires the employer to inform employees as to working conditions, occupational hazards, and production safety conditions.[32]

a. Safety Rights and Obligations

The Work Safety Law provides that the principal manager shall be responsible for workplace safety,[33] whereas unions or other employee organizations have a right to supervise safety matters.[34] Safety inspections by a local safety board are also mandated, and authority is given to order corrective measures for safety deficiencies or even a cessation of business activities pending those corrections.[35]

The government appears to give these remedies a higher profile than it does violations of some other labor and employment laws. Safety specialists are required for mining, construction, and other dangerous industries, and

---

[27] Su Z, Wang S., & Levine S.P., *Occupational Health Hazards Facing China's Workers and Possible Remedies*, 37 WORLD BANK TRANSITION NEWSLETTER 37 (2002); For more recent data, see *China Records, supra* note 24.

[28] Work Safety Law, *supra* note 4.

[29] *Id.*

[30] Tim E. Pringle & Stephen D. Frost, *The Absence of Rigor and the Failure of Implementation: Occupational Health and Safety in China*, 9 INT. J. OCCUP. ENVIRON. HEALTH 309, 313 (2003).

[31] LCL, art. 17.

[32] LCL, art. 8.

[33] Work Safety Law, art. 5.

[34] *Id.* art. 7.

[35] *Id.* art. 56.

most enterprises are required to designate safety control personnel.[36] The employer has a duty to report any safety accidents,[37] and local governments have a duty to disclose work safety accident statistics.[38] Government and other personnel withholding or concealing safety accidents or conducting fraudulent inspections[39] could face criminal penalties.[40] Employees engaged in conduct causing a serious accident also can be criminally liable.[41] Other remedies include civil penalties for the failure to comply with safety regulations[42] and tort damages for safety-related accidents.[43]

Certain rights are accorded employees, such as a right to receive work safety education and training and to learn of hazards,[44] the right to be provided and trained with "articles for labor protection that meet national standards,"[45] the right to report any safety violations without retaliation by the employer,[46] and the right to refuse to perform any dangerous task without protection.[47] In addition, employees "who are suffering injuries due to work safety accidents shall not only enjoy the occupational insurance and social insurance in accordance with the law, but also have the right to claim for compensation from the employing units if they have the right to obtain compensation in accordance with the appropriate civil law."[48]

Administration and enforcement of the Work Safety Law is undertaken by SAWS. Enforcement is now receiving increasing attention, and fines and penalties provided in the law are being used more readily to redress violations. In China there is also the availability of criminal penalties for safety violations.[49] Likewise, employees may initiate the enforcement mechanism and may even refuse to work in operations that place them in harm.[50] The law provides that it is illegal for an employer to seek to exculpate itself from liability under this law by prior contractual agreements.[51] Trade unions also have the

[36] *Id.* art. 19.
[37] *Id.* art. 70.
[38] *Id.* art. 76.
[39] *Id.* art. 79.
[40] *Id.* art. 92.
[41] *Id.* art. 90.
[42] *Id.* arts. 82–5.
[43] *Id.* art. 48.
[44] *Id.* arts. 45, 50.
[45] *Id.* art. 37.
[46] *Id.* arts. 46, 51.
[47] *Id.* art. 47.
[48] *Id.* art. 48.
[49] John Balzano, *Criminal Liability for Labor Safety Violations in the People's Republic of China*, 3 WASH. U. GLOBAL STUD. L. REV. 503 (2004).
[50] Work Safety Law, arts. 45, 46.
[51] *Id.* art. 44.

right to supervise the employer's workplace safety operations,[52] and employees and the union have a role in enforcement.[53] Article 48 of the Work Safety Law[54] also preserves the right of an injured employee to sue in tort for safety accidents, notwithstanding the worker's compensation that is otherwise available.

b. Occupational Health Rights and Obligations

The 2001 Law on the Prevention and Treatment of Occupational Diseases (1) requires employers to protect the health of employees through preventive measures and by providing accident insurance; (2) provides for the rights of employees to information, education, and training; and (3) authorizes their participation in monitoring.[55] It specifically mandates the employer to "provide equipment to individual workers to guard against such diseases"[56] and in many cases to provide employees' physical exams.[57] It also places responsibilities on the trade union and the government at all levels to prevent and protect against occupational diseases.[58]

Occupational diseases are defined to include exposure of employees to industrial dusts, radioactive substances, and other harmful substances in the workplace. Many more specific regulations have been promulgated to further enumerate the risks and the standards for compliance.[59]

Overall administration and enforcement are the responsibility of the State Council's Work Safety Commission, whose working body is the SAWS.[60] Its function is to supervise and manage safety nationwide, including supervision of coal mine safety and the State Administration of Coal Mine Safety.[61] It must also

> "oversee and inspect industrial hygiene at the workplace of industrial, mining and commercial operations . . . and to be in charge of the management of issuance of occupational safety and health licenses; to oversee the monitoring, control and correction of major sources of hazards and to investigate and penalize those . . . that are not equipped with proper conditions for safe production."[62]

---

[52] *Id.* arts. 7, 52.

[53] *Id.*

[54] *Id.* art. 48; *see also* Law on Prevention and Treatment of Occupational Disease, *supra* note 3, art. 52.

[55] Law on Prevention and Treatment of Occupational Disease, *supra* note 3, art. 30.

[56] *Id.* art. 20.

[57] *Id.* arts. 32, 34, 54; Labor Law, art. 54.

[58] Law on Prevention and Treatment of Occupational Disease, *supra* note 3, art. 37.

[59] Pringle et al., *supra* note 30, at 313.

[60] *Id.*

[61] State Administration of Work Safety, http://english.gov.cn/2005-10/20/content_80531.htm.

[62] Main Duties of State Administration of Work Safety, http://english.gov.cn//2005-10/20/content_80534.htm.

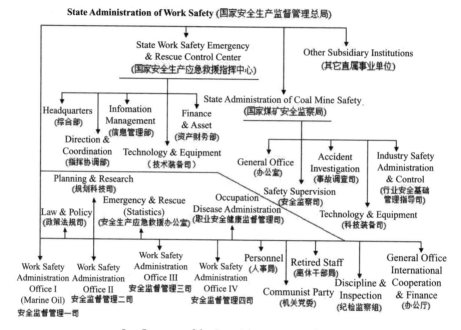

FIGURE 8.1. Structure of the State Administration of Work Safety.

Such large areas of responsibilities obviously leave much of the oversight and supervision at the local levels, and there are critics who claim there is an "absence of rigor and failure of implementation,"[63] as well as widespread underenforcement.[64] Much of this failure is said to be caused by inspections and related functions being under the authority and performed by *local* safety boards. Figure 8.1 shows the administrative structure of SAWS.[65]

In protecting occupational health, the State Council, through its Safety Committee, oversees the MOHRSS, the MOH, and the ACFTU.[66] The MOH oversees local Health Bureaus, local Institutes for Occupational Health and Poisoning Control, and the China Center of Disease Control and Prevention (CCDC), which, in regulatory coordination with the MOHRRS and ACFTU, oversee the health and safety committees in the workplaces of employers.[67]

---

[63] Pringle et al., *supra* note 30, at 309.

[64] Peter Shen, *Industrial Hygiene Practice in China – an Overview*, http://www.aiha.org/aihce07/handouts/po120shen.pdf.

[65] SAWS organizational structure, *see* http://www.chinasafety.gov.cn/newpage/zzjg/zzjg.htm.

[66] Xing Gao & Li Sun, *Current Status of the Occupational Health and Safety Countermeasures in Beijing, China*, 42 INDUSTRIAL HEALTH 116, 118 (2004) (Figure 1).

[67] *Id.* The MOH is in charge of drafting occupational health statutes and regulations; setting up occupational health criteria; standardizing the prevention, health care, oversight, and

Enforcement of the Law on the Prevention and Treatment of Occupational Disease is implemented by the health departments at the county level and above, wihch have the responsibility to inspect and supervise the measures undertaken by employers.[68] Violations may result in victim compensation, warnings, and orders to correct them as well as fines (up to 500,000 yuan). For "serious" violations the health department can order partial or full cessation of operations.[69] Finally in 2006, enhanced criminal sanctions were added of three to seven years imprisonment for personnel directly involved in serious violations, which include forcing an employee to do risky work, providing deficient working conditions, not meeting regulations regarding dangerous materials, and failing to meet construction standards.[70]

medical treatment of occupational disease; and providing qualification certification for occupational health service agencies, occupational health assessment, and poisonous chemical assessment. SAWS, as a nonministry agency directly under the State Council, is in charge of the overall supervision and regulation of work safety work, issuing occupational health and safety permits, and investigation of work accidents and relevant violations of the work safety rules. Discussion (in Chinese), http://www.moh.gov.cn/publicfiles/business/htmlfiles/zwgkzt/pjggk/200804/621.htm. The MOHRSS is in charge of policy research, work skill training, work safety insurance, and related dispute resolution. *See* http://www.mohrss.gov.cn/mohrss/Desktop.aspx?path=/mohrss/InfoView&gid=a0d4dfb0-c94b-48cb-ace2-444787468af9&tid=Cms_Info.

[68] Zhi Su, *Occupational Health and Safety Legislation and Implementation in China*, 9 INT. J. OCCUP. ENVIRON. HEALTH 302, 305 (2004).

[69] *Id.* at 306; Law on the Prevention and Treatment of Occupational Disease, art. 57.

[70] Law on the Prevention and Treatment of Occupational Disease, art. 76 ("If the administrative department of health and its law enforcement personnel of occupational health supervisions has committed any of the acts listed in Article 60 of this Law, and caused the happening of any occupational diseases and constituted a crime, the criminal responsibilities shall be investigated into; if a crime hasn't been constituted, the principal of the unit, the personnel-in-charge held directly responsible, and other directly responsible personnel shall be given the administrative punishment of demotion, dismissal, or discharge according to law"); Xing fa [Criminal Law] (Promulgated by the 8th Sess. Nat'l People's Cong., Mar. 14, 1997, amended on June 29, 2006), arts. 134–137, 139 (PRC).

Article 134. Where anyone violates the provisions concerning the safety management in production or operations and thus causes any serious casualty or any other serious consequences, he shall be sentenced to fixed-term imprisonment of not more than three years or detention. If the circumstances are extremely severe, he shall be sentenced to fixed-term imprisonment of not less than 3 years but not more than 7 years.

Where anyone forces any other person to conduct risky operations by violating the relevant provisions so that any serious casualty or any other serious consequence is caused, he shall be sentenced to fixed-term imprisonment of not more than five years or detention. If the circumstances are extremely severe, he shall be sentenced to fixed-term imprisonment of five years or more.

Article 135. Where the facilities or conditions for safe work fail to meet the relevant provisions of the state so that any serious casualty or any other serious consequence is caused, the persons-in-charge who are held to be directly responsible and other directly liable persons

(Footnote 70 continued)

shall be sentenced to fixed-term imprisonment of not more than three years or detention. If the circumstances are particularly severe, he shall be sentenced to fixed-term imprisonment of not less than three years but not more than seven years.

Where, any of the provisions concerning safety management is violated in the holding of large-scale activities of the masses so that any serious casualty or any other serious consequence is caused, the persons-in-charge who are held to be directly responsible and other directly liable persons shall be sentenced to fixed-term imprisonment of not more than three years or detention. If the circumstances are particularly severe, they shall be sentenced to fixed-term imprisonment of not less than three years but no more than seven years.

Article 136. Whoever violates the regulations on the control of articles of an explosive, combustible, radioactive, poisonous or corrosive nature, thereby giving rise to a major accident in the course of production, storage, transportation, or use and causing serious consequences, is to be sentenced to not more than three years of fixed-term imprisonment or criminal detention; when the consequences are particularly serious, the sentence is to be not less than three years and not more than seven years of fixed-term imprisonment.

Article 137. When construction, design, working, and engineering supervision units violate the state's regulations by reducing the quality standard of the projects, thereby giving rise to a major safety accident, those who are directly responsible are to be sentenced to not more than five years of fixed-term imprisonment or criminal detention, in addition to a fine; when the consequences are particularly serious, the sentence is to be not less than five years and not more than ten years of fixed-term imprisonment, in addition to a fine.

Article 139. Where, after any safety accident occurs, the person who is obliged to report it fails to report it or makes a false report so that the rescue of the accident is affected and if the circumstances are severe, he shall be sentenced to fixed-term imprisonment of not more than three years or detention. If the circumstances are extremely severe, he shall be sentenced to fixed-term imprisonment of not less than three years but not more than seven years.

9

Injury Compensation

1. Injuries in the Workplace

In 2006, government statistics showed that there were 627,158 workplace injuries at a cost of US$12.5 billion in direct losses and US$25 billion in indirect losses.[1] A 2007 study reported the gruesome finding that about 40,000 fingers are severed every year in the Pearl River Delta Region; about 300 clinics in Kai County, Sichuan Province, specialize in reattaching severed fingers and arms for returning migrants. Another study in the Pearl River Delta Region showed that of 259 injured workers, 210 reported finger injuries, 23 reported hand or wrist injuries, 11 reported arm injuries, and the rest had leg, foot, ankle, or other injuries. Ninety percent of all injuries were of workers' hands or arms, with severity ranging from cuts and burns to severe nerve damage, permanent paralysis, and the loss of entire digits and limbs. The most common injuries reported were broken or severed fingers on the dominant hand.[2] Reports like these have helped bring about labor reforms in the area of work-related injuries.

In 2004, China put in place its Work-Related Injury Insurance Regulations, which cover work-related injuries, disability, or death, as well as occupational diseases.[3] The scope of coverage is broad, including work-related accidents occurring before, after, and during work – even covering motor vehicle

---

[1] 2006 Quan guo ge lei shang wang shi gu qing kuang [Report on Work Injury Accidents Nationwide in 2006], State Administration of Work Safety, Jan. 11, 2007, http://www.chinasafety. gov.cn/anquanfenxi/2007-01/11/content_214963.htm (112,822 workers died in work injury accidents in 2006); *China's Workers at Greater Risk of Illness, Injury on Job*, XINHUA NEWS AGENCY, July 17, 2006, http://fuzhou.china.com.cn/english/MATERIAL/174890.htm.

[2] *The Long March: Survey and Case Studies of Work Injuries in the Pearl River Delta Region*, CHINA LABOR WATCH (Feb. 2007), http://www.chinalaborwatch.org/ 2007FinalWorkInjuryReport.pdf [hereinafter The Long March].

[3] Gong shang baoxian tiao li [Regulations on Work-Related Injury Insurance] (promulgated by the State Council, April 27, 2003), art. 1 (PRC) [hereinafter WIR].

accidents that occur coming to and from work.[4] Awards can include a lump sum payment or other subsidies, a pension, or living expenses. Remedies are exclusive, but the law permits a suit in tort for employer safety violations.[5] Employee waivers of coverage are prohibited,[6] though negotiated settlements for injuries are permitted if not deemed unfair by the courts.[7] The law requires employers to pay the medical expenses of employees suffering from work-related injuries as well as a disability allowance based on the seriousness of the injuries.[8] Employers are responsible even after the employee's labor contract expires or the employee chooses to terminate the contract; absent a settlement, the employer must still pay for the medical expenses as well as the lump sum disability allowance.[9] The insurance is financed by employer-paid premiums, which include experience ratings. Local governments administer and determine the amount of awarded benefits, which are paid from the employee compensation fund mandated by the law.[10]

By the end of 2004 (the first year the law was effective), 68,230,000 employees were covered by worker's compensation and 510,000 persons had claimed benefits.[11] Although coverage has continued to increase since then, there also is much underenforcement of the current law, as well as a great need for more employee education regarding it. The study cited earlier of injured workers in the heavily commercial area of the Pearl River Delta Region found that the most frequent causes of injuries were carelessness (perhaps related to little or no job training) and fatigue (related to working overtime and long hours).[12] It also found that only 65 percent of the workers had labor contracts and

---

[4] WIR, art. 14.

[5] An quan sheng chan fa [Law on Work Safety] (promulgated by the Stand. Comm. of the Nat'l People's Cong., June 29, 2002, effective Nov. 1, 2002), art. 48 (PRC); Zhi ye bing fang zhi fa [Law on Prevention and Treatment of Occupational Disease] (promulgated by the Stand. Comm. of the Nat'l People's Cong., Oct. 27, 2001, effective May 1, 2002), art. 52 (PRC).

[6] Labor Law, arts. 70, 72. *See also* Work Safety Law, art. 44.

[7] The court found the original settlement of 3,000 yuan inequitable due to later evidence of more severe injury (level 6) and modified the settlement agreement to have the employer pay an additional 10,000 yuan. The injury occurred in December, 2007, and the court decision was April 8, 2008; http://www.nmglawyer.com/Article/8000.html.

[8] WIR, arts. 33–5 (provide for range of payments from lump sum disability subsidy or a monthly disability allowance).

[9] WIR, art. 35(b); LCL, arts. 42, 45.

[10] WIR, art. 10.

[11] 2004 News Release of MOLSS, http://w1.mohrss.gov.cn/gb/news/2006–01/19/content_103600.htm. In 2007, in a study by an American professor, it was reported that 120 million workers are under the protection of worker's compensation, up from 85 million at the end of 2005; *see* http://advance.uconn.edu/2007/071113/07111308.htm.

[12] *The Long March, supra* note, at 6; *see also* Michael Pareles, *Crushed: A Survey of Work Injuries and Treatment in the Pearl River Delta,* CHINA LABOR WATCH (Sept. 2005), http://www.chinalaborwatch.org/upload/workinjuryreport.pdf.

only 73 percent had work injury insurance, though both are required by law; in addition, only 13 percent received full pay during their hospitalization, as mandated by law.[13]

2. Coverage

All types of enterprises – public or private, private household economy units with employees,[14] and even those illegal enterprises without licenses or registration[15] – are covered by the Regulations on Work-Related Injury Insurance.[16] The Work Safety Law prohibits an employer from having an agreement with the employee that seeks to exclude or limit the employer's liability for injuries or death covered by this law,[17] and the LCL and EPL further clarify the extension of equal labor rights to many of the formerly excluded categories of employees. In addition, employees in a de facto employment relationship[18] and migrant workers[19] are covered; temporary workers may be covered under some local rules. For example, under Article 50, Shanghai Workers' Compensation Regulation (2004), non-full-time workers are not provided mandatory coverage, but can opt in with employer-provided funding.[20] Dispatched workers are also covered

---

[13] LCL, art. 10; Labor Law, arts. 70, 72; *The Long March, supra* note 2, at 4 and 7

[14] WIR, art. 2.

[15] Fei fa yong gong dan wei shang wang ren yuan yi ci xing bu chang ban fa [The Measures for Compensation in a Lump Sum to the Disabled or Deceased Employee of an Illegal Employing Entity] (promulgated by the MOLSS, Sept. 23, 2003, effective Jan. 1, 2004), art. 2, http://www.chinacourt.org/flwk/show1.php?file_id=88922 [hereinafter 2003 Measure].

[16] WIR, art. 2; 2003 Measure, art. 2.

[17] Art. 44; *See also*, An quan sheng chan wei fa xing wei xing zheng chu fa ban fa [Measures for Administrative Penalties against Illegal Acts Concerning Work Safety] (promulgated by the SAWS, Nov. 9, 2007, effective Jan. 1, 2008), art. 46, http://www.gov.cn/ziliao/flfg/2007-12/12/content_832069.htm.

[18] WIR, art. 61 ("Workers mentioned in the present regulation shall refer to the laborers who keep a labor relation (including de facto labor relation) with the employing entity in all forms of employment and within all forms of employment period"). The test of de facto relationship is the degree of control. Guan yu que li lao dong guan xi you guan shi xiang de tong zhi [Notice on pertinent issues related to establishing labor relations] (promulgated by the MOLSS, May 25, 2005), art. 1(2), http://www.law-lib.com/law/law_view.asp?id=92395; and the burden of proof will shift to the employer. *Id.* art. 2.

[19] Guan yu nong min gong can jia gong shang bao xian you guan wen ti de tong zhi [Notice on Migrant Workers' Rights to Participate in Work Injury Insurance] (promulgated by MOLSS, June 1, 2004), art. 2, http://www.molss.gov.cn/gb/ywzn/2004-06/01/content_213986.htm.

[20] Shanghai shi gong shang bao xian shi shi ban fa [Shanghai Implementing Measures for Work Injury Insurance] (promulgated by the Shanghai Labor and Social Security Bureau, Jan. 5, 2004, effective July 1, 2004), art. 50, http://www.law-lib.com/law/law_view1.asp?id=85516.

by the national law.[21] However, individuals working *as* independent contractors are not employees of the employer, nor are those working *for*
independent contractors similarly engaged by the employer.[22] In a recent
court decision, a student intern killed in traffic en route to work was found
not to be protected under WIR as an employee because of student status and a
written agreement that the employer, not otherwise liable, agreed to be liable
only for work-related injuries for which it was responsible.[23]

The scope of work-related injuries under WIR is broad and includes several
categories of injuries: (1) injuries arising from an accident occurring within the
workplace and during working times, (2) injuries caused by violence within
the workplace, (3) injuries sustained in motor vehicle accidents when going
to or from work, and (4) occupational disease.[24] The law specifically excludes
from coverage an injury incurred while committing a crime, violating the
public security order, or causing self-injury because of being intoxicated or
committing a deliberate act, or committing suicide.[25]

3. Administrative Requirements

Generally, as the law reads, each province shall establish its own worker's
compensation reserve fund and special account, subject to the central government's supervision.[26] It is mandatory for employers to pay the insurance

---

[21] WIR, art. 41.
[22] Guan yu si ren bao gong fu ze ren gong shang dai yu zhi fu wen ti de fu han [Reply on Payment
and Treatment for Work Injury by Private Contractors] (promulgated by the Ministry of Labor,
Jan. 14, 1995), http://www.ldzc.com/laborlaw/ShowArticle.asp?ArticleID=5261.
[23] Shi xi sheng shang ban tu zhong che huo shen wang, dan wei bei pan mian ze [Intern
Died in Traffic Accident on the Way to Work, Court Said Employer Had No Liability],
http://www.yongzhou.gov.cn/Article/2008-04-09/29195.htm.
[24] WIR, art. 14. "A worker shall be ascertained to have suffered from work-related injury if:
  (a) he is injured from an accident within the working hours and the working place due to his
     work;
  (b) he is injured from an accident within the working place before or after the working hours
     for doing preparatory or finishing work related to his job;
  (c) he suffers from violence or other unexpected injury within the working hours and working
     place due to implementation of his duties;
  (d) he suffers from an occupational disease;
  (e) his whereabouts are unknown due to his injury or accident during his trip for performing
     his duties;
  (f) he is injured from a motor vehicle accident on his way to or back from work; or
  (g) other circumstances provided for in laws and administrative regulations under which
     work-related injuries shall be ascertained."
[25] WIR, art. 16.
[26] WIR, arts. 9, 12, 13.

premium[27] to the local taxation department.[28] Payment of these taxes by employers helps ensure continued coverage and is enforced by the taxation department, which can bring about sanctions for payment defaults, including suspension or revocation of business licenses.[29]

The insurance rate of all insured enterprises is based on their classification as low risk, median risk, or high risk.[30] The base rate for each category is 0.5 percent, 1 percent, and 2 percent of total payroll expenses, respectively.[31] The local province can adjust the base rate every one to three years.[32] Enterprises in the low-risk category pay the fixed base rate, no matter how many injuries occur.[33] Depending on the risk-injury data from the previous year, the local Labor Bureau can adjust the enterprise's median- or high-risk rate downward to 50 percent and 80 percent of the base rate, or upward to 120 percent and 150 percent of the base rate, respectively.[34]

---

[27] WIR, art. 2.

[28] E.g., Fujian shi shi gong shang bao xian tiao li ban fa [Fujian Implementing Measures for Regulations on Work Injury Insurance] (promulgated by the Fujian provincial government, April 30, 2004), art. 4, http://china.findlaw.cn/laodongfa/gsbxtl/12189.html.

[29] Under the 2001 Tax Administration Law, the taxation department can request the State Administration for Industry and Commerce to revoke business licenses, http://202.108.90.130/n6669073/n6669088/6887981.html (art. 60); *see also* Lao dong xing zheng chu fa ruo gan gui ding [Certain Regulations Concerning Administrative Punishments with respect to Labor] (promulgated by the Ministry of Labor, Sept. 27, 1996, effective Oct. 1, 1996), art. 5. Generally, for violations of various labor laws, the government has available the sanction of revoking business licenses in accordance with the law; *see e.g.*, Lao dong bao zhang jian cha tiao li [Regulation on Labor Security Supervision] (promulgated by the State Council, Nov. 1, 2004, effective Dec. 1, 2004), art. 28, http://www.chinacourt.org/flwk/show1.php?file_id=97457. The issue of nonpayment is discussed in Pushkar Maitra, Russell Smyth, Ingrid Nielsen, Chris Nyland, & Cherrie Zhu, *Firm Compliance with Social Insurance Obligations Where There Is a Weak Surveillance and Enforcement Mechanism: Empirical Evidence from Shanghai*, 12 PAC. ECON. REV. 577 (2007).

[30] Guan yu gong shang bao xian fei lv wen ti de tong zhi [Notice on Work Injury Insurance Rate Issues] (promulgated by the MOLSS, Oct. 29, 2003), art. 1, http://www.cnlss.com/MolssLaw/InjuryOnJob/200610/MolssLaw_20061015172816_158.html.

[31] *Id.*

[32] *Id.*

[33] *Id.*

[34] *Id.* Example of Shanghai, Shanghai shi gong shang bao xian fu dong fei lv guan li zan xing ban fa [Notice on Shanghai Worker's Compensation Rate] (2005). Cost factor: total claimed benefit / total paid premium. All enterprises (except low-risk category) are placed in a floating rate system of five levels: 0.5%, 1%, 1.5%, 2%, 2.5%, and 3% of total wage expense. The fixed rate of five levels will be revised every year.

Based on the previous year's cost factor of each insurer, the next year's rate will be raised one level if the cost factor is greater than 200%, but no more than 400%; two levels if the cost factor is greater than 400%, but no more than 600%; three levels if the cost factor is greater than 600%, but no more than 800%; four levels if the cost factor is greater than 800%, but no more than 1,000%; and five levels if the cost factor is greater than 1,000%.

Claims by employees for work-related injury or occupational disease compensation can be made only after the degree of their disability is assessed
and officially certified by the local government's labor appraisal committee.
Thereafter, the employer must file the claim with the government agency
within thirty days.[35] If the employer fails to file a claim, the employee or labor
union can file within one year of the diagnosis.[36] The claim must show the
existing employment relationship and the diagnosis of the work-related injury
or disease.[37] The employer has the right to challenge any claim and also has
the burden of proof.[38] The local labor administration must investigate the
claim and render its decision within sixty days of filing. This applies to claims
seeking[39] permanent disability benefits as well.[40]

After a disability has been certified, it is graded for the purpose of determining the level of benefits. There are ten grades, with grade 1 being the most
severe and grade 10 the mildest.[41] There is a right to appeal to the provincial
labor authorities within fifteen days after the initial decision, but their decision
is final.[42]

4. Disability Benefits

Disability benefits paid from the work-related insurance fund cover medicine,
diagnosis, hospitalization, rehabilitation, permanent disability benefits, and
death benefits.[43] In cases of partial/temporary disability, the employer pays full
wages for a period up to twelve months.[44] The employer also covers the cost of
travel for medical treatment[45] and caregiving during the temporary disability
period.[46] The employer must also pay benefits to those working in illegal
enterprises: at least six times the average annual wages for permanent disability
benefits[47] and ten times the average annual wages for death benefits,[48] and all
the medical and living costs.[49]

---

[35] WIR, art. 17.
[36] *Id.*
[37] WIR, art. 18.
[38] WIR, art. 19.
[39] WIR, art. 20.
[40] WIR, arts. 21–5
[41] WIR, art. 22.
[42] WIR, art. 28.
[43] WIR, arts. 29–43.
[44] WIR, art. 31.
[45] WIR, art. 29.
[46] WIR, art. 31.
[47] 2003 Measure, art. 5, *supra* note 15.
[48] *Id.* arts. 6, 3.
[49] *Id.* art. 4.

The ten grades of disability are as follows.[50] Grades 1 to 4 are the most serious and indicate the employee no longer has any ability to work; grades 5 and 6 indicate an employee has lost most of the ability to work; and workers with grade 7 to 10 injuries are classified as partially disabled.[51] The amount of employee compensation for work-related injuries or death is fixed in the law,[52] as specified in the Standard Assessment of the Seriousness of Work-Related Injuries and Occupational Diseases (See Table 9.1). For coal-mine–related deaths, 200,000 yuan seems to have become a "national benchmark" for compensation payments, notwithstanding the law's lower requirement.[53] Negotiated settlements are possible, and where not undertaken will be enforced through mediation and arbitration procedures.[54] Negotiated settlements are enforceable by the court, but may be modified by the courts if deemed unfair.[55]

5. Enforcement

One avenue to deal with some disputed claims, those dealing with such topics as certification or classification of disabilities is to file an administrative appeal to require enforcement of the law against possible violators. For example, action can be taken against a recalcitrant employer who refuses to properly process a claim or accept the certified level of disability[56] or against one who misclassifies the level of disability.[57] This action may include administrative litigation.[58]

---

[50] Zhi gong gong shang yu zhi ye bing zhi can cheng du jian ding biao zhun [Standard Assessment of the Seriousness of Work-Related Injuries and Occupational Diseases] (promulgated by the Ministry of Labor, Mar. 14, 1996, effective Oct. 1, 1996), http://www.yljf.com/FAGUI/12/1211.asp [hereinafter Standard]; *Compensation for Work-Related Injury and Occupational Disease in China*, CHINA LABOR BULLETIN, http://www.clb.org.hk/en/node/100207.

[51] WIR, arts. 33–7.

[52] *Id.*

[53] The 200,000 yuan compensation standard was first introduced on November, 30, 2004, by the Shanxi government in its *Regulations on Enforcing Responsibility for Mine Safety to Prevent Exceptional Loss of Life in Accidents*. This provincial legislation stipulated that the operator of a mine that had been the scene of a fatal accident must pay out at least 200,000 yuan in compensation for each worker killed. After their promulgation, these provisions were approved by the central government's State Administration of Work Safety and reproduced by regional governments in other areas. Liaoning, Guizhou, Hebei, Jiangxi, Yunnan, and Shaanxi provinces all drafted similar legislation, and 200,000 yuan very quickly became the "national benchmark" for compensation payments. *Compensation for Work-Related Injury and Occupational Disease in China*, CHINA LABOR BULLETIN, http://www.clb.org.hk/en/node/100207.

[54] Lao dong zheng yi tiao jie zhong cai fa [The Law on Labor Dispute Mediation and Arbitration] (promulgated by the 31st session of the Standing Comm. of the Tenth NPC, Dec. 29, 2007, effective May 1, 2008), arts. 4, 5 (PRC) [hereinafter LMA].

[55] *See* http://www.nmglawyer.com/Article/8000.html.

[56] WIR, art. 17.

[57] WIR, art. 53.

[58] *Id.*

TABLE 9.1. *Standard assessment of the seriousness of work-related injuries and occupational diseases (work disability scale in full detail); see WIR, arts. 33–5 (amount of compensation)*

The Work Disability Scale

Grade 1: Loss of an organ or complete or irreplaceable loss of organ function; requiring special medical care and support; complete loss or serious loss of the ability to care for oneself, e.g., severe damage to cognitive functions and intelligence, loss of sight in both eyes.

Grade 2: Severe damage to or deformity of an organ; serious functional deficiencies or complications; requiring special medical care and support; complete loss or serious loss of ability to care for oneself, e.g., serious damage to cognitive intelligence; loss of sight in one eye and less than or equal to eight percent of normal vision in the other.

Grade 3: Severe damage to or deformity of an organ; serious functional deficiencies or complications; requiring special medical care and support; partial loss of ability to care for oneself, e.g., loss of a hand, dangerous and impulsive behavior caused by psychotic disorders; serious disfiguration on the face.

Grade 4: Severe damage to or deformity of an organ; serious functional deficiencies or complications; requiring special medical care and support but capable of self-care, e.g., psychotic diseases leading to social skills deficiencies; medium level of facial disfiguration and scars over 70 percent or more of the body.

Grade 5: Major damage to or deformity of an organ; major functional deficiencies or complications; requiring general medical care but capable of self-care, e.g., complete loss of speech due to motor speech disorders; complete loss of ability to read and write (agraphia); moderate facial disfiguration, loss of thumb.

Grade 6: Major damage to or deformity of an organ; moderate level of functional deficiencies or complications; requiring general medical care but capable of self-care, e.g., incomplete loss of speech, serious colorization or discoloration on the face.

Grade 7: Major damage to or deformity of an organ; moderate functional deficiencies or complications; requiring general medical care but capable of self-care, e.g., partial damage to thumb; loss of toes, except the big toe; removal of half the small intestine.

Grade 8: Partial damage to or deformity of an organ; moderate functional deficiencies; requiring moderate medical care but capable of self-care, e.g., change of personality due to psychotic disorders; speech difficulties.

Grade 9: Partial damage to or deformity of an organ; moderate functional deficiencies that do not require medical care, e.g., damage of skull with an area of less than 25 square centimeters, no loss of function; able to eat after an esophagectomy.

Grade 10: Partial damage to or deformity of an organ; no functional deficiencies; not requiring medical care, and capable of self-care, e.g., damage to skull with an area of less than 9.24 square centimeters; moderate colorization or dis-colorization on the face.

TABLE 9.1 *(continued)*

The Amount of Compensation

Disability Grades 1 to 4

The employee shall retain their labor relationship with the employer, but retire from their position and receive:

1. A lump sum disability payment equivalent to:
    Grade 1: 24 months' wages;
    Grade 2: 22 months' wages;
    Grade 3: 20 months' wages;
    Grade 4: 18 months' wages;
2. A disability allowance paid each month and equivalent to:
    Grade 1: 90 percent of their monthly wage;
    Grade 2: 85 percent of their monthly wage;
    Grade 3: 80 percent of their monthly wage;
    Grade 4: 75 percent of their monthly wage.

Grades 5 and 6

The employee shall receive:
A lump sum disability payment equivalent to:
Grade 5: 16 months' wages;
Grade 6: 14 months' wages;
The employee's labor relationship shall be retained and the employer shall arrange for suitable employment. If a suitable post cannot be arranged, the employer shall pay a disability allowance each month equivalent to:
Grade 5: 70 percent of the employee's monthly wage;
Grade 6: 60 percent of the employee's monthly wage.
If the employee wishes to terminate their labor relationship, their employer shall pay the cost of medical treatment together with the lump sum disability allowance.

Grades 7 to 10

The employee shall receive:
A lump sum disability payment equivalent to:
Grade 7: 12 months' wages;
Grade 8: 10 months' wages;
Grade 9: 8 months' wages;
Grade 10: 6 months' wages.

Fatal Accidents

In the case of a fatal accident, the employee's relatives will be entitled to:

1. A lump sum compensation payment equivalent to between 48 and 60 months' average salary in the region in which the fatality occurred.
2. A lump sum funeral subsidy equivalent to six months' average salary in the region in which the fatality occurred;
3. A monthly pension for relatives who have no capability to work or who were dependent on the employee who died:
    40 percent of the deceased employee's monthly wage for the spouse;
    30 percent of the deceased employee's monthly wage for other relatives;
    An additional 10 percent of the deceased employee's monthly wage for the aged or orphaned.

The total sum of the pensions paid shall not exceed the wage of the deceased worker.

Another avenue of enforcement is in Article 52 of WIR, which provides that labor disputes over the treatment of work-related injury obligations shall be settled in the usual processes of labor dispute resolution, as provided in the 2008 Labor Mediation and Arbitration Law. This law states that the arbitration award will be final and binding in "disputes involving recovery of labor remuneration, medical bills for a work-related injury, severance pay or damages, in an amount not exceeding the equivalent of twelve months of the local minimum wage rate."[59] For other claims falling outside the above final and binding coverage, there may be resort to the courts after arbitration.[60] However, according to studies by advocacy groups, practical deficiencies in implementing arbitration of work injury disputes caused by some employers' intransigence to comply with obligations the appropriate treatment of injured workers.[61]

[59] LMA, art. 47.
[60] *Id.*
[61] *The Long March, supra* note 2.

10

Wages and Hours

Minimum wages standards and guidelines are set out in the 2004 Regulations on Minimum Wage (RMW), which follow the 1994 Labor Law.[1] The RMW specifies required wage payments, deductions, and overtime, though some issues occasionally arise regarding exempted categories of workers, such as managers. In addition, variations in coverage and wage levels occur as implementing standards are fixed and administered at local levels.[2] Local governments are also primarily responsible for administration and enforcement, but aggrieved workers must bring their labor dispute to arbitration to recover unpaid wages. Unfortunately, the transition to a market economy has been accompanied by underpayment and nonpayment of wages to many workers, especially to migrant workers. Likewise, studies have shown that minimum wages, originally targeted at 40 to 60 percent of the average monthly wages, often fall below the 40 percent level.[3] For example, in 2006 in Beijing, the level was reported to be at around 20 percent, creating a gap of nearly 600 yuan per month.[4]

---

[1] Zui di gong zi gui ding [Regulations on Minimum Wage] (promulgated by the MOLSS, Jan. 20, 2004, effective Mar. 1, 2004) [hereinafter RMW].

[2] *Minimum Wage Rates are Proposed by Local Governments after Tripartite Consultation for Approval by the State Council.* OECD EMPLOYMENT OUTLOOK 38 (2007). *See also* Zhang Jianguo, *Chinese Trade Unions Actively Promoting Development of Tripartite Consultation and Collective Contract Mechanism*, Dec. 29, 2006, http://www.acftu.org.cn/template/10002/file.jsp?cid=70&aid=125.

[3] *Wages in China*, CHINA LABOUR BULLETIN, www.clb.org.hk/en/node/100206, at 2. *The Labor Statistical Yearbook* only provides average wage data, whereas minimum wages are generally set by local regulations. For further discussion on minimum wages, *see* Moming Zhou, *China Raises Minimum Wages to Calm Consumers*, http://www.marketwatch.com/news/story/china-raises-minimum-wages-calm/story.aspx?guid=%7BB120D814-3C01-468A-9C11-B7596BCE1A35%7D.

[4] *Id.*

1. Societal Disparities

In the late 1980s, the economic developments following the Four Moderniza-tions of 1979 produced workplaces that were increasingly regulated by labor contracts, replacing the "iron rice bowl" model of earlier years.[5] The tran-sition to a socialist market economy in the 1990s coincided with a growing assumption of managerial control by employers.[6] Because of market forces, employers were forced to maximize profits if they hoped to survive without the government subsidies provided in the former planned economy, and law-makers responded by allowing greater employer autonomy. This liberalization of employee management tended to result in cutting labor costs and, all too frequently, ignoring labor laws. This trend was particularly prevalent among employers outside the state-owned enterprise (SOE) system, and the usual victims of unpaid wages were migrant workers in the urban areas, especially in the construction industry.[7]

Yet this market transition has had both positive and negative economic con-sequences. One bright side has been phenomenal economic growth and devel-opment for the country as a whole; however, a dark side has been its impact on individual workers, manifested in layoffs, unemployment, and emerging wage disparities. There are dramatic wage differences between urban and rural workers as well as between regions – especially between the Special Economic Zones (SEZs) in the coastal areas and the non-SEZs in the Western inland provinces.[8] Large wage disparities also exist, as they do in many countries, between management staff and workers.[9] According to former World Bank

---

[5] Jaeyoun Won, *Withering Away of the Iron Rice Bowl? The Reemployment Project of Post-Socialist China*, 39 STUD. IN COMP. INT'L DEV. 71, 71 (2004). *See also* Randall Peerenboom, *Globalization, Path Dependency and the Limits of Law: Administrative Law Reform and Rule of Law in the People's Republic of China*, 19 BERKELEY J. INT'L L. 161, 208 (2001).

[6] Victor Nee & Yang Cao, *Market Transition and the Firm: Institutional Change and Income Inequality in Urban China*, 1 MGMT. & ORG. REV. 23 (2005). *See also* Jonathan P. Hiatt & Deborah Greenfield, *The Importance of Core Labor Rights in World Development*, 26 MICH. J. INT'L L. 39, 40 (2004).

[7] Sean Cooney, *Making Chinese Labor Law Work: The Prospects for Regulatory Innovation in the People's Republic of China*, 30 FORDHAM INT'L L. J. 1050 (2007).

[8] *See generally* Bjorn Gustafsson & Li Shi, *The Anatomy of Rising Earnings Inequality in Urban China*, 29 J. COMP. ECON. 118 (2001). *See also* Cliff Waldman, *The Labor Market in Post-Reform China: History, Evidence, and Implications*, 39 BUS. ECON. 50, 54–6 (2004).

[9] Guo wu yuan fa zhan yan jiu zhong xin [The Development Research Center of the State Council], Zhongguo qi ye ren li zi yuan guan li diao cha bao gao [Report of Chinese Enterprises on Human Resource Management] (2004), cited in Lao zong yuan gong shou ru cha ju zui da chao 50 bei [Manager Earns Fifty Times More than Staff], GUANGZHOU DAILY, Apr. 25, 2004, at A2, http://gzdaily.dayoo.com/gb/content/2004-04/25/content_1517025.htm.

president James Wolfenson, these wage gaps are increasing at an alarming rate, and he warns that such gaps could lead to social unrest and protests.[10]

Nevertheless, average monthly wages in urban areas in China have increased every year since the late 1980s, with an average salary of 2,078 yuan per month in 2007.[11] However, the gap between urban and rural households has also continued to increase: urban households in 2006 had an average disposable income of 11,759 yuan versus 3,587 yuan for rural households.[12] The minimum monthly wages and average monthly wages also vary widely among urban areas. For example, in 2007, minimum wage standards in urban areas were as follows: Chongqing had a low of 480; Wuhan, 460; Guangzhou, 690; Shenzhen, 700; Beijing, 730; and Shanghai, 840. In September 2008, it was reported that minimum wage standards were as follows: Chongqing had a low of 680; Guangzhou, 860; Shenzhen Inner, 1,000; Shenzen Outer, 900; Beijing, 800; and Shanghai, 960.[13] Just as wages vary, so do recent gains. Some highly

---

[10] David Murphy, *The Dangers of Too Much Success*, 167 FAR E. ECON. REV. 28–29 (2004). The Chinese government has taken notice of the increase in mass protests. It is reported that Zhou Yongkang, the Public Security Chief and State Councilor, stated that the "rising conflicts among the people" had been triggered by domestic economic factors, the behavior of cadres, and by a lack of justice with the number of mass protests increasing from about "10,000 in 1994 to more than 74,000 last year [2004]." Shi Ting, *Acceptance of Rights Replacing Reflex Fear of Protests*, S. CHINA MORNING POST, July 7, 2005, at 1.

[11] *Average Salary Increase of Urban Workers Rises to Six-Year High*, XINHUA NEWS AGENCY, April 2, 2008, http://www.china.org.cn/government/central_government/2008-04/02/content_14111192.htm (According to the year's No. 1 statement released by the National Bureau of Statistics (NBS) on Tuesday, the average annual salary increase hovered around 14 percent from 2001 to 2006. The 2007 average annual salary of urban workers was 24,932 yuan and the daily average was 99.31 yuan (14.15 U.S. dollars), up 18.72 percent over the previous year. Taking into account price rises, the average salary increase hit a six-year-high); *see also Wages in China, supra* note 3.

[12] *Wages in China, supra* note 3.

[13] *Wage/Unemployment Standards in Selected Provinces/Municipalities/Cities*, CHINA LABOR WATCH (Aug 2007). *See* Resources on Labor Rights in China, ILRF, http://www.laborrights.org/creating-a-sweatfree-world/rule-of-law/china-program/resources/1806, http://www.chinalaborwatch.org/2007wagestand.htm. In the first nine months of 2008, at least nineteen Chinese provinces and cities raised their minimum wage by an average of about 15 percent. However, in November, China's labor ministry directed local governments not to increase minimum wage levels in a bid to help companies cope with the global financial crisis. *China Freezes Minimum Wage to Help Companies*, Nov. 18, 2008, http://www.google.com/hostednews/afp/article/ALeqM5jYfsN_1RznSoTVPi3G22BmEDkL_w. The minimum wage hike during the first half of 2008 was partly due to labor shortages and partly due to inflation. *See* Liang Qiwen, *Minimum Wage Hike Planned to Plug Labor Shortage*, CHINA DAILY, June, 21, 2008, http://www.chinadaily.com.cn/china/2008-06/21/content_6784122.htm; *Beijing City Hikes Minimum Wage as Inflation Soars*, THE CHINA POST, June 29, 2008, http://www.chinapost.com.tw/china/local-news/beijing/2008/06/29/163216/Beijing-city.htm.

industrialized areas, such as Shenzhen and Guangzhou, had 15 to 20 percent rises from the prior year.[14]

2. Law on Wages

The 1994 Labor Law first established a comprehensive minimum wage system for China, with local governments setting the wage levels according to enumerated factors.[15] This law also requires the employer to pay wages in cash and to pay for statutory holidays, marriage or funeral leaves, or periods of "social activities" required by law.[16] The 2008 Labor Contract Law requires that employment contracts include a term on labor compensation.[17]

In 2004, the Regulations on Minimum Wages (RMW) issued by the MOLSS provided further stipulations as wages.[18] It defined the "minimum wage" standard as "the least labor remuneration paid by the employers required by law on condition that the laborers have provided normal labor during the legal working hours or working hours agreed by the labor contract."[19] These working hours include periods during "annual vacation, home leaves, wedding leave and leave for arranging funeral, maternity leave and leave for contraceptive operation, as well as attending social activities in accordance with law within working hours."[20] In January 2008 the MOLSS increased the number of statutory holidays from ten to eleven and issued a circular on pro rata wage calculations.[21]

The method of wage distribution remains within the discretion of the employer, whereas the minimum and maximum standards are adjusted at least every two years by the government.[22] A monthly rate is to be used for

---

[14] *Minimum Wage Standard Implemented in Guangzhou*, April 6, 2007, http://www.chinacsr. com/en/2007/04/06/1207-minimum-wage-standard-implemented-in-guangzhou/.

[15] Labor Law, art. 48; RMW, art. 7.

[16] Labor Law, arts 50, 51.

[17] LCL, art. 17.

[18] RMW, *supra* note 1.

[19] RMW, art. 3.

[20] *Id.* Social activities include legally exercising the right to vote and the right to be voted for; representing county, distinct level on upper level government, labor union, youth union, women's association, etc. to participate in meetings; taking the witness stand in court; taking part in workers award on excellent worker's meeting; labor union activities allowed under the Trade Union Law, etc. Gong zi zhi fu zan xing qui ding [Interim Rules on Wage Payment] promulgated by MOL, Dec. 6, 1994, eff. Jan. 1, 1995), art. 10.

[21] Guan yu zhi gong quan nian yue ping jun gong zuo shi jian he gong zi zhe suan wen ti de tong zhi [Circular on Issues Concerning the Annual Average Monthly Working Hours of Staff and Workers and the Pro Rata Calculation of Their Wages] (issued by the MOLSS, Jan. 3, 2008), available at CHINA LAW & PRACTICE 91 (Mar. 2008).

[22] RMW, art. 10.

full-time employees and an hourly rate for other employees.[23] New draft wage payment regulations, expected to be approved by the State Council in late 2009, would authorize employees and the union to have "consultations' on the wages to be paid and allow employers to give compensatory time off in lieu of overtime compensation.[24] That part-time workers are to be paid the minimum wage is confirmed by the LCL.[25] However, students working part-time as student interns or under institutional agreements are held not to be employees, and thus the employer is not required to pay them minimum wages.[26]

Exclusions from wages for the purposes of calculating the minimum wage include payments from employers for social insurance, protective clothing or equipment, travel-related expenses, overtime, and subsidies related to working conditions.[27] *Deductions* from wages are limited to those permitted by statute, such as income tax and social security, or by contractual provisions or employer rules that are in accordance with the law, such as employee misconduct that causes economic loss.[28] Local regulations regarding exclusions and deductions vary widely.

3. Law on Hours

The Labor Law originally established the standard working-hour system of eight hours per day and forty-four hours per week, but that has since been

---

[23] LCL, art. 68.

[24] "Gong zi tiao li" cao an zhu ti wan cheng, gong zi zeng zhang you wang xie shang jie jue [Wage Regulations Draft Almost Finished, Consultation to be Used for Wage Increase], Mar. 9, 2008, http://news.xinhuanet.com/fortune/2008-03/09/content_7749752.htm. *See also Draft Wage Regulations Emphasize Importance of Consultation*, www.internationallawoffice. com/Newsletters/ (subscription); *Trade Unions and Multinational Companies in China*, CHINA LAW & PRACTICE (Sept. 2008) ("A recent draft for a national wage regulation issued by the Ministry of Human Resources and Social Security (MOHRSS) provides that, unless an employer engages in collective wage negotiation, the company will not be allowed to include employees' wages as pre-tax business expenses").

[25] LCL, art. 68.

[26] Where the student is an intern or a participant in a work/study program in a college (excluding vocational colleges) pursuant to an agreement between the enterprise and the college. 1995 Labor Law Implementing Opinion, art. 12. *Students Not Covered by Minimum Wage Laws*, www.chinaeconomicreview.com/cer/2007_05/KFC_cleared.html; Shanghai lao dong ju ren ding Mai Dang Lao Ken De Ji mei you wei fa yong gong wen ti [Shanghai Labor Bureau declared that McDonald's and KFC are Not in Violation of Labor Laws], April 17, 2007, http://finance1.jrj.com.cn/news/2007-04-17/000002160061.html (regarding the issue of not paying minimum wage to student interns working at McDonald's and KFC in Shanghai).

[27] RMW, art. 12. Further discussion of social security benefits is in Chapter 11.

[28] Gong zi zhi fu zan xing gui ding [Interim Regulations on Wage Payment] (promulgated by the Ministry of Labor, Jan. 1, 1995), arts. 15, 16.

amended to forty hours per week, including night work.[29] The LCL requires
a description of the employee's working hours in the labor contract.[30] A day of
rest during the week is mandated, and a daily rest period (excluded from work
hours) is typically provided, often as the lunch break.[31] The LCL mandates that
any employer formulations, revisions, or decisions on its rules regarding hours
(and other employee interests) must first be discussed with all employees or
their representative congress.[32] This is to be followed by a responsive proposal
and comments that the employer must then bring to the labor union for
consultations.[33]

An alternative to the standard working-hour system is available where the
employer has a "special nature of production," such as seasonal industry
workers.[34] This "Comprehensive Working-Hour System" typically applies to
transportation, telecommunications, fisheries, and seasonal industries, and it
permits longer working hours during peak periods, subject to prior government
approval, as long as the average number of hours worked in the prescribed
period does not exceed the limit of that system.[35] Overtime payment is required
for work in excess of the system's requirements.[36]

4. Law on Overtime

Overtime pay generally is required for hours worked by employees in excess of
the hourly limits ("extended hours"), absent exceptions, which are discussed in

[29] Labor Law, art. 34; Guo wu yuan guan yu zhi gong gong zuo shi jian de gui ding [Decision of
State Council Regarding Working Hours of Staff and Workers] (issued by the State Council
on Feb. 3, 1994, amended on Mar. 25, 1995, effective May 1, 1995), art. 3.
[30] LCL, art. 17.
[31] Labor Law, art. 3; "Guo wu yuan guan yu zhi gong gong zuo shi jian de gui ding" wen ti jie da
[Question and Answers on Decision of State Council Regarding Working Hours of Staff and
Workers] (issued by the Ministry of Labor, April 22, 1995), art. 1.
[32] LCL, art. 4.
[33] *Id.*
[34] Labor Law, art. 39.
[35] Lao dong bu guan che "guo wu yuan guan yu zhi gong gong zuo shi jian de gui ding" de shi
shi ban fa [Implementing Measures for "Decision of State Council Regarding Working Hours
of Staff and Workers"] (promulgated by the Ministry of Labor, Mar. 26, 1995), art. 7; Guan yu
qi ye shi xing bu ding shi gong zuo zhi he zong he ji suan gong shi gong zuo zhi de shen pi ban
fa [Measures Concerning Examination and Approval of Implementation by Enterprises of the
Flexible Working Hour System and the Comprehensive Working Hour System] (promulgated
by the Ministry of Labor, Dec. 14, 1994, effective Jan. 1, 1995), arts. 4, 5; Interim Regulations on
Wage Payment, *supra* note 28, art. 3.
[36] Implementing Measures for "Decision of State Council Regarding Working Hours of Staff and
Workers," *supra* note 35, art. 8; Interim Regulations on Wage Payment, *supra* note 28, art. 13.

this section.[37] These payments are to be 150 percent for each hour of overtime worked on a normal work day, 200 percent for excess hours worked on a rest day or day off, and 300 percent for excess work on a statutory holiday.[38] Employees working on a piece-rate basis are expected to have their wage rate set on the expectation that reasonable quotas match an amount of work that would normally be accomplished in a forty-hour work week covered by the minimum wage requirements.[39]

Certain employees, such as high-level managerial staff, field staff, sales staff, and security staff, may not receive overtime pay if there has been prior government approval.[40] This "Flexible Working-Hour System" excludes ("exempts") these employees from the requirements of overtime, with working hours limited only by the employer's general obligation to protect their health.[41] Some local regulations, such as in Beijing, vary the approval and obligation provisions, and there are distinctions among locales on how low the management rank can be and still fit the exception.[42] In China, as in other countries, there is an economic incentive to misclassify an employee as management to avoid meeting overtime and other labor law obligations while obtaining many extended hours of work.[43]

5. Enforcement

Local government administrations enforce the laws dealing with wages and hours, and disagreements between the employer and employee on violations

---

[37] Labor Law, art. 44; RMW, art. 12.

[38] Labor Law, art. 44; Interim Regulations on Wage Payment, *supra* note 28, art. 13.

[39] RMW, art. 12.

[40] Measures Concerning Examination and Approval of Implementation by Enterprises of the Flexible Working Hour System and the Comprehensive Working Hour System, *supra* note 35, art. 4.

[41] *Id.*, art. 6. See Chapter 3, Exemptions, discussion in text *accompanying* footnotes 48–63.

[42] Beijing regulations use the same language, "high level management staff," as the national regulations, but have a special Article 8, which provides payment for more prolonged work hours based on the Labor Law, art. 44, and there is a ceiling monthly limit of thirty-six hours. Guan yu yin fa Beijing shi qi ye shi xing zong he ji suan gong shi gong zuo zhi he bu ding shi gong zuo shi ban fa de tong zhi [Notice on Beijing Measures Concerning Examination and Approval of Implementation by Enterprises of the Flexible Working Hour System and the Comprehensive Working Hour System] (issued by the Beijing Labor and Social Security Bureau, Dec. 9, 2003), art. 11, http://www.bjld.gov.cn/LDJAPP/search/fgdetail.jsp?no=1673.

[43] Chinese company officials have noted that McDonald's in Japan recently lost a court case on misclassified "managers" and began paying many of its "managers" overtime pay. *McDonald's Japan to Pay Overtime to Store Managers*, uk.reuters.com/article/consumerProducts/idUKT2939620080520.

are treated as labor disputes. These disputes arise when the employer refuses to pay, and they must be resolved under the Law on Labor Mediation and Arbitration.[44]

The Labor Contract Law also provides for administrative penalties when the employer has violated the wage requirements or failed to pay overtime that is due.[45] The statutory penalty is "damages to the worker at a rate of not less than 50 percent and not more than 100 percent of the amount payable."[46]

[44] *See e.g.*, RMW, art. 14.
[45] LCL, art. 85.
[46] *Id.*

PART V

EMPLOYEE BENEFITS: LEAVES, MEDICAL, MATERNITY, WORK-RELATED, UNEMPLOYMENT, AND PENSION INSURANCE

Mandated and Nonmandated Employee Benefits

1. Social Security System

China's social security "safety net" system comprises five insurance benefit programs: medical, maternity, work-related injury, unemployment, and pension. Most employee benefits are mandated by law and are administered by government programs. A new national law on social insurance is now in draft form and is expected to be passed in late 2009.[1] These include social insurance programs, housing funds, labor union funding, and certain leave policies for employees, such as holiday leave, home leave and/or annual leave, and medical leave. Employees may also receive nonmandated benefits that are discretionary or negotiated and included in contracts, such as seniority, merit increases, bonuses, parking, travel, and special allowances, such as for hazardous work.

Mandated social security benefits programs are nationally devised and locally implemented. Medical insurance is available under a unified insurance program in which both employers and employees contribute a certain percentage of payroll and individual income, respectively, into a general fund consisting of a pooled fund and a personal account. Maternity insurance is employer funded and provides financial support for the mother during an authorized time period. Employer-funded occupational (work-related) injury insurance is also provided under local government systems and is funded by employer contributions. The unemployment and pension programs are a massive undertaking still taking shape, but every year additional millions of employees come under their protective umbrella. Both programs are funded by joint contributions of the employer and employee.

---

[1] China Expected to Promulgate Social Security Law, HUNAN GOVERNMENT, www. enghunan.gov.cn/www.Home/200903/t20090310-153804.htm; Social Insurance Law Draft, http://www.eucss.org.cn/fileadmin/content/pdf/C1report/social.

2. Mandated Social Insurance Programs and Funds

a. Medical Benefits

National regulations create a unified medical insurance system that creates a Basic Medical Insurance Fund, which includes a pooled fund and personal accounts, funded by mandated contributions from the employer of about 6 percent and from the employee of 2 percent.[2] The amount of the employer's contribution can vary by region; for example, Shanghai has a 10 percent employer contribution and Chengdu has 7.5 percent.[3] Some local programs also provide "supplemental" medical benefits, financed by additional employer contributions.[4] Seventy percent of the employer's contribution goes into the pooled fund and 30 percent into each employee's personal account; 100 percent of the employee's contribution is placed in his or her personal account.[5]

Only urban employers, but not rural employers, participate in the medical insurance program.[6] The self-employed and their workers are usually covered, and township employment units may be covered as determined by local governments.[7] Part-time employees have the authority to participate in the medical program, but the final determination is left to the local

---

[2] Guo wu yuan guan yu jian li cheng zhen zhi gong ji ben yi liao bao xian zhi du de jue ding [Decision of the State Council on Establishing the Urban Employees' Basic Medical Insurance System] (promulgated by the State Council, Dec. 14, 1998), http://www.gov.cn/banshi/2005-08/04/content_20256.htm [hereinafter State Council Decision].

[3] Shanghai shi cheng zhen zhi gong ji ben yi liao bao xian ban fa [Measures on Basic Medical Insurance of Shanghai Urban Workers] (promulgated by the Shanghai municipal government, Oct. 20, 2000, effective Dec. 1, 2000), art. 6, http://www.shanghai.gov.cn/shanghai/node2314/node3124/node3125/node3127/userobject6ai269.html [hereinafter Shanghai Measure]; Chengdu shi cheng zhen zhi gong ji ben yi liao bao xian zan xing ban fa [Interim Measures on Basic Medical Insurance of Chengdu Urban Workers] (promulgated by the Chengdu municipal government, Dec. 11, 2000), art. 8, http://www.wsj.chengdu.gov.cn:88/webnew%5Czcfg.nsf/%E4%B8%BB%E8%A7%86%E5%9B%BE/E03D096FC9D2DA3148256D1F000D3E74?opendocument.

[4] Shanghai Measure, *supra* note 2, art. 27.

[5] State Council Decision, *supra* note 1.

[6] *Id.* The Draft Social Security Law provides that rural residents working in urban areas participate in the social security programs under the law, and unemployed rural residents whose land has been condemned can participate in the basic pension plan and the basic medical insurance plan. She hui bao xian fa (Cao an) [Social Security Law (Draft)], arts. 89, 90, http://www.npc.cn/npc/xinwen/syxw/2008-12/28/content_1465140.htm (in Chinese) [hereinafter Draft Social Security Law].

[7] *Id.* Individual business owners without employees and part-time workers can participate in the basic pension plan under Article 9 of the Draft Social Security Law, but they make the contributions themselves.

governments.[8] Coverage of unemployed workers varies with local governments, but they are often covered for at least some time.[9]

Benefits, as a general rule, are paid as follows. Small claims are paid from the employee's personal account; big claims are partially paid from the general pooled fund. To trigger reimbursement from the general fund, the claim must exceed a "threshold level," which is 10 percent of the employee's annual wage.[10] Reimbursement of medical costs or prescriptions is limited by a ceiling, which is 400 percent of the employee's annual wage.[11] For claims above the coverage ceiling, the employee may seek reimbursement from other commercial insurance. It is up to the province to decide for each claim the amount of reimbursement from the general fund.[12]

Certain remedies are available when an employer has not paid the insurance premium. In Beijing, the local government issues a warning and then a final notice. If the employer fails to comply, the local agency seeks enforcement and collects a daily 0.2 percent penalty (73% APR).[13] If an employee's personal account has inadequate funds because of the employer's overdue premium payment, the employee can pay his medical costs and then seek indemnification of those costs from the employer.[14]

As of June 2008, it was reported that 249.07 million persons were covered by the basic urban medical insurance program.[15]

b. Maternity Benefits

The 1994 Labor Law provided that female employees are entitled to not less than ninety days of maternity leave, are protected from discharge or discrimination because of their condition, and may not be subjected to certain onerous work conditions, such as overtime and hazardous work.[16] In 1995, national

---

[8] Lao dong bao zhang bu guan yu fei quan ri zhi yong gong ruo gan wen ti de yi jian [Opinions of MOLSS on Questions about Part-Time Workers] (promulgated by the MOLSS, May 30, 2003), art. 11, http://www.jincao.com/fa/law12.s16.htm.

[9] Beijing shi ji ben yi liao bao xian gui ding [Beijing Regulations on Basic Medical Insurance] (promulgated by Beijing municipal government, Feb. 20, 2001, amended June 6, 2005), art. 24, http://www.china.com.cn/chinese/PI-c/909632.htm [hereinafter Beijing Reg].

[10] State Council Decision, *supra* note 1.

[11] *Id.*

[12] *Id.*

[13] Beijing Reg, *supra* note 8, art. 59.

[14] *Id.*, art. 58.

[15] *China Expands Its Social Security System*, XINHUA NEWS AGENCY, Aug. 1, 2008, http://en.chinagate.com.cn/news/2008-08/01/content_16111209.htm.

[16] Labor Law, arts. 29(3), 61, 62.

regulations confirmed the earlier-established maternity insurance fund that was created to compensate the employee for part of any wages lost during her maternity leave.[17] The fund is financed by employer contributions of not more than 1 percent of the total payroll, as determined by local governments.[18] The funds may be used for maternity allowances and related medical fees, as fixed by local governments.[19]

As of the end of June, 2008, it was reported that 84.52 million women were covered by maternity insurance.[20]

c. Work-Related Injury Insurance

The current national insurance program for work-related injuries was established in 2004.[21] As of the end of June 2008, it was reported that 130.25 million employees were covered by this insurance.[22]

The insurance is financed by employer-paid premiums, based on experience ratings. Local governments primarily administer and determine the amount of awarded benefits, which are paid from the employee compensation fund mandated by law.[23] The law also requires employers to establish reserve funds for large-scale work injuries.[24] Employers must pay the medical expenses of employees suffering from work-related injuries as well as a disability allowance based on the seriousness of the injuries, according to a schedule of ten levels of disability.[25] If the employee's labor contract expires or the employee chooses to terminate the contract, absent a settlement, the employer must still pay for the medical expenses as well as the lump sum disability allowance if the disability level is grade 7 to 10.[26]

---

[17] Qi ye zhi gong sheng yu bao xian shi xing ban fa [Trial Measures for Maternity Insurance of Staff and Workers of Enterprises] (promulgated by the Ministry of Labor, Dec. 14, 1994, effective Jan. 1, 1995), http://www.china.com.cn/chinese/zhuanti/sybx/685832.htm.

[18] *Id.*

[19] Beijing shi qi ye zhi gong sheng yu bao xian gui ding [Beijing Regulations on Maternity Insurance of Staff and Workers of Enterprises] (promulgated by the Beijing municipal government, Jan. 5, 2005, effective July 1, 2005), http://www.chinacourt.org/flwk/show1.php?file_id=99516.

[20] *China Expands Its Social Security System, supra* note 16.

[21] Gong shang bao xian tiao li [Regulations on Work-related Injury Insurance] (promulgated by the State Council, April 27, 2003) (PRC) [hereinafter WIR].

[22] *China Expands Its Social Security System, supra* note 16.

[23] WIR, art. 10.

[24] WIR, art. 13.

[25] WIR, arts. 29–35.

[26] WIR, art. 35.

d. Unemployment Benefits

The Unemployment Regulations covered more than 120 million people, with the official number of unemployed at 4 percent (8.25 million workers), though some argue the real figure is more than double that.[27]

The government's definition of an "unemployed" person is (1) an urban resident who possesses a nonagricultural residence card, (2) within a certain age range (16–retirement), (3) able and willing to work, and (4) registered with the government to work.[28] Migrant workers in urban areas are allowed to apply for unemployment benefits as well.[29] In 2007, the Employment Promotion Law was passed to regulate the labor market, encourage reemployment training, and expand workers' employment potential, as the gap between the number of new jobs and the number of those needing employment continues to widen.

In 1999, a national unemployment insurance (UI) system was created for urban workers and operated by local governments, which were also granted the authority to expand coverage.[30] The UI system is financed by employer and employee contributions of 2 percent of payroll and 1 percent of wages, respectively, and the funds are pooled within regions.[31] In some local areas, the UI funds may be used not only for benefits but also for vocational training, medical and childcare subsidies, and funeral expenses.[32]

There are system-wide standards of eligibility: an employee must be registered for UI benefits; the employer must have paid premiums for at least one year, and the employee must have been involuntarily separated from

[27] *China Records Urban Unemployment Ratio of 4%*, CHINA DAILY, April 28, 2008, http://www.chinadaily.com.cn/bizchina/2008-04/28/content_6649291.htm. *China Expands Its Social Security System*, XINHUA NEWS AGENCY, Aug. 1, 2008, http://en.chinagate.com.cn/news/2008-08/01/content_16111209.htm.

[28] *China Statistical Yearbook 2007*, http://www.stats.gov.cn/tjsj/ndsj/.

[29] Shi ye bao xian tiao li [Regulations on Unemployment Insurance] (promulgated by the State Council, Jan. 22, 1999), arts. 6, 21 (PRC), http://www.gov.cn/banshi/2005-08/04/content_20258.htm [hereinafter RUI]; Jiu ye fu wu yu jiu ye guan li gui ding [Provisions on Employment Services and Employment Management] (promulgated by the MOLSS, Nov. 5, 2007), art. 63 (PRC) (Migrant workers who have been employed for a consecutive six months in the cities can register for unemployment insurance there).

[30] *Id.*, arts. 2, 32.

[31] *Id.*, arts. 6, 7; Vickey Lee, *Unemployment Insurance and Assistance Systems in Mainland China* 23 (June 2000), http://www.legco.gov.hk/yr99-00/english/sec/library/e18.pdf.

[32] *E.g.*, Shanghai shi ye bao xian ban fa [Shanghai Regulations on Unemployment Insurance] (promulgated by the Shanghai municipal government, April 1, 1999), http://www.unn.com.cn/GB/channel335/337/829/200010/13/936.html.

employment, be able and willing to accept work, and be actively seeking work.[33] The maximum duration of benefits is twenty-four months.[34]

By the end of 2007, nationwide, 116,450,000 persons were covered by UI.[35] Among those covered, 2,860,000 persons received UI benefits. In other words, 15 percent of total employees (urban and rural) or 36 percent of urban employees were covered in the UI system. Fewer than 2.5 percent of the total number covered or fewer than 1 percent of urban employees received benefits.[36]

e. Pension Insurance

The 1994 Labor Law provided for the development of a social security system that included retirement and pension benefits.[37] These were developed at the local levels, and eventually, in 1997, the State Council announced a national scheme for all urban enterprises, but that excluded town-village enterprises and the entire rural areas.[38] It has a three-tier structure: (1) a basic pension plan, which is mandatory and contributed to by employer and employee; (2) a supplementary pension plan, which is optional and is maintained by enterprises; and (3) a personal savings account.[39]

---

[33] RUI, *supra* note 28, art. 14.

[34] Duration varies based on the length of the premium payment. *Id.*, art. 17. Draft Social Security Law Article 42 provides that the duration of unemployment insurance is twelve months for unemployed persons whose premium contribution was over a year but fewer than five years; eighteen months for contribution over five years but fewer than ten years, and twenty-four months for contribution over ten years. If after getting unemployment insurance, the job seeker gets a job but gets fired again, the premium contribution period will be recalculated, and the combined duration of the two unemployment insurance enjoyment cannot last more than twenty-four months.

[35] *China Expands Its Social Security System, supra* note 14.

[36] The National Statistical Bureau issued the following report: "[P]opulation covered in the unemployment insurance at the year-end hit 116.45 million persons, an increase of 4.58 million persons. Of the total, the migrant workers grew to 11.50 million persons. A total of 22 provinces (autonomous regions, municipalities) and Xingjian Production and Construction Corps adjusted unemployment insurance standards. The number of beneficiaries of unemployment insurance valued at 2.86 million persons, declined 410 thousand persons, year-on-year. The revenue and expenses of unemployment insurance fund reached 47.2 and 21.8 billion yuan, up by 17.5 and 9.0 percent, year-on-year. The accumulated balance of the unemployment insurance fund at the year-end is valued at 97.9 billion yuan." Statistical Communiqué on Labor and Social Security Development in 2007 (issued by the National Statistical Bureau), http://bg2.mofcom.gov.cn/aarticle/aboutchina/economy/200806/20080605604088.html. The number of workers in the urban versus rural labor force was 293,500,000 and 476,400,000, respectively.

[37] Labor Law, arts. 70, 73.

[38] Draft Social Security Law Article 18 provides that China will gradually establish a separate basic pension system for town-village enterprises and the rural areas.

[39] *White Paper: China Basically Establishes Social Security System*, April 29, 2002, http://english.peopledaily.com.cn/200204/29/eng20020429_94947.shtml. For discussion on

The basic pension plan is funded by employers and employees through the payroll withholding system; the amount of contributions is determined by the local government, and the funds go into both a pooled fund and a personal account for each employee.[40] The employer's contribution is to be no more than 20 percent of the total cost of employee's wages, whereas the employee's contribution is about 8 percent of his or her salary.[41] Every month the personal account's balance shall be 11 percent of the employee's total wages received during covered employment, with all of the employee's deductions deposited into this account and the employer's contribution partially deposited into this account until it reaches this 11 percent balance.[42] This personal account is maintained by the designated state-owned bank, and saving interests will be credited to it.[43] The personal account shall not be used for purposes other than a pension plan, and the account should be able to be transferred when an employee changes a job or moves to another city.[44] Early withdrawal is not permitted,[45] and funds from the personal account can be withdrawn only after a certain period of time.

Benefit eligibility, limits, and payouts vary by region, and participation in supplemental plans is encouraged by the government, particularly at the local levels. Enforcement of employer contributions has been one of the biggest obstacles facing local governments. For any default payment by the employer, the local labor government can charge a daily 0.2 percent penalty,[46] not to exceed 10,000 RMB.[47] The local government can also impose a judicial lien to garnish the default payment from the employer's other property.[48]

---

implementation of China's pension system, *see* Mark Frazier, China's *Pension Reform and Its Discontents*, in ENGAGING THE LAW IN CHINA: STATE, SOCIETY, AND POSSIBILITIES FOR JUSTICE (Neil J. Diamant, Stanley B. Lubman, & Kevin J. O'Brien eds., 2005).

[40] Guo wu yuan guan yu jian li tong yi de qi ye zhi gong ji ben yang lao bao xian zhi du de jue ding [Notice on Establishing Uniform Enterprise Basic Pension Plan, State Council] (promulgated by the State Council, July 16, 1997), art. 1, http://www.people.com.cn/GB/shizheng/252/7486/7498/20020228/675965.html [hereinafter Pension Notice].

[41] Pension Notice, art. 3.

[42] Pension Notice, art. 4.

[43] *Id*. Taxation on interest payments for individual pension accounts is exempted under the Draft Social Security Law, art. 13.

[44] *Id*.

[45] *Id*. Article 13 of the Draft Social Security Law provides that the balance in the individual pension account is inheritable.

[46] She hui bao xian fei zheng jiao zan xing tiao li [Interim Regulations on Social Security Payment] (promulgated by the State Council, Jan. 22, 1999), art. 13, http://www.gov.cn/banshi/2005-08/04/content_20250.htm.

[47] *Id*. art. 23.

[48] *Id*. art. 26.

The Labor Contract Law addresses the pressing issue of portability of individual accounts in the various social insurance plans, including the pension insurance plan. It states that the government "will take measures to establish a comprehensive system that enables workers' social insurance accounts to be transferred from one region to another and to be continued in such other region." No early withdrawal is permitted.[49]

The benefit structure of the pension insurance plan varies by locality, but general principles of the plan allow retirement as of qualifying ages, which are generally at age sixty for men and fifty or fifty-five for women. If employees have contributed to the plan for longer than fifteen years, then on retirement, their monthly pension benefit includes both the basic pension, paid from pension fund, and a personal benefit, paid from their personal account.[50] The basic pension is determined by local government, but generally benefits are at 20 percent of the average wage of local workers. The personal benefit account is the total personal account balance divided by 120 (months).[51] Pension benefits due after that period are paid from the reserve fund.[52]

If the employee has been contributing for fewer than fifteen years, then he or she receives no basic pension paid from the pension fund, but a lump sum payment is provided, which is the balance in his or her personal account.[53]

Other voluntary contribution-based programs include enterprise annuity programs (less than 20 percent of local enterprises are estimated to participate in such programs) funded either by employer or by employer and employee contributions; there is also a voluntary rural worker pension program.[54]

The pension insurance program is still expanding at the local levels and has not yet been fully implemented. By the end of June 2008, it was reported that 210.29 million people were covered by the pension insurance program, up from 201.37 million at the same time in 2007.[55]

---

[49] LCL, art. 49. The Draft Social Security Law allows the portability of individual accounts for the basic pension plan (Article 17), the basic medical plan (Article 28), and for unemployment insurance (Article 48).

[50] *Id.* art. 5.

[51] *Id.*

[52] US Social Security Administration Office of Policy, Social Security Programs throughout the World: Asia and the Pacific, 2006, China – Old Age, Disability, and Survivors, http://www.ssa.gov/policy/docs/progdesc/ssptw/2006-2007/asia/china.html.

[53] Pension Notice, *supra* note 39, art. 5.

[54] Qi ye nian jin shi xing ban fa [Trial Measures for Enterprise Annuities] (promulgated by MOLSS, Dec. 30, 2003, effective May 1, 2004), http://news.xinhuanet.com/zhengfu/2004-04/05/content_1401243.htm.

[55] *China Expands Its Social Security System, supra* note 16.

f. Housing Fund

An additional nationally mandated social program, though not an insurance system, is the Housing Provident Fund.[56] It is funded by employer and employee contributions, as determined by local governments, and is designed to provide assistance to employees in buying, building, or renovating homes or in paying rent.[57] Unused individual account monies, with interest, are to be available to employees on retirement.[58]

g. Union Fund

Employers with labor unions are required to contribute 2 percent of the payroll to the labor union fund.[59] These funds are to be used by the union to serve "the staff and workers and for labor union activities."[60]

3. Mandated Leave Benefits

a. Legal Holidays

By law, employees receive seven paid holidays falling over eleven workdays: one-day holidays for New Year's Day, Tomb Sweeping Day, Labor Day, Dragon Boat Festival Day, and Mid-Autumn Festival and three-day holidays for Spring Festival and National Day. However, traditionally employers rearrange work schedules so seven consecutive days off are provided for Spring Festival and National Day, thus giving employees so-called Golden Weeks.[61] Another paid holiday is Women's Day (April 8), on which employers are required to provide women with one-half day off work.[62]

---

[56] Guo wu yuan guan yu shen hua cheng zhen zhu fang zhi du gai ge de jue ding [Decision of the State Council on the Deeping of Urban Housing Reform] (promulgated by the State Council, July 18, 1994), http://news.xinhuanet.com/ziliao/2005-03/16/content_2705571.htm.

[57] *Id.*; Guo wu yuan guan yu xiu gai zhu fang gong ji jin guan li tiao li de jue ding [Decision of the State Council on Amending Regulations for the Administration of Housing Funds] (promulgated by the State Council, Mar. 24, 2008), http://news.xinhuanet.com/zhengfu/2002-03/28/content_334893.htm.

[58] *Id.*

[59] Gong hui fa [Labor Union Law] (promulgated by the Standing Comm. of Nat'l People's Cong., April 3, 1992, amended on Oct. 27, 2001), art. 42 (PRC).

[60] *Id.*

[61] Quan guo nian jie ji ji nian ri fang jia ban fa [Measures for Holidays on National Festivals and Commemorative Days] (promulgated by the State Council, Dec. 23, 1949, amended on Dec. 14, 2007, effective on Jan. 1, 2008), art. 2, http://www.gov.cn/zwgk/2007-12/16/content_835226.htm.

[62] *Id.* art. 3.

b. Paid Leave: Annual, Medical, and Maternity

Annual Leave

The 1994 Labor Law provides that employees working continuously for one year are to be provided paid annual leave "in accordance with state regulations."[63] As of January 1, 2008, a new national minimum annual leave regulation based on accrued service came into effect: five days for employees who have worked one but fewer than ten years; ten days if worked ten but fewer than twenty years; and fifteen days if worked more than twenty years.[64] Unused leave may be carried over or paid out at 300 percent of the employee's daily average wage.[65] Offsets of accrued annual leave are permitted where certain other types of leave have been taken during the year.[66]

Medical Leave

Employees who are sick or become ill or injured from a non–work-related injury are entitled to job protection[67] and leave for medical treatment.[68] The leave may be intermittent or consecutive within time limits. The length of the leave is fixed by national standards and varies with the length of service in the workforce and with the employer.[69] For example, for an employee who has been in the workforce for fewer than ten years, the employer must provide up to six months of medical leave annually for employees working for more than five years and up to three months for those working fewer than five years.[70] For employees who have been in the workforce ten years or more, the employer's obligation ranges from six months to 24 months (over a thirty-month period).[71]

Wages must be paid during the medical leave at not less than 80 percent of the *local minimum wage*, though the actual amount paid by a given employer

[63] Labor Law, art. 45.
[64] Zhi gong dai xin nian xiu jia tiao li [Regulation on Paid Annual Leave for Staff and Workers] (promulgated by the State Council, Dec. 14, 2007, effective Jan. 1, 2008), art 3., http://www.gov.cn/flfg/2007-12/16/content_835527.htm.
[65] *Id.* art. 5.
[66] *Id.*
[67] Labor Law, art. 29(2).
[68] Qi ye zhi gong huan bing huo fei yin gong fu shang yi liao qi gui ding [Regulations Concerning the Period of Medical Treatment for Enterprise Employees Who Fall Ill or Become Injured Off Duty] (promulgated by the Ministry of Labor, Dec. 1, 1994, effective Jan. 1, 1995), http://www.circhina.com/labour/298-4845.htm.
[69] *Id.*
[70] *Id.*
[71] *Id.*

may be higher and will vary by locale.[72] If an employee is injured in a work-related accident, he or she is entitled to medical treatment, and the costs will be paid from the work-related injury insurance fund.[73] If the employee must take a leave of absence for medical treatment for the accident or occupational disease, his or her wages and social benefits will be paid by the employer during the absence for up to one to two years.[74] After that period, only medical benefits but not wages will continue.[75] When a disabled employee is assessed and the injury graded, the insurance fund will cover the related costs as stipulated by law.[76] If an employee dies from a work-related injury, relatives are entitled to a lump sum subsidy, as well as a dependent's pension and a funeral subsidy paid from the insurance fund.[77]

Maternity Leave

The Labor Law provides that female employees are entitled to ninety days of paid maternity leave,[78] with some extensions permitted depending on the mother's medical condition.[79] Full wages must be paid during maternity leave. Employees must be in compliance with government birth control regulations to be eligible for maternity leave and its benefits.[80] After the birth, the employer must allow the mother to take two half-hour breaks per day to feed and attend to her child who is younger than one year of age.[81] There is no paternity leave policy at the national level, though some local governments have provided it.[82]

[72] Guan yu guan che zhi xing "Lao dong fa" ruo gan wen ti de yi jian [Opinion Concerning Some Issues Related to the Implementation of the Labor Law] (promulgated by the Ministry of Labor, Aug. 4, 1995), art. 59, http://www.chinalaw.gov.cn/jsp/contentpub/browser/contentpro.jsp?contentid=c01762522273.

[73] WIL, *supra* note 20, art. 29.

[74] *Id.* art. 31.

[75] *Id.*

[76] *Id.* arts. 32–5.

[77] *Id.* art. 37.

[78] Labor Law, art. 62.

[79] Nv zhi gong lao dong bao hu gui ding [Regulations on Labor Protection for Female Workers] (promulgated by the State Council, July 21, 1988, effective Sept. 1, 1988), art. 8, http://www.china.com.cn/chinese/funv/228556.htm.

[80] *Id.* art. 15.

[81] *Id.* art. 9.

[82] E.g., Changsha shi ji hua sheng yu jiang li you hui zheng ce shi shi ban fa [Implementing Measures of Changsha on Reward Policy for Childbirth Planning] (promulgated by the Changsha municipal government, June 24, 2005), art. 11(3) (For enterprise workers who only give birth to one child, the father could get a fifteen-day paternity leave).

c. Other Leaves Not Clearly Mandated: Home, Marriage, and Bereavement

Home Leave

In 1981, regulations were adopted mandating to provide paid leave and travel costs home for employees to visit their relatives. Those employees who had worked longer than a year and who are single could visit their parents for twenty days per year or forty-five days over two years. Married employees could visit their spouse (thirty days), and every four years, married employees could leave for twenty days to visit their parents.[83] This regulation was never changed, and there is uncertainty whether it imposes duties today for all employers, particularly in view of the 2008 legal requirement for annual leaves.

Marriage and Bereavement Leave

Another leave policy written in 1980 for SOEs provided that paid leave would be granted by the employer for one to three days (but no travel expenses) for an employee getting married or to attend a funeral of a direct relative who lived at an out-of-town location.[84] This regulation was never changed, and there is uncertainty whether it imposes enforceable duties today for all employers, particularly in view of the 2008 legal requirement for annual leaves.

4. Nonmandated Employee Benefits

Voluntary benefits for employees, such as incentives and allowances, have long been used around the world to enhance employee performance and retention, particularly where unattractive working conditions exist. In China, from 2001 to 2005, average annual employee turnover rates were reported to increase from under 9 percent to around 14 percent,[85] and in response, employers are increasingly using incentives, such as bonuses, share options, and profit sharing.[86] The landscape of employee benefits is expanding with employers

---

[83] Guo wu yuan guan yu zhi gong tan qin dai yu de gui ding [Regulations on Treatment for Employees Who Visit Their Relatives] (promulgated by the State Council, Mar. 14, 1981), http://www.51labour.com/LawCenter/lawshow-15959.html.

[84] Guan yu zhi ding "Guo wu yuan guan yu zhi gong tan qin dai yu de gui ding" shi shi xi ze de ruo gan wen ti de yi jian [Opinions of the State Labor Bureau on Several Issues Concerning the Formulation of the Detailed Implementing Rules for the Regulations on Treatment for Employees Who Visit Their Relatives] (promulgated by the State Labor Bureau, Mar. 26, 1981), http://china.findlaw.cn/fagui/sh/23/57635.html.

[85] *Best Practices: Human Resources: Strategies for Recruitment, Retention, and Compensation*, U.S.-China Business Council (October 2006), www.uschina.org/info/chops/2006/hr-best-practices.html (last visited Oct. 14, 2008).

[86] Fang Lee Cooke, HRM WORK AND EMPLOYMENT IN CHINA 82 (Routledge, 2005).

unilaterally or through negotiations with labor unions adding contractual employee benefits.[87]

Incentives are as simple and inexpensive as employee recognition and seniority for job bidding or may involve monetary bonuses and rewards, including paid life insurance, travel, education or training opportunities, and wage increases above the minimum wage.[88]

Allowances (sometimes referred to as *subsidies*) are also used by employers as a means of retaining and compensating employees. For example, employers may supplement mandatory benefits, such as sick leave, and may provide allowances for travel, meals, clothing, or childcare.[89] Working conditions are also often addressed by premium pay/allowances for undesirable jobs and the provision of special protective equipment.

Occasionally, a mandatory benefit is mixed in with what might be thought to be a voluntary benefit. An example is the *warm weather subsidy* issued by the government in June 2007, which mandates subsidies for employees working outdoors when temperatures reach 35 degrees Centigrade.[90] Some local governments limit the number of work hours during times of high temperatures.[91]

---

[87] *See* Maggie Rauch, *Year of Carrot: Incentives in China*, Oct. 31, 2006, www.allbusiness.com/services/business-services-advertising/4214858-1.html (last visited Oct. 14, 2008) (Illustrative individual and collective contractual benefit provisions on file with the author)

[88] *E.g., China Social Security and Private Employee Benefits*, Chinese Graduate Recruitment, February 15, 2008, www.cambridgenetwork.co.uk/news/article/default.aspx?objid=44203.

[89] *Employing Local Personnel in China*, JLJ Group, www.jljgroup.com/uploads/Information_Guides/Employing_Local_Personnel_in_China.

[90] Guan yu jin yi bu jia qiang gong zuo chang suo xia ji fang shu jiang wen gong zuo de tong zhi [Notice on Further Improvement of the Work on Summer Sunstroke Prevention at the Workplace] (promulgated by MOH, MOLSS, SAWS, & ACFTU, June 8, 2007), art. 4(7), http://www.gov.cn/gzdt/2007-06/08/content_641702.htm.

[91] *Employee Entitled to Warm Weather Subsidies*, China Employment Law Update 2 (June 2007), http://www.bakernet.com/NR/rdonlyres/10A2F3A2-1CD9-4BFB-98E6-742FB43857C9/0/china_employmentlaw_ca_jun07.pdf. *See also* 37°C yi shang, bu fa gao we bu tie wei fa [Warm Weather Subsidy Required in Law When the Temperature Is Higher Than 37°C], http://politics.people.com.cn/GB/14562/5705134.html.

PART VI

DISCIPLINE AND TERMINATION UNDER EMPLOYMENT AGREEMENTS

12

Employer Work Rules, Discipline, and Termination

1. Employer Work Rules and Discipline

The Labor Law and Labor Contract Law require employers to establish labor rules and regulations to ensure that workers enjoy their rights and perform their labor obligations; the LCL further requires the employer to have certain "consultations" with employees about those rules.[1] Under the LCL, the employer first has a duty of "discussion" with the worker's Congress or all of the employees when it "formulates, revises or decides on rules and regulations or material matters that have a direct bearing on the immediate interests of its workers."[2] These topics include "labor compensation, work hours, rest, leave, work safety and hygiene, insurance benefits, employee training, work discipline, or work quota management."[3] The Congress or employee group shall put forward a "proposal and comments," whereupon the matter shall be determined by "consultations" between the employer and the labor union or the employee representatives. If there is disagreement on the rules' appropriateness, the employer is to seek to improve the rules by amendments. Interestingly, the law does not explicitly require consent before the rules are implemented.[4] Handbook rules and regulations on the above topics that are in conflict with the law are invalid.[5]

Employers' work rules on conduct typically lay out conduct standards with consequences for violations, including warnings, suspensions, terminations, loss of pay, and demotions. They also provide a basis for employers and arbitrators in evaluating the performance of employees, and they offer justifications

---

[1] Labor Law, art. 4; LCL, art. 4.
[2] LCL, art. 4.
[3] *Id.*
[4] *Id.* The rules should be made public or communicated to the workers.
[5] LCL, art. 80.

for personnel decisions other than discipline, such as granting leaves and bonuses. An example of an employer's disciplinary rules with fines for their violation is as follows. An employer making toys in the Pearl River Delta had rules with the following penalties: for "warnings" (e.g., "failure to meet quality requirements," RMB 10–30); for "minor mistakes" (e.g., "reckless work and concealing defective items," RMB 30–90); and for "major mistakes" (e.g., ignoring quality control guidelines, leading to "defective products," RMB 90–170).[6] For these employees, who earned an average of RMB 500–800 per month, the amount of the fine was significant.[7] Issues will arise when an employer rule seems to violate existing laws (e.g., coercing work by intimidation) or is unreasonable. In addition, after implementation of the LCL, an employer's failure to properly incorporate these rules into the labor contract and otherwise follow the required procedures of consultation can render them invalid and unenforceable as illegal rules.

The following illustrative language (though not necessarily *model* language) has been used to incorporate employer rules into a labor contract:

Labor Discipline

1. Party B shall strictly comply with the various Rules and Regulations prepared by Party A in accordance with law.
2. In the event that Party B has complied with rules and regulations in an exemplary manner or in the event that Party B has violated such rules and regulations, Party A shall reward or discipline Party B, as the case may be.[8]

Before the LCL, the rules and their enforcement were typically left to the discretion of the employer. Abuses by some employers, as illustrated by the following rules, which were put in operation prior to the LCL, helped hasten the LCL reforms that require some employee participation in the rule making.

Worker rules at one factory included the following: "If a worker is injured either through his own fault or by mistake, no medical leave is permitted." In the section on rules pertaining to safety, employees were told, "No chatting is allowed during work hours, no matter whether workers are engaged in single-machine production or line work." Employees were also instructed how to line up to enter the premises to start work, how to line up in the cafeteria, how to pick up their food, and how to spend their downtime in the dormitory (no fighting, no gambling, no chess or poker, no smoking, no unauthorized lights, etc.).

---

[6] Stephen Frost, *Rules and Regulations in Chinese Factories*, 9 J. Occupational & Environmental Health 317–318 (2003).
[7] *Id.* at 317–19. It may also raise issues of meeting minimum wage obligations.
[8] Onecle, www.contracts.onecle.com/ctrip/emp.shtml.

At Mattel's Number Two Toy Factory in Chang'an, management reserved the right to fire workers for what was termed "a physical problem" (which included work-related injuries and illnesses) and to keep their pay. In addition, workers had to pay for electricity and water used in the dormitory and a factory ID card; make a deposit on the equipment provided by management that they used to perform job tasks; and contribute to a medical fund, even though company-paid medical care could be denied if it was found that the workers were negligent or their injury or illness was the result of a "mistake."[9] New employees also had to pay for the eleven-chapter, ninety-three-page employee handbook.[10]

Many of these rules, even had they been imposed following the LCL-required procedures of consultation, would be deemed unenforceable as illegal rules. Others, however, could provide the basis for discipline or termination if materially violated. In a case in Hangzhou, an employee was terminated following a quarrel with a supervisor because it violated an employer rule that an employee should never "publicly contradict a supervisor." The discharge was upheld by the labor arbitration tribunal and the court on appeal.[11] These standards then, can determine rights and duties, such as entitlement to severance pay, continuing employment, and damages.[12]

Failure to have "authorized" rules to deal with certain employment situations also could foreclose an employer from acting unilaterally against an employee, as any unincorporated and unauthorized rules would be unenforceable. A 2007 case in Beijing found that the employer, absent any authority in the contract (not in conflict with the law), acted in violation of its employee's labor contract when it unilaterally lowered his pay and demoted him.[13] Although this action took place during a reorganization, it would appear analogous and applicable to a disciplinary case on the issue of employer authority. The court enforced the arbitration remedy of reinstatement and restoration of position and pay.[14] A similar holding in a Shanghai court found that the employer

9 Sandy Smith, *China: Out with the Old and In with the Old?* www.occupationalhaards.com/articles/10952, quoting from Frost, *supra* note 6, at 317–19.

10 Frost, *supra* note 6, at 319.

11 Lu Shihua, *Employee Handbook Challenges Labor Law*, CHINA LABOR AND SOCIAL SECURITY NEWS (March 6, 2004).

12 LCL, art. 39(2).

13 *Beijing Court Rules Unilateral Pay Cut, Demotion Illegal*, Baker & McKenzie, CHINA EMPLOYMENT LAW UPDATE (Oct. 2007), at 4, http://www.bakernet.com/NR/rdonlyres/615192A9-2233-475D-AC67-7D1D12BD7097/0/china_employment_lawupdate_octo7.pdf; *see also* Guo Jingxia & Wu Xiaoxiang, Beijing – Gong hui zhu xi wei quan an zhong shen sheng su [Beijing – Chairman of the Enterprise Labor Union Finally Won His Case], April 24, 2007, http://acftu.people.com.cn/GB/67575/5656126.html.

14 *Id.*

violated the labor contract by unilaterally reducing the salary of an employee without the employee's consent or other authorization.[15] In addition, some local government regulations place limitations on the amounts of economic punishments used by employers.[16]

2. Termination under Labor Contracts

a. When a Labor Contract Ends versus Terminates

Some labor contracts automatically end (*zhongzhi*) at a certain time (e.g., when fixed-term or project contracts expire) or when a condition occurs (e.g., the employee dies), as opposed to there being a termination (*jiechu*) by mutual agreement or by dismissal.[17] The significance of this distinction – under the Labor Law, severance pay is not required on expiration of a fixed-term contract – has been diminished under the LCL, as it requires severance pay at the end of any fixed-term labor contract unless the employee refuses to extend the contract under the same or better terms.[18] The prohibitions on terminating employees under Article 42 of the LCL, discussed in the next section, mandate the extension of a term contract "until the relevant circumstance ceases to exist," at which point the contract ends, except for work-related injuries, which are covered by separate legislation.[19]

b. Termination by Employer without Notice or Severance Pay

Termination of an employee by the employer may or may not require notice and the payment of severance pay. Summary termination by an employer

[15] Reinstatement was awarded under regulations protecting pregnant women and must be at former wages, not at a lower level; therefore, any employer rules on rehiring to the contrary would be illegal. *Pregnant Employee Wins Reinstatement after Having Agreed to Terminate Employment*, Baker & McKenzie, CHINA EMPLOYMENT LAW UPDATE (June 2008), at 6; see also Jie yue hou fang zhi huai yun, su qing che xiao jie yue he tong [Learning about Pregnancy after Termination of Labor Contract, Employee Sued for Reinstatement], April 23, 2008, http://sh.xinmin.cn/shehui/2008/04/23/1126729.html.

[16] The amount of each individual fine or cumlative fines in a month may not exceed 30 percent of the monthly wage of the worker punished. Also, the same violation may not be punished more than once. Shenzhen jing ji te qu he xie lao dong guan xi cu jin tiao li [Regulations for the Promotion of Harmonious Labor Relations in the Shenzhen Special Economic Zone (SEZ)] (promulgated by the Shenzhen Municipal Peopls's Cong., Oct. 6, 2008, effective November 1, 2008), art. 16, http://www.npc.gov.cn/npc/xinwen/dfrd/guangdong/2008-10/08/content_1452415.htm.

[17] LCL, art. 44(1–6).

[18] LCL, art. 46(5).

[19] LCL, arts. 45, 42(2).

without severance pay (or prior notice) is allowed by statute in six instances: (1) during the probationary period; (2) for material or serious breach of employer rules and regulations; (3) for a serious dereliction of duty or graft causing substantial damage to the employer; (4) where there is a employment relationship with another employer that materially affects the employee's duties, which the employee will not rectify on the employer's request; (5) the party's use of deception or coercion to induce the making of a labor contract; (6) the employee's criminal liability is being pursued.[20]

Probationary employees, those not satisfying the "conditions of employment," may be terminated without severance pay. To prove that there exists an employment relationship more than an "at-will" relationship, the employer would need to produce evidence, such as job advertisements and a job description, that the employee's performance was measured and found wanting.

Material breaches of employer rules and regulations center around two issues – whether the rules are valid and whether the breach was "material." The issue of materiality may ultimately need to be decided in each case by the labor arbitration process. In a recent case in which materiality was found, an employee was dismissed for making excessive phone calls at work in violation of employer rules.[21] The rule limited personal phone calls to one hour per week, but the employee was proven to have made more than twenty hours of such phone calls during a two-week period.[22] In another case, a court in Ningbo, Zhejiang, held that the employer's rules, first posted on a bulletin board in 2003, were invalid because the recently enacted LCL consultation procedures were not followed.[23] Therefore, terminating the employee for excessive absences under the old rules was invalid.[24]

A *serious dereliction of duty or graft causing substantial harm to the employer* can justify a summary termination without severance pay.[25] Again, "serious dereliction" will be determined on a case-by-case basis in the labor arbitration process. But there is some guidance that suggests that a finding of "substantial harm caused to the employer" will generally be resolved in the employer's favor, as legal rules state that determination is left to the employer and its

---

[20] LCL, art. 39(1–6); items 1, 2, 3, and 6 are also contained in Labor Law, art. 25(1–4).
[21] *Dismissal for Excessive Personal Calls Upheld*, Baker & McKenzie, CHINA EMPLOYMENT LAW UPDATE (Dec. 2007), at 3–4, www.bmhk.com/PRC/2007-534.pdf.
[22] *Id.*
[23] *Court Invadidates Company Rules*, Baker & McKenzie, CHINA EMPLOYMENT LAW UPDATE (June, 2008), 4, www.bakernet.com/BakerNet/Resources/Publications/Recent+ Publications/ChinaEmploymentLawUpdateJun08.htm.
[24] *Id.*; LCL, art. 4.
[25] LCL, art. 39(3).

internal rules.[26] An illustration of the difficulty of determining issues under this section of the law is presented by a widely publicized Beijing case in which a management employee who was also a union leader was terminated for a "serious" violation; the employee caused the employer sufficient "harm" by failing to obtain a drinking water supply qualification, resulting in the employer having to pay a modest fine.[27] The employee ultimately prevailed in labor arbitration, and the Beijing Shuiyi District Court upheld the arbitration, finding the employer had failed to meet its burden of proof on sufficient harm.[28] Employee graft cases also fall under this provision or the above section on material breach of employer rules, and rulings will likely turn on intent and the amounts involved in the graft.[29]

An *employment relationship with more than one employer* is not prohibited unless it adversely affects performance or is contractually limited, such as by a covenant not to compete, moonlighting prohibition, etc.[30] This statutory provision could serve as an explicit duty of loyalty even on noncompetitive outside work done during the term of the labor contract, without the employer having to obtain agreement to it and pay for it.[31]

The LCL prohibits the use of deception or coercion by an employee to induce the making of a labor contract.[32] A recent illustration is the ruling in a case of an employee who was fired for resume fraud. In November 2007 the Beijing Chongwen District Court upheld the firing of a Japanese national who had falsified his resume.[33] The court reportedly cited Article 18 of the Labor Law – the same provisions as those in LCL Article 39(5)[34] – to rule that the

---

[26] Guan yu "Lao dong fa" ruo gan tiao wen de shuo ming [Explanations of Several Articles of the Labor Law] (promulgated by the Ministry of Labor, Sept. 5, 1994), art. 25, http://china.findlaw.cn/laodongfa/zfemghghgldf/1533.html [hereinafter Labor Law Explanation].

[27] Pan yue, Wai qi gong hui zhu xi wei quan bei chao zhuang gao gong si sheng su [Union Leader in FIE Fired due to Bargaining for Labor Rights, Sued the Company and Won], http://content.chinahr.com/laodongfayuan/Article(49147)ArticleInfo.view. Case discussed in Lily Wei Zhou, *Labor Union Leader's Wrongful Employment Termination Case*, CHINA LAW & PRACTICE (May 2007), http://www.chinalawandpractice.com/Article/1690272/Search/Results/Labour-Union-Leaders-Wrongful-Employment-Termination-Case.html?Keywords=Employment.

[28] *Id.*

[29] LCL, art. 39(3).

[30] LCL, arts. 23, 24 (The covenant not to compete must be negotiated and paid for).

[31] An action was found to lie in contract and tort; *see Interesting Case on Non-Competition Clauses in Employment Contracts*, http://lawprofessors.typepad.com/china_law_prof_blog/2008/06/interesting-cas.html.

[32] LCL, art. 39(5).

[33] *False Resume Leads to Firing of Foreign National*, Baker & McKenzie, CHINA EMPLOYMENT LAW UPDATE (Dec. 2007), at 4, www.bmhk.com/PRC/2007-534.pdf.

[34] *Id.*

employee's labor contract was invalid because the employee had committed fraud to enter into the contract. Because the contract was invalid as of the date of execution, the employer in this case arguably would not have been required to comply with statutory termination requirements, such as notifying the union of the termination. In another resume fraud case, Tsinghua University fired an assistant dean after discovering misrepresentations on his resume about his academic publications.[35]

Summary termination without severance pay is permitted where an employee's *criminal liability* is being pursued.[36] The implementing regulations further provide that the worker shall pay to the employer the liquidated damages stipulated in the employment contract if the worker has criminal liability pursued in accordance with the law.[37] An illustrative case under the current law arose in March 2008; an employer's summary termination was upheld at the labor arbitration level because the employee had been prosecuted and convicted for assault, but no criminal penalty had been imposed because of his crime's minor nature.[38] The court on appeal affirmed the arbitration decision, specifically citing LCL Article 39(6) as the basis for its decision.[39]

c. Termination by Employer with Notice and Severance Pay

Article 40 of the LCL authorizes the employer to terminate the employee on three grounds with thirty-day notice or with one month's wages in lieu of notice. Article 46(3) requires severance pay in these three instances. Article 41 provides a fourth ground that allows termination with severance pay for qualifying mass terminations[40] and requires thirty-day notice.[41]

The *first ground* allows termination (1) at the end of the set period of medical care for an illness or non–work-related injury, and (2) if the employee is unable to work at the original or employer-arranged work, which the employee is required to first attempt.[42] Reimbursement for the costs of medical care

---

[35] Vivian Wu, *University Fires Fibbing Professor*, SOUTH CHINA MORNING POST (March 28, 2006).

[36] LCL, art. 39(6).

[37] Lao dong he tong fa shi shi xi ze [Implementing Regulations for the Labor Contract Law] (promulgated by the State Council, Sept. 18, 2008), arts. 25, 26(5) (PRC).

[38] *Lack of Criminal Penalties Ruled No Bar to Terminate Employee*, Baker & McKenzie, CHINA EMPLOYMENT LAW UPDATE (April 2008), at 5–6.

[39] *Id.* Note, LCL, art. 43 requires advance notice to the union as to the reason for the unilateral termination.

[40] LCL, art. 46(5).

[41] LCL, art. 41(1–4).

[42] LCL, art. 40(1).

is available for three to twenty-four months, depending on the length of employment.[43]

The *second ground* that requires notice and severance pay is when an employee is determined to be incompetent even after training or adjustment of his or her position.[44] There likely needs to be some factual basis for that determination, such as deficiencies in measured performance in view of announced job expectations, as well as evidence of attempts to retrain or reassign the employee.

The *third ground* allowing termination with notice and severance pay occurs when there is a major change in "objective circumstances relied upon at the time of the conclusion of the labor contract" that renders performance unperformable (impossible, *force majeure*, etc.), and after consultations, the parties cannot agree on amending the contract.[45] Fact-intensive issues may arise on a number of issues ranging from new government restrictions, loss of licenses, relocations, reorganizations, transfers, mergers, and acquisitions; even loss of a major customer might fall under this category.[46] In mergers, the surviving entity may offer a new labor contract that, on the employee's consent, serves as an amendment to the original.[47] Legal liabilities of employers in this area, as in many others, can be adjusted by legal provisions addressing certain contingencies, such as transfer or reassignment provisions.

The *fourth ground* allows for workforce reductions by mass terminations and requires payment of severance pay and thirty-day notice.[48] Prerequisites for using this ground require a termination of twenty employees or 10 percent of the employer's total workforce, prior explanation to the union or all employees, consideration of their opinions, and reporting the workforce reduction plan to government authorities.[49] There are four qualifying circumstances: (1) restructuring pursuant to the Enterprise Bankruptcy Law; (2) serious difficulties in production or business operations; (3) changes in production, business methods, or technological innovations and, after amendment of labor contracts,

---

[43] Labor Law, art. 29; Qi ye zhi gong huan bing huo fei yin gong fu shang yi liao qi gui ding [Regulations Concerning the Period of the Medical Treatment for Enterprise Employees Who Fall Ill or Become Injured Off Duty] (promulgated by the Ministry of Labor, Dec. 1, 1994, effective Jan. 1, 1995), http://www.circhina.com/labour/298-4845.htm.

[44] LCL, art. 40(2).

[45] LCL, art. 40(3).

[46] Labor Law Explanation, *supra* note 25, art. 26.

[47] Guan yu guan che zhi xing "Lao dong fa" ruo gan wen ti de yi jian [Opinions on Several Questions Regarding Implementing of the Labor Law] (promulgated by the Ministry of Labor, Aug. 14, 1995), arts. 13, 37, http://www.chinalaw.gov.cn/jsp/contentpub/browser/contentpro.jsp?contentid=c01762522273; LCL, arts. 34, 35.

[48] LCL, art. 41(1–4).

[49] LCL, art. 41.

a continued need to reduce the workforce; and (4) a major change in the objective circumstances relied on at the time of the conclusion of the labor contracts, rendering them unperformable.[50]

In meeting the above grounds, employers have some guidance at the national level, but most of the detailed requirements on terms such as "seriousness," "hardship," "objective economic circumstances," and "unperformable" are left for local determination. In making those decisions, local governments consider such factors as the length of an employer's economic downturn, its ability to pay debts, and other evidentiary documentation.[51]

When reducing the workforce, certain employees receive preference for retention.[52] They are employees (1) with relatively long fixed-term contracts, or (2) with open-ended contracts, or (3) who are the only family member to be employed and whose families have an elderly person or a minor for whom they need to provide.[53] When rehiring within six months of mass terminations, the employer must first give notice to those terminated and, if all things are equal, give these employees preference in hiring.[54]

d. Limits and Prohibitions on Unilateral Termination by the Employer

Employers face certain procedural *limitations* before they may terminate an employee. Article 43 of the LCL requires the employer to provide advance notice to the labor union before any unilateral termination of an employee. The labor union has the right to respond, and the employer must consider this response and provide the union with written notification of how it will deal with the matter.[55]

Employers are *prohibited* from unilaterally terminating employees who fall under the following categories, even including those who can be terminated with notice and severance pay under Articles 40 and 41, discussed earlier[56]: (1) those exposed to occupational disease hazards and who have not undergone a predeparture occupational check-up or are suspected of having contracted an occupational disease and are being diagnosed or under medical observation;

---

[50] LCL, art. 41(1–4).
[51] Qi ye jing ji xing cai jian ren yuan gui ding [Regulations for Personnel Reductions by Enterprises on Economic Grounds] (promulgated by the Ministry of Labor, Nov. 14, 1994, effective Jan. 1, 1995), arts. 2, 4, http://www.molss.gov.cn/gb/ywzn/2006-02/15/content_106668.htm; LCL, art. 41.
[52] LCL, art. 41.
[53] *Id.*
[54] LCL, art. 41.
[55] *Id.*
[56] LCL, art. 42 (notice the prohibition does not prohibit terminations under art. 39).

(2) those confirmed as having lost or partially lost their capacity to work because of an occupational disease contracted or a work-related injury sustained with the employer; (3) those who have contracted an illness or sustained a non–work-related injury, and the set period of medical care has not expired; (4) those who are pregnant, confined, or nursing; (5) those working for the employer continuously for not fewer than fifteen years and are fewer than five years away from legal retirement age; and (6) those with other circumstances stipulated in laws.[57]

3. Termination by the Employee

An employee's employment relationship may come to an end in several ways. It may come by employer termination, mutual agreement, end of the labor contract, or by the employee's unilateral termination through resignation. Under the LCL, the employee must usually give thirty-day notice to the employer before unilaterally terminating employment.[58] An exception to the notice requirement occurs where the employer uses violence, threats, or unlawful restrictions of personal freedom to compel a worker to work or if a worker is ordered by the employer to perform dangerous operations that threaten his or her personal safety.[59]

Grounds for an employee's unilateral termination include failure by the employer to (1) provide the contracted labor protection and working conditions, (2) pay full compensation on time, (3) pay social insurance premiums, (4) the employer provides invalid rules, harming the employee's rights and interests; (5) there is an invalid labor contract under Article 26 (deception, disclaimer of liability, violation of laws); and (6) other circumstances exist in which laws permit employee termination.[60]

4. Liabilities: Remedies and Severance Pay

Employers' liabilities on termination of the employment relationship, as discussed earlier, will vary for a variety of reasons. The law requires the employer to issue a proof of termination within fifteen days to effectuate the transfer of the employee's file and social insurance account.[61] For unlawful terminations,

[57] LCL, art. 41(1–6).
[58] Three-day notice is required during the probationary period. LCL, art. 37.
[59] LCL, art. 38.
[60] LCL, art. 38(1–6).
[61] LCL, art. 50.

the employer must continue the employee, if requested (in effect, reinstatement); if there is no request or it is not possible to continue the employee, the employer is liable for damages.[62] Where the employer terminates or ends the contract in violation of the law, there is employer liability for damage of "twice the rate of the severance pay provided in Article 47."[63] Even without termination, the employer may be liable for damages; for example, where there is a failure to pay proper compensation for wages, overtime, or severance pay, damages must be paid to the employee "at a rate of not less than 50 percent and not more than 100 percent of the amount payable."[64]

Employer liability for severance pay may arise for different reasons on the ending of the employment relationship.[65] As discussed earlier, the LCL provides for severance pay in the following circumstances: (1) per Article 38, employee termination; (2) per Article 36, mutual termination; (3) per Article 40, employer termination with notice; (4) per Article 41, first paragraph, mass reduction of the workforce; (5) per Article 44(1), fixed-term contract ending; (6) per article 44(4–5) contract ends per bankruptcy, license revocation, or early liquidation; and (7) other circumstances specified in laws.[66]

The LCL specifies the amount of severance pay to be awarded.[67] An employee is entitled to severance pay based on the number of years worked with the employer at the rate of one month's wage for each full year worked, with caps placed on high-earning employees (those earning more than three times the average monthly wage of employees in the area).[68] The monthly wage is defined as the average monthly wage for the prior twelve months; time worked between six months and one year shall be counted as one year.[69] Some variations occur in the case of permitted terminations for injury or illness.[70]

Employees may also be liable for damages for violations of the LCL. Under Article 90, if an employee terminates his or her labor contract in violation of the LCL and doing so causes the employer to suffer loss, the employee will

---

[62] LCL, arts. 48, 86–9.
[63] LCL, art. 87.
[64] LCL, art. 85.
[65] LCL, art. 46(1–7).
[66] *Id.*
[67] LCL, art. 47.
[68] *Id.*
[69] *Id.*
[70] Wei fan he jie chu lao dong he tong de jing ji bu chang ban fa [Measures Regarding Economic Compensation for Breach and Early Termination of Employment Contracts] (promulgated by the Ministry of Labor, Dec. 3, 1994, effective Jan. 1, 1995), arts. 6, 11, http://www.molss.gov.cn/gb/ywzn/2006-02/15/content_106667.htm.

be liable for damages. These damages can include recruitment and training costs, and the employer may recover liquidated damages related to funded contractual training programs and provisions dealing with restricting confidential information, trade secrets, and competition.[71]

---

[71] LCL, arts. 25, 22–24; Wei fan "Lao dong fa" you guan lao dong he tong gui ding de pei chang ban fa [Measures for Compensation in Connection with Violations of Provisions of the Labor Law on Labor contracts] (promulgated by the Ministry of Labor, May 10, 1995), http://www.law-lib.com/law/law_view.asp?id=41048. *See also* airline sued former employee pilot for leaving the company before the expiration of the contract in violation of contract term, court awarded 2,030,000 yuan in favor of airline in Henan., and damages included repayment of company training costs. Bin Zhou, 2008 shi da xin xing lao dong zheng yi an jie xi [Analysis of Ten New Types of Labor Disputes in 2008], Sept. 26, 2008, http://www.cworksafety.com/101812/101941/101691.html (in Chinese).

13

Restrictive Covenants

Employee Loyalty and the Employer's Protectable Interests

1. Legal Regulation

Traditionally in China, there has been no legally recognized duty of employee loyalty, though to be sure criminal limits existed, such as theft.[1] With China's entry into a market economy came the development of employee mobility and private employers' interests in protecting confidential matters and restricting employees from moving to competitive companies; in response, by the early 1990s legislative protections for the employer began to be implemented.[2] In 1994, the Labor Law authorized labor contract protections for "business secrets," and more specific provisions followed both at the national and local levels.[3] By 2006, laws clearly prohibited certain employees – "directors and senior management personnel" – from disclosing company secrets.[4] In 2008, the LCL expanded on the Labor Law's protection of business secrets to allow

---

[1] Xing fa [Criminal Law] (promulgated by the Nat'l People's Cong. Mar 14, 1997, effective Oct. 1, 1997, amended on June 29, 2006), art. 264 (PRC).

[2] E.g., protection of business secrets. Fan bu zheng dang jing zheng fa [Anti-Unfair Competition Law] (promulgated by the Standing Comm. of Nat'l People's Cong., Dec. 1, 1993), art. 10 (PRC); He tong fa [Contract Law] (promulgated by the Nat'l People's Cong., Mar. 15, 1999, effective Oct. 1, 1999), art. 43 (PRC).

[3] Labor Law, art. 22; Lao dong bu guan yu qi ye zhi gong liu ding ruo gan wen ti de tong zhi [Notice of Ministry of Labor on Several Issues Concerning Mobility of Enterprise Staff and Workers] (promulgated by the Ministry of Labor, Oct. 31, 1996), art. 2 (business secrets and restrictive covenants on competition), http://www.law-lib.com/lawhtm/1996/63564.htm; Guan yu jin zhi qin fan shang ye mi mi xing wei de ruo gan gui ding [Several Regulations Concerning Prohibitions of Acts of Infringement of Business Secrets] (promulgated by the State Administration for Industry & Commerce, Nov. 23, 1995, amended on Dec. 3, 1998), http://www.law-lib.com/lawhtm/1995/61463.htm; and e.g., Jiangsu sheng lao dong he tong tiao li [Jiangsu Labor Contract Regulations] (promulgated by the Jiangsu Provincial People's Cong., Oct. 25, 2003, effective Dec. 1, 2003), art. 17 (restrictions relating to noncompetition agreements), http://www.molss.gov.cn/gb/ywzn/2006-04/10/content_151358.htm.

[4] Gong si fa [Company Law] (promulgated by the Standing Comm. of the Nat'l People's Cong., Oct. 27, 2005, effective Jan. 1, 2006), art. 149 (PRC).

more specific contractual protection of "confidentiality matters" relating to trade secrets and intellectual property and a restriction on competition for those workers who signed a confidentiality agreement.[5]

However, there are limits on which employees and what interests may be legally restricted by contract. The LCL authorizes contract provisions restricting disclosure of confidential matters, such as trade secrets and intellectual property.[6] Article 24 stipulates that competition restrictions may also be agreed to (compensation is required) and are limited to "senior management, senior technicians and other personnel with a confidentiality obligation."[7] Although this wording appears to limit competition restrictions to senior personnel, the LCL in Article 24 adds "and other personnel with a confidentiality obligation." Therefore, a *dual* provision protecting confidentiality and restricting competition might seem to be efficient if provided to the employees actually needing the restrictive limitation; however, it may also present the employer with unexpected legal consequences and costs. It has been suggested, as a human resource management defensive strategy, to extend competition restrictions to many more employees than those who have a potential for violating confidentiality and, if valid, enforce as needed.[8] A practical difficulty of a dual provision is that noncompetition agreements require compensation, whereas confidentiality agreements by themselves do not. Thus, from an employer's point of view, a separate agreement for each, as is required, would avoid unnecessary compensation, though arguably, it may be possible for an employer to rescind the dual provision before compensation is due, especially if it is a separate agreement.

2. Protectable Interests: Confidentiality and Competition

The confidentiality obligation, agreed to by contractual provision, is designed to save from harm an employer's protectable interests. The term "protectable interest" is a fluid concept and can relate to definitions of a trade secret, which can have a broad scope, encompassing technical, management, marketing and pricing strategies, customer lists, etc.[9] A protectable interest, under Article 24

---

[5] LCL, arts. 23–4.

[6] LCL, art. 23.

[7] LCL, art. 24.

[8] *See* Edward Lehman, *Does China's New Labor Contract Law Better Protect Intellectual Property Owners?* 4 China L. Reptr. 4 (2008).

[9] Anti-Unfair Competition Law, *supra* note 2, art. 10 (providing broad definition); Several Regulations Concerning Prohibitions of Acts of Infringement of Business Secrets, *supra* note 3, arts. 2–3 (defining scope and limiting employees' infringement).

of the LCL, also specifically includes intellectual property rights, such as patents and copyrights, which have legal definitions of their own.[10]

Assuming there will be some legal coherency to the term "confidential matters," Article 24 provides that a valid noncompetition clause is available for those with the confidentiality obligation. These noncompete provisions have legal limits on their duration and the scope of employment restricted, and possibly the geographical limits placed on the employee. The LCL, Article 24, fixes duration as not exceeding two years. It defines the scope of work restriction from the termination or the ending of the contract as working for a competing employer, or an employer that produces the same type of products, or is engaged in the same type of business as the current employer or when the employee establishes his or her own competitive business.[11] The LCL-sanctioned anticompetition provision has been upheld by a recent court decision to cover the employee's registration of a new competing business while still employed, with the court awarding the employer the contractually agreed liquidated damages amount of RMB 120,000 and requiring the employee to return compensation paid to him by the employer.[12] There is no explicit geographical limitation; that term is left to the contractual negotiations of the parties.[13]

There appears to be no requirement for separate compensation by the employer for the confidentiality provisions by themselves.[14] These could be separate provisions in the labor contract. As described earlier, noncompetition provisions (for which post-termination compensation must be paid) are sometimes combined in the same labor contract with a confidentiality provision (no extra compensation is required). Consideration should be given to separating the two provisions, confidentiality and noncompete, in those cases where only a confidentiality provision is needed.

The amount of compensation to be paid to the employee, after termination, for inclusion of the non-competition provision has no statutory standard in

---

[10] Zhuan li fa [Patent Law] (promulgated by the Standing Comm. of the Nat'l People's Cong., Mar. 12, 1984, effective April 1, 1985, amended on Aug. 25, 2000) (PRC); Zhu zuo quan fa [Copyright Law] (promulgated by the Standing Comm. of the Nat'l People's Cong., Sept. 7, 1990, effective June 1, 1991, amended Jan. 27, 2001) (PRC). See general discussion of treatment of protected interests in Chaowu Jin & Wei Luo, COMPETITION LAW IN CHINA (2002).

[11] LCL, art. 24; additionally, LCL, art. 39(4) addresses the issue of working for a second employer during the current employment.

[12] *Registration of Company Held to be in Violation of Non-Compete Restriction*, Baker & McKenzie, CHINA EMPLOYMENT LAW UPDATE 4 (April 2008), http://www.bakernet.com/NR/rdonlyres/B333CEB3-AF4D-4D31-A53A-9E13A091A57A/0/china_employment_la_apr08.pdf.

[13] LCL, art. 24.

[14] LCL, art. 23.

the LCL and is fixed in the labor contract by the parties.[15] In local practice, it has ranged from one-third to two-thirds of the total remuneration that the employee received in the prior year of employment.[16] This compensation must be paid to the employee after the employment relationship ends and not as part of the salary while currently employed. The compensation is to be paid in monthly installments.[17] Local governments may have varying requirements on the amount of compensation required; therefore, care should be taken to ensure the contract is valid under local laws.

Article 90 of the LCL provides for damages for an employee's breach of either the confidentiality or the noncompetition agreement, or both.[18] If there is a breach by the employee of the noncompetition provision, then the employee must pay an amount in liquidated damages (an amount agreed to in the contract).[19]

3. Remedies for Breach

If there is a dispute over a breach by the employer or the employee of a provision *contained within the labor contract*, the dispute arguably could be resolved in arbitration as a labor dispute or possibly directly in court if it fits the exceptions to exhausting labor arbitration as a prerequisite to a court action.[20] This raises a related issue of whether it is preferable to include restrictive covenants in an agreement separate from the labor contract. Breach of these provisions in a *separate* agreement should authorize the employer to proceed directly to court under the 1999 Contract Law.[21]

In cases where a new employer hires an employee before that employee has terminated or ended his or her contract with the original employer,[22] the new

---

[15] LCL, art. 24.

[16] Jiangsu Labor Contract Regulations, *supra* note 3, art. 17; Zhejiang sheng ji shu mi mi bao hu ban fa [Zhejiang Protection of Technical Secrets Measures] (promulgated by the Zhejiang provincial government, Sept. 30, 2005, effective Jan. 1, 2006), art. 15, http://www.chinacourt.org/flwk/show1.php?file_id=105884.

[17] LCL, art. 23.

[18] LCL, art. 90.

[19] LCL, art. 23.

[20] LCL, art. 77; LMA, arts 5, 44; Anti-Unfair Competition Law, *supra* note 2, art. 20.

[21] He tong fa [Contract Law] (promulgated by the Nat'l People's Cong., Mar. 15, 1999, effective Oct. 1, 1999), art. 128 (PRC); it is reported that in 2005 (before the LCL), in the Haidian Court, a contract and tort action (under unfair competition) was successfully brought against the employee and the competitor, cited in *Interesting Case on Non-Competition Clauses in Employment Contacts*, lawprofessors.typepad.com/china_law_prof_blog/2008/06/interesting-cas. html (See original court decision in Chinese at http://lawprofessors.typepad.com/china_law_prof_blog/files/unfair_competition_case.pdf); *see also* http://news. xinhuanet.com/legal/2005-08/09/content_3329571.htm.

[22] LCL, art. 50 requires formalities evidencing the end of employment.

employer is liable to the original employer for any damages suffered.[23] Therefore, if a new employer were to prematurely hire an employee who had a restrictive covenant with a liquidated damage provision, thereby causing that employee to breach his or her restrictive covenant, liability could lie with the new employer. However, some employers may calculate this as an "opportunity cost" and be willing to pay the liquidated damages fee to acquire "confidential matters," even if they have to pay extra for the employee.

Foreign employees, who are (seconded) to work in China or otherwise have an employment contract made in the sending country and using home-country law, may present an issue of whose law governs. Although it appears that either the LCL or the 1999 Contract Law will apply to the employee (or labor service contractor), the home-country contract law may also be applicable. For example, in the recent highly-publicized employment case involving a Microsoft employee hired by Google to work in China in alleged violation of a noncompetition clause, U.S. courts and law were used to settle the case.[24]

Finally, criminal penalties are available against an employee whose breach of restrictive covenants involves an infringement of trade secrets that causes the employer serious losses.[25] A recent criminal prosecution against an employee for disclosing trade secrets of a former employer to a new employer in violation of employer rules occurred in Sichuan, resulting in a five-year prison term and a fine of RMB 1 million.[26]

---

[23] LCL, art. 91.

[24] LCL, arts 2, 57–67; *See, Gates' Microsoft and Google Settle Employee Row,* www.forbes.com/2005/12/23/gates-microsoft-google-ex_cn_1223autofacescan02.html; *see discussion in* Marisa Anne Pagnattaro, *"The Google Challenge": Enforcement of Noncompete and Trade Secret Agreements for Employees Working in China,* 44 AM. BUS. J. 603 (2007)

[25] Criminal Law, *supra* note 1, art. 219 (as amended June 29, 2006); a "serious" breach has a monetary threshold of RMB 500,000 for individuals and RMB 1.5 million for businesses, *see* Gao fa gao jian fuan yu ban li qin fan zhi shi chan quan xing shi an jian ju ti ying yong fa lv ruo gan wen ti de jie shi [Interpretations of the SPC and SPP on Several Issues Concerning the Specific Application of the Law in Handling of Criminal Cases Involving Intellectual Property Infringement] (promulgated by the SPC and SPP, Dec. 22, 2004), art. 7, http://www.china.com.cn/chinese/law/734357.htm.

[26] *Employee Sentenced to Five Years for Disclosure of Trade Secrets,* Baker & McKenzie, CHINA EMPLOYMENT LAW UPDATE 6 (April 2008). Similarly, in the United States, a naturalized U.S. citizen from China became employed by a new employer in China, taking with her proprietary information and documents from her U.S. employer. The U.S. employer had her prosecuted for theft rather than use the alternative civil remedy of contractual restrictive covenant, Dawn Mertineit, *Chicago Area Women Indicted for Theft of Trade Secrets Intended for China,* April 7, 2008, http://www.tradesecretslaw.com/2008/04/articles/trade-secrets/chicagoarea-woman-indicted-for-theft-of-trade-secrets-intended-for-china/.

14

Resolving Labor Disputes by Mediation, Arbitration, and Litigation

1. Legal Regulation of Labor Disputes

Labor disputes arising from statutory or contractual bases are resolved by the governmental labor mediation and arbitration process. The mediation process traditionally occurs within the enterprise and is voluntary. Arbitration is available, but claims must be filed within time limits. The Labor Mediation and Arbitration Law (LMA) became effective on May 1, 2008.[1] It provides increased accessibility for employees and greater finality to the arbitration process. It also clarifies the relationship of arbitration awards to judicial appeal. Certain exceptions to the usual exhaustion requirement are now included where direct access to the court is permitted. The new law seems to have spurred an increased use of arbitration: "Guangdong's courts and arbitrators handled more than twice as many labor disputes this May than a year earlier, after introduction of rules giving workers more rights and making arbitration free."[2]

The evolving legal regulation of labor arbitration, resulting in the current, primary regulations, began in 1993 with Regulations on Settlement of Labor Disputes in Enterprises, which were followed by the 1994 Labor Law and two Supreme People's Court Judicial Interpretations in 2001[3] and

[1] Lao dong zheng yi tiao jie zhong cai fa [Law on Labor Dispute Mediation and Arbitration] (promulgated by the Standing Comm. of the Nat'l People's Cong., Dec. 29, 2007, effective May 1, 2008) (PRC) [hereinafter LMA].

[2] The number of labor disputes handled by Guangdong's arbitration agencies tripled and court cases jumped 160 percent in recent months. Ninety percent of the cases were brought in the major Pearl River Delta manufacturing hubs of Guangzhou, Dongguan, Shenzhen, Zhongshan, Foshan, and Huizhou. Fiona Tam, *Caseloads Surge as Laborers Air Gripes*, SOUTH CHINA MORNING POST (July 9, 2008).

[3] Guan yu shen li lao dong zheng yi an jian shi yong fa lv ruo gan wen ti de jie shi [Interpretation of the Supreme People's Court Concerning Several Issues Regarding the Application of Law to the Trials of Labor Dispute Cases] (promulgated by the People's S. Ct., April 16, 2001) [hereinafter S.Ct. Interpretation I].

2006.[4] The LMA and the Labor Contract Law (LCL) were passed in 2007 and became effective in 2008. On January 1, 2009, new Labor and Personnel Dispute Arbitration Procedure Rules were issued by the MOHRSS.[5] Altogether, the laws make available a three-step process of mediation, arbitration, and litigation.[6] The employee may also lodge a complaint with the local Labor Bureau where there is a violation of law over arrears in paying remuneration, medical bills for work-related injuries, severance pay, or damages, and the government will "handle the matter in accordance with the laws."[7]

The scope of labor arbitration is large and increasing, often varying by region.[8] The number of labor arbitration cases grew from 10,326 in 1989 to about 350,000 in 2007,[9] an increase of more than 3,000 percent and an annual rise of 10.4 percent from 2006 to 2007.[10] In 2007 the 350,000 cases involved 650,000 workers. At the same time the number of arbitration cases has been increasing, the number of *collective* labor disputes has declined. It decreased from 14,000 cases in 2006 involving 350,000 workers to 13,000 cases in 2007 involving 270,000 workers, or about 41.5 percent of the total workers involved in labor disputes.[11] Collective disputes often lead to collective actions indicative of social unrest, such as demonstrations, strikes, or even violence.[12]

---

[4] Guan yu shen li lao dong zheng yi an jian shi yong fa lv ruo gan wen ti de jie shi (II) [Interpretation of the Supreme People's Court Concerning Several Issues Regarding the Application of Law to the Trials of Labor Dispute Cases (2)] (promulgated by the People's S. Ct., Aug. 14, 2004) [hereinafter S.Ct. Interpretation II].

[5] Lao dong ren shi zheng yi zhong cai ban an gui ze [Labor and Personnel Dispute Arbitration Procedure Rules] (promulgated by MOHRSS, Jan. 1, 2009) [hereinafter Arbitration Procedure Rules]. The new Procedure Rules apply to both labor dispute arbitration and personnel dispute arbitration; for example, disputes involving civil servants and People's Liberation Army (PLA) nonmilitary staff. The new Procedure Rules are drafted based on LMA, Civil Servants Law, and Regulations on PLA Nonmilitary Staff. These supersede the Labor Dispute Arbitration Commission Procedure Rules, issued by the Ministry of Labor on Oct. 18, 1993, and the Personnel Dispute Resolution Procedure, issued by the Ministry of Personnel on September 6, 1999.

[6] Labor Law, art. 77; LCL, art. 77; LMA, arts. 4, 5.

[7] LMA, art. 9.

[8] Ronald Brown, *China Labor Dispute Resolution*, RULE OF LAW IN CHINA: CHINESE LAW & BUSINESS, The Foundation for Law, Justice and Society, at 2 (2008), http://www.fljs.org/uploads/documents/Brown%231%23.pdf.

[9] China Statistics Bureau, China Statistical Communiqué on Labor and Social Security Development in 2007, http://bg2.mofcom.gov.cn/aarticle/chinanews/200806/20080605584560.html.

[10] National Bureau of Statistics of China, China Statistical Communiqué on Labor and Social Security Development in 2007, http://bg2.mofcom.gov.cn/aarticle/chinanews/200806/20080605584560.html; Statistical Communiqué on Labor and Social Security Undertakings in 2006, http://www.stats.gov.cn/english/newsandcomingevents/t20070524_402406436htm.

[11] *Id.*

[12] Brown, *supra* note 8.

In the first three quarters of 2008, China's labor dispute arbitration committees accepted 520,000 new cases, a 50 percent increase over the same period in
2007. This figure is expected to increase sharply in the fourth quarter, reflecting the rise in the number of factory closures and mass layoffs in the southeast
coastal region.[13]

There are significant regional disparities in which labor arbitration cases
arise. As might be expected, where industry, investment, and economic development activity are high, there is a correspondingly high incidence of labor
disputes. In 2005, Jiangsu, Guangdong, Shandong, Shanghai, Beijing, and
Zhejiang each had between 15,000 and 61,200 labor arbitration cases. Regions
of heavy industry (involving mostly SOEs, which are making the transition to
a market economy and are undergoing restructuring, which affect significant
numbers of workers) also have a relatively large number of labor disputes.
These include Liaoning, Hubei, Fujian, Chongqing, and Sichuan, which
typically have between 8,000 and 10,000 cases per year, compared with fewer
than 2,000 cases per year in many of the provinces.[14]

The characteristics of labor arbitration cases vary widely. Topics of labor disputes include (in order of the number of cases) wages, termination, insurance,
and work injury. In 2006, 64 percent of Shanghai's 24,000 labor arbitration
cases involved the failure to pay wages or social insurance. The type of ownership is also an identifiable characteristic, with most labor disputes being with
either an SOE or a foreign-invested enterprise (FIE). An interesting side note
is that, although more large-scale mass *protests* occur with SOEs, more *work
stoppages* and strikes occur in the FIEs. Moreover, in Guangdong most of
the labor disputes have occurred in Japanese, Taiwanese, Hong Kong, and
Korean invested enterprises, where workers' rights are reported to be more
often violated. Lastly, although the worker is the complainant in nearly 95
percent of the cases, the employer may bring a claim as well. Over the years,
employers have filed as the moving party in 4 to 13 percent of the arbitration
cases, usually on topics dealing with deliberate damage to employer property
or other labor contract violations.[15]

In China, labor disputes involve violations of contractual and statutory labor
rights. Generally speaking, resolving a labor dispute between an employee
and an employer through labor arbitration is mandatory, if initiated by either
party, and in most cases is a prerequisite for a court to have jurisdiction. The

[13] *Government Proposals to Speed Up Labor Dispute Arbitration Lack Clout*, Jan. 12, 2009,
http://www.china-labour.org.hk/en/node/100366.
[14] *Id.*
[15] *Id.*

LMA, Article 2, defines a "labor dispute" as one arising from formation of an employment relationship. The LCL provides further definition, stating that "an employment relationship with an employee is established on the day it starts using the employee.[16] Thus, "applicants," not yet having formed an employment relationship, would seem to fall outside this definition, whereas "retired employees" may have residual rights to use arbitration over pensions and other benefit entitlements.[17] The LMA, Article 2, continues, stipulating the following as labor disputes: (1) disputes arising from the confirmation of a labor relationship; (2) disputes arising from the conclusion, performance, amendment, termination, or ending of a labor contract; (3) disputes arising from dismissal or from a formal or de facto resignation; (4) disputes arising from working hours, rest and leave, social insurance, benefits, training, or labor protection; (5) disputes arising from labor compensation, medical bills for a work-related injury, severance pay, or damages; and (6) other labor disputes specified in laws or statutes.

2. Mediation

The 1994 Labor Law, Section 80, states that enterprises may establish internal mediation committees to assist in resolving labor disputes. The 2008 LMA broadens this to also include local mediation organizations.[18] Within each enterprise, guidance for the mediation procedures comes from its own rules. If filed, the process must be reconciled within the legal time requirement of filing for arbitration, within one year.[19] The mediation process is voluntary, and usually the employee has no explicit right to an individual representative. If no mediation settlement agreement is reached within fifteen days of submission, then either party may file for arbitration.[20] If a mediation agreement is reached, it is legally binding.[21] If either party fails to fulfill the mediation agreement, the other party may apply for arbitration.[22] However, a mediation agreement on certain subjects, including agreements on payment of overdue labor remuneration, medical bills for a work-related injury, severance pay, or damages, is directly enforceable by the courts.[23]

[16] LCL, art. 7.
[17] S.Ct. Interpretation I, *supra* note 3, art. 1.
[18] LMA, art. 10.
[19] LMA, art. 27.
[20] LMA, art. 14.
[21] LMA, art. 14.
[22] LMA, art. 15.
[23] LMA, art. 16.

Under the LMA, there is a tripartite mediation committee, with one representative each appointed from the employer, the workers, and the trade union.[24] However, many enterprises do not have a union, and those who do typically provide no meaningful training in mediation and are said to lack the ability or credibility to mediate labor disputes. In fact, this process can be, and often is, bypassed, and the claiming party may directly proceed to arbitration.[25]

As early as 1997, the number of cases being taken directly to arbitration was the same as the number being processed from enterprise mediation. The number of enterprise-mediated settlements continues to decline even as the number of arbitration cases rises.[26] However, even with dramatically declining numbers of cases using enterprise mediation, the percentage of cases settled remains high.

3. Arbitration

Labor arbitration has proven quite successful in resolving cases; the resolution rate is higher than 92 percent, including conciliation/mediation and arbitration awards, which in 2006 were 34 and 46 percent of the total settlements, respectively.[27] Of a total of 310,780 cases filed and settled in the arbitration process, 104,435 cases were mediated, whereas 141,465 cases were settled by arbitration. The other 20 percent were dispensed with by withdrawals, rejections, and the like. Workers prevailed in 146,028 cases, employers in 39,251, and there were split decisions in 125,501 cases.[28] Since 1999, the annual number of arbitration awards has exceeded the number settled by conciliation/mediation. Statistics show workers win nearly four cases for every one by the employer, and win partial victories in a majority of the split decisions.

The LMA has 34 articles in Chapter 3 that outline the arbitration requirements and process. They increase accessibility to employees by extending the

---

[24] LMA, art. 10.

[25] Yunqiu Zhang, *Law and Labor in Post-Mao China*, 14(04) JOURNAL OF CONTEMPORARY CHINA, 525, 530 (Aug. 2005).

[26] Brown, *supra* note 8, at 3; for an argument that mediation is underutilized, *see* Aaron Halegua, *Getting Paid: Processing the Labor Disputes of China's Migrant Workers*, 26 BERKELEY J. INT'L L. 254 (2008).

[27] CHINA STATISTICAL YEARBOOK (2006). Statistical Communique on Labor and Social Security Development in 2007, May 23, 2008, National Bureau of Statistics of China, http://www.stats.gov.cn/was40/gjtjj_en_detail.jsp?searchword=labor+dispute+arbitration&channelid=9528&record=1.

[28] *Id.*

TABLE 14.1. *Disposition of labor disputes in 2006 and 2007*

	2006	2007
Number of cases left over from last period	22,165	25,424
Cases accepted		
Number of cases	317,162	350,182
Number of collective labor disputes	13,977	12,784
Number of cases appealed by laborers	301,233	325,590
Number of persons involved overall	679,312	653,472
Number of persons involved in collective disputes	348,714	271,777
Cause of the disputes		
Change the labor contract	3,456	4,695
Relieve the labor contract	55,502	67,565
End the labor contract	12,366	12,696
Cases settled		
Number of cases settled	310,780	340,030
Manner of settlement		
by mediation	104,435	119,436
by arbitration lawsuit	141,465	149,013
Others	64,880	71,581
Result of settlement		
Won by units	39,251	49,211
Lawsuit won by laborers	146,028	156,955
Lawsuit won partly by both parties	125,501	133,864

Source: China Statistical Yearbook 2007 and 2008.

filing deadline from sixty days to one year and eliminating any fees.[29] The law affirms the use of the previously established, government-based Labor Arbitration Commission (LAC).[30] Pursuant to the Organization Rules of the Labor Dispute Arbitration Commission,[31] the LAC is staffed by representatives from the labor administrative authorities (labor bureau), the labor union, and a government-appointed representative with management authority.[32] It is in charge of the following functions: (1) retaining and dismissing full- and part-time labor dispute arbitrators, (2) accepting and hearing labor arbitration

[29] LMA, arts. 27, 53.
[30] LMA, arts. 17.
[31] Lao dong zheng yi zhong cai wei yuan hui zu zhi gui ze [Organization Rules of Labor Dispute Arbitration Commission] (promulgated by the Ministry of Labor, Nov. 5, 1993) [hereinafter Organization Rules].
[32] Organization Rules, art. 7; LMA, art. 19.

cases, (3) discussing major or difficult labor arbitration cases, and (4) oversee-ing labor arbitration activities.[33] The total number of commission members must be an odd number.[34]

Arbitrators who serve on the LAC's Labor Arbitration Tribunals must meet certain qualifications under the LMA. In addition to being "just and upright," they must have: (1) once served as a judge; (2) been engaged in legal research or education with a mid-level or higher title; or (3) possess legal knowledge and been professionally engaged in human resource management, labor union work, or other such work for at least five years; or (4) practiced as a lawyer for at least three years.[35]

Earlier qualification standards for arbitrators do not appear to have been explicitly displaced by the LMA. A 2008 Notice by the Beijing Labor Dispute Arbitration Commission on referring part-time labor arbitrators provides a good example on how the two sets of standards may be currently applied. The qualifications for the nominees are (1) labor arbitrators who have been licensed since 2004; (2) labor union public lawyers; (3) previous experience as a judge; (4) been engaged in law research or a professor with a mid-level or higher professional title; (5) a bar license and more than two years of experience in labor union work; (6) legal knowledge and more than five years of experience with labor union legal aid or legal counseling; or (7) a law degree and labor union work experience for more than five years.[36]

---

[33] Organization Rules, art. 10; LMA, art. 19.

[34] Organization Rules, art. 7. Usually the head of the local labor administrative bureau is the president of the commission. Art. 8. One or two vice presidents will be voted in by members of the commission. More than two-thirds of members must attend any commission meeting. *Id.* The appointment and dismissal of labor arbitration commission members have to be approved by the local government. Art. 9.

[35] LMA, art. 20.

[36] Guan yu zuo hao xiang Beijing shi lao dong zheng yi zhong cai wei yuan hui tui jian jian zhi lao dong zhong cai yuan gong zuo de tong zhi [Notice on Referring Part-time Labor Arbi-trators] (promulgated by the Beijing Labor Dispute Arbitration Commission, Sept. 1, 2008), http://www.bjzgh.gov.cn/template/10002/file.jsp?cid=436&aid=13821. An example of a recom-mendation form (2008) can be found on the Beijing Municipal Trade Union's Web page, http://www.bjzgh.gov.cn/template/10002/file.jsp?cid=436&aid=13821. Earlier mandates, such as the Measures on Labor Arbitrators Hiring and Management, issued by the Ministry of Labor in 1995, appear to still be effective; Lao dong zhong cai yuan pin ren guan li ban fa [Measures on Labor Arbitrators Hiring and Management] (promulgated by the Ministry of Labor, Mar. 23, 1995) [hereinafter Measure]. Because the LMA is not retroactive and there is no clear annulment of the 1995 measures, Labor Bureaus will need to clarify the continuing qualifi-cations of arbitrators selected under them and determine whether they must meet the new qualifications. Professional labor arbitrators under the 1995 measure are hired from govern-ment staff working on labor dispute resolution in local labor administrative bureaus. *Id.*, art. 2. Part-time labor arbitrators can be hired from other government staff working in local labor administrative bureaus or other government entities, labor union staff, scholars, or lawyers. *Id.*

Labor arbitrators must undergo training and take a qualification exam; there is a permit system for labor arbitrators as well.[37] Anyone with the background and experience described in the previous paragraph has the right to apply to be a labor arbitrator.[38] For example, the Beijing Labor Dispute Arbitration Commission issued a notice on referring part-time labor arbitrators on September 1, 2008.[39] The notice asked all local levels of the labor union, the city's various industry departments, workers' committee, employee University, and legal service centers to nominate part-time labor arbitrators to the city-level labor union for approval. Each permit is effective for three years.[40] However, LAC members, once nominated by the government, automatically receive this permit.[41]

The LAC will convene Labor Arbitration Tribunals as needed, composed of one, two, or three arbitrators, or if the case is a collective arbitration (involving more than thirty claimants), an odd number of more than three arbitrators is selected.[42] Most arbitration cases are handled by one arbitrator under simplified procedures.[43] Arbitrators may be full- or part-time, with the former usually drawn from the administrative staff of the Labor Bureau.[44] Training of arbitrators is often provided, but few had legal education before the LMA. At the end of 2007, it was reported that there were 7,424 full-time and 12,906 part-time arbitrators nationally.[45] In addition to conducting the arbitration,

---

[37] Measure, art 4

[38] Measure, art. 3.

[39] Guan yu zuo hao xiang Beijing shi lao dong zheng yi zhong cai wei yuan hui tui jian jian zhi lao dong zhong cai yuan gong zuo de tong zhi [Notice on Referring Part-time Labor Arbitrators] (promulgated by Beijing Labor Dispute Arbitration Commission, Sept. 1, 2008), http://www.bjzgh.gov.cn/template/10002/file.jsp?cid=436&aid=13821. An example of a recommendation form (2008) can be found on the Beijing Municipal Trade Union's Web page, http://www.bjzgh.gov.cn/template/10002/file.jsp?cid=436&aid=13821.

[40] Measure, art. 6.

[41] *Id.*

[42] Lao dong zheng yi zhong cai wei yuan hui ban an gui ze [Working Rules of Labor Arbitration Commission] (promulgated by the Ministry of Labor, Oct. 18, 1993), arts. 36–7 [hereinafter Working Rules].

[43] Qi ye lao dong zheng yi chu li tiao li [Regulations for the Handling of Enterprise Labor Disputes] (promulgated by the State Council, Aug. 1, 1993), art. 16, http://www.gov.cn/ziliao/flfg/2005-08/06/content_20937.htm; Andreas Lauff, EMPLOYMENT LAW & PRACTICE IN CHINA 311 (2008).

[44] Lao dong zhong cai yuan pin ren guan li ban fa [Measures for the Administration of the Engagement of Labor Arbitrators] (promulgated by the Ministry of Labor, Mar. 22, 1995), http://www.chinalaw.gov.cn/jsp/contentpub/browser/contentpro.jsp?contentid=c01762442932; Lao dong zheng yi zhong cai wei yuan hui zu zhi gui ze [Rules of Organization of the Labor Arbitration Commission] (promulgated by the Ministry of Labor, Nov. 5, 1993), http://www.chinalaw.gov.cn/jsp/contentpub/browser/contentpro.jsp?contentid=c01762513861.

[45] Lin Ling, Ying dui lao dong zheng yi an jian jing ben yao you shi ce [Measures to be Taken to Deal with Massive Labor Dispute Cases], CHINA LABOR & SOCIAL SECURITY DAILY, April 24, 2008, http://www.cnss.cn/xwzx/zl2/ldzyf/qjzw/200804/t20080424_187145.html.

arbitrators are also called on to attempt mediation before rendering the arbitration award.[46] In 2006, more than one-third of the decided cases filed in arbitration were mediated.[47]

Arbitrator fees vary according to local standards. Under the old system, the party who lost the labor arbitration paid for the arbitration fees. Now, under the LMA, labor arbitration is free for the parties, and local governments pay the fees. Several provinces have issued special local regulations on labor arbitration fees (e.g., Hunan,[48] Fujian,[49] and Guangdong[50]). Under those local rules, the local ministry of finance at the same level as the labor arbitration authority reimbursed the labor arbitration fees from May 1, 2008, to December 31, 2008; the labor arbitration fees became part of the government-spending budget in 2009. In most cases, this amount is relatively modest. For example, the standard in Taizhou, a small city in Jiangsu Province, which is relatively wealthy, depends on the labor arbitrator's qualification: at the senior level, 120 yuan per case; at the junior level, 100 yuan per case; at the associate level, 80 yuan per case; and at the assistant level, 50 yuan per case.[51] In Guangxi province, which is relatively poor, labor arbitrators receive a flat subsidy of 30 yuan per case, and there is a ceiling of 60 yuan per month for each arbitrator.[52]

Because the majority of the full-time labor arbitrators are actually public servants working for the Labor Bureau, they typically do not receive additional compensation for arbitration, but this can vary by locale. Part-time arbitrators usually receive only a nominal reimbursement or subsidy. This is quite different from commercial arbitration in China, in which the Chinese arbitrator can get paid a very high hourly rate and/or a percentage of the total amount under dispute.

4. Arbitration Process

Arbitration is mandatory if requested by either party and has three phases: filing, the hearing, and the award. The applicant for arbitration must file

---

[46] LMA, art. 42.
[47] *China Statistical Yearbook* (2006).
[48] http://www.gov.cn/gzdt/2008-10/06/content_1112531.htm.
[49] http://www.fjlss.gov.cn/PubDir/PubView.asp?vid=577&TB_iframe=true&width=768& height=450.
[50] http://www.gd.gov.cn/govpub/zwdt/bmdt/200811/t20081125_74103.htm.
[51] http://www.ggld.gov.cn/read.php?wid=182. In Shanghai, it is reported that arbitrators earn an average 2,800 yuan ($410.23) a month. Dong Zhen and Wang Xiang, Workers' disputes cause headaches for arbitrators, http://www.shanghaidaily.com/sp/article/2009/20090422/article_98441.htm.
[52] http://www.51labour.com/lawcenter/lawshow-26917.html.

with the LAC within one year of the alleged violation, and there is no prior requirement to use mediation.[53] As described earlier, since the LMA became effective on May 1, 2008, labor arbitration is free of charge.[54]

MOLSS published its latest working rules on labor and personnel disputes arbitration on January 1, 2009.[55] These rules supersede all previous procedural rules, and although there are few major changes, they provide more details and instructions.[56] Article 4 provides that the Labor Dispute Arbitration Commission will give priority to disputes involving more than ten workers or to collective contracts. Article 8 allows shareholders, mother companies, or supervisory departments to be joined as co-defendants when the employer in dispute has its business license revoked, is shut down or dismissed, and is unable to be responsible for the liability. Article 20 provides that when parties cannot collect evidence by themselves because of objective reasons, the Labor Dispute Arbitration Commission can collect evidence based on the PRC Civil Procedure Law. Article 26 provides that the case records of the LAC are open to the parties or their representatives for review and copying, except for those cases involving national or military secrets.[57]

The filing deadline of one year may be tolled in certain circumstances, such as when an applicant is currently seeking a remedy from a relevant government authority, or there has been an intervention of *force majeure*, or if the labor dispute involves overdue remuneration during the ongoing employment relationship.[58] The applicant must provide pertinent information in the arbitration application, including the nature of the claim, supporting evidence, and witnesses.[59] The LAC must accept or reject the application (with a stated reason) within five days from its receipt, or else the applicant may proceed directly to court, as is also the case if the application is

[53] LMA, art. 27; also see Supreme People's Court's guidance, if the matter should be in court. S.Ct. Interpretation II, *supra* note 4.

[54] LMA, art. 53. News media report that the fee cancellation greatly increased the number of labor arbitration cases. http://www.chinadaily.com.cn/china/2008-12/11/content_7292345.htm; *China Social Security Daily*, Feb. 16, 2009, http://www.lm.gov.cn/gb/salary/2009.

[55] Lao dong ren shi zheng yi zhong cai ban an gui ze [Labor and Personnel Dispute Arbitration Procedure Rules] (promulgated by MOHRSS, Jan. 1, 2009) [hereinafter Arbitration Procedure Rules]. http://news.xinhuanet.com/legal/2009-01/09/content_10630599.htm.

[56] *Id.*

[57] *Id.*

[58] LMA, art. 53.

[59] LMA, art. 28. The application has to provide (1) the name, occupation, address, and employer of the employee, as well as the name, address, and title of the legal representative or principal of the employee; (2) arbitral claims, supporting facts and reasons, evidence, sources of evidence, witnesses' names and addresses; and (3) the attorney's engagement letter and signature. The new LMA allows oral application, and commission staff will help record the application and serve the party when it has difficulty in writing an application. *Id.*

rejected.[60] The respondent is notified within five days after acceptance of the application and has ten days to respond.[61]

The LAC first designates a Labor Arbitration Tribunal (LAT) and notifies the applicant of its composition within the five-day period from receipt of the application.[62] The one to three arbitrators are bound by ethical standards and must recuse themselves or be challenged by the parties for violating any listed areas of impropriety, such as being related to a party, having a material interest in the case, etc.[63] The LAT will attempt mediation before issuing its award, and if a resulting written mediation agreement is signed by the arbitrator(s) and the parties, it is enforceable in the courts.[64]

The arbitration hearing process allows for the parties to cross-examine, argue, and make final comments, and a record is maintained.[65] Evidence accepted as genuine by the LAT is used as "the basis for determining the facts," and the burden of production, if not proof, is on each party, except where the evidence is in the possession or under the control of the employer and the employee is unable to submit it, in which case the employer must produce it by a deadline, and failure to do so will be held against the employer's burden of proof.[66] Although there is some guidance available on determining

---

[60] LMA, art. 29. All following "days" in the procedure means "workdays." The commission decides whether to accept the labor arbitration application. The review determines (1) whether the applicant has standing, (2) whether it is a labor dispute, (3) whether the commission has jurisdiction, (4) whether the one-year statute of limitation has run, and (5) whether the application and other relevant materials meet the requirements. If the application is incomplete, the commission will send a request to complete the application. If all the conditions are met, staff will prepare a case file opening approval form and let the person in charge sign the form. Then the commission will send notice to the applicant about its decision within five days.

[61] LMA, art. 30. Even if the commission does not receive the complaint, the labor arbitration proceeding will continue. *Id.*

[62] LMA, arts. 31, 32.

[63] LMA, art. 33.

[64] LMA, arts. 42, 51; private settlement by the parties is also authorized. LMA, arts. 4, 41. A mediation agreement reached under labor dispute mediation commission with contents of labor rights and obligations has the binding force of an employment contract and can be the basis for the judgment of the people's court. Where the parties involved only reach a mediation agreement under the labor dispute mediation commission, if the employer fails to perform the payment obligation determined in the mediation agreement and the laborer lodges a lawsuit directly with the people's court, the people's court can accept it as a common civil dispute. Guan yu shen li lao dong zheng yi an jian shi yong fa lv ruo gan wen ti de jie shi (II) [Interpretation of the Supreme People's Court Concerning Several Issues Regarding the Application of Law to the Trials of Labor Dispute Cases (2), art. 17] (promulgated by the People's S.Ct., Aug. 14, 2004). If during the proceeding the parties settle their case, the arbitration application will be deemed withdrawn. LMA, art. 41.

[65] LMA, arts. 38, 40.

[66] LMA, arts. 6, 39.

the "burden of proof" in court cases, it is not expressly binding on arbitrators in the arbitration process.[67]

The arbitration award must be rendered within forty-five to sixty days from the date of acceptance by the LAC of the application for arbitration.[68] When the LAT is composed of more than one arbitrator, the written award is based on majority opinion, or if none can be reached, it will be in accord with the opinion of the chief arbitrator, along with dissent(s) also placed in the record.[69] The award is final and legally effective on the date it is rendered in two areas of labor disputes: (1) labor remuneration, medical bills for work-related injuries, severance pay, or damages, in any amount not exceeding the equivalent of twelve months of the local minimum wage[70] and (2) working hours, rest, leave, social insurance, etc., arising from the implementation of state standards.[71]

An employee dissatisfied with an award in those two areas may appeal to the court within fifteen days, whereas an employer within thirty days may seek to vacate the order in intermediate court only on errors in law, jurisdiction, or statutory procedure; fabricated or concealed evidence; or if the arbitrator demanded a bribe or committed graft.[72] All other non–Article 47 appeals may be brought to court by either party within fifteen days from the date of the receipt of the written ruling.[73] In 2008, in the first reported case under the LCL, a district court in the Chaoyang District of Beijing upheld an arbitration ruling that awarded an employee an open-ended labor contract based on her circumstances, including her prior employment with the employer, and notwithstanding her leave of absence.[74]

Arbitration awards tend to be brief, without elaborate analysis, as contrasted with, for example, longer American arbitration decisions. Access to Chinese awards is limited, with only the appealing parties granted access to the award.[75] In 2009, new Procedure Rules provided that the case records of Labor

---

[67] S.Ct. Interpretation I, *supra* note 3, art. 13.

[68] LMA, art. 43.

[69] LMA, arts. 45, 46.

[70] LMA, art. 47(1); *see* LMA, art. 44 (advance execution and transfer to court).

[71] LMA, art. 47(2).

[72] LMA, art. 49(1–6).

[73] *Id.*

[74] *Employee Wins First Reported Employment Contract Law Case*, Baker & McKenzie, CHINA EMPLOYMENT LAW UPDATE, at 7 (Feb. 2008), http://www.bakernet.com/NR/rdonlyres/E8862D4F-16FC-402E-B8AD-A7B2F5D157FE/0/china_employment_la_febo8.pdf.

[75] Gu Weixia, *Recourse against Arbitral Awards: How Far Can A Court Go? Supportive and Supervisory Role of Hong Kong Courts as Lessons to Mainland China Arbitration*, 4(2) CHINESE J. INT. L. 481 (2005).

Arbitration Commission are open to the parties or their representatives for review and copying.[76]

There are mixed views about whether the new law will resolve the growing number of labor disputes. Most see it as a further improvement[77]; whereas advocacy groups argue the LACs are ill-equipped to deal with the surging workload.[78]

5. Litigation

The number of labor dispute cases appealed to the courts from labor arbitration decisions has grown dramatically from 28,285 in 1995 to 114,997 in 2004 and to 122,480 in 2005 (involving about 2.37 billion yuan).[79] In 2005, about 94 percent of appeals were initiated by workers, and they prevailed in more than half of them; in some courts, such as in Ningbo in Zhejiang and Zhongshan in Guangdong, as many as 90 percent of the appeals were settled in favor of the worker. The LMA seeks to add more finality to arbitration decisions in stipulated areas, as discussed in this section.

In 2005, 121,516 court cases were settled (resolved) – 62,608 by court judgment, 27,944 by mediation, – and 20,998 were withdrawn, with 7,115 rejected.[80] Interestingly, the court successfully mediated nearly one-third of the settled cases.

---

[76] There is an exception for those cases involving national or military secrets. Lao dong ren shi zheng yi zhong cai ban an gui ze [Labor and Personnel Dispute Arbitration Procedure Rules] (promulgated by the MOHRSS, Jan. 1, 2009) [hereinafter Arbitration Procedure Rules], art. 26. http://news.xinhuanet.com/legal/2009-01/09/content_10630599.htm.

[77] Li Jiangang, *PRC Law on Mediation and Arbitration of Labor Disputes: Further Improvement in Handling Labor Issues in China*, CHINA LAW & PRACTICE 31 (May 2008). In the first three months of 2009, the following increases in labor disputes handled by courts occurred; Guangdong, 42 percent; Jiangsu, 50 percent; Zhejiang, 64 percent; Shandong, 19 percent. China cares soar as workers seek redress, http://english.people.com.en/90001/90776/90882/66452282.html.

[78] They argue that the situation in the Haizhu District in the Pearl River Delta is typical. Their LAC has only three staff members, working six days and three evenings a week to keep pace with the dramatic number of new cases. *Help or Hindrance to Workers: China's Institutions of Public Redress, China Labor Bulletin Research Report,* http://www.clb.org.hk/en/files/share/File/research_reports/Help_or_Hindrance.pdf. In Shanghai there are 20 labor dispute arbitration offices with 162 full-time arbitrators; in the first nine months of 2008 workers filed 52,930 cases, more than double the previous year's number. It was reported by the union that each arbitrator handled more than 226 cases last year, whereas a "reasonable work load would be 50 cases." Arbitrators are said to be working excessive overtime and delays in the arbitration process have occurred due to too few arbitrators. Dong Zhen and Wang Xiang, Workers' disputes cause headaches for arbitrators, *supra* note 51.

[79] Brown, *supra* note 8, at 4.

[80] *Id.*

Chinese law ordinarily distinguishes between "labor contracts" and "contracts for work," with the latter treated as a civil contract case able to be taken directly to court. In contrast, the former is treated as a labor case in which resolution of the labor dispute through labor arbitration is required before court access is granted.[81] The LCL and a 2006 SPC Interpretation (preceding the LMA) authorize direct lawsuits in court on certain limited topics, such as back wages owed for which the amount is not in dispute.[82] A recent court case in Shanghai, basing its holding on the Civil Procedure Law (CPL) Article 191, ordered a wage payment of RMB 200,000 to an employee whose employer had agreed the money was due, and the date for payment was past.[83]

There may be some question as to how best to reconcile this narrow exception with Article 44 of the LMA, which requires first going to arbitration and requesting authorization for "advance execution," as discussed in this section.[84] However, a limited number of nonperformed mediation agreements (settlements) may be taken directly to court for enforcement,[85] and the LMA

---

[81] Yin Wu, Lao dong he tong yu lao wu he tong bi jian [Comparison between Labor Contract and Contract for Services], http://www.lawbooks.com.cn/lw/lw_view.asp?no=3946; *see also* He tong fa [Contract Law] (promulgated by the Nat'l People's Cong., Mar. 15, 1999, effective Oct. 1, 1999), art. 128 (PRC). A recent regulation in Shenzhen placed a prohibition on lawyers using contingent fees in civil labor dispute cases. Shenzhen Jing ji te qu he xie lao dong guan xi cu jin tiao li [Regulations for the Promotion of Harmonious Labor Relations in the Shenzhen Special Economic Zone (SEZ)] (promulgated by the Shenzhen Municipal People's Cong., Oct. 6, 2008, effective November 1, 2008), art. 57, http://www.npc.gov.cn/npc/xinwen/dfrd/guangdong/2008-10/08/content_1452415.htm.

[82] LCL Article 30 provides a fast and simple procedure – "order to pay" for wage default cases; *see also* S.Ct. Interpretation II, *supra* note 4, art. 3.

[83] *Employee Obtains Court Order for Wage Payment in Four Days*, Baker & McKenzie, CHINA EMPLOYMENT LAW UPDATE, at 3–4 (April 2008), http://www.bakernet.com/NR/rdonlyres/B333CEB3-AF4D-4D31-A53A-9E13A091A57A/0/china_employment_la_apr08.pdf; *see also* Pan Wenjie, Gong si fu zong bei qian xin 20 wan, Shanghai fa chu shou ge lao dong bao chou zhi fu ling [VP Wage Defaulted 200K, Shanghai Issued The First Payment Order], April 22, 2008, http://www.chinacourt.org/html/article/200804/22/297768.shtml (in Chinese).

[84] Article 44 allows "advance execution" in labor arbitration cases seeking wage defaults, payment for work injury medical bills, or severance payment and when execution after the arbitration decision would be detrimental to the applicant's living situation where the obligations are obvious. *See* Lao dong zheng yi tiao jie zhong cai fa jie xi: di 44 tiao (xian yu zhi xing) [Interpretation of LMA: Art. 44 (Advance Execution)], Mar. 16, 2008, http://www.laodonghetong.org/1094a.html (in Chinese). In contrast, the order to pay is available for all wage default cases under the LCL when the debtor-creditor relationship is clear, no matter whether the employee has difficulty maintaining a life without the procedure. Min shi su song fa [Civil Procedure Law] (promulgated by the Nat'l People's Cong., April 9, 1991, amended by the Standing Comm. of the Nat'l People's Cong., Oct. 28, 2007, effective April 1, 2008), arts. 191–4 (P.R.C.) [hereinafter Civil Procedure Law], and *see* Xiao Chengchi, Ru he zheng que shi yong zhi fu ling [How to Use the Order to Pay Correctly], Nov. 14, 2005, http://www.chinacourt.org/html/article/200511/14/185400.shtml (in Chinese).

[85] LMA, art. 16.

authorizes other nonconflicting related laws to continue in force.[86] Some of these related laws, such as the Women's Rights and Interests Law (Women's Law) and the Employment Promotion Law, specifically grant the right to "institute a legal action in a People's Court."[87] Whether that precludes first exhausting this "labor dispute" in labor arbitration is doubtful, though debatable, in view of current court cases.[88]

Uncontested arbitration awards, except those falling under Article 47, or those qualifying for *advance execution* under Article 44, will be final after the fifteen-day appeal period.[89] Under new provisions of the LMA, the usual right of appeal and full review, largely de novo, of the arbitration award by the court can be avoided either by a successful application for advance execution[90] or an arbitration award in two stipulated areas under Article 47.[91]

An advance execution can be made in qualifying cases involving recovery of "labor remuneration, medical bills for a work-related injury, severance pay or damages."[92] The employee applies to the LAT for an award for advance execution and transfer of the case to the court for execution.[93] Two conditions are required: (1) the rights and obligations are clear and (2) the failure to grant will "materially affect the livelihood of the applicant." Article 47 provides for "final and legally effective" arbitration awards on the date they were rendered in two areas: (1) labor remuneration, medical bills for a work-related injury, severance pay, or damages "not exceeding the equivalent of twelve months of the local minimum wage rate" and (2) disputes over working hours, rest, leave, social insurance, etc. arising from the implementation of government labor standards.[94]

If an employee is dissatisfied with the arbitration award under Article 47, he or she may make an appeal to the Intermediate People's Court within fifteen days.[95] An appeal by an employer to vacate the award is limited to six circumstances: (1) error in the application of laws; (2) the LAC lacked

---

[86] LMA, art. 52.

[87] Fu nv quan yi bao zhang fa [Women's Rights and Interests Law] (promulgated by the Nat'l People's Cong., Aug. 28, 2005, effective Dec. 1, 2005), art. 52; Jiu ye cu jin fa [Employment Promotion Law] (promulgated by the Standing Comm. of the Nat'l People's Cong., Aug. 30, 2007, effective Jan. 1, 2008), art. 62.

[88] Ronald C. Brown, *China's Employment Discrimination Laws during Economic Transition*, 19 Colum. J. Asian L. 361, 409–11, 423–4 (2006).

[89] LMA, art. 50.

[90] LMA, art. 44. There is no need to provide a security in such cases.

[91] LMA, art. 47(1–2).

[92] LMA, art. 44.

[93] *Id.*

[94] LMA, art. 47.

[95] LMA, art. 48.

jurisdiction; (3) a statutory procedure was violated; (4) evidence on which award was based was fabricated; (5) the other party concealed evidence sufficient to affect the fairness of the award; and (6) the arbitrator demanded or accepted a bribe, committed graft, or rendered an award that perverted the law.[96] If the award is vacated, it will be final unless either party, within fifteen days, takes the labor dispute to the People's Court.[97]

There are certain requirements for and barriers to court review of labor disputes. As discussed earlier, an appellant first must have a "labor dispute" arising from an employment relationship and, second, must have first exhausted the labor arbitration procedures, except where this requirement has been excluded. A mediation agreement reached in court, like a mediation agreement reached in arbitration, is binding, except on the legality of the agreement.[98]

Arbitrated labor dispute cases, taken by the courts, unless otherwise directed by laws or Supreme People's Court (SPC) guidance, will be enforced in accordance with the law. The Civil Procedure Law includes rules on evidence, review standards, appeals, etc.,[99] and, according to the SPC's 2001 Labor Dispute Interpretation, the employer has a burden to produce evidence within its control, and in cases of termination, reduction of compensation, or recalculation of an employee's length of service, it has the burden of proof.[100]

---

[96] LMA, art. 49.

[97] *Id.*

[98] Where mediation is possible prior to the rendering of a judgment, a session of mediation may be conducted. Civil Procedure Law, art. 128.

[99] Civil Procedure Law, arts. 147, 158, 213.

[100] S.Ct. Interpretation I, *supra* note 3, art. 13; this burden of production is similar to that in the arbitration process. LMA, arts. 6, 39. Alternatives to arbitration are available to aggrieved employees. For example, they may petition (xin fang) the Letters and Visits Offices to resolve labor conflicts. They also "can withdraw by shifting to another enterprise or locality, or endure the treatment faced, or attempt to negotiate directly with the employer, or file a lawsuit [if permitted]. A survey carried out by the Shenzhen Labor Bureau in 1996 revealed that 1,537 of 2,789 migrant workers had encountered some labor-related problem during the previous year. The survey found that 4 percent of the migrant workers had turned to either arbitration committees, courts, or Letters and Visits Offices, although the survey did not distinguish among these three routes. Another 39 percent of the migrant workers had tried to take up their problem directly with their employer, 26 percent had given up trying to improve their situation, 23 percent had initiated some form of mediation process within the enterprise, 5 percent had quit the enterprise over the problem, and 1.5 percent had launched an appeal to the local news media." Isabelle Thireau & Linshan Hua, *The Moral Universe of Aggrieved Chinese Workers: Workers' Appeals to Arbitration Committees and Letters and Visits Offices*, 50 THE CHINA J. 83, 84 (2003). Although current labor laws better support the employees' choice to arbitrate, these other alternatives are still available.

PART VII

RIGHTS, REMEDIES, AND MULTIPLE FORUMS

15

Working Labor and Employment Law Illustrations

1. Rights, Remedies, and Multiple Forums

Labor rights in China, as elsewhere in the world, may emanate from a variety of sources, including international, national, statutory, and contractual law. From these sources come alternative avenues of regulation and enforcement: administrative, labor arbitration, and the courts. The use of these varied approaches can be seen from a brief illustration. Suppose a female employee with a labor contract is discriminated against at work by her employer. Under the Women's Rights and Interests Law, she may complain to administrative authorities, which may investigate and impose sanctions[1]; under this law, she also has a right to proceed to court,[2] but because it is a "labor dispute," she also has a right (if not a duty) to go to labor arbitration.[3] Similar alternatives are available for an employer that has a trade secret compromised by an employee. The Law against Unfair Competition prohibits infringement of trade secrets, and the employer may take the matter to the State Administration of Industry and Commerce (SAIC), which is empowered to deal with and resolve disputes related to trade secrets.[4] If a labor contract protects confidential information,

---

[1] Fu nv quan yi bao zhang fa [Women's Rights and Interests Law] (promulgated by the Nat'l People's Cong., Aug. 28, 2005, effective Dec. 1, 2005), art. 52 (PRC).

[2] *Id.*; Jiu ye cu jin fa [Employment Promotion Law] (promulgated by the Standing Comm. of the Nat'l People's Cong., Aug. 30, 2007, effective Jan. 1, 2008), art. 62.

[3] Lao dong zheng yi tiao jie zhong cai fa [Law on Labor Dispute Mediation and Arbitration] (promulgated by the Standing Comm. of the Nat'l People's Cong., Dec. 29, 2007, effective May 1, 2008), art. 5 (PRC); Lao dong he tong fa [Labor Contract Law] (promulgated by the Nat'l People's Cong., June 29, 2007, effective Jan. 1, 2008), art. 77 (PRC).

[4] Guan yu jin zhi qin fan shang ye mi mi xing wei de ruo gan gui ding [Several Regulations Concerning Prohibitions of Acts of Infringement of Business Secrets] (promulgated by the State Administration for Industry & Commerce, Nov. 23, 1995, amended on Dec. 3, 1998), http://www.law-lib.com/lawhtm/1995/61463.htm.

the labor arbitration process will also be available. Access to the court could arise under either avenue.

Another example is a work-related injury that may need an assessment by the administrative agencies for labor security (usually the local bureau of labor and social security) of the percent of permanent injury; once that administrative agency determines the percent of injury, the employer may dispute the assessment or the duty to pay the employee. The first dispute involves administrative matters dealing with the government's treatment of a legally protected right, such as decisions and review; the second deals with a labor dispute between the employer and employee. Each has its own avenue of redress.

The point is that there is great interplay, and often overlap, on labor rights among the multiple forums provided by the administrative, labor arbitration, and judicial processes. In China, each labor right has with it a bundle of these administrative, statutory, and likely contractual overlays that must be understood and dealt with. Each administrative agency administers and supervises compliance with particular labor rights and duties, and each has its own set of requirements under particular laws at the national and local levels. Additionally, there are a number of general administrative laws pertinent to labor laws and their enforcement. First, the MOHRSS has Labor Bureaus throughout China that inspect compliance with labor law duties and have sanctions available for enforcement. Its regulations provide for inspections, investigation, and supervision of employers' labor practices.[5] The scope of inspection encompasses most, if not all, aspects of the employment relationship from wages to employer rules and extends the right to make a complaint for all employees.[6] If violations are found, an employer must rectify them and is subject to fines and administrative penalties, including revocation of the business license and civil and criminal sanctions.[7] For individual disputes, the employee must seek redress through the labor arbitration process.[8]

The penalties authorized for use by administrative agencies are enumerated and limited by the Administrative Penalties Law.[9] Dissatisfied employers are

---

[5] Lao dong bao zhang jian cha tiao li [Regulation on Labor Security Supervision] (promulgated by the State Council, Nov. 1, 2004, effective Dec. 1, 2004), art. 10, http://www.chinacourt.org/flwk/show1.php?file_id=97457.

[6] *Id.* arts. 9, 10.

[7] *Id.* arts. 23, 28, 32, and 33.

[8] *Id.* art. 21.

[9] Xing zheng chu fa fa [Law on Administrative Penalties] (promulgated by the Standing Comm. of the Nat'l People's Cong., Mar. 17, 1996, effective Oct. 1, 1996) (PRC), http://www.law-lib.com/law/law_view.asp?id=307; Wei fan "lao dong fa" xing zheng chu fa ban fa [Measures Concerning Administrative Penalties for Violations of the Labor Law] (promulgated by the Ministry of Labor, Dec. 24, 1994, effective Jan. 1, 1995), http://w1.mohrss.gov.cn/gb/ywzn/2006–02/20/content_107422.htm.

authorized to seek an administrative appeal through review by a higher level agency or by the courts.[10] Administrative review of social insurance disputes is authorized when administrative determinations are challenged by aggrieved parties.[11]

Among these alternatives, aggrieved parties choose an appropriate alternative to resolve their disputes, mindful that prerequisites and procedural delays and obstacles are rampant and often inevitable when seeking administrative, labor arbitration, and judicial redress in the enforcement of labor rights and duties. Parties may need to involve more than one forum, which may affect their rights and duties, such as where there are differing filing or appeal deadlines, duties of exhaustion, costs, or remedies.

2. Illustrative Cases

a. Labor Arbitration

The First Intermediate Court of Beijing recently issued a decision arising after the new Labor Mediation and Arbitration Law became effective on May 1, 2008. Under this law, only employees can appeal certain arbitration decisions, and on those decisions the employer is only able to petition the court to vacate arbitration decisions on certain limited grounds.

The plaintiff in this case began work in November 2007 for a medical technology company in Beijing; his probationary period ended in January 2008. In February 2008, he was terminated for incompetence. He filed for labor arbitration and was awarded RMB 3,600 compensation under the Labor Contract Law. The court vacated this decision on the grounds that the LCL (which became effective on January 1, 2008) did not apply retroactively to the case at hand. It determined that the arbitrator had improperly applied the LCL retroactively on a severance calculation.[12]

b. Restrictive Covenant

A recent court decision in Beijing highlights the significance of restrictive covenant provisions in labor contracts and their legal use by employers. The following case was decided before the new LCL became effective.

---

[10] Xing zheng su song fa [Law on Administrative Litigation] (promulgated by the Nat'l People's Cong., April 4, 1989, effective Oct. 1, 1990) (PRC), http://www.law-lib.com/law/law_view.asp?id=5641&page=5.

[11] She hui bao xian xing zheng zheng yi chu li ban fa [Measures for Handling Social Insurance Administrative Disputes] (promulgated by the Ministry of Labor and Social Security, May 27, 2001), http://www.molss.gov.cn/gb/ywzn/2006–02/20/content_107415.htm.

[12] *See* case reference at *China Law Insight*, www.chinalawinsight.com/2008/09/articles/corporate/labor-employment/labor-arbitration-decision-vacated/.

The Beijing No. 1 Intermediate Court issued two decisions involving non-compete and nondisclosure agreements between Beijing Aptech Beida Jade Bird Information Technology Co., Ltd. and two of its former employees, Xia and Yin.[13] Xia and Yin signed an employment agreement with their employer when they started work. Two years later, each left the employer to work for a competitor. The employer sued for breach of the noncompete covenants, requesting termination of the employment relationship with the new employer and claiming RMB 500,000 in compensation.

The Beijing Court upheld the validity of the employment relationship and the nondisclosure covenants generally, but the employer was unsuccessful in enforcing the noncompete and nondisclosure obligations. The court held that, to enforce noncompete obligations against former employees, the employer must have provided compensation to the former employee for that restriction. The amount of compensation, according to local regulations in Beijing, was to be no less than 50 percent of the final annual income of the former employee. Because the employer failed to provide sufficient evidence that it had compensated Yin or Xia in this way, neither employee was deemed to be bound by the noncompetition agreements. Therefore, no compensation was payable, and they were not restricted in their new employment.

As this case was decided before the LCL's effective date, consideration may be given to the likely application of Articles 23 and 24 of the LCL that require compliance with the following provisions:

1. Restrictive covenants are voluntary and negotiable as to scope (new employment with the same type of enterprise activities), geographical limits, and duration (not to exceed two years).[14]
2. They are limited to certain senior personnel.[15]
3. The employer must provide *post*-termination[16] compensation to the employee who agrees to the restrictive covenant provision, paid out on a monthly basis.[17]

---

[13] *See* case reference and discussion in Patti Walsh & Sophie Chen, *Non Compete Agreements and the New Labor Contract Law in the Peoples' Republic of China*, www.minterellison.com/public/connect/Internet/Home/Legal±Insights/Articles/A-Non-compete±agreements.

[14] LCL, art. 24

[15] *Id.*

[16] In a *pre*-LCL court case, a court held an employee and the new hiring employer liable in contract and tort for violation of the no-compete restrictive covenant, even though the compensation paid to the employee was paid during the labor contract and not post-termination, lawprofessors.typepad.com/china_law_prof_blog/2008/06/interesting-cas.html. This holding appears contrary to LCL, art. 23. A case in the Beijing Second Intermediate People's Court in March 2009 enforced such a provision against an employer. China Employment Law update, April 2009, at 4, Baker & McKenzie.

[17] *Id.* art. 23

4. An employee who breaches the covenant must compensate the employer according to the contractually negotiated liquidated damages.[18]

The national law does not specify the amount of compensation to be paid to employees, and this decision is made at the local level. For example, in Beijing, regulations require the compensation to be no less than 50 percent of the last year's annual income of the employee[19]; in Shenzhen it is to be no less than two-thirds of the employee's last year's income.[20]

Applying the LCL to the facts of the above case brings the same result in that the employer failed to provide the employee with the compensation required under Article 23, thus rendering the restrictive covenant unenforceable. How the decision might have resolved the validity of the liquidated damages provision is unknown, as no national law gives guidance on this issue.[21]

Another illustrative case is the noncompetition restriction placed on Kai-Fu Lee, a former executive at Microsoft who jumped to Google to run its China operations in alleged violation of a restrictive covenant in his employment contract with Microsoft. This case raises an issue of possibly two countries' labor laws applying to the labor dispute, which is discussed more fully in the case presented in the next section, of a foreign national living and working in China (or a Chinese employee working in a foreign location). Depending on how the employment contract(s) is drafted, Chinese or foreign labor laws or both may be applicable to an individual employee.

Forbes Magazine described the facts of this case as follows:

> To recap the heavyweight tussle, Lee had worked at Microsoft since 2000 and helped develop its MSN Internet search technology, including desktop search software rivaling Google's. Lee joined Google in July to lead the search engine's

[18] *Id.* and art. 90.

[19] Zhongguancun ke ji yuan qu tiao li [Beijing Zhongguancun Industrial Technology Park Regulations] (promulgated by the Standing Comm. of the Beijing People's Cong., Dec. 8, 2000, effective Jan. 1, 2001), arts. 43, 44, http://www.bjdch.gov.cn/n1569/n2458434/n2462161/2573918.html.

[20] Shenzhen jing ji te qu qi ye ji shu mi mi bao hu tiao li [Regulations of Shenzhen Special Economic Zone on the Protection of Technical Secrets of Enterprises] (promulgated by the Standing Committee of the Shenzhen People's Cong., Nov. 3, 1995, effective Jan. 1, 1996), art. 17, http://fzj.sz.gov.cn/laws/2LAW10a3.asp.

[21] According to Tianjin Bureau of Labor & Social Security, liquidated damages should be legal, equitable, and appropriate; in theory, they should not exceed the twelve-month standard wage. Guan yu bao shou shang ye mi mi xie yi, zhi fu wei yue jin he jiu ye bu zhu jin deng you guan lao dong he tong wen ti de tong zhi [Notice on Labor Contract Issues about Protecting Business Secrets, Liquidated Damages, and Employment Subsidy, etc.] (promulgated by the Tianjin Bureau of Labor & Social Security, Sept. 5, 2005), http://ldrsj.tjftz.gov.cn/system/2006/12/15/010007924.shtml. In a 2009 case in a Jiangsu People's Court, a decision rewrote the amount of compensation due an employee and awarded a higher amount pursuant to Jiangsu legal requirements. China Employment Law update, *supra* note 16.

expansion into China, prompting Microsoft's suing of both Google and Lee, contending that Lee's duties at Google would violate the terms of a non-compete agreement he signed as part of his Microsoft employment contract. The software leviathan said Lee's contract prohibited him from taking a job with a competitor within a year of leaving Microsoft and accused Google of "intentionally assisting" Lee. "Google is fully aware of Lee's promises to Microsoft, but has chosen to ignore them, and has encouraged Lee to violate them," Microsoft said in its lawsuit.

Google hit back with its own lawsuit, contending that Microsoft's clause was "clearly an illegal restraint of trade" since it violated laws in California, where Google is based, giving workers the right to change jobs.[22]

Although the case was finally settled in 2005, this question can be addressed: how would this type of case be resolved in China if the parties found the jurisdiction applicable? To begin, Microsoft, in its employment agreement with Lee, would have had to comply with the stipulations of Articles 23 and 24 of the LCL presented earlier. If properly drafted, the labor contract would be valid and enforceable. Because the employee, Lee, appears to have left mid-contract without a proper basis for termination, he would be liable for the negotiated liquidated amount of damages. In addition, Google would have possible joint and several liability under the LCL if it hired Lee before his employment contract had been validly terminated.[23]

c. Individual Employment Contract

Labor Arbitration vs. Courts
In an illustrative case arising under an individual employment contract, a union leader acted as a representative for an employee who was suing his employer.[24]

Cai was an employee at Wal-Mart's Nanchang Bayi Square store. In October 2007, Wal-Mart unilaterally terminated its labor contract relation with Cai, alleging that Cai, without paying, ate work meals during nonwork hours and

---

[22] *Gates' Microsoft and Google Settle Employee Row,* www.forbes.com/2005/12/23/gates-microsoft-google-cx_cn_1223autofacescano2.html.

[23] LCL, art. 91. For more detailed discussion of this case, *see* Marisa Pagnattaro, *"The Google" Challenge": Enforcement of Noncompete and Trade Secret Agreements for Employees Working in China,* 44 AM. BUS. L. J. 603 (2007), www.ingentaconnect.com/content/bsc/ablj/2007/00000044/00000004/art00002?crawler=true; *see also* Marisa Pagnattaro, *Protecting Trade Secrets in China: Update on Employee Disclosures and the Limitations of the Law,* 45 AM. BUS. L. J. 399 (2008).

[24] Li Jingying, Yuan gong bei ci tui, zhuang gao Wal-Mart Nanchang Bayi guang chang dian yi shen sheng su [Fired Employee Sued Wal-Mart Nanchang Bayi Square Store and Won on Trial], Sept. 26, 2008, http://www.chinacourt.org/html/article/200809/26/323163.shtml.

that such dishonest behavior seriously violated the employee handbook drafted by the company, causing losses to the company. Cai, supported by the store union chair, Gao Haitao,[25] filed a labor arbitration application on December 16, 2007, with Gao as his representative.

In Gao's opinion, Wal-Mart neither gave the required thirty-day written notice nor told the labor union of the termination in advance; such unilateral termination violated the procedures required by the Trade Union Law. In addition, Cai only inappropriately ate three work meals, which were worth merely 11.5 yuan, and the punishment was too great. Finally, the employee handbook was created without any negotiation or collective bargaining with the employees, as required under the LCL.[26]

On February 18, 2008, the Nanchang Labor Dispute Arbitration Committee rejected Cai's arbitration application. The next day, Gao prepared a civil complaint and filed in Donghu People's Court in Nanchang. The court vacated the labor arbitration decision and ordered Wal-Mart to pay Cai a lump sum of 800 yuan in wages plus a 400-yuan severance payment within three days from the day the judgment became effective. [27]

Material Breach of Rules or Serious Dereliction of Duty Causing Substantial Harm to the Employer

In another illustrative case involving wrongful employment termination, an FIE dismissed Mr. Tang, who was not only a mid-level manager of the company but also the president of the company's labor union.[28] The employer dismissed Tang on the grounds that administrative penalties assessed against the company for sanitary water supply problems were caused by Tang's negligence in his role as manager of the general affairs department at the company; his negligence thus resulted in significant damages to the company. Tang claimed instead that he was retaliated against for his actions as union president. In that role, he had raised concerns over issues of poor water quality with the company's top management on many occasions, and when he could not get any official response from the company, he filed a formal complaint with

[25] Gao resigned from his position to protest Wal-Mart's circumvention of the collective bargaining process for his store at Nanchang Bayi. *See* Paul Garver, *Wal-Mart Wins Round Three against Chinese Union Federation*, http://talkingunion.wordpress.com/2008/09/27/is-union-reform-possible-in-china/.

[26] LCL, art. 4.

[27] Li Jingying, *supra* note 24.

[28] Case discussed in Lily Wei Zhou, *Labor Union Leader's Wrongful Employment Termination Case*, CHINA LAW & PRACTICE (May 2007), http://www.chinalawandpractice.com/Article/1690272/Search/Results/Labour-Union-Leaders-Wrongful-Employment-Termination-Case.html?Keywords=Employment.

the government, which caused the administrative penalties and, Tang argued, his termination.

After going to labor arbitration, the case was taken to court, where Tang prevailed. In April 2007, before the LCL was law, the court found the termination unlawful under Article 25 of the Labor Law[29] and ordered reinstatement and 60,000 yuan in compensation.[30] The court found both that the employer had provided insufficient evidence of the seriousness and harmfulness of Tang's actions and that the employer had supervising responsibility over the water issue.[31]

If the case had arisen after the effective date of the LCL, the same result likely would have occurred, though for additional reasons. First, the LCL requires that the employer's rules and regulations be sent to the union for review and comment before they are adopted and applied, and the union must be notified before the termination, neither of which was apparently done in the Tang case.[32] Additionally, the LCL, like the Labor Law, does provide that the employer may dismiss an employee for *material* breach of rules and regulations or committing a *serious* dereliction of duty that causes *substantial* harm to the employer.[33] On the basis of these unproven violations, the aggrieved employee can obtain damages and reinstatement. In this particular case, Tang, as a union leader, also has protection and redress under the Trade Union Law, Article 52, which requires damages and reinstatement where the union representative is terminated for performing union duties.[34]

A Foreigner Working in China

Another illustration is provided to address the legal issues of a foreign person working in China who is both under contract with a foreign-based, home-country employer and under contract with a China-based corporation. This individual could be contracted for labor services as a consultant or as an

---

[29] Labor Law art. 25(1) and (2) provides that an employer may terminate an employee for serious violations of labor discipline and regulations of the employer or for causing great losses to the employer through gross neglect of duty.

[30] Lily Wei Zhou, *supra* note 28.

[31] *Id.*

[32] LCL, arts 4, 43. According to a reported 2009 draft of the Supreme People's Court Interpretation, at least in court cases, employer rules made without employee consultation may still be valid if not contrary to law. China Employment Law update, at 1, *supra* note 16; For discussion of Judicial Interpretations, see RONALD C. BROWN, *Understanding Chinese Courts and Legal Process: Law with Chinese Characteristics* (67–70), (1997).

[33] LCL, art. 39.

[34] According to the law, for this violation the union should seek redress with the "labor administrative authority," rather than the courts. Trade Union Law, art. 52.

employee and is likely working in management, but not necessarily. Assume that the individual has an employment contract with the home-country office and another employment contract with the local affiliated Chinese company during the assignment in China. For the sake of discussion, further assume that the individual, while working in China, is accused of theft of company property. How should or must an employer deal with this case, and what are the legal consequences? A checklist and an analysis of legal issues follow.

If the matter were dealt with under Chinese law, the issues would be as follows:

- The first issue is determining whether there is an employment relationship. If not, then Contract Law would apply and the question would be whether the theft "materially" breached the agreement. This would be decided by the courts. If there is an employment relationship as determined by a labor arbitration commission, then the LCL would apply.
- If governed by the LCL, the employer can terminate the employee where the employee has engaged in a serious dereliction of duty causing substantial damage to the employer or materially breached the rules and regulations of the employer. Whether that has occurred will depend on the facts and the type and amount of the theft.[35] Additionally, it will depend on whether the employer has complied with the LCL in issuing its rules and regulations.[36]
- Under the LCL, the employee may resign after providing thirty-day notice.[37] In such cases, severance pay is not required.
- The parties may also terminate by mutual agreement. In such cases, the employer is required to pay severance pay only if the employer proposes such a termination.[38]

Analysis of these issues shows the difficulties of enforcing termination if the employer failed to meet the LCL Article 4 obligation of consultation with the union before issuing its rules and regulations. Providing sufficient evidence to show "serious" violation and "substantial" harm to the employer is also very difficult. Termination by mutual agreement is possible, though the employer will be required to pay severance pay if it is found that the employer proposed termination. Therefore, the best choice for the employer is to obtain evidence of a voluntary resignation, preferably drafted by the employee. If the LCL is inapplicable and contract law governs, there will be a requirement to follow

---

[35] LCL, art. 39 and Implementation Rules of the LCL, art. 19.
[36] LCL, art. 4.
[37] LCL, art. 37.
[38] LCL, arts 36, 46(2).

the valid provisions of the agreement and to show that there was a "material" breach, often an arduous task.

A similar and possibly duplicative analysis of lawful rights and liabilities might also take place in the arbitration forums and courts of the employee's home country. This being so, employers usually seek a global settlement of the legal issues that covers China and the home-country contracts and laws. The important point is to know the full extent of applicable labor and employment laws as potential settlements are negotiated.

Employment Relationship and Remedies

A final illustration of an individual labor dispute involves a Chinese worker who performed routine maintenance work over the past five years for a foreign entity. He was originally engaged by an entity, a Representative Office since 2000, through a dispatch agency, which was the nominal employer under Chinese law. After a year or so the worker became directly engaged by the Representative Office and was no longer working for the dispatch/staffing agency. In 2005, the parent company of the Representative Office also registered as a wholly owned foreign enterprise (WOFE). In 2007, the worker continued in the same job, but claimed that he was employed by and working for the WOFE. There was no written employment contract, the worker was paid a monthly wage, and his work was performed during regular business hours with relatively little supervision. He was terminated at the end of 2008. Thereafter, he filed for arbitration, claiming the employer had violated pertinent provisions of the labor laws and he was owed unpaid wages, penalties for having no written labor contact, payment for insufficient notice of termination, severance pay, and pension insurance benefits for the period they should have been but were not paid.

Certain questions must be addressed to determine whether the case would be accepted for arbitration and to evaluate the possible outcome(s):

1. Was there an *employment relationship* and, if so, with whom?
2. What are the *liabilities*, if any, if there is an employment relation?
3. Will *judicial review* be available?

There are no definitive criteria under the labor laws for defining an employment relationship. Many factors can be considered, such as the presence of a labor contract, payment of wages and benefits, duration of work, supervision, and the like. In this case the employment relationship with the Representative Office appears somewhat clear, but the relationship with the WOFE may be less obvious. Different legal liabilities flow from the determination of the existence and location of the employment relationship. If the Labor Arbitration Commission (LAC) determines the worker was in fact working for the Representative Office, there is no liability under the labor laws because it is not a "legal person" authorized to act as an employer directly; rather, it acts only in a liaison capacity, and any workers hired must be through a staffing firm.[39] Therefore, it is not an "employer" within the meaning of the Labor Law or the LCL. Liabilities to the Representative Office will then lie in two areas: civil liability under contract law, but only for any unpaid wages, and potential administrative sanctions if a complaint is brought for unauthorized direct local hiring.[40]

If the "employer" is the WOFE, as determined by the LAC or by a strategic management decision to agree to such a designation so as to avoid possible sanctions by the government, then labor laws are applicable. The LCL would cover the employer and liabilities would follow, except as possible defenses might apply.[41] Depending on the available evidence, defense arguments could be that the worker is an independent contractor under a labor service arrangement[42] or is a part-time worker excluded from most coverage.[43] Liabilities under the LCL include violations of having no written contract (and the related penalty of double salary),[44] illegal termination with accompanying severance pay (double if wrongful termination),[45] and social insurance payments.[46]

---

[39] Interim Regulation on Foreign Enterprise Representative Office, art. 11 (1980) (requires a Representative Office to hire all workers through designated staffing firms). Regulation on Foreign Enterprise Representative Office Registration, art. 10 (1983) (requires a Representative Office to follow Article 11 of Interim Regulation on Foreign Enterprise Representative Office to recruit any local workers through designated staffing firms).

[40] E.g., in Beijing see *Implementation Rules of Regulation on Foreign Enterprise Representative Office*, art. 28 (1995) (authorities may issue administrative sanctions against a Representative Office for violation of relevant regulations, such as unauthorized direct local hiring. Administrative sanctions may include written warning, suspension of license, or revocation of registration).

[41] LCL became effective January 1, 2008; prior labor laws would need to be consulted as to any prior liabilities.

[42] LCL, art. 69; *See* textual discussion in Chapter 3, at footnote 35.

[43] LCL, arts. 68–72 (special provisions on part-time workers). For example, minimum wage standards for part-timers are optional at the local levels of government. Part-timers can participate in the basic pension or medical system, but they have to pay the premiums themselves; however, employers have to pay work injury insurance for them. Guan yu fei quan ri zhi yong gong ruo gan wen ti de yi jian [Opinions on Several Issues Regarding Part-Time Workers] (promulgated by the Ministry of Labor and Social Security, May 30, 2003), Ž3, arts. 10–12. *See* textual discussion of pension insurance in Chapter 13, at footnotes 38–55. See textual discussion of part-time workers in Chapter 3, at footnotes 36–38.

[44] LCL, art. 10 (written contract required); Implementation Rules of PRC Employment Contract Law, art. 6 (2008) (penalties for no written contract after first month).

[45] LCL, art. 47 (termination) and art. 48 (double payment for wrongful termination).

[46] LCL, art. 17 (social insurance is mandatory for individual labor contracts).

Recourse to judicial review in this case is governed by the type and amount of the claim as provided under the LMA. Requests for judicial review of arbitration awards on labor disputes must be submitted to the court within fifteen days, unless, as here, the claim was for unpaid salary and severance, in which case the award is final as long as the total is below the amount of twelve months' local minimum wages.[47]

As described earlier, the vast majority of labor law cases are usually determined on the facts and the labor laws, as determined by an arbitrator, not a judge in the courts. As can be seen in the previous illustration, the work of human resources personnel in China, as elsewhere, in developing the proper employment relationships and personnel practices can usually control outcomes as much or more than lawyers and the laws themselves.[48]

d. Collective Contract

According to the 2006 ACFTU Blue Paper on the Protection of Workers' Rights and Interests by Chinese Trade Unions, by the end of 2005, there were 754,000 collective contracts signed, covering 104 million workers.[49] In 2007 there were about 13,000 *collective* labor disputes (down from 14,000 in 2006) involving 270,000 workers (350,000 in 2006), or about 41.5 percent of the total number of workers involved in labor disputes.[50] Collective disputes often lead to collective actions indicative of social unrest, such as demonstrations, strikes, or even violence.[51] Rights arising under these agreements are basically treated like individual labor contract disputes, with resolution of the labor dispute

---

[47] LMA, art. 47. Awards for social insurance are also final. *Id.* For discussion on the finality of arbitration awards and the relationship with the courts, *see* text in Chapter 14 accompanying footnotes 5–77.

[48] Anecdotal common trouble spots precipitating labor arbitration claims are firing an employee for a reason not explicitly entimed in the labor contacts or employer manual; for non-payment of overtime for not having a writtern contract; and firing an employee for whom the employer did not make the required social insurance or pension payments. Wanna Get Sued in China? Your Ex-Employees Can Help, Harris & Moure, Chena Law Blog, http://www.chinalawblog.com/2009/04/wanna_get_sued_in_china_your_e.html.

[49] Blue Paper on the Protection of Workers' Rights and Interests, http://english. acftu.org/template/10002/file.jsp?cid=114&aid=264.

[50] National Bureau of Statistics of China, China Statistical Communique on Labor and Social Security Development in 2007, http://bg2.mofcom.gov.cn/aarticle/chinanews/200806/20080605584560.html; Statistical Communiqué on Labor and Social Security Undertakings in 2006, http://www.stats.gov.cn/english/newsandcomingevents/t20070524_402406436 htm.

[51] Ronald Brown, *China Labor Dispute Resolution*, FOUNDATION FOR LAW, JUSTICE AND SOCIETY, at 2 (2008).

coming through the usual channels of labor arbitration and the courts, though the decisions affect many employees, such as in an unpaid wage claim by many workers.[52]

---

[52] Labor Law, art. 84; LCL, art. 56; LMA, art. 27. For commentary, *see The Need for Legal Muscle to Enforce China's Collective Labour Contracts*, CHINA LABOUR BULLETIN, www.clb. org.hk/en/node/100269.

16

Illustrative Contracts

1. Individual Employment Contract

Employment contracts are required by the LCL, Article 17, to include the following items:

1. The employer's name, domicile, legal representative, or major person-in-charge
2. The employee's name, domicile, identity card number, or other valid identity certificate number
3. The time limit for the labor contract
4. The job descriptions and work locations
5. The work hours, break time, and vacations
6. The remunerations
7. The social security
8. The employment protection, work conditions, and protection against and prevention of occupational harm
9. Other items that shall be included in the labor contract under any laws or regulations

In addition to those essential clauses, the employer and the employee may stipulate the "probation time period, training, confidentiality, supplementary insurances, welfares and benefits, and other items."

An illustrative (not model) employment contract is translated below to provide insight into practical applications of the labor laws. Obviously, the sophistication of the agreements can vary widely among employers and those receiving advice from HRM personnel and legal advisors. How the labor and employment laws in this book are translated into labor contracts is a practical lesson in itself.

Illustrative Labor Contract (used in the manufacturing industry in 2008; on file with author)

Employer enterprise (party A): _____

Operation address: _____

Legal representative main representative): _____

Laborer (party B): _____ Gender: _____

Nationality (zone):_____

Address of registered residence: _____

Existing detailed address: _____

ID card no. (other valid ID card no.): _____

As per "labor law of the People's Republic of China" (hereafter referred to "labor law"), "labor contract law of the People's Republic of China" (hereafter referred to "labor contact law"), and the legal requirements of nation and municipality, party A and party B sign this contract on the basic of legality, equality, voluntariness, negotiation and faithfulness, comply with all the listed items of this contract.

I. Contract Term

Party A and party B can define the contract term as follows:

1. Fixed term: It totals ____years, begins from _____ (date) to_____(date).
2. Non-fixed term: It begins from (date).
3. The term for certain work begins from _____ (date) to _____ (date): If a probation period is needed, the probation period begins from _____ (date) to_____ (date).

The contract term includes a probation period. If the contract term is less than three months and is measured by the term of certain work, a probation period cannot be stipulated.

II. Work Content and Workplace

1. Party A should arrange party B to work as_____ (job), according to the requirements of production or the task.
2. Workplace_____

3. Party A should define party B's work responsibilities, production requirements' quality targets, and working arrangements on the basis of work
quotas and labor weave, meaning compliance with legal requirements.
See Shaoxing China, Labor and Social Security Bureau, http://www.
sx.gov.cn/anportal/dept_label.jsp?catalog_id=20050920000019. According
to the product technology and organization:

4. Party B must diligently improve his or her working skills and accomplish
the tasks required by party A. Working content _____.

5. Party A can put into writing labor's position or task according
to working requirements after negotiating mutually.

III. Working Protection and Working Condition

1. Party A must set up and publish work safety and sanitation principles, safety
rules, and work regulations; educate party B on work safety and hygiene;
and provide safe and sanitary conditions.

2. Party A must, in the hiring process, offer party B necessary working protection and healthy food according to party B's tasks, rank working condition
and periodically provide health checkups, inform party B of workplace
dangers and risks, protection measures taken, and available treatment for
occupational diseases.

3. Party A must specially protect female labor and infant persons according to
law.

4. Party B must strictly abide by safety operation regulations and other kinds
of working safety and sanitation principles.

5. It is not defined as breach of the contract when party B refuses employer
directives which may violate the rules and regulations. Party B has a right to
criticize, prosecute, and sue regarding working conditions that harm health
and life.

IV. Working Hours, Rest, and Vacations

1. Party B executes _____working system
   (1) According to the standard working-hour system, the normal working
   hours of party B shall be eight hours per day, for an average of forty
   hours per week. If Party A must arrange for party B to do overtime work
   due to work requirements, Party A shall negotiate with the labor union
   and with party B; meanwhile, the extended working hour for a day shall
   generally not exceed one hour. If such extension is called for due to
   special reasons, the extended time shall not exceed three hours per day;

however, the total extension in a month shall not exceed thirty-six hours so as to ensure party B's health.

(2) According to the comprehensive working-hour system approved by the Department of Labor and Administration, the average working time of day and week are not excess legal working times.

(3) According to nonfixed working-hour system approved by the Department of Labor and Administration, working time should be executed by national principle.

2. Party B is entitled to the rests and legal vacations in accordance with laws.

V. Payment of Labor

1. Party A should abide by the principle of "distribution according to one's performances," execute the same salary for the same work fairly, and set up the salary level and distribution methods (if a group contract is established, salary is not less than as stipulated by the provision of the contract) in accordance with the operations, condition, and finances of its own company; this should be an attachment to this contract.

2. Party A should pay party B who finishes the required tasks a monthly salary by legal tender. It should be paid at least once monthly.

The monthly salary is _____ in probation, _____ after probation, and paid on _____ (date).

3. Party A cannot avoid paying the standard minimum salary in _____ City regarding party B's salary and shall increase the salary level step in accord with improvements in the company's operational results.

4. Party A arranges overtime work for party B to meet working requirements; overtime salary should be paid according to the provision of the state.

5. Party A should pay party B's salary or living expenses by laws if the company is shut down for a reason not caused by party B.

VI. Social Insurance and Welfare

1. Party A and party B must participate in the social insurance system and respectively pay all kinds of social insurance fees, such as pension insurance, medical insurance, work injury insurance, maternity insurance, and unemployment insurance, according to the state provision on social insurance.

2. Party A must pay party B legal allowances and subsidy.

3. The treatment of female workers during pregnancy, confinement, and nursing periods is in accordance with the relevant provisions of the state and autonomous region.

4. Party B shares the costs of welfare treatment according to the relevant principles of the state and autonomous region.

VII. Job Training

1. Party B should be educated and trained before assuming a normal and technical task and should get special job qualification via special training before taking up a specialized industrial job.
2. Party A pays for training expenses incurred by party B. For specific technology training, Party A can sign a contract with party B to specify the training period. In the process of implementing the contract, party B should compensate party A for breaching contract. Compensation amount cannot exceed the training expenses and the amount should be paid in installments.

VIII. Implementation, Amendment, Renewal, Termination, and End of the Labor Contract

1. Party A and party B must implement their obligations according to the provisions of the contract.
2. The contract may be amended by party A and party B in accordance with the principle of equality, voluntariness, and negotiation. Parties cannot violate the relevant laws and should go through the proper amendment procedure. The agreement should be signed.
3. The contract can be renewed through negotiation by parties. It needs to go through the proper procedure.
4. The contract can be terminated according to negotiation by party A and party B.
5. The contract can be terminated by party A under the following conditions:
    (1) Where the company proves that the employee has failed to meet the recruitment requirement during the probation period;
    (2) Where the employee has seriously violated the labor policies of the company;
    (3) Where the employee has committed a serious dereliction of duty or practices graft, causing substantial damage to the interests of the company;
    (4) Where the employee has established an additional employment relationship with another employing unit that materially affects the completion of the tasks assigned by the company, or refuses to rectify the situation after the same is brought to his or her attention by the company;
    (5) The contract is invalid due to the situation stipulated by the first line, first clause, of the 26th item of the Labor Contract Law;
    (6) Where the employee is subject to criminal liabilities.

6. The contract can be ended by party A by giving notice in written form 30 (thirty) days in advance or paying an additional one-month salary.
   (1) Where the employee suffers from illness or a non–work-related injury and is unable to take up the original work or any other work assigned by the company to him or her on the conclusion of his or her medical treatment leave;
   (2) Where the employee is incompetent at his position and remains incompetent after undergoing training or being assigned to another position;
   (3) Where there is a major change to the objective circumstances under which this contract was executed that has rendered this contract unenforceable and the parties have failed to reach an agreement on an amendment to this contract after consultation.
7. If any of the following circumstances make it necessary to reduce the workforce by 20 persons or more or by a number of persons that is less than 20 but accounts for 10 percent or more of the total number of the enterpriser's employees, the employer may reduce the workforce after it has explained the circumstances to its labor union or to all of its employees 30 days in advance, has considered the opinion of the labor union or the employees, and has consequently reported the workforce reduction plan to the labor administration department.
   (1) Restructuring pursuant to the Enterprise Bankruptcy Law;
   (2) Serious difficulties in production or business operations;
   (3) The enterprise switches production, introduces a major technological innovation, or revises its business method and, after amendment of employee contracts, still needs to reduce its workforce; or
   (4) Another major change in the objective economic circumstances relied on at the time of conclusion of the employment contracts renders them unperformable.
   When reducing the workforce, party A shall retain, with priority, persons
   (1) Who have concluded with the employer fixed-term employment contracts with a relatively long term;
   (2) Who have concluded open-ended employment contracts with the employer; or
   (3) Who are the only ones in their families to be employed and whose families have an elderly person or a minor for whom they need to provide.
   If the employer that has reduced its workforce pursuant to the first paragraph hereof hires again within six months, it shall give notice to the persons dismissed at the time of the reduction and, all things being equal, hire them on a preferential basis.

8. An employer may not terminate an employment contract pursuant to clause 6 and 7 under Chapter 8 if party B
   (1) Is engaged in an operation exposing him or her to occupational disease hazards and has not undergone a predeparture occupational health checkup, or is suspected of having contracted an occupational disease and is being diagnosed or under medical observation;
   (2) Has been confirmed as having lost or partially lost his capacity to work due to an occupational disease contracted or a work-related injury sustained with party B;
   (3) Has contracted an illness or sustained a non–work-related injury and the set period of medical care therefore has not expired;
   (4) Is a female employee in her pregnancy, confinement, or nursing period;
   (5) Has been working for Party A continually for not less than 15 years and is less than 5 years away from his legal retirement age;
   (6) Finds himself in other circumstances stipulated in laws or administrative statutes.

9. When Party A is to terminate an labor contract unilaterally, it shall give the labor union advance notice of the reason thereof. If party A violates laws, administrative statutes, or the employment contract, the labor union has the right to demand that party A rectify the matter. Party A shall study the labor union's opinions and notify the labor union in writing as to the outcome of its handling of the matter.

10. The contract can be terminated by party B via giving notice to party A 30 days in advance. If it is during the probation term, then 3-day notice in advance is required.

11. Under the following circumstances, the employee may immediately terminate this contract by serving a written notice to the company.
    (1) Where the company fails to provide labor protection or safe working conditions as provided by this contract;
    (2) Where the company fails to pay remunerations in full and on time;
    (3) Where the company fails to make social insurance contributions for the employee in accordance with the laws;
    (4) Where the company's labor policies conflicts with the laws or regulations and thereby harms the employee's rights and interests;
    (5) Where the company uses such means as deception or coercion or takes advantage of the employee's difficulties to cause the employee to sign this contract or to make an amendment thereto that is contrary to the employee's true intent; or
    (6) In other circumstances stipulated by laws or administrative statutes.

If the employer uses violence, threats, or unlawful restriction of personal freedom to compel the employee to work, or if the employee is instructed to violate rules and regulations or is peremptorily ordered by the company to perform dangerous operations that threaten his or her personal safety, the employee may terminate this contract with immediate effect without serving prior notice to the company.

12. The contract can be ended if:
    (1) The contract term expires;
    (2) The employee has begun to receive his or her basic retirement pension in accordance with the law or has reached his or her statutory retirement age;
    (3) The employee dies or is declared dead or missing by the People's Court;
    (4) The company is declared bankrupt;
    (5) The company has its business license revoked, is ordered to close, is closed down, or decides on early liquidation;
    (6) Other circumstances specified by laws or administrative statutes occur.

13. If a labor contract expires and any of the circumstances specified in 8.8 hereof occur, the term of the labor contract shall be extended until the relevant circumstance ceases to exist, at which point the contract shall end. However, matters relating to the ending of the employment contract of a worker who has lost or partially lost his or her capacity to work as specified in item 8.2 hereof shall be handled in accordance with state regulations on work-related injury insurance.

14. On the termination or ending of this contract, the company will issue the termination or end certification to the employee and transfer his or her personnel archives and social insurance within 15 days.

LX. Other Appointed Items Stimulated by Parties

IX. *Severance Pay and Compensation*

1. In any of the following circumstances, Party A shall pay party B severance pay:
   (1) The labor contract is terminated by party A pursuant to 8.4, 8.6, or 8.7 hereof;
   (2) The labor contract is terminated by party B pursuant to 8.11;
   (3) The labor contract is terminated pursuant to 8.12.4 or 8.12.5 hereof;
   (4) The labor contract is a fixed-term contract that ends pursuant to 8.12.1, unless party B does not agree to renew the contract, even though the

conditions offered by party A are the same as or better than those stipulated in the current contract;

(5) Other circumstances specified in laws or administrative statues.

2. If party B breaches the provisions of this contract, the labor policies of the company, or the regulations of the other appointed items such as confidential information or noncompetition and thereby has caused economic losses to the company, party B shall compensate the company for such losses.

3. If Party A breaches the provisions of the contract and thereby has caused economic loss to party B, party A shall compensate party B accordingly for such loss.

X. Labor Dispute

For any disputes between parties arising from this contract, either party may apply to the labor dispute conciliation committee for conciliation. Either or both parties may directly apply to the labor dispute arbitration committee for arbitration.

XI. The Matters Not Mentioned in the Contract Shall Be Handled According to the Relevant Regulations of the State

XII. When There Are Differences Between the Contract in Chinese and the English Version for Foreigner Labor, the Chinese Version Is the Basis

XIII. This Contract Is Made in Duplicate. Party A and Party B Each Keep One Copy

Employer enterprise (party A): (stamp)
Legal representative (authorized agent): (signature)
Labor (party B): (signature)
Date of signing:

2. A Model Collective Contract (for Trial Implementation)

Issued by Beijing Municipal Federation of Trade Unions (December 2007)

Table of Contents

Chapter One   General Principles

Article 1   This contract is signed by and between the worker and the enterprise (including institutions under corporate management and nonenterprise units under civilian auspices), with unanimity reached through consultation in accordance with the *Labor Law of the People's Republic of China, the Labor Contract Law of the People's Republic of China, the Trade Union Law of the People's Republic of China, the Collective Contract Regulations of the Beijing Municipality*, and relevant laws and regulations for the purpose of safeguarding the legitimate rights and interests of the workers and enterprises, giving impetus to the development of enterprises and to the improvement of workers' interests and constructing harmonious and stable labor relations.

Article 2   This contract determines various labor standards and working conditions, including payment for labor, working hours, leaves and holidays, labor safety and health, job training, insurance and welfare, etc.

Article 3   This contract is legally binding upon the enterprise and all its workers.

Article 4   The enterprise shall operate itself according to law, carry out this contract conscientiously, show respect and provide backing for trade union work, positively carry out the *Work Rules for Enterprise Trade Unions*, appropriate and pay trade union funds on time and in their full amount in accordance with the law, and ensure the exercise of various trade union duties.

Article 5   Enterprise trade unions shall safeguard the legitimate rights and interests of workers, coordinate labor relations, and organize workers to participate in democratic management and supervision in enterprises. Trade unions should educate workers to conscientiously observe the rules and regulations and labor disciplines as laid down by the enterprises; to take good care of enterprise properties, guard enterprise secrets, and devote themselves to work; to conscientiously carry out labor contracts and collective contracts and be scrupulous in doing their duties; to positively give backing to and participate in enterprise reform; to consciously abide by the important decisions and resolutions reviewed and adopted at the Worker's Congress or Worker's Conference; and to fulfill their duties based on their own jobs.

Chapter Two   Payment for Labor

Article 6   Wage Distribution System

The enterprise shall set up the wage distribution system mainly based on job responsibility, achievements in work, and risks in operation; strictly carry out the minimum wage security system set up by the state, and abide by the state labor laws with regard to wages and workers' welfare.

The enterprise wage distribution system follows the principle of equal pay for equal work and more pay for more work, with laws observed and prominence given to knowledge and skill, and it links wages with responsibility, benefits, and risk. The system includes principles and modes for wage distribution among workers as well as the specific methods for distributing wages, bonuses, subsidies, and allowances; and ensures transparency.

In drawing up and adjusting rules and regulations as well as enforcement measures concerning workers' rights and interests such as wage distribution and work appraisal, the enterprise should heed the opinions of the trade union, and such rules and regulations should not come into force unless they are reviewed and adopted by the Worker's Congress or Worker's Conference.

Article 7 Wage System

Different wage systems are carried out for workers on different jobs, such as time wage (including duty wage, job salary, and engagement salary), piece-rate wage, yearly salary, and wages for a certain amount of work done.

Other forms for income distribution include earnings from undertaking contracted scientific and technological projects; commissions from profits of new products, scientific and technological achievements, and technology patents converted into stock; fixed-base assessment; and commissions from sales.

Article 8 Wage Income

The wage incomes incurred in enterprises include seniority wage, duty wage, scale wage, job salary, skill wage, piece-rate wage, overtime wage, special wage, bonus (achievement wage), allowance, and subsidy, etc.

The seniority wage, duty wage, scale wage, job salary, skill wage, allowance, and subsidy determined by an enterprise constitute the base pay for workers on different jobs.

The workers, female or male, will get equal pay for equal types of work or jobs.

The enterprise shall enforce other distribution systems in light of its relevant regulations, such as yearly wage system, contracting-out system, and commission system, etc.

Article 9 Methods for Wage Payment

The enterprise will take monthly (hourly, daily, or weekly) payment as the cycle for payment of wages on the principle of paying wages on time and in their full amount and with precedence. Wages for a certain amount of scheduled work should be paid as soon as it is done.

The enterprise should make at least one wage payment to the worker in each month. The enterprise shall pay wages to the worker in the form of currency (which can be done through bank) on_____day and_____month. The wages should be paid in advance before holidays, festivals, and the two-day (days off), and the enterprise should not embezzle or default on the payment of wages.

The enterprise, when not in a position to pay wages on time owing to the difficulty in production or operation, should make that situation clear to workers, and such a deferment is allowed only after unanimity is reached through consultation with the trade union or at the Worker's Congress and should not exceed 30 days at the maximum. In case of the enterprise unable to pay wages after 30 days, the trade union or workers' representatives can resolve it with the enterprise; if they fail to resolve it through consultation, they can report it to labor security departments or apply to the people's court for a payment order.

Article 10   Workers' Wage Increase Mechanism

The enterprise shall conduct a collective wage consultation, sign a special wage agreement, and establish a mechanism for normal increase and adjustment of workers' wages with the trade union on the basis of the change in economic benefits, consumer price index (CPI), the minimum wage pattern, the guidance wage spread on the labor market, the wage guideline, the average workers' wage level of the Beijing municipality and the average levels in different trades and professions, and the labor productivity of the enterprise, so as to enable the workers' wages to increase regularly with the increase of economic benefits. And the percentage (_____%) of increase in economic benefits of the enterprise will be the percentage (_____%) for the increase of workers' wages.

Article 11   Rules on Workers' Wage Increase

When economic benefits increase, the enterprise will raise the workers' wage level year by year in accordance with the methods for wage distribution. And the wage increase shall be inclined toward the core members in production and operation, the urgently needed personnel, and the workers who have made outstanding contributions; wage increases of the low-income workers and technicians at the production front line shall not be less than wage increases of the persons in charge of the enterprise, and the overall wage level of workers should be raised gradually.

Article 12   The Minimum Wage Pattern

The workers, who have provided normal labor in prescribed working hours, should enjoy a monthly salary no less than the minimum wage as set by the enterprise. The minimum wage set by the enterprise should be higher than the minimum wage set by the Beijing municipality, which shall amount to_____yuan per month or_____yuan per hour. And such a minimum wage should be adjusted every year according to the operation of the enterprise and based on the change of the minimum wage pattern of the Beijing municipality.

Article 13   Per Capita Enterprise Wage Level

The workers' per capita wage realized by the enterprise in the previous year was_____yuan, and the annual workers' per capita wage during_____ (year) will arrive at_____yuan on the condition that the economic benefits of the enterprise increase.

Article 14   Seniority Wage

The seniority wage prescribed by the enterprise is_____yuan per year, based on December 31 of the same year as the deadline for the accounting.

Article 15   Duty Wage

The enterprise shall determine duty wages according to different operational and management jobs (unless otherwise stipulated by law). The administrative posts in an enterprise include_____, _____, and_____, etc. Posts for party and mass affairs in an enterprise correspond to administrative posts according to regulation. The posts are subject to appointments or removals by the party or government. (See attached table for the duty wage pattern.)

Article 16   Scale Wage

For the same post, the enterprise will determine different wage scales based on job features and in accordance with the number of years a worker held the post, the number of his or her working years, and the titles for technical personnel. (See attached table for the scale wage.)

Article 17   Job Salary

The job salary shall be established based on job appraisal, with equal pay to be granted for equal work and wages to vary with jobs. The job salary is determined by such factors as job responsibility, complexity, and working conditions, including worker posts, technical posts, ordinary management posts, and auxiliary rear-service posts, totaling_____scales, with the amount of wages ranging from _____. (See attached table for jobs and job salaries.)

One who has worked at the same post for_____ consecutive years can enjoy the job salary of a higher level after he or she qualifies through examination.

Article 18   Skill Wage

The enterprise shall formulate the skill wage pattern to encourage workers to learn and gain more skills, and the skill wage pattern shall be formulated on the basis of the knowledge and abilities acquired by the workers in light of the assessable or possessed knowledge and skills, educational background, and titles and on the principle of whether the enterprise will engage the worker or not.

In accordance with the occupational qualifications, the worker post can be divided into junior worker, middle-rank worker, senior worker, technician, and senior technician. (See attached table for the graded wages.)

In accordance with the occupational qualifications, the technical post can be divided into primary professional title, intermediate professional title, high-level professional title, and chief high-level professional title. (See attached table for the graded wages.)

The worker who satisfies the conditions of any two grades will enjoy the wages of the higher level.

One who has worked under the same wage pattern for_____ consecutive years can enjoy the skill wage of a higher level after he or she qualifies through examination.

For those who have made technical advances and given great impetus to the production and operation of the enterprise, enabling it to achieve immediate economic benefits, and who have achieved outstanding results, their wages can be promoted with the approval of the enterprise to_____ scales after examination by the skill assessment committee of the enterprise.

Article 19   Bonus (Achievement Wage)

The enterprise shall appraise and decide the bonus base and distribution pattern according to economic benefits and production quotas fulfilled by the workers during the assessment period. (See attached table for bonus bases.)

Article 20   Piece-Rate Wage

The enterprise shall formulate the piece-rate wage posts and wage pattern through consultation with the trade union and shall appraise, decide, and grant piece-rate wages according to the production quotas fulfilled by the workers. (See attached table for piece-rate wage posts and the wage pattern.)

Article 21   Overtime Wage

The enterprise shall pay for the overtime work done by the worker in accordance with the Beijing municipal and state regulations. The monthly overtime wage base shall be determined by the enterprise and the trade union through consultation and shall not be less than the average monthly basic wages earned by the worker in the previous year. The piece-rate overtime wage base shall be assessed as per the daily production quota of the worker.

Article 22   Relevant Allowances and Subsidies

Allowances to be granted by the enterprise include high-temperature allowance, full work attendance allowance, and wages to be paid under special circumstances.

High-temperature allowance: persons who work outdoors shall enjoy a monthly allowance no less than_____yuan; and persons who work indoors shall enjoy a monthly allowance no less than_____yuan. The high-temperature work means work that is done outdoors by workers in high temperatures (with the highest daily temperature to be 35° Celsius and above) or the work done in workplaces where effective measures cannot be taken to bring the temperature under 33° Celsius (exclusive of 33° Celsius).

Full work attendance allowance: allowance for work in shifts shall amount to_____yuan per month, night shift to_____yuan per month, and day shift to_____yuan per month; those who are late for work, come off duty earlier than their prescribed working hours, or are released from their regular posts for_____times and above or ask for leave for_____days in the same month shall not enjoy the full work attendance allowance.

Wages to be paid under special circumstances: as per state stipulations (such as allowances for work in mine shafts, high above the ground, in the open air, in high or low temperatures and under noxious and harmful circumstances and conditions, as well as model worker allowance). (For details, see attached table.)

Various subsidies: food allowance, transportation subsidy, communication subsidy, clothing allowance, and housing allowance.

Article 23   Production Quota

The enterprise shall work out production quotas through consultation with the trade union, and the workload to be fulfilled by more than 90 percent of the workers on the same job within prescribed working hours and under the same working conditions will be taken as the production quota.

Where production quotas need to be amended due to technical innovation, technological transformation, change of working conditions, personnel adjustment, cost reduction, change of raw materials, and wage increase, the enterprise shall work out a scheme according to state and trade regulations and in line with the actual conditions of the enterprise, and shall finalize the scheme through consultation with the trade union. (See attached table for production quotas.)

Article 24　Other Stipulations

For a worker who takes a sick leave or is on leave for non–work-related injuries, his or her actually paid-out monthly wages, after deducting personal payable social insurance premiums and the housing accumulation funds (exclusive of model worker allowance), shall by no means be less than 80 percent of the minimum pay as prescribed by the enterprise.

The enterprise shall, after deducting personal payable social insurance premiums and the housing accumulation funds, pay basic living expenses no less than 70 percent of the minimum pay as prescribed by the enterprise to the personnel awaiting job assignment.

Wages of a worker on probation shall by no means come under the lowest scale of wages for the same job or under 80 percent of the wages as agreed to in the labor contract and shall by no means be less than the minimum pay as prescribed by the enterprise.

For a worker who takes a home leave, a marriage leave, or a funeral leave, his or her wages shall by no means come under the minimum pay as prescribed by the enterprise.

The enterprise shall pay wages for normal work to the female workers who enjoy maternity leave and get involved in regular breast-feeding, who enjoy holidays according to law for childbirth under the family planning scheme or receive family planning operations (married workers), or who receive antenatal examinations and engage in breast-feeding.

The living expenses of the personnel in early retirement should be paid in accordance with the relevant regulations laid down by the enterprise.

The enterprise shall fine the workers who offend against the discipline according to the rules and regulations, with their remaining monthly salaries not to come under 70 percent of the minimum pay as prescribed by the enterprise after the deduction of the personal payable social insurance premiums and the housing accumulation funds.

Chapter Three   Working Hours

Article 25   Standard Working-Hour System

The enterprise shall carry out the standard working-hour system, with workers to work 8 hours a day and the weekly working hours not to exceed 40 hours.

The workers shall have one hour for dinner each day and shall have a 15-minute break after a four-hour work period. The time for dinner for the workers should be specified, and a dinnertime should be arranged after a five-hour work period.

Article 26   Irregular Working-Hour System

The enterprise may implement the irregular working-hour system as need arises to arrange workers of some sectors or on some jobs as well as workers involved in some special jobs to work on Saturdays, Sundays, or at night alternately, or to work flexible hours. The enterprise shall report such a system to labor and administrative departments for approval and shall make it known to the trade union.

Article 27   Comprehensively Calculated Working-Hour System

The enterprise, where the standard working-hour system cannot be carried out because of production features, can practice the comprehensively calculated working-hour system; namely, the working hours are calculated comprehensively based on the week, month, quarter, or year as a cycle, but the average daily working hours and the average weekly working hours should equal the prescribed standard working hours as a whole, with rewards to be paid for extended working hours. The enterprise shall report such a system to labor and administrative departments for review and approval before implementation and shall make it known to the trade union.

The enterprise should consult with the trade union for specific work arrangement on the basis of paying full attention to workers' opinions, and should adopt such measures as centralized working, centralized rest, having holidays by turns, and working in shifts to fulfill production quotas and work tasks. The enterprise should arrange holidays for workers no fewer than_____days a year to safeguard the workers' right for holidays and vacations.

The enterprise can practice part-time employment with flexible hours for flexible work arrangements in line with the production features, special work requirements, or scope of responsibility. Working hours for a worker employed for a part-time pattern shall not exceed 4 hours per day on the average and shall not exceed an accumulated total of 24 hours each week.

For workers involved in piecework, the enterprise shall consult with the trade union to determine reasonable production quotas and piece-rate wage patterns with reference to the standard working-hour system, protect workers' right for holidays and vacations, and ensure that the workers can have at least_____days off within each week.

Article 28   Overtime Work Arrangement

The enterprise, through consultation with the trade union, workers, or workers' representatives, can extend the working hours for no more than one hour per day on average; if the working hours need to be extended due to special causes, the maximum of the hours to be prolonged shall not exceed 3 hours per day on the condition that the workers' physical health is protected, but the monthly maximum shall not exceed 36 hours.

Article 29   Definition of the Extra Working Hours

Time in excess of the average daily 8 working hours; time in excess of the average weekly 40 working hours; working hours arranged for workers during official holidays.

Article 30   Procedures and Agreement on Overtime Work

1. The enterprise shall consult with the trade union or workers' representatives to decide on the working hours, number of personnel, and content for the overtime work.
2. The worker has the right to turn down any overtime work imposed on him or her by the enterprise if no consultation is conducted between the enterprise and the worker.
3. The worker who needs to work overtime shall ask the responsible department for approval and then he or she can get the overtime pay.
4. The trade union can look into the records of overtime work in the enterprise at any time and check up on implementation of workers' leaves by turns and on payment of overtime pay to workers.
5. The trade union has the right to reflect and report on behalf of the workers on the overtime work, which is done in excess of prescribed hours or endangers workers' physical and mental health, to the enterprise or to higher competent authorities.

Article 31   Agreement on Overtime Work

The enterprise, in addition to paying overtime wages in accordance with the state regulation, shall observe the following agreements:

1. Except for *force majeure* or normal extra work, the enterprise shall give day/days off and pay overtime wages as agreed to workers for having worked overtime on holidays; if the extra working hours are less than 4 hours, the worker should receive a 4-hour overtime pay no less than the hourly overtime wage base.
2. The enterprise shall pay overtime wages to workers based on working hours for demanding workers to wait for work in a flexible way and not to leave their work without permission.
3. The trade union has the right to check on behalf of workers the acts endangering workers' physical health and personal safety or exceeding the prescribed extended working hours or extended working hours as stipulated by rules and regulations.

Article 32   Day/Days Off for Having Worked Overtime

The enterprise should arrange day/days off for the worker for having worked overtime within_____working days in accordance with the stipulation; the enterprise, being unable to arrange day/days off for the worker, should pay out overtime wages. The worker can suggest the dates off for having worked overtime according to his or her own needs. If the worker's application for day/days off is turned down by the enterprise, then the day/days off can be held valid within one year.

Chapter Four   Labor Contract Management

Article 33   Labor Contract System

The enterprise shall standardize the labor employment according to law, strengthen the management of labor contracts, and establish the labor contracts system through consultation with the trade union. The trade union should help and guide workers to sign and carry out labor contracts with the enterprise in accordance with the law and should supervise the implementation of the labor contract system in the enterprise.

Article 34   Recruitment of Workers

With a view to further development, the enterprise has decided to recruit workers and shall recruit workers in accordance with the required conditions on the principles of openness, fairness, equitableness, and employment based on competitive selection. The enterprise, when laying down conditions for recruitment, should detail, specify, and quantify the conditions and make them operable and known to the trade union to facilitate the recruitment of workers and assessment of probationers' job proficiency by the enterprise.

The enterprise, when laying down conditions for recruiting or enrolling workers, should not incur any discrimination due to sex, nationality, belief, religion, marriage, or age.

Article 35   Forms of Recruitment

1. Full-time workers: The enterprise shall sign labor contracts with all its workers and staff members in labor relations and shall make work arrangements for the workers according to types of work, contents of work, working hours, and criteria as stipulated in the labor contracts.
2. Contract workers: The enterprise shall sign agreements with labor service companies to recruit contract workers to do temporary, auxiliary, or replaceable work. Jobs of a protracted nature provided by the enterprise are not suitable for contract workers, and the number of contract workers cannot exceed_____percent of the total number of workers in the enterprise.
3. Part-time workers: The enterprise can enroll part-timers for seasonal, temporary, or auxiliary work, and both parties can enter into oral agreements. The number of the part-timers cannot exceed_____percent of the total number of workers. The labor payment for part-timers is based on hourly calculation.

Article 36   Probation Period

1. In case the worker on probation has_____day/days off more than stipulated due to leave of absence or sick leave, then the number of days for the probation period should be extended accordingly. The one who continues to work after the probation period will become the full-time worker of the enterprise, and his or her working age should be counted from the date of employment.
2. The enterprise shall inform the worker of the termination of the labor contract during the probation period at least_____days prior to the termination and should give written reasons for the dismissal.
3. The enterprise, when recruiting workers, should give priority to recruiting the job applicants who once worked in the same enterprise, with his or her probation period reaching one month and above.

Article 37   Labor Contract Period

The enterprise shall determine the labor contract period in accordance with the type of work, work demands, and nature of the work and shall divide the period into fixed period, unlimited period, and period for accomplishing a certain amount of work.

Workers who have won titles of model worker or advanced worker at the municipal level and above can conclude unlimited-period labor contracts.

Article 38   Conclusion of the Labor Contract

1. When the enterprise formulates or modifies the labor contract, the parties to the contract should consult with each other about the specific contents of the contract and should heed the opinions of the trade union. Texts of the labor contract can be submitted to the Worker's Congress or Worker's Conference for discussion.
2. The trade union should give publicity to laws and regulations relating to the labor contract among workers, help workers learn about the texts, and enhance the workers' self-protection awareness in carrying out the labor contracts and safeguarding their rights and interests according to law.
3. The trade union shall supervise and examine the management, signing, and execution of the labor contracts.
4. Contents such as restricting female workers from getting married or giving birth to children shall not be stipulated in the labor contracts signed between the enterprise and the female workers.

Article 39   Change of the Labor Contract

The enterprise, after reaching unanimity through consultation with the workers, can change the contents agreed on in the labor contracts and shall record the changes in written form, which will come into force on signature or stamp by both parties.

The trade union should supervise the validity of changing the procedures stipulated in the labor contracts and should help workers learn about the changed substantive contents in the labor contracts and the possible effects in the future.

Article 40   Termination of the Labor Contract

1. The enterprise shall inform the trade union in advance of the reasons for unilaterally terminating the labor contract. Where it is inappropriate, the

trade union has the right to put forward opinions. When the enterprise violates laws, regulations, or rules as agreed on in the labor contract, the trade union has the right to ask the enterprise to make rectification. The enterprise should accept the opinions of the trade union and should inform the trade union of the rectification results in writing.

2. If a worker stays ill after medical treatment is completed, his or her ability to work should be authenticated by the Beijing Municipal Committee for Labor Ability Appraisal. If the ability to work is identified to be between the first degree and the fourth degree, then the worker should withdraw from his or her post with the labor contract to be terminated, and he or she should go through formalities for ill-health retirement, leaving his or her post for retirement due to illness or non–work-related injuries; if the ability to work is identified to be between the fifth degree and the tenth degree, the enterprise can then terminate the labor contract and shall pay economic compensations and medical allowances in accordance with the regulations.

3. The state-owned enterprises, when practicing staff reduction, shall submit the staff reduction plans to the Worker's Congress for review and adoption.

4. When reducing the staff, the enterprise should put priority on retaining the following staff members:
   (1) Those who have won titles of model worker or advanced worker at the municipal level and above;
   (2) Those who have concluded labor contracts for an unlimited period;
   (3) Those who have concluded labor contracts for a long fixed period;
   (4) Those with their other family members being unemployed, with aged people or minors to support;
   (5) The destitute workers and needy workers of the enterprise.

5. The trade union should supervise the enterprise in terminating the labor contracts and ensure that the contract termination is lawful, the reasons for termination are adequate, and the workers have the right of petition.

Article 41   Renewal of the Labor Contract

The trade union should supervise the validity of the renewed labor contracts and the standardization of the renewal procedures. If the number of workers at the expiration of their labor contracts exceeds 30 percent of the total number of workers and the contract renewal rate is lower than 80 percent, the trade union should report the case to labor security departments and to higher trade unions in order to ensure stable labor relations in the enterprise.

Article 42   *Other Agreed Terms*

1. If the contract workers and part-timers recruited by the enterprise have worked at important posts for_____consecutive years and more, then the enterprise should arrange its full-time workers to take over such posts or turn the contract workers and the part-timers into full-time workers.
2. In case of concluding, executing, changing, terminating, abrogating, or renewing the labor contract, the enterprise should observe the laws, regulations, and the stipulations as agreed on in the contract, and both parties to the contract should conduct equal consultation about the specific contents of the contract.
3. The labor contract period for full-time trade union chairmen, vice chairmen, or union committee members will extend automatically from the date of their term of office, and this period is equivalent to their tenure of office; the labor contract period for nonprofessional chairmen, vice chairmen, or union committee members will extend automatically from the date of their term of office until the labor contract expires, if the unexecuted contract period is shorter than the term of office. However, those who have committed serious mistakes during their tenure of office or who have reached the legal retirement age are exceptions.

   If the term of office of the trade union chairman and vice chairmen has not expired, the enterprise shall not change their jobs or transfer them to other posts at will. In case of any job change or post transfer demanded by the work, the enterprise should ask permission in advance from the trade union committee of the same level and from the trade union at a higher level.

Chapter Five   Leaves and Holidays

Article 43   *General Provisions*

Workers must have one day off each week.

Holidays of the workers are subject to postponement in case of state official holidays.

The enterprise can arrange_____day/days off for workers according to actual conditions during special holidays such as Youth Day (May 4), Children's Day (for workers who have children under 14), and the Double Ninth Festival and during the traditional festivals of the minority nationalities, with full wages to be paid out as usual.

The wages will be paid to the worker based on assessment rules during his or her sick leave, marriage leave, funeral leave, maternity leave, family planning leave, baby-care leave, home leave, leave of absence, and industrial injury leave, etc.

Reimbursement of the traveling expenses for home leave to and fro between cities or provinces shall be handled according to state regulations; if no regulations are laid down, the enterprise shall reimburse_____percent of the traveling expenses in line with the actual conditions and at its discretion.

Article 44   Sick Leave

If the worker falls ill and goes out to seek medical advice, he or she should present on the same day the certificate for sick leave written out by the hospital.

If the worker is on sick leave, he or she should let the enterprise know it on the same day and inform the enterprise of the duration of the sick leave and should present the medical record, doctor's advice, and certificate for sick leave written out by the hospital to the enterprise when he or she comes back to work.

If the worker needs a long suspension of work for medical treatment or recuperation due to illness or non–work-related injuries, he or she should apply to the enterprise for the work suspension_____days in advance and submit a doctor's certificate. The enterprise should go through the formalities for the worker to receive the medical treatment and grant a sick leave based on the patient's condition and the number of his or her working years.

Article 45   Marriage Leave

When the worker gets married, he or she can have_____day/days off for the marriage leave. If the couple get married late, apart from the marriage leave laid down by the state, they could enjoy another 7–14 days of marriage leave as awards. If the couple do not work in the same place when they get married, their marriage leave will not include the time for the distance traveled.

Article 46   Funeral Leave

When parents of the worker or of his or her spouse, the worker's spouse, children, sisters and brothers, grandparents, grandchildren, and guardians pass away, the enterprise should grant a funeral leave of_____days to the worker according to the actual conditions. If the arrangements need to be made for the funeral in another place, then the duration of the funeral leave will not include the time for the distance traveled.

Article 47   Maternity Leave

Female workers enjoy the maternity leave as stipulated by the state. If the female worker has not recovered yet from childbirth and cannot come back to work in time, she should submit the doctor's certificate to the enterprise, and the maternity leave can be extended for another_____days according to actual conditions on verification.

Holidays for female workers who become pregnant and abort after using intrauterine contraceptive rings will be treated as maternity leaves.

Article 48   Family Planning Leave

Female workers enjoy family planning leave. _____extra day(s) will be added as the maternity leave for women who use intrauterine devices during the maternity leave.

Article 49   Baby-Nursing Leave

Right after the birth of the child, the male worker can take the baby-nursing leave for_____ consecutive days; if the newborn baby becomes physically ill, the male worker can present the certificate written out by the hospital to the enterprise_____days in advance, and on verification and approval, the baby-nursing leave can be extended for another_____days. A leave awarded to the female worker for her late childbirth can be enjoyed by her spouse.

Article 50   Home Leave

One year after he or she starts work, the worker whose spouse or parents live in a different province or city can enjoy the home leave to visit his or her spouse and parents.

The worker can visit his or her spouse on a home leave once a year for_____days, not including the traveling time.

An unmarried worker can visit, on principle, his or her parents on a home leave once a year for_____days, not including the traveling time; if the enterprise cannot arrange such a home leave in the same year due to need of work, or if the worker volunteers to take a home leave once every two years, then the enterprise can arrange such a leave for_____days, not including the traveling time.

A married worker can visit his or her parents on a home leave once every four years for_____days, not including the traveling time.

A home leave abroad shall be handled according to relevant state regulations.

Article 51   Leave of Absence

If the worker has personal affairs to do, he or she can ask for a leave of absence on condition that the leave will not interfere with the work, and the worker should apply orally or in writing to the leader(s) of his or her workplace for the leave____days ahead of time. The accumulated number of days for the leave of absence during a whole year cannot exceed____days. If something unexpected should occur, the worker should inform the enterprise by phone in no time.

The worker can ask for a leave of absence for____day(s) due to attendance at the parent meeting, house repairs by real estate department, building demolition, and participation in social examinations for a private purpose.

If the worker needs to accompany and look after his or her spouse, lineal relative(s), or parents of the spouse hospitalized for serious disease, he or she should submit a written application to the enterprise for the leave of absence, and on verification and approval, he or she can take the leave for____days.

If the worker is not in a position to return to the enterprise on time due to certain reason(s), he or she should apply to the leader(s) of his or her workplace for the extension of the leave of absence____day(s) ahead of time; if the leave surpasses____day(s), the worker should submit a written explanation to the enterprise, and on approval, he or she can continue the leave of absence.

Article 52   Industrial Injury Leave

If the worker is injured during work or contracts an occupational disease and needs medical treatment, he or she can apply for an industrial injury leave. On verification by the medical department, an industrial injury leave for an ambulatory injury should not exceed 6 months; and an industrial injury leave for a serious injury should not exceed 12 months. The leave for serious injuries or for special cases authenticated by the Beijing Municipal Committee for Labor Ability Appraisal can be extended accordingly, with the maximum extension not exceeding 12 months, unless otherwise stipulated by laws and regulations. If the worker remains ill after an extension of 12 months and needs further treatment or recuperation, he or she can consider a sick rest.

Article 53   Paid Annual Leave

The enterprise shall set up the paid annual leave system. The worker who continues to work in the enterprise for more then one year can enjoy the paid annual leave and the leave cannot be used for the next year. (See specific rules in the attached table.)

Article 54   Arrangement of the Annual Leave

1. The enterprise, in January of each year, will announce to all workers the time slots to be selected as time for paid annual leave, the number of days to be taken by the workers as paid annual leave, and the deadline for workers to submit application for the paid annual leave, and the workers will choose the time for the leave on their own and submit their written applications to the enterprise or to the trade union for the annual leave.
2. The enterprise and the trade union will jointly work out the plans in accordance with the actual conditions for workers to have holidays and will paste up a notice to announce the yearly holiday arrangements for the workers.
3. If the worker is unable to take the leave as scheduled due to special reasons, or needs to adjust the holiday plan for the moment due to special reasons, he or she should submit an application to the enterprise or to the trade union_____days ahead of time, and the enterprise and trade union will discuss it together and will make a reply within_____days.
4. All announced holiday arrangements shall be strictly carried out.

Article 55   Overtime Work on Holidays

The enterprise, when requiring the worker to work during his or her marriage leave, home leave, or baby-nursing leave, should pay for the overtime work based on 200 percent to 300 percent of the worker's daily (or hourly) wages.

The enterprise that is not in a position to arrange the annual leave for the worker because of a real need of work will not arrange the leave for the worker with the worker's consent, and the enterprise shall pay the worker a reward equivalent to 300 percent of his or her daily wages for the unused holidays.

1. The enterprise should inform the trade union of the actual conditions at least_____days ahead of time and should work out the plan for overtime work jointly with the trade union.
2. The enterprise shall work out plans for overtime work on holidays, the workers shall fill out the application forms on a voluntary basis, and the enterprise shall arrange the overtime work jointly with the trade union according to the actual needs; if the applicants for overtime work are not enough in number, the enterprise, after consultation is made between the

enterprise, the trade union and the workers, can arrange the overtime work among the workers who have not set forth their applications.

3. At least 4 hours and relevant overtime pay should be ensured for the overtime work during holidays.

Article 56   Other Regulations

1. If the worker falls ill on his or her annual leave, he or she can submit a hospital certificate to the enterprise, and on verification, such an occasion can be regarded as a sick leave and the annual leave can be postponed accordingly.

2. If the worker gets married on his or her annual leave, he or she should submit a written certificate to the enterprise, and on verification, he or she can take marriage leave during the annual leave and the annual leave can be postponed accordingly.

3. Except that the home leave, marriage leave, funeral leave, maternity leave, and official holidays can be used together with the annual leave, two paid leaves cannot be taken in succession, and there should be at least_____days apart between the two leaves.

4. If the marriage leave or home leave has not been fully used within a year, then the remaining number of days for the leave can be added to the annual leave to be used up.

5. The trade union will organize the model workers, advanced individuals, and pacesetters at various levels to recuperate by stages and in batches for at least_____days every year.

6. The worker can consult with the enterprise about being released from work for study or for refresher courses for private purposes.

Chapter Six   Labor Safety and Health

Article 57   The enterprise shall carry out safety production management and set up a permanently effective mechanism for safety production to protect workers' lives and physical health according to relevant state laws and regulations and in accordance with the safety production rules as prescribed in *Safety Production Law, Occupational Disease Prevention and Treatment Law,* and the *Trade Union Law.*

The enterprise should set down safety production targets at the beginning of the year, such as number of fatal accidents to be 0, number of serious injuries to be 0, number of conflagrations to be 0, and number of occupational poisoning accidents to be 0. It should set up a labor safety and health responsibility system and work out safety management skills and measures and the relevant methods for implementation. The enterprise should also set up the safety production guaranteeing system; safety management system; safety production training system; safety management skills, measures, and requirements; safety production inspection methods; and casualty accident reporting system.

The enterprise should improve the safety production supervision and management facilities and draw up annual safety production and work plans with full and accurate contents, clear purposes, and effective measures. The enterprise should hold the safety production regular meeting at least once a month and convene working conferences at regular intervals for controlling serious accidents, probing into safety production work and working out measures to guard against the accidents.

The enterprise shall establish and improve the labor safety and health responsibility system; carry out the laws, rules, and government regulations concerning labor protection; establish and improve the management systems and organizational systems concerning labor safety, fire prevention, environmental protection, public order, public security, and public health in line with the production features; and implement the safety production responsibility system.

The enterprise must provide the production and operation places, equipment, and facilities that conform to state relevant laws, rules, and regulations concerning safety production and meet state standards or guild criteria.

The enterprise shall set aside special funds for the supervision and management of safety production in order to ensure the start of the safety production work. The enterprise should withdraw safety production and environmental protection funds as per stipulated proportions for the improvement of working conditions and enhancement of workers' safety awareness so as to guard against the occurrence of accidents and to reduce occupational hazards.

Article 58 The leading cadre in charge of the safety production in the enterprise shall be held responsible for the following duties in the safety production work of the enterprise:

1. To build, improve, and supervise the implementation of the safety production responsibility system;
2. To organize the formulation and supervise the implementation of the safety production rules and regulations as well as the operating rules and regulations;
3. To ensure the effective implementation of the safety production system;
4. To study safety production issues on a regular basis;

5. To supervise and examine the safety production work and eliminate the hidden troubles in production in time;
6. To organize the formulation and implementation of emergency and reinforcement plans against the occurrence of accidents in production;
7. To report the accidents in production timely and accurately.

Article 59 The enterprise shall set forth annual plans and measures for safety production each year and should set aside funds, designate personnel, and fix the time for implementing and fulfilling the measures.

In carrying out new construction, extending existing projects, and exercising reconstructions and technological transformations in accordance with the state regulations, the enterprise shall enforce simultaneous design, simultaneous construction, and simultaneous production after acceptance test in providing working conditions and safety and health facilities. In popularizing new techniques, new craftsmanship, and new products, the enterprise must adopt reliable safety and health measures and should inform the trade union to organize personnel for the participation.

The trade union has the right to supervise the use of safety facilities in construction projects; has the right to supervise the simultaneous design, simultaneous construction, and simultaneous production of the principal projects; and has the right to put forward opinions.

Article 60 The enterprise should improve safety and health conditions, enhance labor protection, and strengthen the protection of female workers and workers on special jobs. The enterprise must conduct training among the special personnel involved in_____ and qualify them for the special jobs.

The trade union, when finding that leaders of the enterprise compel workers to do risky work by giving instructions in violation of the rules or discover apparently serious hidden perils, occupational hazards, and things endangering the safety of workers' lives in the process of production, has the right to put forward proposals for settlement of the problems and has the right to propose that the enterprise organize workers to evacuate the dangerous workplaces, and the enterprise should make the decisions for the settlement as soon as possible.

Article 61 The enterprise, in line with seasonal climate change, should take specific measures to do a good job of preventing heatstroke and lowering the temperature, preventing coldness and keeping the warmth, and should grant health care articles in time. In case of high temperature in summer or under other special circumstances, when the trade union proposes that the working hours be reduced, the enterprise should take it into consideration.

Article 62   The enterprise should provide labor safety and health conditions that conform to state regulations and necessary labor protection articles; grant health care allowances and labor protection articles to workers involved in noxious and harmful jobs; and grant the allowances on time each month in accordance with the regulations on health care allowances for workers at different workplaces and on different jobs. The enterprise should set up necessary places of rest for workers involved in different types of work or laboring in different working environments and should provide labor protection articles that conform to labor health regulations by the schedule's time.

Article 63   For workers involved in jobs vulnerable to occupational diseases, the enterprise should organize pre-work, on-the-job, and off-work occupational health examinations for them in accordance with the rules and regulations set down by the administrative health departments of the State Council and should make the real examination results known to the workers. Expenses for the health examinations will be borne by the enterprise.

Special health examinations will be provided once a year by the enterprise to workers involved in jobs risking occupational hazards.

Article 64   The enterprise shall give support to the management of labor protection in the enterprise and be of assistance in examining and supervising the labor protection work.

The enterprise and the trade union have the responsibility to educate workers to strictly observe various production rules and regulations and the operating rules and regulations and to educate and organize workers to receive safety skill training and management. The trade union should provide backing to the enterprise for the punishment of conduct impairing the safety of the enterprise and workers.

The trade union should positively cooperate with the enterprise in supervising the implementation of the systems, rules, and regulations concerning labor protection and labor safety and health.

Article 65   When an accident takes place in the process of production, persons on the spot should immediately report it to the leaders of the enterprise.

Leaders of the enterprise, on receipt of the report on the accident, should immediately take effective measures to organize rescues, guard against the expansion of the accident, reduce casualties and damage to properties, and should give an accurate account of the accident at once to the local department in charge of safety production supervision and management in accordance with relevant state regulations. The enterprise should not withhold the truth, lie about the accident, or procrastinate reporting the accident and should not destroy the scene of the accident and the relevant evidence on purpose.

The enterprise should inform the trade union of the accident on time, and the trade union has the right to participate in the investigation of the accident according to law, to set forth opinions to the department concerned with tackling the accident, and to demand that the responsibility of the person(s) in charge for the accident be investigated and affixed.

Article 66   The enterprise should strengthen the labor safety and health education and training given to workers. The enterprise has the obligation to spread safety education among workers, and the workers have the right to receive safety education. Safety education at the factory, workshop, and production squad or team levels should be conducted among the new recruits; and the pre-work training must be carried out among personnel to be involved in special types of work (subject to the types of work as defined by the state) to qualify them for the said types of work through examinations.

The trade union should actively cooperate with the enterprise to start safety education and training among workers, to improve workers' technical competence and safety awareness, to set up safety production propaganda and education systems, to organize a good job in launching "Health Cup" campaigns and "Safety Production Month" activities, and to start safety production propaganda and education activities in various forms.

Article 67   The enterprise should set up the trade union labor protection supervision and examination committee and designate trade union labor protection examiners in production squads and teams. The trade union should establish and improve the supervision and examination system, the serious hidden perils and occupational hazards filing and follow-up system, and the mass's whistle-blower system; set up the labor protection job responsibility system; participate in investigation and settlement of the work-related casualties among workers and other problems seriously endangering workers' health in accordance with the law; and assist and supervise the enterprise to endow the trade union and the workers with the right to know, the right to participate, the right to supervise, and the right to avoid serious dangers with regard to safety production as prescribed by law.

Article 68   The enterprise should set up the working system for the Worker's Congress or Worker's Conference to supervise safety in production. The legal representative of the enterprise should make a special report on safety production to the Worker's Congress at least once a year, with the main content including status of the safety production in the enterprise, safety production targets and the fulfillment of the targets, duties performed by the leaders of the enterprise in carrying out safety production, hidden perils and rectification of the perils, preventive measures against accidents and settlement of the casualty problems, safety production propaganda and education and the training among workers, formulation and implementation of the fund plans for enforcing safety skills and measures, etc.

Chapter Seven   Insurance and Welfare

Article 69   Social Insurance

The enterprise shall pay various social insurance premiums for workers according to state and municipal regulations, such as old age insurance, medical insurance, unemployment insurance, industrial injury insurance, and birth insurance, with the payment rate to reach 100 percent, and shall make public the payment of insurance premiums made by both workers and the enterprise among the workers once a year. Specific rules to follow are hereunder:

Old-Age Insurance
The enterprise shall pay 20 percent of the sum of all workers' wage bases payable in the previous year as the old age insurance premiums.

The worker shall pay 8 percent of his or her average monthly wage in the previous year as the premiums. If the base is lower than 60 percent of the workers' average monthly wage in the previous year, then 60 percent of the workers' average monthly wage in the previous year will be taken as the base for insurance premiums. (The municipal regulations will be carried out in the interim.) The part of a worker's average monthly wage in the previous year higher than 300 percent of the workers' average monthly wage in the previous year will not be taken as the base for insurance premiums.

Medical Insurance
The enterprise shall pay 9 percent of the sum of all workers' wage bases payable in the previous year as the basic medical insurance premiums, and 1 percent should be paid as mutual funds for large medical expenses.

Any individual worker shall pay 2 percent of his or her average monthly wage in the previous year as basic medical insurance premiums; and shall pay 3 yuan every month as mutual funds for large medical expenses. Should the worker's average monthly wage in the previous year be any lower than 60 percent of the workers' average monthly wage in the previous year, then the 60 percent of the workers' average monthly wage in the previous year will be taken as the base for insurance premiums. The part of a worker's average monthly wage in the previous year higher than 300 percent of the workers' average monthly wage in the previous year will not be taken as the base for insurance premiums.

Unemployment Insurance

The enterprise shall pay 1.5 percent of all workers' wage bases payable in the previous year as the unemployment insurance premiums.

    The worker shall pay for the medical [sic] [unemployment] insurance based on 0.5 percent of his or her average monthly wage in the previous year. The part of a worker's average monthly wage in the previous year higher than 300 percent of the workers' average monthly wage in the previous year will not be taken as the base for insurance premiums. The contract rural workers will not pay for unemployment insurance.

Industrial Injury Insurance

The enterprise shall pay the product of the sum of all workers' wage bases multiplied by the payment rate as the industrial injury insurance premiums, and the workers will not pay the premiums by themselves.

Birth Insurance

The enterprise shall pay 0.8 percent of the sum of all workers' wage bases payable in the previous year as the birth insurance premiums. If the base is lower than 60 percent of the workers' average monthly wage in the previous year, then the premiums will be calculated based on 60 percent of the workers' average monthly wage in the previous year, and the part of a worker's average monthly wage in the previous year higher than 300 percent of the workers' average monthly wage in the previous year will not be taken as the base for birth insurance premiums. The workers will not pay the premiums by themselves.

    Old age, medical, and unemployment insurance premiums to be paid by workers themselves will be deducted by the enterprise from their salaries.

    The wage earned by the new recruit of the enterprise in the first month will be taken as the base for the insurance premiums to be paid in the same year; from the second year on, the premium base will be determined according to his or her actual average monthly wage in the previous year.

Article 70   *Housing Accumulation Fund*

The enterprise shall set aside a housing accumulation fund in accordance with the *Housing Accumulation Fund Management Rules*. The enterprise shall pay 8 percent to 12 percent of the total amount of the workers' average monthly wages in the previous year as the housing accumulation fund on a monthly basis.

    The worker shall pay 8 percent to 12 percent of his or her average monthly wage in the previous year as the housing accumulation fund on a monthly basis, and the sum will be deducted by the enterprise from his or her salary.

Article 71   Annuity

The enterprise, through discussion at the Worker's Congress or among the workers, shall set forth plans and opinions in accordance with the relevant state and municipal regulations for the collective consultation with the trade union or with workers' representatives in order to set up the annuity system in the enterprise. Relevant contents will be agreed on in the *Annuity Plan of the Enterprise* and will be submitted to the Worker's Congress or Worker's Conference for discussion, adoption, and a final formation.

Sources of the Annuity and the Rule for Paying the Annuity
The annuity will be paid by the enterprise and the workers themselves. The enterprise will withdraw, on a yearly basis, no more than 1/12 of the total amount of the workers' wages in the previous year; and the worker will pay, on a yearly basis, no more than 1/12 of the total amount of his or her wages in the previous year.

Management and Bookkeeping
A complete system accumulation system [fully funded] will be carried out for enterprise annuity, and the use of the personal account will be taken as a kind of management. Personal payments will all be entered in the personal accounts; payments to be made by the enterprise will be calculated as per the ratio prescribed in the annuity plan of the enterprise and in accordance with the types of work and length of the worker's service and will be entered in the worker's personal annuity account. (The enterprise shall work out and implement specific methods according to relevant state regulations.)

Treatment
When the worker reaches the state-stipulated age of retirement, he or she can draw the annuity from his or her personal account once and for all or on a monthly basis. If he or she does not reach the state-stipulated age of retirement, then he or she may not draw the annuity ahead of time. Those who go abroad for permanent settlement can draw the annuity from their personal accounts once and for all.

Article 72   Supplementary Medical Insurance

The enterprise shall set up the supplementary medical insurance and shall list the supplementary medical insurance of no more than 4 percent of the total amount of workers' wages into cost in accordance with relevant state and municipal regulations.

The specific methods for the management of the supplementary medical insurance and the annual budgetary plans shall be considered by the Worker's Congress or Worker's Conference, and such methods and plans, if in a joint-stock enterprise, shall be considered by the general meeting of shareholders and by the board of directors. Implementation of the supplementary medical insurance is subject to the examination by the Worker's Congress or by the Worker's Conference and shall be made public among the workers.

Ratio and source of the supplementary medical insurance: The enterprise will draw, on a yearly basis,_____ from the total amount of the workers' wages in the previous year as supplementary medical insurance premiums.

Management and bookkeeping: The enterprise will bring the supplementary medical insurance premiums drawn on a yearly basis into the supplementary medical insurance fund for special management.

Treatment: The treatment will be practiced in accordance with relevant regulations.

Other agreements: The enterprise can cover commercial medical insurance for workers each year to lighten the medical burdens on the workers.

Article 73   Workers' Mutual Aid Insurance

The enterprise, on the principle of voluntary participation by the workers, patronage by the enterprise, and organizing by the trade union, shall organize workers to participate in a mutual aid insurance campaign initiated by All-China Federation of Trade Unions. The workers shall pay by themselves, and the trade union shall submit the insurance premiums to the Beijing Office of Chinese Workers' Mutual Aid Insurance Association. Mutual Aid insurance includes the following:

1. Medical Mutual Aid Insurance for Hospitalized In-Service Workers: The insurance premium comes to 50 yuan for each person in each year. The insurance can be used only once, and the insurance period lasts one year.
2. Mutual Aid Insurance for In-Service Workers with Serious Diseases: The insurance premium comes to 90 yuan for the insurance used once in every insurance period that lasts 3 years, and the insurance can be used twice at the most, with the insurance covered each time to amount to 5,000 to 10,000 yuan.
3. Mutual Aid Insurance for In-Service Workers with Injuries by Accident: The insurance rates will be separately determined according to jobs and

types of work undertaken by the workers. See detailed rates laid down by Chinese Workers' Mutual Aid Insurance Association. The insurance period lasts 1 year.

4. Mutual Aid Insurance for Female Workers with Special Diseases: The trade union of an organization can provide the insurance in a unified way for the in-service female workers of the organization who have joined the Chinese Workers' Mutual Aid Insurance Association, can work normally, are in good health, and aged between 16–60. Insurance to be covered each time amounts to 36 yuan, and the insurance can be used one to two times, with an insurance period of 2 years and the insurance amount for each time to be 10,000 yuan.

5. Mutual Aid Insurance for In-Service Workers' Children with Injuries by Accident: The premium comes to 50 yuan for each person in each year, and the insurance can be used four times at the most, with an insurance period of 1 year.

Article 74 Withdrawal and Use of Workers' Welfare Funds

The welfare funds disbursed by the enterprise according to stipulation will be specially used to improve and increase various types of welfare for the workers. *The Plan for Use of Enterprise Workers' Welfare Funds* should be discussed at the Worker's Congress or among all workers, and the plans and opinions should be put forward for equal consultation with the trade union or among workers' representatives before they become effective.

Article 75 Workers' Welfare

1. Tenant Allowance: The enterprise will provide a tenant allowance to workers in accordance with relevant municipal policies of Beijing.
2. Food Allowance: The enterprise will grant food allowances to workers based on_____yuan per month per person.
3. Transportation Subsidy: The enterprise will grant transportation subsidies to workers according to the location of the workers' homes.
4. Communication Subsidy: The enterprise will grant communication subsidies to workers according to the nature of the work undertaken by the workers.
5. Physical Examination among Workers: The enterprise will organize the general physical examination once a year for the workers.
6. Cultural, Sports, and Recreational Activities among Workers: The enterprise will organize cultural and recreational activities for workers, such as

excursions or ball games, interesting sports meets, and karaoke singing, once every half a year to relax the workers and to facilitate contact and communication among the workers.

Article 76   *Warmth-Delivering Fund*

The enterprise will set up the Warmth-Delivering Fund. The enterprise will provide_____yuan (unit: 10,000 yuan), and the trade union will raise_____yuan (unit: 10,000 yuan), to jointly form the fund.

The enterprise and the trade union will jointly draw up the *Measures on Management and Use of the Warmth-Delivering Fund* to set down detailed aiding measures and criteria, and will submit the measures to the Worker's Congress or the Worker's Conference for consideration and approval. The fund will be earmarked for special use under special management for tackling the sudden and temporary serious difficulties that crop up in workers' daily lives and for helping workers tide over the hardships.

Chapter Eight   Special Protection of Female Workers and Underage Workers

Article 77   In accordance with the *Law on Protection of Women's Rights and Interests* and in compliance with relevant government laws and policies on female workers' labor protection, the enterprise shall practice labor protection among female workers, strictly carry out the *Regulations on Women Workers' Scope of Taboo Labor* promulgated by the Ministry of Labor, and bring female workers' labor safety and health protection into the occupational safety and health management system for simultaneous implementation.

Article 78   The enterprise should maintain the equality of men and women in providing opportunities for vocational training, rise in rank, promotion to a higher office, appraisal of professional titles, welfare enjoyment, and implementation of state rules and regulations on personnel retirement.

Article 79   *Protection of the Female Worker during Her Menstrual Period*

1. For the female worker working at a high place, in a low temperature, with cold water, or under a third-degree labor intensity as defined by the state, the enterprise should reduce the workload or change the work for the time during her menstrual period.
2. The female worker can take one-day leave for her dysmenorrhea during the menstrual period after diagnosis by the medical institution or the maternity and child care center, and the leave can be regarded as working hours.

Article 80   *Protection of the Female Worker during Her Pregnancy*

1. The enterprise shall not demote the female worker or reduce her wages owing to her pregnancy.
2. The enterprise shall not arrange pregnant female workers to work in the open air with the temperature higher than 35° Celsius or at workplaces with the temperature higher than 33° Celsius.
3. If the pregnant female worker takes a prenatal examination during the working hours, the time spent on the examination will be regarded as the working hours and her production quota should be reduced accordingly.
4. The leave taken by the female worker to prevent miscarriages after pregnancy will be regarded as a sick leave.

Article 81   *Protection of Female Worker's Childbirth Period*

1. The premature delivery or extended parturition by the female worker after at least 7 months of pregnancy will be regarded as normal parturition.
2. When the maternity leave expires, the enterprise should resume the female worker's previous work, and should give_____days for the female worker to gradually adapt to the previous workload. If the female worker is not used to the previous workload, then she can be transferred to another work post after she has agreed.
3. If the female worker needs further medical treatment after the maternity leave expires, on certification by the medical institution, she can enjoy the disease medical treatment stipulated by the state.
4. The family planning expenses spent by the female worker shall be reimbursed according to stipulation, and the female worker will be given a leave according to the doctor's advice and the leave will be regarded as working hours.
5. The female worker will not enjoy the economic privileges during the childbirth period if she violates the family planning stipulations.

Article 82   *Protection of Female Workers during the Breastfeeding Period*

1. The female worker who has received the *Honor Certificate for One-Child Parents* can enjoy another three months of maternity leave on approval after her official maternity leave expires (but the three-year money awards for one-child parents shall be reduced or canceled).
2. The female worker should enjoy a proper extended period for breast-feeding not exceeding 6 months on condition that her child is diagnosed by a

medical organization at the municipal, prefectural, or county level to be in poor health.

3. The female worker with a baby younger than 1 year old can pool her breast-feeding time on a voluntary basis if she is virtually unable to ensure her everyday breast-feeding time due to special reasons, and the pooled breast-feeding time can be regarded as the working hours.

4. Under special circumstances, the female worker can enjoy the extended maternity leave with unanimity reached through consultation with the enterprise. The extended maternity leave cannot exceed the breast-feeding period, and the wage incomes for the extended leave shall by no means come under the minimum pay set down by the enterprise.

Article 83   Protection during Female Workers' Climacteric

If the female worker is diagnosed by a general medical institution or a maternity and child care center above the prefectural and county levels (including those at the prefectural and county levels) to suffer from the climacteric syndrome and cannot evidently recover from the syndrome after treatment and is unable to undertake the previous work, the enterprise should reduce her workload to a certain extent or arrange some other suitable work for her for the time being.

Article 84   The enterprise will carry out the *Regulations on Childbirth Insurance for Workers of Enterprises in Beijing.*

After the female worker receives a family planning operation, gives birth to a child, or suffers an abortion, the enterprise, with the female worker's application and presentation of relevant medical certificate, will apply to the social insurance authority for childbirth allowances in accordance with the regulation and will reimburse the medical expenses for her prenatal examinations and family planning outpatient operation.

The payment base in the month of the female worker's childbirth divided by 30 and then times the number of days for maternity leave will result in the childbirth allowances. The childbirth allowances are wages of the female worker during her maternity leave. If the childbirth allowances are lower than the standard wage, then the enterprise will make up the balance.

The enterprise shall give the appropriate childbirth allowances and the related insurance premiums to the worker as soon as it receives them. (The enterprise will work out unified measures for the reimbursement of the expenses in excess of the appropriate birth insurance premiums in accordance with relevant regulations.)

Article 85   The enterprise will bear the expenses incurred during childbirth for the female workers who not covered by insurance in accordance with the *Regulations on Childbirth Insurance for Workers of Enterprises in Beijing.*

1. For retired personnel and workers without Beijing household registers, if they have covered the basic medical insurance, the basic medical insurance fund will bear their medical expenses incurred in family planning operations according to regulation; if they are not covered by the basic medical insurance, then the enterprise will pay the expenses.
2. When the female worker who does not participate in medical insurance becomes pregnant and receives an examination or gives birth to a child at the medical institution of the enterprise or at a designated medical institution,the examination expenses, the midwifery expenses, the operation expenses, the hospitalization expenses, and the medicine expenses will be borne by the enterprise.

Article 86   The enterprise shall grant money awards to one-child parents in accordance with the *Regulations of the Beijing Municipality on Population and Family Planning* at 10 yuan per month. The child care fees for the only child will be reimbursed by the organization to which the couple belongs according to relevant regulations. _____ percent of the medical expenses paid by the workers for their children younger than the age of 18 after participation in the municipal unified medical insurance will be reimbursed by the enterprise.

Article 87   The enterprise should provide funds every year to arrange the gynecology examinations for female workers once a year and should appoint personnel in charge of establishing physical examination files for female workers.

Article 88   *Other Special Protections*

1. The enterprise should give overtime pay to female workers for at least 4 hours of extra work completed during the Women's Day.
2. The enterprise should provide female workers with locker rooms, bathrooms, and squatting toilets in line with the number of female workers and should keep the environment clean and hygienic.
3. The enterprise should provide female workers with sanitary necessities on a monthly basis valued at_____yuan.
4. Married female workers using intrauterine contraceptive rings will receive the ring-roentgenoscopy examination once a year, and the expenses will be borne by the enterprise.

5. The enterprise shall support the female workers in having female health insurance.
6. The enterprise should take effective measures to guard against, look into, and check for sexual harassment.

Article 89   Special Protection of Underage Workers

1. For underage workers who are 16 years of age but not 18 years of age, the enterprise shall carry out the rules and regulations set down by the state in terms of work type, working hours, labor intensity, and protection measures and shall not arrange labor or dangerous work that impairs the physical and mental health of the underage workers.
2. The enterprise shall arrange physical examinations for underage workers on a regular basis at the time before job assignment, after a full year's work, and a half-year after the previous physical examination when the worker has reached the age of 18.
3. The enterprise will arrange suitable work for the underage workers according to the results of the physical examinations and shall reduce the workload or arrange other types of work for those who are unable to undertake the previous jobs in accordance with the certificates issued by the medical departments.

Article 90   Protection of Female Workers and Female Workers' Organizations under Trade Unions

1. The enterprise shall heed the opinions of the female workers' committee under the trade union when formulating and modifying the rules and regulations with regard to the rights and interests of the female workers.
2. The enterprise shall give support to female workers' organizations under the trade union in starting mobile quality education classes in line with the needs of female workers.
3. The enterprise shall encourage female workers' organizations under the trade union to participate in democratic management, and the female workers' representatives should make up a proportion in the Worker's Congress or union members' congress.

   There should be representatives of female workers in the labor dispute mediation committee, the labor protection and supervision committee of the trade union, and the labor law supervision and examination committee of the trade union.

4. The enterprise shall consult with the trade union about the special protection of female workers and can conclude special agreements or special collective contracts.

Chapter Nine   Professional Skill Training

Article 91   Vocational Training System

The enterprise will establish the vocational training system according to the features, conditions, and requirements of the posts and will carry out planned training among the workers with a view to bringing up a contingent of workers imbued with solid rudimentary knowledge and job proficiency and constantly enhancing the vitality of the enterprise in production.

Article 92   Withdrawal and Use of Education and Training Funds

The enterprise will withdraw 1.5 percent to 2.5 percent from the total amount of the workers' wages to be used as education and training funds and to have the cost listed and will use the funds to arrange the workers to take part in various types of professional skill training. The funds used for the training of the management staff shall not be any higher than 30 percent of the total amount, and the funds used for the training of the workers at the production front line shall not be any lower than 60 percent of the total amount. The annual scheme for use of the education and training funds in the enterprise and the training plan should be submitted to the Worker's Congress or the Worker's Conference for discussion and adoption.

Article 93   Time for Training

1. The mid-level and high-level management staff shall have an accumulated total of at least_____days of study and training every year;
2. Staff members at mid-level or high-level technical posts shall have an accumulated total of at least_____days of study and training every year;
3. Workers at the average posts or at the production front line shall have an accumulated total of at least_____days of study and training every year.

Article 94   Types of Professional Skill Training and Relevant Regulations

1. The enterprise should encourage workers to take an active part in various kinds of training for academic credentials and technical skills conducted

under civilian auspices. The worker, if the courses he or she majors in are closely linked with his or her job and can directly improve his or her working competence, can have the cost for the acquired credentials and the tuition fees reimbursed not less than_____ percent on approval of the enterprise.

2. The enterprise will give proper encouragement to workers who have participated in relevant training with their personal abilities being improved in real earnest and who have acquired certain technical competence and been engaged in terms of job arrangement and rise in rank and wage incomes, with a view to arousing the enthusiasm of the workers to the full tapping of their potential and facilitating the improvement of the overall labor productivity of the enterprise.

Article 95   Technological Transformation

When the enterprise uses new technology, new equipment, new craftsmanship, and new conditions to change the working environment, including the creation of new posts, it should inform the trade union in written form of the changes to thereby arise in production quotas, working hours, working conditions, number of workers, and wage incomes before the changes take place. When significant new technical transformations take place or new equipment is introduced, the enterprise should inform the superior trade union ahead of time.

Article 96   Training at the New Posts

When the new posts come into being or the existing posts change due to technological transformation and introduction of equipment, the enterprise should first provide in-service workers with_____days' of on-the-job training; and no fewer than_____days of training withdrawn from work can be arranged for workers at technically specific posts. The enterprise should strengthen vocational training among workers who have stopped work for the time being or who are waiting for reassignment of jobs and should guarantee the workers' employment.

Article 97   Recruitment through Talent Competition

1. Within one week before the recruitment through talent competition, the enterprise should inform the trade union of the plan for the recruitment and should make public the details to the workers to ensure equal chances among the workers. Conditions for the recruitment through talent

competition mainly include working competence, specialties and working experience, knowledge possessed, and physical condition.

2. The enterprise should give priority to employing those who can satisfy the following conditions under the same background: model workers and advanced workers at the municipal and district levels, those who have been chosen as the advanced individuals or who have made an outstanding contribution in three consecutive year, and workers with a protracted length of service and seniority.

Article 98 Task Adjustment and Job Change

When making adjustment and reassignment of the tasks among workers, the enterprise should inform the trade union of the relevant situation, discuss the task assignment jointly with the trade union, and reach unanimity with the workers_____day(s) before the adjustment or reassignment takes place. When a worker is assigned to another department or a new post, he or she should be informed of it at least_____ day(s) ahead of time and should have_____ day(s) for adaptation, so as to gradually meet the production quotas and the job requirements.

Chapter Ten   Rules and Regulations, Award and Punishment

Article 99   When formulating, modifying, or deciding on the rules and regulations or important matters directly relating to the immediate interests of the laborers, such as payment for labor, working hours, leaves and holidays, labor safety and health, insurance and welfare, training among workers, labor discipline and production quota management, etc., the enterprise should start discussion at the Worker's Congress or among all workers and set forth plans and opinions to be determined through equal consultation with the trade union or with workers' representatives.

Article 100   The enterprise must inform the workers in a proper way of the rules and regulations set up by the enterprise in accordance with the law and shall modify and supplement the rules and regulations in time according to the objective situation.

Article 101   The enterprise will adopt the principle of combining encouragement with restraint toward workers and will award material reward and moral encouragement to workers who have made outstanding contributions to society and to the enterprise. The enterprise and the trade union will work out specific methods for implementation through consultation.

Article 102   Workers should abide by labor discipline and rules and regulations of the enterprise; learn and grasp literacy, techniques, professional knowledge, and skills needed in the work; establish fine professional ethics; strive to work well; actively participate in production emulation campaigns and various economic and technical innovative activities launched by the enterprise; and promote technological advance and economic development of the enterprise.

Article 103 The trade union shall organize workers to start the mass economic and technical innovative activities such as emulation campaigns, rationalization proposals, technical innovations, technological breakthroughs, technical cooperations, inventions and creations, on-the-job training, and skill contests, etc.

Article 104 The enterprise should set up the labor emulation committee to lead the emulation campaigns in a unified way. The main duties and responsibilities of the committee include examining and approving emulation programs, formulating relevant policies, coordinating and controlling the emulation funds, examining/appraising/commending/rewarding, and listening to the report on the emulation campaigns.

Article 105 The enterprise should provide backing for the mass economic and technical innovative activities started by the trade union and should create conditions to foster the activities. The enterprise should set up a labor emulation encouragement fund and should withdraw the encouragement funds at no less than_____percent of the total amount of workers' wages after consultation with the trade union and should account for the funds used as wages for strict management and use.

Article 106 Funds for labor emulation campaigns should be granted to advanced groups and advanced workers selected through appraisal during the year for economic and technical innovations in various forms centered on the improvement of economic performance (or service quality).

Article 107 Examination, assessment, and appraisal of the labor emulation campaigns should be conducted in an open, impartial, and fair way and should be subject to data. The economic value of the emulation achievements, if any, should be worked out accurately and should be approved by the enterprise.

Article 108 Appraisal and commendation of the labor emulation campaigns should be focused on their innovative, progressive, effective, and demonstrative features, and the number of appraisals and commendations should be brought under strict control. Labor emulation appraisal, commendation, and rewarding should usually be conducted once a year. Awarding the honorable titles of Advanced Group and Advanced Individual in Emulation Campaign should be standardized in a unified way.

Article 109 The award criteria for labor emulation campaigns will be determined in accordance with the value created, relevant policies and regulations, and the actual conditions of the enterprise. And those who have made outstanding contributions should be amply rewarded.

Article 110 The enterprise will stick to the principle of combining education with punishment of workers who have violated the discipline and will impel them to correct their mistakes. Some punishment should be inflicted in accordance with the rules and regulations on workers who have violated labor discipline, technology discipline, or other rules and regulations; who have made serious mistakes in work and dereliction of duties; or who have committed other serious mistakes.

Article 111 Punishment Procedures

1. The organization where the worker belongs or a relevant department will be responsible for inflicting punishment (including economic punishment) on the worker if he or she has violated the discipline, and on the basis of finding out the facts and obtaining the evidence, the organization or the department will put forward suggestions about the punishment according to the nature and level of the mistake committed, in line with the worker's performance at ordinary times, and his or her realization of the mistake and in accordance with the prescribed regulations, and will hand over the suggestions about the punishment, the information about the mistake committed by the worker, the worker's consistent performance, and his or her realization of the mistake in written form to the assessment department of the enterprise.
2. The assessment department of the enterprise will put forward opinions after a complete investigation, submit the opinions to the enterprise for study and decision making, and inform the trade union in written form. If the trade union thinks the punishment unreasonable, it has the right to put forward different opinions, and the enterprise should make a written reply to the trade union on their opinions.
3. The worker should be informed in written form of the public reprimand or disciplinary sanction inflicted on him or her, and relevant regulations will be carried out in case of the labor contract being terminated.

Article 112 The worker who has committed general mistakes will be criticized and the economic punishment will be inflicted on him or her according to actual conditions and in accordance with the rules and regulations.

Article 113 If the worker does not agree with the public reprimand or disciplinary sanction inflicted on him or her, he or she can make it known to the enterprise; if he or she appeals the disciplinary sanction, he or she can apply to the labor dispute mediation committee of the enterprise for the mediation; if he or she is to be expelled or his or her labor contract will be terminated, he or she can submit a written application to the local labor dispute arbitration committee for arbitration_____ day(s) after the decision on punishment has been made public. The case will be executed in accordance with the original decision before the arbitration committee has decided to change the original decision on punishment.

Chapter Eleven   Settlement of Labor Disputes

Article 114   When labor disputes arise between workers and the enterprise, either party can demand a settlement through consultation. If one party demands the settlement through consultation, the other party should respond within_____day(s).

Article 115   If settlement through consultation is agreed on by both parties, then the consultation will be conducted between workers and_____(the legal representative/persons in charge or authorized persons of the enterprise). The trade union can be asked to appoint personnel for the consultation. And the trade union should supervise both parties' conscious implementation of the written agreement reached between the workers and the enterprise through consultation.

Article 116   If both parties to the labor dispute are reluctant to start consultation or are unable to start the consultation, they can apply for mediation or arbitration in accordance with the law.

Article 117   The enterprise will set up the labor dispute mediation committee. The mediation committee will be composed of_____workers' representative(s), _____representative(s) of the enterprise, and_____ representative(s) of the trade union. The workers' representative(s) will be elected at the Worker's Congress or the Worker's Conference; representative(s) of the enterprise will be designated by the legal representative or persons in charge of the enterprise; and the representative(s) of the trade union will be appointed by the trade union committee. The representative of the trade union will act as director of the mediation committee, and the office will be set up in the trade union.

Article 118   When receiving the application for the mediation, the mediation committee should seek the opinions of the other party, and if the other party is reluctant to accept mediation, then the mediation committee should make careful records and inform the applicant in written form within 3 working days. The mediation committee should make the decision within 4 working days on whether to accept and hear the case or not and should explain to the applicant if the case is not accepted and heard.

Article 119   If there is a failure to start the mediation, either party can apply for arbitration. And the party to the dispute can directly apply for arbitration.

Article 120   Both parties can commission solicitors or other people to participate in the arbitration. The legal agents or authorized agents can participate in the arbitration on behalf of the workers with civil disability or with restrictive civil disposition capability or on behalf of the decreased workers.

Article 121   Both parties should carry out the arbitration award and arbitration verdict of legal provision.

If the parties to the labor dispute do not agree with the arbitration decision, they can bring the case to the people's court in the place where the enterprise registers itself at the authority of industry and commerce 15 days after receipt of the arbitration verdict.

Chapter Twelve   Alteration, Cancellation, Termination, and Renewal of the Collective Contract

Article 122   The collective contract can be altered or terminated with unanimity reached through consultation between representatives of both parties and through adoption by voting at the Worker's Congress or union members' conference.

Article 123   The collective contract will be terminated due to any of the following reasons:

1. The enterprise goes bankrupt, dissolves, or gets merged.
2. One of the parties does not agree to renew the collective contract when it expires.

Article 124
Procedures for the Enterprise to Renew the Collective Contract:

1. Both parties will put forward the intention to renew the collective contract three months before the collective contract expires.
2. Representatives of both parties will consult with each other about the content of the previous collective contract and will make relevant amendments and supplements to form a new draft collective contract.
3. Both parties will go through the formalities to renew the collective contract in accordance with the procedures for collective contract conclusion.

Chapter Thirteen   Settlement of the Disputes in the Course of Contract Execution

Article 125   When disputes arise in contract execution, both parties should settle the disputes on the basis of equal consultation and cooperation. If the chief representative of one party proposes a settlement through consultation, both parties should hold a meeting for consultation within_____day(s), and a written agreement should be concluded once a consensus has been reached.

Article 126   In case no consensus can be reached through consultation, the workers can apply for arbitration at the_____labor dispute arbitration committee in the place where the enterprise registers itself at the authority of industry and commerce 60 days after the occurrence of the collective disputes.

Article 127   If either party appeals the arbitration award, the party can conduct a prosecution at the people's court in the place where the enterprise registers itself at the authority of industry and commerce 15 days after receipt of the arbitration verdict. If no legal action has been taken within 15 days, then the arbitration verdict will become legally effective.

Article 128   If the enterprise violates the collective contract and infringes on the labor rights and interests of the workers, the trade union can ask the enterprise to undertake the responsibilities in accordance with the law; if disputes arise from the execution of the collective contract and cannot be solved through consultation, the trade union can apply for arbitration and conduct a prosecution in accordance with the law.

Chapter Fourteen   Supervision and Inspection of the Collective Contract

Article 129   In order to ensure that this contract will be carried out fully and completely, the enterprise and the trade union should jointly set up a collective contract supervising and inspecting team_____days after this contract has been concluded, and the members of the team will be composed of_____, _____, _____, and_____of the enterprise to be led by the chairman of the trade union.

Article 130   After this contract becomes effective, the representatives of the enterprise and the trade union or the workers can point out the practices violating this contract discovered by them to the chief representatives of both parties. After consultation, both parties should report the results of disposition within_____day(s).

Article 131   The supervising and inspecting team should examine the implementation of this contract on a regular or irregular basis and should solve the discovered problems on time through consultation. The chief representatives of both parties should report the implementation of the collective contract to each other every half-year.

Article 132   The supervising and inspecting team should give a written report to the Worker's Congress or union members' conference on a regular basis (according to the time and numbers of the convered Worker's Congress on the implementation of the collective contract, the inspection results, and the measures of rectification).

Chapter Fifteen   The Collective Contract Period

Article 133   The period of this contract is_____year(s), and the contract will be terminated once it expires.

Article 134   When the enterprise meets with an emergency or encounters a special occasion and is unable to renew the contract on schedule, the collective contract can be extended for another six months through consultation and with the consent of both parties.

Chapter Sixteen   Supplementary Articles

Article 135   If the labor security administrative department lodges an objection against the content of this contract, then the enterprise and the trade union should conduct further consultation, make amendments, and carry out the procedures as agreed on in the collective contract.

Article 136   The *Special Agreement on Collective Wage Consultation*, *Special Agreement on Protection of Female Workers*, and *Special Agreement on Labor Safety and Health* concluded by the enterprise in accordance with this contract are equally authentic.

Article 137   If the contractual clauses contravene the state laws, regulations, and policies in the course of implementation, then the state laws, regulations, and policies will be taken as final.

Article 138   This contract shall be in quadruplicate to be held each by the parties hereto and shall have one copy kept by the labor administrative department for the record and another copy submitted to the higher trade union.

APPENDIX

1. Labor Low of the People's Republic of China

The Labor Law of the People's Republic of China that has been adopted at the Eighth Meeting of the Standing Committee of the Eighth National People's Congress on July 5, 1994, is promulgated now, and shall enter into force as of January 1, 1995.

Table of Contents

Chapter 1   General Provisions

Article 1   This Law is hereby formulated in accordance with the Constitution in order to protect the legitimate rights and interests of laborers, readjust labor

---

Law Info China is the source of the five laws presented in the Appendix.

relationships, establish and safeguard the labor system suiting the socialist market economy, and promote economic development and social progress.

Article 2 This Law applies to enterprises, individually owned economic organizations (hereinafter referred to as the employer) and laborers who form a labor relationship with them within the boundary of the People's Republic of China.

State departments, institutional organizations, and social groups and laborers who form a labor relationship with them shall follow this Law.

Article 3 Laborers have the right to be employed on an equal basis, choose occupations, obtain renumerations for labor, take rests, have holidays and leaves, receive labor safety and sanitation protection, get training in professional skills, enjoy social insurance and welfare treatment, and submit applications for settlement of labor disputes, and other labor rights stipulated by law.

Laborers shall fulfill their tasks of labor, improve their professional skills, follow rules on labor safety and sanitation, and observe labor discipline and professional ethics.

Article 4 The employer shall establish and perfect rules and regulations in accordance with law and guarantee that laborers enjoy labor rights and fulfill labor obligations.

Article 5 The State shall take various measures to promote employment, develop vocational education, formulate labor standards, regulate social incomes, perfect social insurance, coordinate labor relationships, and gradually raise the living level of laborers.

Article 6 The State shall advocate laborers' participation in social voluntary labor, labor competition, and activities of forwarding rational proposals; encourage and protect laborers in scientific research, technical renovation, and invention; and commend and award labor models and advanced workers.

Article 7 Laborers shall have the right to participate in and organize trade unions in accordance with law.

Trade unions shall represent and safeguard the legitimate rights and interests of laborers, and stage activities independently in accordance with law.

Article 8 Laborers shall take part in democratic management through worker's congress, worker's representative assembly, or any other forms in accordance with law, or consult with the employer on an equal footing about protection of the legitimate rights and interests of laborers.

Article 9 The labor management department under the State Council shall take charge of the management of labor of the whole country.

Local people's governments above the county level shall take charge of the management of labor in areas under their jurisdiction.

Chapter 2   Promotion of Employment

Article 10 The State shall create employment conditions and expand employment opportunities through promotion of economic and social development.

The State shall encourage enterprises, institutional organizations, and social groups to start industries or expand businesses within the scope allowed by stipulations of laws and administrative decrees for the purpose of increasing employment.

The State shall support laborers to organize and employ themselves on a voluntary basis and to get employed in individual businesses.

Article 11 Local people's governments at various levels shall take measures to develop various kinds of job agencies and provide employment services.

Article 12 Laborers shall not be discriminated against in employment due to their nationality, race, sex, or religious belief.

Article 13 Women shall enjoy equal rights as men in employment. Sex shall not be used as a pretext for excluding women from employment during recruitment of workers unless the types of work or posts for which workers are being recruited are not suitable for women according to State regulations. Nor shall the standards of recruitment be raised when it comes to women.

Article 14 Any special stipulations in laws and regulations about the employment of the disabled, minority people, and demobilized soldiers shall be observed.

Article 15 The employer shall be banned from recruiting juveniles under the age of 16.

Art, sports, and special-skill units that plan to recruit juveniles under the age of 16 shall go through examination and approval procedures according to relevant State regulations and guarantee the right of the employed to receive compulsory education.

Chapter 3   Labor Contracts and Collective Contracts

Article 16 Labor contracts are agreements reached between laborers and the employer to establish labor relationships and specify the rights, interests, and obligations of each party.

Labor contracts shall be concluded if labor relationships are to be established.

Article 17 Conclusion and alteration of labor contracts shall follow the principle of equality, voluntariness, and agreement through consultation. They shall not run counter to stipulations in laws or administrative decrees.

Labor contracts shall become legally binding once they are concluded in accordance with law. The parties involved shall fulfill obligations stipulated in labor contracts.

<u>Article 18</u> The following labor contracts shall be invalid:

(1) Labor contracts concluded against laws or administrative decrees;
(2) Labor contracts concluded through cheating, threat, or any other means.

Invalid labor contracts shall not be legally binding from the very beginning of their conclusion. If a labor contract is confirmed as being partially invalid, the other parts shall be valid if the parts that are invalid do not affect the validity of these other parts.

The invalidity of a labor contract shall be confirmed by a labor dispute arbitration committee or a people's court.

<u>Article 19</u> Labor contracts shall be concluded in written form and contain the following clauses:

(1) Time limit of the labor contract;
(2) Content of work;
(3) Labor protection and labor conditions;
(4) Labor remunerations;
(5) Labor disciplines;
(6) Conditions for the termination of the labor contract;
(7) Liabilities for violations of the labor contract.

Apart from the necessary clauses specified in the preceding clause, the parties involved can include in their labor contracts other contents agreed upon by them through consultation.

<u>Article 20</u> The time limits of labor contracts shall be divided into fixed and flexible time limits and time limits for the completion of certain amounts of work.

Labor contracts with flexible time limits shall be concluded between the laborers and the employer if the former requests for the conclusion of labor contracts with flexible time limits after working continuously with the employer for more then 10 years and with agreement between both of the parties involved on prolonging their contracts.

<u>Article 21</u> Probation periods can be agreed upon in labor contracts. These probation periods shall not, however, exceed six months at the longest.

<u>Article 22</u> The parties involved in a labor contract can reach agreements in their labor contracts on matters concerning the keeping of the commercial secrets of the employer.

Article 23 Labor contracts shall terminate upon the expiration of their time limits or the occurrence of the conditions agreed upon in labor contracts by the parties involved for terminating these contracts.

Article 24 Labor contracts can be revoked with agreement reached between the parties involved through consultation.

Article 25 The employer can revoke labor contracts should any one of the following cases occur with its laborers:

(1) When they are proved during probation periods to be unqualified for employment;
(2) When they seriously violate labor disciplines or the rules or regulations of the employer;
(3) When they cause great losses to the employer due to serious dereliction of duties or engagement in malpractices for selfish ends;
(4) When they are brought to hold criminal responsibilities in accordance with law.

Article 26 The employer can revoke labor contracts should any one of the following cases occur, with its laborers to be notified, in written form, of such revocation 30 days in advance:

(1) The laborers can neither take up their original jobs nor any other kinds of new jobs assigned by the employer after completion of medical treatment for their illnesses or injuries not suffered during work;
(2) The laborers are incompetent at their jobs and remain so even after training or after readjusting the work posts;
(3) No agreements on an alteration of labor contracts can be reached through consultation between and by the parties involved when major changes taking place in the objective conditions serving as the basis of the conclusion of these contracts prevent them from being implemented.

Article 27 In case it becomes a must for the employer to cut down the number of workforce during the period of legal consolidation when it comes to the brink of bankruptcy or when it runs deep into difficulties in business, the employer shall explain the situation to its trade union or all of its employees 30 days in advance, solicit opinions from its trade union or the employees, and report to the labor administrative department before it makes such cuts.

If the employer cuts its staff according to stipulations in this Article and then seeks recruits within six months, it shall first recruit those who have been cut.

Article 28 The employer shall make economic compensations in accordance with relevant State regulations if it revokes labor contracts according to stipulations in Article 24, Article 26, and Article 27 of this Law.

Article 29 The employer shall not revoke labor contracts in accordance with stipulations in Article 26 and Article 27 of this Law should any one of the following cases occur with its laborers:

(1) Those who are confirmed to have totally or partially lost their labor ability due to occupational diseases or work-related injuries;
(2) Those who are receiving treatment for their diseases or injuries during a prescribed period of time;
(3) Women employees during pregnancy, puerperium, and nursing periods;
(4) Others cases stipulated by laws and administrative decrees.

Article 30 The trade union shall have the right to air its opinions if it regards as inappropriate the revocation of a labor contract by the employer. If the employer violates laws, regulations, or labor contracts, its trade union shall have the right to ask for handling the case anew. If laborers apply for arbitration or raise lawsuits, the trade union shall render support and help in accordance with law.

Article 31 Laborers planning to revoke labor contracts shall give a written notice to their employer 30 days in advance.

Article 32 Laborers can notify, at any time, their employer of their decision to revoke labor contracts in any one of the following cases:

(1) During their periods of probation;
(2) If they are forced to work by the employer through means of violence, threat, or deprival of personal freedom in violation of law;
(3) Failure on the part of the employer to pay labor remunerations or to provide labor conditions as agreed upon in labor contracts.

Article 33 The employees of an enterprise as one party may conclude a collective contract with the enterprise as another party on labor renumerations, work hours, rests and leaves, labor safety and sanitation, insurance, welfare treatment, and other matters.

The draft collective contract shall be submitted to the workers representative assembly or all the employees for discussion and passage.

Collective contracts shall be signed by and between the trade union on behalf of the employees and the employer. In an enterprise that has not yet set up a trade union, such contracts shall be signed by and between representatives recommended by workers and the enterprise.

Article 34 Labor contracts shall be reported to labor administrative departments after their conclusion. Labor contracts shall take effect automatically if no objections are raised by these labor administrative departments within 15 days after they are received.

Article 35 Labor contracts concluded in accordance with law shall be binding on both the enterprise and all of its employees. The standards on labor conditions and labor payments agreed upon in labor contracts concluded between individual laborers and their enterprises shall not be lower than those stipulated in collective contracts.

Chapter 4   Working Hours, Rests, and Leaves

Article 36 The State shall practice a working hour system wherein laborers shall work for no more than eight hours a day and no more than 44 hours a week on average.

Article 37 In case of laborers working on the basis of piecework, the employer shall rationally fix quotas of work and standards of piecework remuneration in accordance with the working hour system stipulated in Article 36 of this Law.

Article 38 The employer shall guarantee that its laborers have at least one day off a week.

Article 39 If an enterprise cannot follow the stipulations in Article 36 and Article 38 of this Law due to special characteristics of its production, it may follow other rules on work and rest with the approval by labor administrative departments.

Article 40 The employer shall arrange rests for laborers in accordance with law during the following holidays:

(1) The New Year's Day;
(2) The Spring Festival;
(3) The International Labor Day;
(4) The National Day;
(5) Other holidays stipulated by laws and regulations.

Article 41 The employer can prolong work hours due to needs of production or businesses after consultation with its trade union and laborers. The work hours to be prolonged, in general, shall be no longer than one hour a day, or no more than three hours a day if such prolonging is called for due to special reasons and under the condition that the physical health of laborers is guaranteed. The work time to be prolonged shall not exceed, however, 36 hours a month.

Article 42 The prolonging of work hours shall not be subject to restrictions of stipulations of Article 41 of this Law in any one of the following cases:

(1) Need for emergency treatment during occurrence of natural disasters, accidents, or other reasons that threaten the life, health, or property safety of laborers;
(2) Need for timely rush-repair of production equipment, transportation lines, or public facilities that have gone out of order and as a result affect production and public interests;
(3) Other cases stipulated in laws and administrative decrees.

Article 43 The employer shall not prolong the work hours of laborers in violation of the stipulations of this Law.

Article 44 The employer shall pay laborers more wage remunerations than those for normal work according to the following standards in any one of the following cases:

(1) Wage payments to laborers no less than 150 percent of their wages if the laborers are asked to work longer hours;
(2) Wage payments to laborers no less than 200 percent of their wages if no rest can be arranged afterward for the laborers asked to work on days of rest;
(3) Wage payments to laborers no less than 300 percent of their wages if the laborers are asked to work on legal holidays.

Article 45 The State follows the system of annual leaves with pay.

Laborers shall be entitled to annual leaves with pay after working for more than one year continuously. Specific rules on this shall be worked out by the State Council.

Chapter 5   Wages

Article 46 Distribution of wages shall follow the principle of distribution according to work and equal pay for equal work.

The level of wages shall be raised gradually on the basis of economic development. The State shall exercise macro regulation and control over total payrolls.

Article 47 The employer shall fix its form of wage distribution and wage level on its own and in accordance with this Law according to the characteristics of its production and businesses and economic efficiency.

Article 48 The State shall implement a system of guaranteed minimum wages. Specific standards on minimum wages shall be stipulated by provincial, autonomous regional, and municipal people's governments and reported to the State Council for registration.

The employer shall pay laborers wages no lower than local standards on minimum wages.

Article 49 Standards on minimum wages shall be fixed and readjusted with comprehensive reference to the following factors:

(1) The lowest living costs of laborers themselves and the number of family members they support;
(2) Average wage level of the society as a whole;
(3) Productivity;
(4) Situation of employment;
(5) Differences between regions in their levels of economic development.

Article 50 Wages shall be paid to laborers themselves in the form of currency on a monthly basis. The wages payable to laborers shall not be deducted or delayed without reason.

Article 51 The employer shall pay wages to laborers in accordance with law when they have legal holidays, take leaves during periods of marriage or mourning, and participate in social activities in accordance with law.

Chapter 6   Labor Safety and Sanitation

Article 52 The employer shall establish and perfect its system for labor safety and sanitation, strictly abide by State rules and standards on labor safety and sanitation, educate laborers in labor safety and sanitation, prevent accidents in the process of labor, and reduce occupational hazards.

Article 53 Labor safety and sanitation facilities shall meet State-fixed standards.

The labor safety and sanitation facilities of new projects and projects of renovation and expansion shall be designed, constructed, and put into operation and use at the same time as the main projects.

Article 54 The employer shall provide laborers with labor safety and sanitation conditions meeting State stipulations and necessary articles of labor protection, and carry out regular health examination for laborers engaged in work with occupational hazards.

Article 55 Laborers to be engaged in special operations shall receive specialized training and acquire qualifications for these special operations.

Article 56 Laborers should strictly follow rules on safe operation in the process of labor.

Laborers shall have the right to refuse to follow orders if the management personnel of the employer direct or force them to work in violation of regulations, and to criticize, expose, and accuse any acts endangering the safety of their life and physical health.

Article 57 The State shall establish a system for the statistical report and treatment of accidents of injuries or deaths and cases of occupational diseases. The labor administrative departments and other relevant departments under the peoples governments at or above the county level and the employer shall, in accordance with law, carry out statistical report and disposition with respect to accidents of injuries or deaths that occurred to laborers in the process of their work and situations of occupational diseases.

Chapter 7   Special Protection for Female Staff and Workers and Juvenile Workers

Article 58 The State provides special protection to female staff and workers and juvenile workers. Juvenile workers refer to laborers up to 16 years old but below 18 years old.

Article 59 It is forbidden to arrange underground work for women workers at mines, or any labor with Grade IV physical labor intensity as stipulated by the State, or other labor forbidden to women.

Article 60 It is forbidden to engage women workers in work high above the ground, under low temperatures, or in cold water during their menstrual periods or labor with Grade III physical labor intensity as stipulated by the State.

Article 61 It is forbidden to engage women workers during their pregnancy in work with Grade III physical labor intensity as stipulated by the State or other work the State prevents them from doing during pregnancy. It is forbidden to prolong the work hours of women workers pregnant for seven months or ask them to work night shifts.

Article 62 Birth-giving women workers shall be entitled to maternity leaves no shorter than 90 days.

Article 63 It is forbidden to engage women workers in work with Grade III physical labor intensity as stipulated by the State during their breast-feeding of babies less than one year old and other labor the Sate prevents them from doing during their breastfeeding periods. Neither shall their work hours be prolonged nor shall they be asked to work night shifts during these periods.

Article 64 It is forbidden to engage underage workers in work under wells at mines, poisonous or harmful work, or Grade IV physical labor intensity as stipulated by the State or any other labor the State prevents them from doing.

Article 65 The employer shall carry out regular physical examinations for underage workers.

Chapter 8   Vocational Training

Article 66 The State shall promote the cause of vocational training through various channels and by various measures to develop the professional skills of laborers, improve their quality, and strengthen their employment and work abilities.

Article 67 People's governments at all levels shall include vocational training into their programs for social and economic development, and encourage and support enterprises, institutional organizations, social groups, and individuals to carry out vocational training in various forms.

Article 68 The employer shall establish a system for vocational training, extract and use funds for vocational training according to State regulations, and provide laborers with vocational training in a planned way and according to its specific conditions.

Laborers to be engaged in technical work shall receive training before taking up their posts.

Article 69 The State shall determine occupational classification, set up professional skill standards for specific occupations, and practice a system of vocational qualification certificates. Examination and appraisal organizations authorized by governments shall be charged to carry out examination and appraisal of the professional skills of laborers.

Chapter 9   Social Insurance and Welfare

Article 70 The State shall promote the development of the cause of social insurance, establish a social insurance system, and set up social insurance funds so that laborers can receive help and compensation when they become old, suffer diseases or work-related injuries, lose their jobs, and give birth.

Article 71 The level of social insurance shall be brought in line with the level of social and economic development and social sustainability.

Article 72 The sources of social insurance funds shall be determined according to the categories of insurance, and the practice of unified accumulation of insurance funds shall be introduced. The employer and individual laborers shall participate in social insurance in accordance with law and pay social insurance costs.

Article 73 Laborers shall be entitled to social insurance treatment in any one of the following cases:

(1) Retire;
(2) Suffer diseases or injuries;
(3) Become disabled during work or suffer occupational diseases;
(4) Become jobless;
(5) Give birth.

The dependents of the laborer who dies shall enjoy, in accordance with law, subsidies provided to these dependents.

The conditions and standards on the eligibility of laborers for social insurance treatment shall be stipulated by laws and regulations.

The social insurance funds for laborers shall be paid in due time and in full.

Article 74 Organizations charged with the task of handling social insurance funds shall collect, keep, and use social insurance funds in accordance with stipulations in laws, and assume the responsibility to guarantee and multiply the value of these funds.

Organizations charged to supervise social insurance funds shall supervise in accordance with law stipulations, the collection, keeping, and use of social insurance funds.

The establishment and functioning of the organizations in the preceding two clauses shall be specified by law.

No unit or individuals shall be allowed to use social insurance funds for other purposes.

Article 75 The State encourages the employer to set up supplementary insurance for laborers according to its practical conditions.

Article 76 The State shall promote the development of the social welfare cause, construct public welfare facilities, and provide conditions for laborers to rest and recuperate and convalesce.

The employer shall create conditions to improve collective welfare and provide laborers with better welfare treatment.

Chapter 10   Labor Disputes

Article 77 In case of labor disputes between the employer and laborers, the parties concerned can apply for mediation or arbitration, bring the case to courts, or settle them through consultation.

The principle of mediation is applicable to arbitration and court procedures.

Article 78 Labor disputes shall be settled according to the principles of justice, fairness, and promptness so as to safeguard the legitimate rights and interests of the parties involved in these disputes in accordance with law.

Article 79 Once a labor dispute occurs, the parties involved can apply to the labor dispute mediation committee of their unit for mediation; if it cannot be settled through mediation and one of the parties asks for arbitration, application can be filed to a labor dispute arbitration committee for arbitration. Any one of the parties involved in the case can also apply to a labor dispute arbitration committee for arbitration. The party that has objections to the ruling of the labor arbitration committee can bring the case to a people's court.

Article 80 A labor dispute mediation committee can be set up inside the employer. This committee shall be composed of worker representatives, the representatives of the employer, and trade union representatives. The chairmanship of this committee shall be held by a trade union representative.

Agreements reached on labor disputes through mediations shall be implemented by the parties involved.

Article 81 Labor dispute arbitration committees shall be composed of the representatives of labor administrative departments, representatives from trade unions at the same level, and the employer's representatives. The chairmanship of such a committee shall be held by the representative of a labor administrative department.

Article 82 The party that asks for arbitration shall file a written application to a labor dispute arbitration committee within 60 days starting from the date of the occurrence of a labor dispute. Generally speaking, the arbitration committee shall produce a ruling within 60 days after receiving the application. The parties involved shall implement arbitration rulings if they do not have any objections to these rulings.

Article 83 If any of the parties involved in a labor dispute has objections to an arbitration ruling, it can raise a lawsuit with a people's court within 15 days after receiving the ruling. If one of the parties involved neither raises a lawsuit nor implements the arbitration ruling within the legal period of time, the other party can apply to a people's court for forced implementation.

Article 84 Cases of disputes resulting from the conclusion of collective contracts shall be handled through consultation by all the parties concerned brought together by the labor administrative department of a local people's government if these cases cannot be handled through consultation between the parties involved.

Cases of disputes resulting from the implementation of collective contracts shall be brought to a labor dispute arbitration committee for arbitration if these cases cannot be solved through consultation between the parties involved. The party that has objections to a ruling can raise a lawsuit with a people's court within 15 days after receiving the ruling.

Chapter 11   Supervision and Inspection

<u>Article 85</u> The labor administrative departments under people's governments at or above the county level shall supervise and inspect efforts by the employer to abide by laws and regulations, and have the power to stop any behavior that runs counter to labor laws and regulations and order correction.

<u>Article 86</u> The supervisors and inspectors of the labor administrative departments under people's governments at or above the county level shall have, while performing their public duties, the right to go to the employer to make investigations about the employer's implementation of labor laws and regulations, consult data they deem necessary, and inspect labor spots.

The supervisors and inspectors of the labor administrative departments under people's governments at or above the county level shall produce their documents of certification while performing public duties, impartially enforce laws, and abide themselves by relevant regulations.

<u>Article 87</u> Relevant departments under people's governments at or above the county level shall supervise, within the range of their duties and responsibilities, the employer in its observance of labor laws and regulations.

<u>Article 88</u> Trade unions at various levels shall safeguard the legitimate rights and interests of laborers, and supervise the employer in its observance of labor laws and regulations.

All units and individuals shall have the right to expose and accuse behaviors that go against labor laws and regulations.

Chapter 12   Legal Responsibilities

<u>Article 89</u> If the rules and regulations on labor formulated by the employer run counter to the provisions of laws and regulations, it shall be given a warning by labor administrative departments, ordered to make corrections, and asked to hold responsibility over harms that may be done to laborers.

<u>Article 90</u> If the employer prolongs work hours in violation of stipulations in this Law, labor administrative departments can give it a warning, order it to make corrections, and may impose a fine thereon.

<u>Article 91</u> The employer involved in any one of the following cases that encroach upon the legitimate rights and interests of laborers shall be ordered

by labor administrative departments to pay laborers wage remunerations or to make up for economic losses, and may even order it to pay compensation:

(1) Deduction or unjustified delay in paying wages to laborers;
(2) Refusal to pay laborers wage remunerations for working longer hours;
(3) Payment of wages to laborers below local standards on minimum wages;
(4) Failure to provide laborers with economic compensations in accordance with this Law after revocation of labor contracts.

Article 92 The employer whose labor safety facilities and labor sanitation conditions fall short of State regulations or who fails to provide laborers with necessary labor protection articles and labor protection facilities shall be ordered by labor administrative departments or other relevant departments to make corrections, or be fined. Those involved in serious cases shall be reported to people's governments at or above the county level so that these people's governments can decide and order it to stop production for consolidation. Criminal responsibilities shall be fixed upon the persons in charge according to stipulations in Article 187 of the Criminal Law should the failure on the part of the employer to take measures against possible accidents result in serious accidents and cause losses of laborers' life or properties.

Article 93 Criminal responsibilities shall be fixed upon the persons in charge in accordance with law if the employer forces laborers to venture to work against regulations and as a result causes major accidents of injuries and deaths and serious consequences.

Article 94 The employer that recruits juveniles below the age of 16 in violation of law shall be ordered by labor administrative departments to make corrections, and be fined. That which results in a serious case shall have its business license revoked by the administration for industry and commerce.

Article 95 The employer that encroaches upon the legitimate rights and interests of women and underage workers in violation of the stipulations of this Law on their protection shall be ordered by labor administrative departments to make corrections, and be fined. That which causes harms to women and underage workers shall assume the responsibility over making compensations.

Article 96 The responsible person of the employer involved in any one of the following cases shall be taken by a public security department into custody for 15 days, fined, or given a warning, and criminal responsibilities shall be fixed upon whoever commits a crime:

(1) Use of violence, threat or illegal deprival of personal freedom to force labor;
(2) Humiliation, corporal punishment, beating, and illegal search or holding of laborers.

Article 97 The employer shall assume the responsibility over compensation for losses caused to laborers by the invalidity of contracts due to reasons on the part of the employer.

Article 98 The employer that revokes labor contracts or purposely delays the conclusion of labor contracts in violation of the conditions specified in this Law shall be ordered by labor administrative departments to make corrections and assume responsibility over compensation for any losses that may be sustained by laborers therefrom.

Article 99 The employer that recruits laborers whose labor contracts have not yet been canceled, thus causing economic losses to the former employer, shall assume joint liabilities for compensation according to law.

Article 100 The employer that refuses to pay social insurance funds shall be ordered by labor administrative departments to pay within fixed periods of time. That which fails to make payments beyond the prescribed time shall be asked to pay arrears.

Article 101 The employer that unjustifiably prevents labor administrative departments and other relevant departments as well as their workers from exercising supervision and inspection powers or retaliates against informers shall be fined by labor administrative departments or other relevant departments. If a crime is committed, the person in charge shall be brought to hold criminal responsibilities.

Article 102 Laborers who revoke labor contracts in violation of the conditions specified in this Law or violate terms on secret-keeping matters agreed upon in labor contracts shall be asked to hold responsibility over compensation in accordance with law if their violation causes economic losses to the employer.

Article 103 Criminal responsibilities shall be fixed upon the workers of labor administrative departments or any other relevant departments if they abuse their powers, neglect their duties, and practice fraud for the benefit of relatives or friends to such a degree that they commit crimes. Those who have not committed crimes shall be disciplined administratively.

Article 104 Public servants and the workers of organizations charged to handle social insurance funds shall be brought to hold criminal responsibilities if they use social insurance funds for other purposes and as a result commit crimes.

Article 105 If other laws or administrative decrees have already specified punishments for encroachment upon the legitimate rights and interests of laborers in violation of the stipulations of this Law, punishments shall be given in accordance with the stipulations of these laws or administrative decrees.

Chapter 13   Supplementary Provisions

<u>Article 106</u> People's governments at the provincial, autonomous regional, and municipal levels shall work out rules on the steps of the implementation of the system of labor contracts according to this Law and their local conditions and report the rules to the State Council for registration.

<u>Article 107</u> This Law shall take effect on January 1, 1995.

2. Labor Contract Law (of the People's Republic of China)

Order of the President of the People's Republic of China (No. 65)

The Labor Contract Law of the People's Republic of China, which was adopted at the 28th Session of the Standing Committee of the Tenth National People's Congress of the People's Republic of China on June 29, 2007, is hereby promulgated and shall come into force as of January 1, 2008.

Table of Contents

Chapter I   General Provisions

Article 1 This Law is formulated for the purposes of improving the labor contractual system, clarifying the rights and obligations of both parties of labor contracts, protecting the legitimate rights and interests of employees, and establishing and developing a harmonious and stable employment relationship.

Article 2 This Law shall apply to the establishment of an employment relationship between employees and enterprises, individual economic organizations, private non-enterprise entities, or other organizations (hereafter referred to as employers), and to the formation, fulfillment, change, dissolution, or termination of labor contracts.

The state organs, public institutions, social organizations, and their employees among them where there is an employment relationship shall observe this Law in the formation, fulfillment, change, dissolution, or termination of their labor contracts.

Article 3 The principles of lawfulness, fairness, equality, free will, negotiation for agreement, and good faith shall be observed in the formation of a labor contract.

A labor contract concluded according to the law shall have a binding force. The employer and the employee shall perform the obligations as stipulated in the labor contract.

Article 4 An employer shall establish a sound system of employment rules so as to ensure that its employees enjoy the labor rights and perform the employment obligations.

Where an employer formulates, amends, or decides rules or important events concerning the remuneration, working time, break, vacation, work safety and sanitation, insurance and welfare, training of employees, labor discipline, or management of production quotas which are directly related to the interests of the employees, such rules or important events shall be discussed at the meeting of employees' representatives or the general meeting of all employees, and the employer shall also put forward proposals and opinions to the employees and negotiate with the labor union or the employees' representatives on a equal basis to reach agreements on these rules or events.

During the process of execution of a rule or decision about an important event, if the labor union or the employees deem it improper, they may require the employer to amend or improve it through negotiations.

The employer shall make an announcement of the rules and important events that are directly related to the interests of the employees or inform the employees of these rules or events.

Article 5 The labor administrative department of the people's government at the county level or above shall, together with the labor union and the representatives of the enterprise, establish a sound three-party mechanism to coordinate the employment relationship and shall jointly seek to solve the major problems related to employment relations.

Article 6 The labor union shall assist and direct the employees when they conclude with the employers and fulfill labor contracts and establish a collective negotiation mechanism with the employers so as to maintain the lawful rights and interests of the employees.

Chapter II   Formation of Labor Contracts

Article 7 An employer establishes an employment relationship with an employee from the date when the employer puts the employee to work. The employer shall prepare a roster of employees for inspection.

Article 8 When an employer hires an employee, it shall faithfully inform him of the work contents, conditions and location, occupational harm, work safety state, remuneration, and other information that the employee requests to be informed of. The employer has the right to know the basic information of the employee that is directly related to the labor contract and the employee shall faithfully provide such information.

Article 9 When an employer hires an employee, it shall not detain his identity card or other certificates, nor require him to provide a guaranty or collect money or property from him under any other excuse.

Article 10 A written labor contract shall be concluded in the establishment of an employment relationship.

Where an employment relationship has already been established with an employee but no written labor contract has been entered simultaneously, a written labor contract shall be concluded within one month from the date when the employee begins to work.

Where an employer and an employee conclude a labor contract prior to the employment, the employment relationship is established from the date when the employee begins to work.

Article 11 Where an employer fails to conclude a written labor contract when the employer put his employee to work, if the remuneration stipulated between the employer and the employee is not clear, the remuneration to the new employee shall conform to the provisions of the collective contract. If there is no collective contract or if there is no such stipulation in the collective contract, the principle of equal pay for equal work shall be observed.

Article 12 Labor contracts are classified into fixed-term labor contracts, labor contracts without a fixed term, and the labor contracts that set the completion of specific tasks as the term to end contracts.

Article 13 A fixed-term labor contract refers to a labor contract in which the employer and the employee stipulate the time of termination of the contract.

The employer and the employee may conclude a fixed-term labor contract upon negotiation.

Article 14 A labor contract without a fixed term refers to a labor contract in which the employer and the employee stipulate no certain time to end the contract.

An employer and an employee may, through negotiations, conclude a labor contract without a fixed term. Under any of the following circumstances, if the employee proposes or agrees to renew or conclude a labor contract, a labor contract without a fixed term shall be concluded unless the employee proposes to conclude a fixed-term labor contract:

(1) The employee has already worked for the employer for 10 full years consecutively;

(2) When the employer initially adopts the labor contract system or when a state-owned enterprise reconcludes the labor contract due to restructuring, the employee has already worked for this employer for 10 full years consecutively and he attains the age that is less than 10 years up to the statutory retirement age; or

(3) The labor contract is to be renewed after two fixed-term labor contracts have been concluded consecutively, and the employee is not under any of the circumstances as mentioned in Article 39 and Paragraphs (1) and (2) of Article 40 of this Law.

If the employer fails to sign a written labor contract with an employee after the lapse of one full year from the date when the employee begins to work, it shall be deemed that the employer and the employee have concluded a labor contract without a fixed term.

Article 15 A labor contract that sets the completion of a specific task as the term to end the contract refers to the labor contract in which the employer and the employee stipulate that the time period of the contract shall be based on the completion of a specific task.

An employer and an employee may, upon negotiation, conclude a labor contract that sets the completion of a specific task to end the contract.

Article 16 A labor contract shall be agreed upon by the employer and the employee and shall come into effect after the employer and the employee affix their signatures or seals to the labor contract.

The employer and the employee shall each hold one copy of the labor contract.

Article 17 A labor contract shall include the following clauses:

(1) The employer's name, domicile, legal representative, or major person-in-charge;
(2) The employee's name, domicile, identity card number, or other valid identity certificate number;
(3) The time limit for the labor contract;
(4) The job descriptions and work locations;
(5) The work hours, break time, and leaves;
(6) The remunerations;
(7) The social security;
(8) The employment protection, work conditions, and protection against and prevention of occupational harm; and
(9) Other items that shall be included in the labor contract under any laws or regulations.

Apart from the essential clauses as prescribed in the preceding paragraph, the employer and the employee may, in the labor contract, stipulate the probation time period, training, confidentiality, supplementary insurances, welfares, benefits, and other items.

Article 18 If remunerations, work conditions, and other criteria are not expressly stipulated in a labor contract and a dispute is triggered, the employer and the employee may renegotiate the contract. If no agreement is reached through negotiations, the provisions of the collective contract shall be followed. If there is no collective contract or if there is no such stipulation about the remuneration, the principle of equal pay for equal work shall be observed. If there is no collective contract or if there is no such stipulation about the work conditions and other criteria in the collective contract, the relevant provisions of the state shall be followed.

Article 19 If the term of a labor contract is not less than 3 months but less than 1 year, the probation period shall not exceed one month. If the term of a labor contract is not less than one year but less than 3 years, the probation period shall not exceed 2 months. For a labor contract with a fixed term of 3 years or more or without a fixed term, the probation term shall not exceed 6 months.

An employer can only impose one probation time period on an employee.

For a labor contract that sets the completion of a specific task as the term to end the contract or with a fixed term of less than 3 months, no probation period may be stipulated.

The probation period shall be included in the term of a labor contract. If a labor contract only provides the term of probation, the probation shall be null and void and the term of the probation shall be treated as the term of the labor contract.

Article 20 The wage of an employee during the probation period shall not be lower than the minimum wage for the same position of the same employer or lower than 80 percent of the wage stipulated in the labor contract, nor may it be lower than the minimum wage of the locality where the employer is located.

Article 21 During the probation period, except when the employee is under any of the circumstances as described in Article 39 and Article 40 (1) and (2), the employer shall not dissolve the labor contract. If an employer dissolves a labor contract during the probation period, it shall make an explanation.

Article 22 Where an employer pays special training expenses for the special technical training of his employees, the employer may enter an agreement with his employees to specify their service time period.

If an employee violates the stipulation regarding the service time period, he shall pay the employer a penalty for breach of contract. The amount of penalty for breach of contract shall not exceed the training fees provided by the employer. The penalty for breach of a contract in which the employer requires the employee to pay shall not exceed the training expenses attributable to the service time period that is unfulfilled.

The service time period stipulated by the employer and the employee does not affect the raising of the remuneration of the employee during the probation period under the normal wage adjustment mechanism.

Article 23 An employer may enter into an agreement with his employees in the labor contract to require his employees to keep the business secrets and intellectual property of the employer confidential.

For an employee who has the obligation of keeping confidential, the employer and the employee may stipulate noncompetition clauses in the labor contract or in the confidentiality agreement and come to an agreement that, when the labor contract is dissolved or terminated, the employee shall be given economic compensations within the noncompetition period. If the employee violates the stipulation of noncompetition, it shall pay the employer a penalty for breaching the contract.

Article 24 The persons who should be subject to noncompetition shall be limited to the senior mangers, senior technicians, and the other employees who have the obligation to keep secrets of employers. The scope, geographical range, and time limit for noncompetition shall be stipulated by the employer and the employee. The stipulation on noncompetition shall not be contrary to any laws or regulations.

After the dissolution or termination of a labor contract, the noncompetition period for any of the persons as mentioned in the preceding paragraph to work for any other employer producing or engaging in products of the same category or engaging in business of the same category as this employer shall not exceed two years.

Article 25 Except for the circumstances as prescribed in Articles 22 and 23 of this Law, the employer shall not stipulate with the employee that the employee shall pay the penalty for breaching contract.

Article 26 The following labor contracts are invalid or are partially invalid if:

(1) A party employs the means of deception or coercion or takes advantage of the other party's difficulties to force the other party to conclude a labor contract or to make an amendment to a labor contract that is contrary to his will;
(2) An employer disclaims its legal liability or denies the employee's rights; or
(3) The mandatory provisions of laws or administrative regulations are violated.

If there is any dispute over the invalidating or partial invalidating of a labor contract, the dispute shall be settled by the labor dispute arbitration institution or by the people's court.

Article 27 The invalidity of any part of a labor contract does not affect the validity of the other parts of the contract. The other parts shall still remain valid.

Article 28 If a labor contract has been confirmed to be invalid, the employer shall pay remunerations to his employees who have labored for the employer. The amount of remunerations shall be determined by analogy to the remuneration to the employees taking up the same or similar positions of the employer.

Chapter III   Fulfillment and Change of Labor Contracts

Article 29 An employer and an employee shall, according to the stipulations of the labor contract, fully perform their respective obligations.

Article 30 An employer shall, under the contractual stipulations and the provisions of the state, timely pay its employees the full amount of remunerations.

Where an employer defers paying or fails to pay the full amount of remunerations, the employees may apply to the local people's court for an order of payment. The people's court shall issue an order of payment according to the law.

Article 31 An employer shall strictly execute the criterion on its production quota; it shall not force any of its employees to work overtime or make any of its employees do so in a disguised form. If an employer arranges overtime work, it shall pay its employee for the overtime work according to the relevant provisions of the state.

Article 32 If an employee refuses to perform the dangerous operations ordered by the manager of his employer, who violates the safety regulations or forces the employee to risk his life, the employee shall not be deemed to have violated the labor contract.

An employee may criticize, expose to the authorities, or make a charge against the employer if the work conditions may endanger his life and health.

Article 33 An employer's change of its name, legal representative, key person-in-charge, or investor shall not affect the fulfillment of the labor contracts.

Article 34 In case of merger or split, the original labor contracts of the employer still remain valid. Such labor contracts shall be performed by the new employer who succeeds the rights and obligations of the aforesaid employer.

Article 35 An employer and an employee may modify the contents stipulated in the labor contract if they so agree upon in negotiations. The modifications to the labor contract shall be made in writing.

The employer and the employee shall each hold one copy of the modified labor contract.

Chapter IV   Dissolution and Termination of Labor Contracts

Article 36 An employer and an employee may dissolve the labor contract if they so agree upon in negotiations.

Article 37 An employee may dissolve the labor contract if it notifies in writing the employer 30 days in advance. During the probation period, an employee may dissolve the labor contract if it notifies the employer 3 days in advance.

Article 38 Where an employer is under any of the following circumstances, its employees may dissolve the labor contract:

(1) It fails to provide labor protection or work conditions as stipulated in the labor contract;
(2) It fails to timely pay the full amount of remunerations;
(3) It fails to pay social security premiums for the employees;
(4) The rules and procedures set up by the employer are contrary to any law or regulation and impair the rights and interests of the employees;
(5) The labor contract is invalidated due to the circumstance as mentioned in Article 26 (1) of this Law; or
(6) Any other circumstances prescribed by other laws or administrative regulations that authorize employees to dissolve labor contracts.

If an employer forces any employee to work by the means of violence, threat, or illegally restraining personal freedom, or an employer violates the safety regulations to order or force any employee to perform dangerous operations that endanger the employee's personal life, the employee may immediately dissolve the labor contract without notifying the employer in advance.

Article 39 Where an employee is under any of the following circumstances, his employer may dissolve the labor contract:

(1) It is proved that the employee does not meet the recruitment conditions during the probation period;
(2) The employee seriously violates the rules and procedures set up by the employer;
(3) The employee causes any severe damage to the employer because he seriously neglects his duties or seeks private benefits;
(4) The employee simultaneously enters an employment relationship with other employers and thus seriously affects his completion of the tasks of

the employer, or the employee refuses to make the ratification after his employer points out the problem;

(5) The labor contract is invalidated due to the circumstance as mentioned in Item (1), paragraph 1, Article 26 of this Law; or

(6) The employee is under investigation for criminal liabilities according to law.

Article 40 Under any of the following circumstances, the employer may dissolve the labor contract if it notifies the employee in writing 30 days in advance or after it pays the employee an extra month's wages:

(1) The employee is sick or is injured for a non–work-related reason and cannot resume his original position after the expiration of the prescribed time period for medical treatment, nor can he assume any other position arranged by the employer;

(2) The employee is incompetent in his position or is still so after training or changing his position; or

(3) The objective situation, on which the conclusion of the labor contract is based, has changed considerably, the labor contract is unable to be performed, and no agreement on changing the contents of the labor contract is reached after negotiations between the employer and the employee.

Article 41 Under any of the following circumstances, if it is necessary to lay off 20 or more employees, or if it is necessary to lay off less than 20 employees but the layoff accounts for 10 percent of the total number of the employees, the employer shall, 30 days in advance, make an explanation to the labor union or to all its employees. After it has solicited the opinions from the labor union or of the employees, it may lay off the number of employees upon reporting the employee reduction plan to the labor administrative department:

(1) It is under revitalization according to the Enterprise Bankruptcy Law;

(2) It encounters serious difficulties in production and business operation;

(3) The enterprise changes products, makes important technological renovations, or adjusts the methods of its business operation, and it is still necessary to lay off the number of employees after changing the labor contract; or

(4) The objective economic situation, on which the labor contract is based, has changed considerably and the employer is unable to perform the labor contract.

The following employees shall be given priority to be kept when the employer cuts down the number of employees:

(1) Those who have concluded a fixed-term labor contract with a long time period;
(2) Those who have concluded a labor contract without fixed term; and
(3) Those whose family has no other employee and has aged or minors to support.

If the employer intends to hire new employees within 6 months after it cuts down the number of employees according to the first paragraph of this Article, it shall notify the employees cut down and shall, in the equal conditions, give a priority to the employees cut down.

Article 42 An employer shall not dissolve the labor contract under Articles 40 and 41 of this Law if any of its employees:

(1) is engaging in operations exposing him to occupational disease hazards and has not undergone an occupational health checkup before he leaves his position, or is suspected of having an occupational disease and has been diagnosed or is under medical observation;
(2) has been confirmed as having lost or partially lost his capacity to work due to an occupational disease or a work-related injury during his employment with the employer;
(3) has contracted an illness or sustained a non–work-related injury and the proscribed time period of medical treatment has not expired;
(4) is a female who is in her pregnancy, confinement, or nursing period;
(5) has been working for the employer continuously for not less than 15 years and is less than 5 years away from his legal retirement age; or
(6) finds himself in other circumstances under which an employer shall not dissolve the labor contract as proscribed in laws or administrative regulations

Article 43 Where an employer unilaterally dissolves a labor contract, it shall notify the labor union of the reasons in advance. If the employer violates any laws, administrative regulation, or stipulations of the labor contract, the labor union has the power to require the employer to make ratification. The employer shall consider the opinions of the labor union and notify the labor union of the relevant result in writing.

Article 44 A labor contract may be terminated under any of the following circumstances:

(1) The term of a labor contract has expired;
(2) The employee has begun to enjoy the basic benefits of his pension;
(3) The employee is deceased, or is declared dead or missing by the people's court;

(4) The employer is declared bankrupt;

(5) The employer's business license is revoked or the employer is ordered to close down its business or to dissolve its business entity, or the employer makes a decision to liquidate its business ahead of the schedule; or

(6) Other circumstances proscribed by other laws or administrative regulations.

Article 45 If a labor contract expires and it is under any of the circumstances as described in Article 42 of this Law, the term of labor contract shall be extended until the disappearance of the relevant circumstance. However, the matters relating to the termination of the labor contract of an employee who has lost or partially lost his capacity to work as prescribed in Article 42 (2) of this Law shall be handled according to the pertinent provisions on work-related injury insurance.

Article 46 The employer shall, under any of the following circumstances, pay the employee an economic compensation:

(1) The employee dissolves the labor contract in pursuance of Article 38 of this Law;

(2) The employer proposes to dissolve the labor contract, and it reaches an agreement with the employee on the dissolution through negotiations;

(3) The employer dissolves the labor contract according to Article 40 of this Law;

(4) The employer dissolves the labor contract according to the first Paragraph of Article 41 of this Law; or

(5) The termination of a fixed-term labor contract according to Article 44 (1) of this Law unless the employee refuses to renew the contract even though the conditions offered by the employer are the same as or better than those stipulated in the current contract;

(6) The labor contract is terminated according to Article 44 (4) and (5) of this Law; or

(7) Other circumstances as proscribed in other laws and administrative regulations.

Article 47 An employee shall be given an economic compensation based on the number of years he has worked for the employer and at the rate of one month's wage for each full year he worked. Any period of not less than six months but less than one year shall be counted as one year. The economic compensation payable to an employee for any period of less than six months shall be one-half of his monthly wages.

If the monthly wage of an employee is higher than three times the average monthly wage of employees declared by the people's government at the level of municipality directly under the central government or at the level of a districted city where the employer is located, the rate for the economic compensation to be paid to him shall be three times the average monthly wage of employees and shall be for no more than 12 years of his work.

The term "monthly wage" mentioned in this Article refers to the employee's average monthly wage for the 12 months prior to the dissolution or termination of his labor contract.

Article 48 If an employer dissolves or terminates a labor contract in violation of this Law but the employee demands the continuous fulfillment of the contract, the employer shall do so. If the employee does not demand the continuous fulfillment of the contract or if the continuous fulfillment of the labor contract is impossible, the employer shall pay compensation to the employee according to Article 87 of this Law.

Article 49 The State shall take measures to establish and improve a comprehensive system to ensure that the employee's social security relationship can be transferred from one region to another and can be continued after the transfer.

Article 50 At the time of dissolution or termination of a labor contract, the employer shall issue a document to prove the dissolution or termination of the labor contract and complete, within 15 days, the procedures for the transfer of the employee's personal file and social security relationship.

The employee shall complete the procedures for the handover of his work as agreed upon between both parties. If relevant provisions of this Law require the employer to pay an economic compensation, it shall make a payment upon completion of the procedures for the handover of the employee's work.

The employer shall preserve the labor contracts, which have been dissolved or terminated, for not less than 2 years for reference purposes.

Chapter V   Special Provisions

Section 1   *Collective Contracts*

Article 51   The employees of an enterprise may get together as a party to negotiate with their employer to conclude a collective contract on the matters of remuneration, working hours, breaks, vacations, work safety and hygiene, insurance, benefits, etc. The draft of the collective contract shall be presented to the general assembly of employees or all the employees for discussion and approval.

A collective contract may be concluded by the labor union on behalf of the employees of an enterprise with the employer. If the enterprise does not have a labor union yet, the contract may be concluded between the employer and the representatives chosen by the employees under the guidance of the labor union at the next highest level.

Article 52 The employees of an enterprise as a party may negotiate with the employer to enter specialized collective contracts regarding the issues of work safety and hygiene, protection of the rights and interests of female employees, the wage adjustment mechanism, etc.

Article 53 Industrial or regional collective contracts may be concluded between the labor unions and the representatives of enterprises in industries such as construction, mining, catering services, etc., in the regions at or below the county level.

Article 54 After a collective contract has been concluded, it shall be submitted to the labor administrative department. The collective contract shall become effective after the lapse of 15 days from the date of receipt thereof by the labor administrative department, unless said department raises any objections to the contract.

A collective contract that has been concluded according to law is binding on both the employer and the employees. An industrial or regional collective contract is binding on both the employers and employees in the local industry or the region.

Article 55 The standards for remunerations, working conditions, etc., as stipulated in a collective contract shall not be lower than the minimum criteria as prescribed by the local people's government. The standards for remunerations, working conditions, etc. as stipulated in the labor contract between an employer and an employee shall not be lower than those as specified in the collective contract.

Article 56 If an employer's breach of the collective contract infringes upon the labor rights and interests of the employees, the labor union may, according to law, require the employer to bear the liability. If a dispute arising from the performance of the collective contract is not resolved after negotiations, the labor union may apply for arbitration or lodge a lawsuit in pursuance of law.

Section 2 *Worker Dispatch Service*

Article 57 A worker dispatch service provider shall be established according to the Company Law and have a registered capital of not less than RMB 500,000 yuan.

Article 58 Worker dispatch service providers are employers as mentioned in this Law and shall perform an employer's obligations for its employees. The labor contract between a worker dispatch service provider and a worker to be dispatched shall, in addition to the matters specified in Article 17 of this law, specify such matters as the entity to which the worker will be dispatched, the term of dispatch, positions, etc.

The labor contracts between a worker dispatch service provider and the workers to be dispatched shall be fixed-term labor contracts with a term of not less than 2 years. The worker dispatch service provider shall pay the remunerations on a monthly basis. During the time period when there is no work for the workers, the worker dispatch service provider shall compensate the workers on a monthly basis at the minimum wage prescribed by the people's government of the place where the worker dispatch service provider is located.

Article 59 To dispatch workers, a worker dispatch service provider shall enter into dispatch agreements with the entity that accepts the workers under the dispatch arrangement (hereinafter referred to as the "accepting entity"). The dispatch agreements shall stipulate the positions to which the workers are dispatched, the number of persons to be dispatched, the term of dispatch, the amounts and terms of payments of remunerations and social security premiums, and the liability for breach of agreement.

An accepting entity shall decide with the worker service dispatch provider on the term of dispatch based on the actual requirements of the positions, and it shall not separate a continuous term of labor use into two or more short-term dispatch agreements.

Article 60 A worker dispatch service provider shall inform the workers dispatched of the content of the dispatch agreements.

No worker dispatch service provider may skimp on any remuneration that an accepting entity pays to the workers according to the dispatch agreement.

No worker dispatch service provider or accepting entity may charge any fee from any dispatched worker.

Article 61 If a worker dispatch service provider assigns a worker to an accepting entity in another region, the worker's remuneration and work conditions shall be in line with the relevant standards of the place where the accepting entity is located.

Article 62 An accepting entity shall perform the following obligations:

(1) To implement state labor standards and provide the corresponding working conditions and labor protection;
(2) To communicate the job requirements and labor compensations for the dispatched workers;
(3) To pay overtime remunerations and performance bonuses and provide benefits relevant to the position;
(4) To provide the dispatched employees who assume the positions with required training; and
(5) To implement a normal wage adjustment system in the case of continuous dispatch.

No accepting entity may in turn dispatch the workers to any other employer.

Article 63 The workers dispatched shall have the right to receive the same pay as that received by employees of the accepting entity for the same work. If an accepting entity has no employee in the same position, the remuneration shall be determined with reference to that paid in the place where the accepting entity is located to employees at the same or a similar position.

Article 64 The workers dispatched have the right to join the labor union of the worker dispatch service provider or of the accepting entity or to organize such unions, so as to protect their own lawful rights and interests.

Article 65 A worker dispatched may, according to Articles 36 and 38 of this Law, dissolve the labor contract between himself and the worker dispatch service provider.

Where a worker dispatched is under any of the circumstances as mentioned in Article 39 and Article 40 (1) and (2), the accepting entity may return the worker to the worker dispatch service provider, and the worker dispatch service provider may dissolve the labor contract with the worker.

Article 66 The worker dispatch services shall normally be used for temporary, auxiliary, or substitute positions.

Article 67 No accepting entity may establish any worker dispatch service to dispatch the workers to itself and to its subsidiaries.

Section 3 *Part-Time Employment*

Article 68 The "part-time employment" is a form of labor in which the remuneration is mainly calculated on an hourly basis, the average working hours of a worker per day shall not exceed 4 hours, and the aggregate working hours per week for the same employer shall not exceed 24 hours.

Article 69 Both parties to a part-time employment may reach an oral agreement.

A worker who engages in part-time employment may conclude a labor contract with one or more employers, but a labor contract concluded subsequently may not prejudice the performance of a labor contract previously concluded.

Article 70 No probation period may be stipulated by both parties for a part-time employment.

Article 71 Either of the parties to part-time employment may inform the other party of the termination of labor at any time. Upon the termination of a part-time employment, the employer will pay no economic compensation to the employee.

Article 72 The criteria for the calculation of part-time employment on an hourly basis shall not be lower than the minimum hourly wage prescribed by the people's government of the place where the employer is located.

The maximum remuneration settlement and payment cycle for part-time employment shall not exceed 15 days.

Chapter VI   Supervision and Inspection

<u>Article 73</u> The labor administrative department of the State Council shall be responsible for the supervision and inspection of the implementation of the system of labor contracts throughout the country.

The labor administrative department of the local people's governments at the county level and above shall be responsible for the supervision and inspection of the implementation of the system of labor contracts within their respective administrative areas.

During the supervision and inspection of the implementation of the system of labor contracts, the labor administrative departments of the people's governments at the county level and above shall solicit the opinions of the labor unions, enterprise representatives, and relevant industrial administrative departments.

<u>Article 74</u> The labor administrative department of the local people's government at the county level or above shall exercise supervision and inspection in respect of the implementation of the system of labor contracts:

(1) The employers' formulation of rules and regulations directly related to the interests of workers, and the implementation thereof;

(2) The formation and dissolution of labor contracts by employers and workers;

(3) The compliance with relevant regulations on dispatch by worker dispatch service providers and the accepting entities;

(4) The employers' compliance with provisions of the state on workers' working hours, breaks, and vacations;

(5) The employers' payment for remuneration as specified in the labor contracts and compliance with the minimum wage criteria;

(6) The employers' participation in social security and the payment for social security premiums; and

(7) Other labor supervision matters as prescribed by laws and regulations.

<u>Article 75</u> During the supervision and inspection process, the labor administrative department of the people's government at the county level or above has the power to consult the materials relevant to the labor contracts and collective contracts and to conduct on-the-spot inspections at the workplaces. The employers and employees shall faithfully provide pertinent information and materials.

When the functionaries of the labor administrative department conduct an inspection, they shall show their badges, exercise their duties and powers pursuant to laws, and enforce the law in a well-disciplined manner.

Article 76 The relevant administrative departments of construction, health, work safety supervision and administration, etc., of the people's governments at the county level and above shall, with the scope of their respective functions, supervise and administer the employers' implementation of the system of labor contracts.

Article 77 For any employer whose lawful rights and interests are impaired, he may require the relevant department to deal with the case, apply for an arbitration, or lodge a lawsuit.

Article 78 A labor union shall protect the employees' legitimate rights and interests and supervise the employer's fulfillment of the labor contracts and collective contracts. If the employer violates any law or regulation or breaches any labor contract or collective contract, the labor union may put forward its opinions and require the employer to make ratification. If the employee applies for arbitration or lodges a lawsuit, the labor union shall support and help him in pursuance of law.

Article 79 Any organization or individual may report the violations of this law. The labor administrative departments of the people's governments at the county level and above shall timely verify and deal with such violations and shall grant awards to the meritorious persons who report the violations.

Chapter VII   Legal Liabilities

Article 80 If the rules and procedures of an employer directly related to the employees' interests are contrary to any laws or regulations, the labor administration department shall order the employer to make rectification and give it a warning. If the rules and procedures cause any damage to the employees, the employer shall bear the liability for compensation.

Article 81 If the text of a labor contract provided by an employer does not include the mandatory clauses required by this Law or if an employer fails to deliver a copy of the labor contract to its employee, the labor administration department shall order the employer to make ratification. If any damage is caused to the employee, the employer shall bear the liability for compensation.

Article 82 If an employer fails to conclude a written labor contract with an employee after the lapse of more than one month but less than one year as of the day when it started using him, it shall pay to the worker his monthly wages at double amount.

If an employer fails, in violation of this Law, to conclude with an employee a labor contract without a fixed term, it shall pay to the employee his monthly wage at double amount, starting from the date on which a labor contract without a fixed term should have been concluded.

Article 83 If an employer stipulates the probation period with an employee to violate this Law, the labor administration department shall order the employer to make rectification. If the illegally stipulated probation has been performed, the employer shall pay compensation to the employee according to the time worked on probation beyond the statutory probation period, at the rate of the employee's monthly wage following the completion of his probation.

Article 84 Where an employer violates this Law by detaining the resident identity cards or other certificates of the employees, the labor administrative department shall order the employer to return the ID and certificates to the employees within a time limit and shall punish the employer according to the relevant laws.

Where an employer violates this Law by collecting money and property from employees in the name of guaranty or with any other excuses, the labor administrative department shall order the employer to return the said property to the employees within a time limit and fine the employer not less than 500 yuan but not more than 2,000 yuan for each person. If any damage is caused to the employees, the employer shall be liable for compensation.

When an employee dissolves or terminates the labor contract in pursuance of law, if the employer retains the archives or other articles of the employees, it shall be punished according to the provisions of the preceding paragraph.

Article 85 Where an employing entity is under any of the following circumstances, the labor administrative department shall order it to pay the remunerations, overtime remunerations, or economic compensation within a time limit. If the remuneration is lower than the local minimum wage, the employer shall pay the shortfall. If payment is not made within the time limit, the employer shall be ordered to pay an extra compensation to the employee at a rate of not less than 50 percent and not more than 100 percent of the payable amount:

(1) Failing to pay an employee his remunerations in full amount and on time as stipulated in the labor contract or prescribed by the state;
(2) Paying an employee the wage below the local minimum wage standard;
(3) Arranging overtime work without paying overtime remunerations; or
(4) Dissolving or terminating a labor contract without paying the employee the economic compensation under this Law.

Article 86 Where a labor contract is confirmed invalid under Article 26 of this Law and any damage is caused to the other party, the party at fault shall be liable for compensation.

Article 87 If an employer violates this Law by dissolving or terminating the labor contract, it shall pay compensation to the employee at the rate of twice the economic compensations as prescribed in Article 47 of this Law.

Article 88 Where an employer is under any of the following circumstances, it shall be given an administrative punishment. If any crime is constituted, it shall be subject to criminal liabilities. If any damage is caused to the employee, the employer shall be liable for compensation:

(1) To force the employee to work by violence, threat, or illegal limitation of personal freedom;
(2) To illegally command or force any employee to perform dangerous operations endangering the employee's life;
(3) To insult, corporally punish, beat, illegally search, or restrain any employee; or
(4) To cause damages to the physical or mental health of employees because of poor working conditions or severely polluted environments.

Article 89 Where an employer violates this Law by failing to issue to an employee a written certificate for the dissolution or termination of a labor contract, it shall be ordered to make a ratification by the labor administrative department. If any damage is caused to an employee, the employer shall be liable for compensation.

Article 90 Where an employee violates this Law to dissolve the labor contract, or violates the stipulations of the labor contract about the confidentiality obligation or noncompetition, if any loss is caused to the employer, he shall be liable for compensation.

Article 91 Where an employer hires any employee whose labor contract with another employer has not been dissolved or terminated yet, if any loss is caused to the employer mentioned later, the employer first mentioned shall bear joint and several liability of compensation.

Article 92 Where a worker dispatch service provider violates this Law, it shall be ordered to make rectification by the labor administrative department and other relevant administrative departments. If the circumstance is severe, it shall be fined at the rate of not less than 1, 000 yuan but not more than 5, 000 yuan per person and have its business license revoked by the administrative department for industry and commerce. If any damage is caused to the workers dispatched, the worker dispatch service provider and the accepting entity shall bear joint and several liability of compensation.

Article 93 Where an employer without lawful business operation qualifications commits any violation or crime, it shall be subject to legal liabilities. If the employees have already worked for the employer, the employer or its capital contributors shall, under the relevant provisions of this Law, pay the employees remunerations, economic compensations, or indemnities. If any damage is caused to the employee, it shall be liable for compensation.

Article 94 Where an individual as a business operation contractor hires employees in violation of this Law and causes any damage to any employee, the contracting organization and the individual business operation contractor shall be jointly and severally liable for compensation.

Article 95 If the labor administrative department, or any other relevant administrative department, or any of the functionaries thereof neglect its (his) duties, does not perform the statutory duties, or exercises its (his) duties in violation of law, it (he) shall be liable for compensation. The directly liable person-in-charge and other directly liable persons shall be given an administrative sanction. If any crime is constituted, they shall be subject to criminal liabilities.

Chapter VIII   Supplementary Provisions

Article 96 For the formation, performance, modification, dissolution, or termination of a labor contract between a public institution and an employee under the system of employment, if it is otherwise provided for in any law, administrative regulation, or by the State Council, the latter shall be followed. If there is no such provision, the relevant provisions of this Law shall be observed.

Article 97 Labor contracts concluded before the implementation of this Law and that continue to exist on the implementation date of this Law shall continue to be performed. For the purposes of Item (3) of the second Paragraph of Article 14 of this Law, the number of consecutive times on which a fixed-term labor contract is concluded shall be counted from the first renewal of such contract to occur after the implementation of this Law.

If an employment relationship was established prior to the implementation of this Law without the conclusion of a written labor contract, such contract shall be concluded within one month from the date when this Law becomes effective.

If a labor contract existing on the implementation date of this Law is dissolved or terminated after the implementation of this Law and, according to Article 46 of this Law, an economic compensation is payable, the number of years for which the economic compensation is payable shall be counted from the implementation date of this Law. If, under relevant effective regulations prior to the implementation of this Law, the employee is entitled to the economic compensation from the employer in respect of a period prior to the implementation of this Law, the matters shall be handled according to the relevant effective regulations at that time.

Article 98 This Law shall come into force as of January 1, 2008.

3. Regulation on the Implementation of the Employment Contract Law of the People's Republic of China

Order of the State Council of the People's Republic of China (No. 535)

The Regulation on the Implementation of the Employment Contract Law of the People's Republic of China, which was adopted at the 25th executive meeting of the State Council on September 3, 2008, is hereby promulgated, and shall come into force on the date of promulgation.

Premier Wen Jiabao
September 18, 2008

Table of Contents

Chapter I   General Provisions

Article 1 This Regulation is formulated to implement the Employment Contract Law of the People's Republic of China (hereinafter referred to as Employment Contract Law).

Article 2 The people's governments at all levels, the labor administrative departments of the people's governments at or above the county level, and the labor unions, etc. shall take steps to promote the implementation of the Employment Contract Law and develop a harmonious employment relationship.

Article 3 Legally established accounting firms, law firms, and other partnerships and foundations are employers defined in the Employment Contract Law.

Chapter II   Conclusion of Employment Contracts

Article 4 A branch office established by an employer as defined in the Employment Contract Law that has obtained its business license or registration certificate according to law may conclude employment contracts with employees in the name of an employer; if it has failed to obtain a business license or registration certificate, it may conclude employment contracts with employees only upon the authorization of the employer.

Article 5 Where any employee, after being notified by the employer in writing, fails to conclude a written employment contract with the employer within one month from the day when he is employed, the employer shall terminate the employment relationship with the employee and notify the employee in writing, in which case the employer is not required to make any economic compensation to the employee, but shall pay the employee for his actual working time.

Article 6 Where an employer fails to conclude a written employment contract with an employee after the lapse of more than one month but less than one year from the date when the employee is employed, it shall pay to the worker his monthly wages in double amount according to Article 82 of the Employment Contract Law, and shall conclude a written employment contract with the employee. Where an employee refuses to conclude a written employment contract with his employer, the employer shall terminate the employment relationship, notify the employee in writing, and make economic compensations to the employee according to Article 47 of the Employment Contract Law.

The start time of the period when an employer is required to pay an employee his monthly wages in double amount shall be the day following the full month from the day when the employee is employed, and the end time shall be the day before the day when the written employment contract is concluded.

Article 7 Where an employer fails to conclude a written employment contract with an employee after the lapse of one full year from the day when the employee is employed, under Article 82 of the Employment Contract Law, the employer shall pay his monthly wages in double amount from the day next to the lapse of a full month to the day before it is a full year since the employee's employment, and it shall be deemed that the employer has concluded an employment contract without a fixed term with the employee on the day when it is a full year since the employee's employment, and a written employment contract without a fixed term shall be concluded with the employee immediately.

Article 8 The roster of employees as mentioned in Article 7 of the Employment Contract Law shall contain the employees' name, gender, citizen's identity number, registered permanent residence address and current address, contact information, form of employment, start time of employment, and term of the employment contract, etc.

Article 9 The start time of the term "10 consecutive years" as mentioned in Paragraph 2 of Article 14 of the Employment Contract Law shall be the day when the employer hired the employee, including the time of employment before the Employment Contract Law came into force.

Article 10 Where an employee is transferred to a new employer for reasons not attributable to himself, his working time with the original employer shall be consolidated into his working time with the new employer. If the original employer has made economic compensations for his working time with the original employer, the new employer shall not consider the employee's working time with the original employer when calculating economic compensations made to such employee for dissolving or terminating the employment contract with him.

Article 11 Where an employee proposes the conclusion of an employment contract without a fixed term with the employer under Paragraph 2, Article 14 of the Employment Contract Law, the employer shall conclude an employment contract without a fixed term with him, unless it is otherwise agreed to by both parties. The contents of an employment contract shall be determined by both parties under the principles of legality, equity, free will, consensus, and good faith. Any dispute over the contents shall be settled according to Article 18 of the Employment Contract Law.

Article 12 For the public welfare posts arranged by the local people's governments at various levels and the relevant departments of the local people's government at or above the county level for people with employment difficulties who enjoy post-based subsidies and social insurance subsidies, the provisions of the Employment Contract Law with respect to employment contracts without a fixed term and economic compensations are not applicable to the employment contracts for those posts.

Article 13 An employer and an employee may not agree on any other term for the termination of the employment contract beyond the circumstances for the termination of employment contracts as prescribed in Article 44 of the Employment Contract Law.

Article 14 Where the place of performance of an employment contract is not the place of registration of the employer, such matters about the employee as the maximum wage level, labor protection, work conditions, prevention against occupational harm, and the local average monthly wages in the last year shall be governed by the relevant provisions of the place of performance of the employment contract. If the relevant standards at the place of registration of the employer are higher than those at the place of performance of the employment contract and both the employer and the employee have agreed on following the relevant provisions of the place of registration of the employer, the relevant provisions of the place of registration of the employer shall apply.

Article 15 An employee's wages during probation shall not be less than 80 percent of the minimum wages for the same post of the employer or 80 percent of the wages stipulated in the employment contract, and shall not be less than the minimum wage level of the place where the employer is located.

Article 16 The training expenses as mentioned in Paragraph 2, Article 22 of the Employment Contract Law include the training expenses spent by the employer on providing professional technical trainings for an employee, the travel expenses during the training, and other direct expenses spent on the employee as a result of the training.

Article 17 Where an employment contract expires when the term of service stipulated by the employer and the employee according to Article 22 of the Employment Contract Law has not expired yet, the employment contract shall be performed until at least the expiration of the term of service, unless it is otherwise stipulated by both parties.

Chapter III   Dissolution and Termination of Employment Contracts

Article 18 Under any of the following circumstances, an employee may, according to the conditions and procedures prescribed in the Employment Contract Law, dissolve an employment contract with a fixed term, an employment contract without a fixed term, or an employment contract that sets the completion of a specific task as the term of the contract concluded with the employer:

(1) The employee and the employer so agree;
(2) The employee has notified the employee of the dissolution in writing at least 30 days in advance;
(3) The employee has notified the employer of the dissolution three days in advance during probation;
(4) The employer fails to provide labor protection or work conditions as it has promised in the employment contract;
(5) The employer fails to pay labor remunerations on schedule or in full amount;
(6) The employer fails to pay social insurance premiums for the employee as required by law;
(7) Some of the employer's rules or procedures have contravened the law and damaged the rights and interests of the employee;
(8) The employer, by means of deception or coercion or by taking advantage of the employee's difficulties, forces the employee to conclude or change the employment contract against the employee's true will;
(9) The employer disclaims its legal liability or denies the employee's rights in the employment contract;

(10) The employer violates the mandatory provisions of any law or administrative regulation;

(11) The employer compels the employee to work by force, threat, or illegally restricting the personal freedom of the employee;

(12) The employer gives orders in violation of the safety regulations or forces the employee to risk his life; or

(13) Other circumstances under which the employee can dissolve the employment contract as set forth in laws or administrative regulations.

Article 19 Under any of the following circumstances, an employer may, according to the conditions and procedures prescribed in the Employment Contract Law, dissolve an employment contract with a fixed term, an employment contract without a fixed term, or an employment contract that sets the completion of a specific task as the term of the contract concluded with an employee:

(1) The employer and the employee so agree;

(2) The employee is proved to have failed to meet the employment conditions during the probation;

(3) The employee seriously violates the rules and procedures set up by the employer;

(4) The employee seriously neglects his duties or engages in malpractice for personal gains and has caused severe damages to the employer;

(5) The employee simultaneously enters an employment relationship with any other employer and thus seriously affects his completion of the tasks assigned by the employer, or the employee refuses to correct after the employer has pointed out the problem;

(6) The employee, by means of deception or coercion or by taking advantage of the employer's difficulties, forces the employer to conclude or change the employment contract against the employer's true will;

(7) The employee is under investigation for criminal liabilities;

(8) The employee is sick or is injured for a non–work-related reason and cannot resume his original position after the expiration of the prescribed time period for medical treatment, nor can he assume any other position arranged by the employer;

(9) The employee is incompetent in his position or is still so after training or being assigned to another position;

(10) The objective situation on which the conclusion of the employment contract is based has changed considerably, which makes it impossible to perform the employment contract, and no agreement on changing the

contents of the employment contract has been reached after negotiations between the employer and the employee;

(11) The employer is being restructured according to the Enterprise Bankruptcy Law;

(12) The employer encounters serious difficulties in production and business operations;

(13) The employer changes its products, makes important technological renovations, or adjusts the way of business operations, and it is still necessary to lay off some employees after modifying the employment contract; or

(14) Other objective economic situations on which the employment contract is based change substantially, which makes it impossible to perform the employment contract.

Article 20 Where an employer decides to dissolve the employment contract with an employee by paying the latter an additional month's wages according to Article 40 of the Employment Contract Law, the amount of the additional month's wages shall be determined according to the employee's wages in the last month.

Article 21 An employment contract shall be terminated when an employee reaches the mandatory age for retirement.

Article 22 Where an employment contract that sets the completion of a specific task as the term of the contract is terminated upon the completion of the specific task, the employer shall make economic compensations to the employee according to Article 47 of the Employment Contract Law.

Article 23 Where an employer terminates the employment contract with an employee injured at work, it shall, apart from making economic compensations according to Article 47 of the Employment Contract Law, pay medical subsidies for the work-related injury and employment subsidies to the disabled once and for all according to the state provisions on work-related injury insurance.

Article 24 An employment contract dissolution or termination certificate issued by an employer shall bear the term of the employment contract, the date when it is dissolved or terminated, the position of the employee, and the working time of the employee with this employer.

Article 25 Where any employer dissolves or terminates the employment contract with an employee against the Employment Contract Law, if it has paid a compensation according to Article 87 of the Employment Contract Law, it is not required to make economic compensations. The working time based on which said compensation is calculated shall be calculated from the day when the employee was hired.

Article 26 If an employer and an employee have stipulated the period of service in the employment contract, when the employee dissolves the employment contract according to Article 38 of the Employment Contract Law, it is not against the stipulation of the period of service, and the employer is not entitled to ask the employee to pay a penalty for breach of contract.

If the employer dissolves the employment contract that has stipulated the period of service under any of the following circumstances, the employee shall pay a penalty for breach of contract to the employer:

(1) The employee seriously violates the rules and procedures set up by the employer;
(2) The employee seriously neglects his duties or engages in malpractice for personal gains and has caused severe damages to the employer;
(3) The employee simultaneously enters an employment relationship with any other employer and thus seriously affects his completion of the tasks assigned by the employer, or the employee refuses to correct after the employer has pointed out the problem;
(4) The employee, by means of deception or coercion or by taking advantage of the employer's difficulties, forces the employer to conclude or change the employment contract against the employer's true will; or
(5) The employee is under investigation for criminal liabilities.

Article 27 According to Article 47 of the Employment Contract Law, the monthly wages for calculating the economic compensation to be paid to an employee shall be the monthly wages that the employee deserves, including the hourly wages or piecework wages and other monetary incomes such as bonuses, allowances, and subsidies. If the average wages of the employee in the 12 months before the employment contract is dissolved or terminated are below the local minimum wage level, the economic compensation shall be calculated based on the local minimum wage. If the working time of the employee is less than 12 months, the average wages shall be calculated based on the actual work time.

Chapter IV   Special Provisions on Labor Dispatch

Article 28 According to Article 67 of the Employment Contract Law, a labor dispatch entity funded by an employer or a subsidiary entity thereof or established in the form of partnership may not dispatch any employee to the employer or the subsidiary entity.

Article 29 An employer shall fulfill its obligations set forth in Article 62 of the Employment Contract Law and safeguard the legitimate rights and interests of the dispatched employees.

Article 30 No labor dispatch entity may employ part-time to-be-dispatched employees.

Article 31 Economic compensations to be made after a labor dispatch entity or a dispatched employee has lawfully dissolved or terminated the employment contract shall be made according to Article 46 or 47 of the Employment Contract Law.

Article 32 Where any labor dispatch entity illegally dissolves or terminates the employment contract with a dispatched employee, Article 48 of the Employment Contract Law shall apply.

Chapter V   Legal Liability

Article 33 Where any employer violates the provisions of the Employment Contract Law on setting up a roster of employees, the competent labor administrative department shall order it to correct within a certain time limit and, if it fails to do so, impose a fine of not more than 20,000 yuan but not less than 2,000 yuan upon it.

Article 34 Where any employer fails to pay an employee his monthly wages in double amount or compensations when it is so required by the Employment Contract Law, the competent labor administrative department shall order it to make the payment.

Article 35 Where any employer violates the provisions of the Employment Contract Law or this Regulation on dispatching employees, the competent labor administrative department or other competent department shall order it to correct and, if the circumstances are serious, impose a fine of 1,000 yuan to 5,000 yuan per dispatched employee. If any damages have been caused to the dispatched employee, the dispatch entity and the employer shall assume joint and several liabilities.

Chapter VI   Supplementary Provisions

Article 36 For the reported or complained acts in violation of the Employment Contract Law or this Regulation, the labor administrative departments of the local people's governments at or above the county level shall handle them according to the Regulation on Labor Security Supervision.

Article 37 For any dispute incurred in the conclusion, performance, modification, dissolution, or termination of an employment contract between an employee and his employer, the Law of the People's Republic of China on the Mediation and Arbitration of Labor Disputes shall apply.

Article 38 This Regulation shall come into force on the date of promulgation.

4. Law of the People's Republic of China on Labor Dispute Mediation and Arbitration

Order of the President of the People's Republic of China (No. 80)

The Law of the People's Republic of China on Labor Dispute Mediation and Arbitration, which was adopted at the 31st meeting of the Standing Committee of the Tenth National People's Congress of the People's Republic of China on December 29, 2007, is hereby promulgated and shall be effective as of May 1, 2008.

President of the People's Republic of China: Hu Jintao
December 29, 2007

(Adopted at the 31st meeting of the Standing Committee of the Tenth National People's Congress of the People's Republic of China on December 29, 2007)

Table of Contents

Chapter I   General Provisions

Article 1   To impartially and timely settle the labor disputes, protect the legal rights and interests of the parties, and promote the harmonious and stable labor relations, this Law has been formulated.

Article 2   This Law shall apply to the following labor disputes arising between an employer and an employee within the territories of the People's Republic of China:

(1) A dispute arising from the confirmation of a labor relationship;
(2) A dispute arising from the conclusion, performance, modification, rescission, or termination of a labor contract;
(3) A dispute arising from the removal or layoff of an employee or the resignation or retirement of an employee;

(4) A dispute arising from the work hours, breaks, vacations, social insurance, benefits, training, or labor safety;

(5) A dispute arising from the labor remunerations, medical expenses for a work-related injury, economic indemnity, compensation, etc.; or

(6) Any other labor dispute as provided for by a law or administrative regulation.

Article 3 A labor dispute shall be settled on the basis of facts and on the principles of legality, fairness, timeliness, and emphasis on mediation so as to protect the legal rights and interests of the parties according to law.

Article 4 Where a labor dispute arises, an employee may consult with his or her employer, or request the trade union or a third party to jointly consult with the employer, so as to reach a settlement agreement.

Article 5 Where a labor dispute arises, if a party does not desire a consultation, the parties fail to settle the dispute through consultation, or a party does not execute a reached settlement agreement, any party may apply to a mediation organization for mediation; if a party does not desire a mediation, the parties fail to settle the dispute through mediation, or a party does not execute a reached mediation agreement, any party may apply to a labor dispute arbitration commission for arbitration; and a party disagreeing to an arbitral award may bring an action in the people's court except as otherwise provided for by this Law.

Article 6 Where a labor dispute arises, a party shall be responsible for adducing evidence to back up its claims. Where the evidence related to the disputed matter is controlled by an employer, the employer shall provide it; and the employer who fails to provide the evidence shall bear the adverse consequences.

Article 7 Where a labor dispute involves more than ten employees and the employees have the same claim, they may recommend their representatives to participate in the mediation, arbitration, or litigation.

Article 8 In conjunction with the trade unions and enterprise representatives, the labor administrative authority of the people's government at or above the county level shall establish a tri-party labor mechanism for coordinating the labor relations, and jointly study and address major issues related to the labor dispute.

Article 9 Where an employer, in violation of state provisions, delays paying or fails to pay in full the labor remunerations, or delays paying the medical expenses for a work-related injury, economic indemnity, or compensation, an employee may complain about it to the labor administrative authority and the labor administrative authority shall deal with it according to law.

Chapter II   Mediation

Article 10   Where a labor dispute arises, a party may apply to any of the following mediation organizations for mediation:

(1) Labor dispute mediation committee of an enterprise;
(2) Grassroots people's mediation organization legally established; and
(3) Organization with the labor dispute mediation function established in a township or neighborhood community.

A labor dispute mediation committee of an enterprise shall comprise the employee representatives and enterprise representatives. The employee representatives shall be members of the trade union or persons recommended by all employees, while the enterprise representatives shall be designated by the person in charge of the enterprise. The chairman of a labor dispute mediation committee of an enterprise shall be a member of the trade union or a person recommended by both parties.

Article 11   A mediator of a labor dispute mediation organization shall be an adult citizen who is fair, decent, connected with the people, and enthusiastic for the mediation work and has a certain level of knowledge of law, policy, and culture.

Article 12   A party may apply for a labor dispute mediation in writing or verbally. For a verbal application, a mediation organization shall record, on the spot, the basic information on the applicant, disputed matters for which the party applies for mediation, the reasons for application for mediation, and the time of application for mediation.

Article 13   In labor dispute mediation, the statements of facts and reasons by both parties shall be fully heard and the parties shall be guided patiently by a mediator so as to help them reach an agreement.

Article 14   Where an agreement is reached through mediation, a mediation agreement paper shall be made.

A mediation agreement paper shall be signed or sealed by both parties, and take effect after the mediator signs it and the seal of the mediation organization is affixed thereon, which shall be binding upon both parties and executed by the parties.

Where a mediation agreement is not reached within 15 days after a labor dispute mediation organization receives a mediation application, a party may apply for arbitration according to law.

Article 15   Where, after a mediation agreement is reached, one party fails to execute the mediation agreement within the period of time prescribed in the agreement, the other party may apply for arbitration according to law.

Article 16 Where a mediation agreement is reached on a matter of delayed payment of labor remunerations, medical expenses for a work-related injury, economic indemnity, or compensation, and the employer fails to execute it within the period of time prescribed in the agreement, the employee may apply to the people's court for a payment order based on the mediation agreement, and the people's court shall issue a payment order according to law.

Chapter III   Arbitration

Section I   Common Provisions

Article 17 The labor dispute arbitration commissions shall be established on the principles of full planning, reasonable layout, and adaptation to the practical needs. The people's government of a province or autonomous region may decide to establish the arbitration commissions in cities and counties; the people's government of the municipality directly under the Central Government may decide to establish them in districts and counties. One or more labor dispute arbitration commissions may also be established in a municipality directly under the Central Government or a city with districts. The labor dispute arbitration commissions shall not be established level by level according to administrative divisions.

Article 18 The labor administrative authority of the State Council shall make arbitration rules according to the relevant provisions of this Law. The labor administrative authorities of provinces, autonomous regions, and municipalities directly under the Central Government shall guide the labor dispute arbitration work within their respective administrative regions.

Article 19 A labor dispute arbitration commission shall comprise the representatives of the labor administrative authority, representatives of trade unions, and representatives of enterprises. The members of a labor dispute arbitration commission shall be in odd numbers.

A labor dispute arbitration commission shall perform the following functions:

(1) Retaining and dismissing full-time or part-time arbitrators;
(2) Accepting and hearing labor dispute cases;
(3) Discussing major or difficult labor dispute cases; and
(4) Overseeing arbitration activities.

A labor dispute arbitration commission shall set up a general office to be responsible for the daily work of the labor dispute arbitration commission.

Article 20 A labor dispute arbitration commission shall maintain a panel of arbitrators.

An arbitrator shall be fair and decent and satisfy any of the following requirements:

(1) Once serving as a judge;
(2) Engaging in legal research or teaching work with a professional title at or above the medium level;
(3) Having knowledge of law and engaging in human resource management or trade union or other professional work for five years; or
(4) Having practiced law as a lawyer for three years.

Article 21 A labor dispute arbitration commission shall be responsible for the labor disputes occurring within its jurisdiction.

A labor dispute arbitration commission at the place of performance of a labor contract or at the place of residence of an employer shall have jurisdiction of a labor dispute. Where the two parties respectively apply to the labor dispute arbitration commissions at the place of performance of a labor contract and at the place of residence of an employer for arbitration, the labor dispute arbitration commission at the place of performance of a labor contract shall have jurisdiction.

Article 22 An employee and an employer, between which a labor dispute arises, shall be the two parties in a labor dispute arbitration case.

Where a dispute arises between a labor dispatch entity or employer and an employee, the labor dispatch entity and employer shall be the joint party.

Article 23 A third party that has an interest relationship with the results of handling of a labor dispute case may apply for participation in the arbitration activities or be notified by the labor dispute arbitration commission to participate in the arbitration activities.

Article 24 A party may appoint an attorney to participate in the arbitration activities. A party who appoints an attorney to participate in the arbitration activities shall submit to the labor dispute arbitration commission a Power of Attorney signed or sealed by the party, and the Power of Attorney shall expressly state the authorized matters and powers.

Article 25 The legal representative of an employee who has lost all or part of his or her capacity of conduct in civil law shall participate in the arbitration activities on behalf of the employee; and where such an employee does not have a legal representative, the labor dispute arbitration commission shall designate a representative for the employee. For a deceased employee, the close relative or attorney of the deceased employee shall participate in the arbitration activities.

Article 26 The labor dispute arbitration shall be conducted openly, except one that shall not be conducted openly as agreed on by the parties or involves a national secret, trade secret, or personal privacy.

Section II Application and Acceptance

Article 27 The time limitation period for application for arbitration of a labor dispute shall be one year. The time limitation period for arbitration shall be counted as of the date when a party knows or should know that its right has been violated.

The time limitation period prescribed in the preceding paragraph shall be discontinued upon one party's claiming a right against the other party or requesting a right's remedy to the relevant authority or the other party's agreeing to perform an obligation. The time limitation period shall be recounted from the time of the interruption.

Where for a *force majeure* or any other proper reason a party cannot apply for arbitration within the time limitation period for arbitration prescribed in the first paragraph hereof, the time limitation period for arbitration shall be suspended. The time limitation period for arbitration shall continue being counted at the date when the reason for suspension of the time limitation period disappears.

Where a dispute arises from the delayed payment of labor remunerations during the period of existence of a labor relationship, an employee's application for arbitration shall not be subject to the time limitation period for arbitration prescribed in the first paragraph hereof; but if a labor relationship is terminated, an employee shall apply for arbitration within one year as of the date of termination of the labor relationship.

Article 28 To apply for arbitration, an applicant shall submit a written application for arbitration and copies thereof as per the number of respondents.

The written arbitration for arbitration shall expressly state the following matters:

(1) Name, gender, age, occupation, work unit and residence of an employee, name and residence of an employer, and names and titles of the legal representative or principal of an employer;
(2) Arbitral claims and supporting facts and reasons; and
(3) Evidence, sources of evidence, and names and residences of witnesses.

Where a party has difficulty in writing an application for arbitration, the party may apply for arbitration verbally, and a labor dispute arbitration commission shall record it in writing and notify the other party.

Article 29 Within five days of receiving an application for arbitration, the labor dispute arbitration commission, if considering that the requirements for acceptance are satisfied, shall accept the application and notify the applicant; or if considering that the requirements for acceptance are not satisfied, shall notify the applicant in writing of the rejection of the application and explain the reasons. Where a labor dispute arbitration commission decides not to accept an application for arbitration or fails to make a decision before the prescribed time limit, an applicant may bring an action in the people's court for matters on the labor dispute.

Article 30 Within five days after accepting an application for arbitration, the labor dispute arbitration commission shall serve a copy of the written application for arbitration on a respondent.

Within ten days after receiving a copy of the written application for arbitration, a respondent shall submit a statement of defense to the labor dispute arbitration commission. Within five days after receiving the statement of defense, the labor dispute arbitration commission shall submit a copy of the statement of defense to the applicant. The failure of a respondent to submit a statement of defense shall not affect the conduct of arbitration procedures.

Section III   Tribunal Hearing and Awarding

Article 31 The arbitral tribunal system shall be adopted for a labor dispute arbitration commission to decide labor dispute cases. An arbitral tribunal shall comprise three arbitrators, including a chief arbitrator. A simple labor dispute case may be arbitrated by a sole arbitrator.

Article 32 A labor dispute arbitration commission shall notify the parties in writing of information on the composition of an arbitral tribunal within five days after the date of accepting an application for arbitration.

Article 33 Under any of the following circumstances, an arbitrator shall recuse himself or herself, and a party shall have the right to apply for recusal verbally or in writing:

(1) Being a party in the case or a close relative of a party or attorney thereof;
(2) Having an interest relationship with the case;
(3) Having any other relationship with a party or attorney thereof in the case, which may affect the rendering of a fair award; or
(4) Meeting in private a party or attorney thereof, or accepting a treat or gift from a party or attorney thereof.

A labor dispute arbitration commission shall timely make a decision on an application for recusal and notify the party verbally or in writing of its decision.

Article 34 Where an arbitrator is under the circumstance of Article 33 (4) of this Law, asks for or accepts bribes, practices favoritism for personal gain, or renders an award by perverting the law, such an arbitrator shall bear the legal liability according to law. A labor dispute arbitration commission shall dismiss such an arbitrator.

Article 35 An arbitral tribunal shall notify both parties of the date and place of hearing at least five days before a hearing. For proper reasons, a party may request the postponement of a hearing at least three days before a hearing. Whether a hearing shall be postponed shall be decided by a labor dispute arbitration commission.

Article 36 Where after receiving a written notice an applicant refuses to participate in a hearing without proper reasons or withdraws in the midst of a hearing without the permit of the arbitral tribunal, the applicant shall be deemed as having dropped the application for arbitration.

Where after receiving a written notice a respondent refuses to participate in a hearing without proper reasons or withdraws in the midst of a hearing without the permit of the arbitral tribunal, an award may be rendered in the absence of the respondent.

Article 37 Where an arbitral tribunal considers that an authentication is necessary for a specialized matter, the arbitral tribunal may delegate the authentication of the specialized matter to an authentication agency as agreed on by the parties; or where the parties do not have or cannot reach an agreement on it, the authentication shall be conducted by an authentication agency designated by the arbitral tribunal.

At the request of a party or as required by an arbitral tribunal, an authentication agency shall send the authenticators to participate in the hearing. With the permit of the arbitral tribunal, the parties may question the authenticators.

Article 38 The parties shall have the right to cross-examination and debate in the process of arbitration. At the end of cross-examination or debate, the chief arbitrator or sole arbitrator shall hear the final statements of both parties.

Article 39 The arbitral tribunal shall invoke evidence that is adduced by the parties and has been found to be true as the basis for determining facts.

Where an employee cannot adduce any evidence that is related to an arbitral claim but controlled by an employer, an arbitral tribunal may require the employer to provide it within a specified period of time. An employer that fails to provide it within the specified period of time shall bear the adverse consequences.

Article 40 All arbitral tribunals shall maintain written records of hearings. A party or any other arbitration participant, considering that there is any omission or mistake in the record of its statements, shall have the right to apply for correction. If the record is not corrected, such an application for correction shall be recorded.

The written record shall be signed or sealed by the arbitrators, recorder, parties, and other arbitration participants.

Article 41 After a party applies for arbitration of a labor dispute, the two parties may reach a settlement on their own. Where a settlement agreement is reached, the application for arbitration may be dropped.

Article 42 Before rendering an award, an arbitral tribunal shall conduct mediation first.

Where an agreement is reached through mediation, an arbitral tribunal shall make a mediation record.

A mediation record shall expressly state the arbitral claims and results of agreement by the parties. A mediation record shall be signed by the arbitrators, on which the seal of the labor dispute arbitration commission shall be affixed, and served on both parties. A mediation record shall take effect after being signed by both parties.

Where mediation fails or one party regrets before a mediation record is served, an arbitral tribunal shall timely render an award.

Article 43 The arbitral tribunal shall render an award for each labor dispute case within 45 days of the date when an application for arbitration is accepted by a labor dispute arbitration commission. Where a case is complicated and requires an extension of the above-prescribed period of time, with the approval of the chairman of a labor dispute arbitration commission, extension may be made and shall be notified in writing to the parties, but the period of extension shall not exceed 15 days. Where an arbitral tribunal fails to render an award before the above or extended period of time, a party may bring an action in the people's court for the labor dispute matters.

When rendering an award in a labor dispute case, the arbitral tribunal may first render an award on the part of facts that have been ascertained.

Article 44 For a case of recovery of the labor remunerations, medical expenses for a work-related injury, economic indemnity, or compensation, upon an application of a party, an arbitral tribunal may render an award of prior execution, and transfer the case to the people's court for execution.

The following requirements shall be satisfied for an arbitral tribunal to render an award of prior execution:

(1) The relationships of rights and obligations between the parties are clear; and
(2) Without prior execution, the living of an applicant will be seriously affected.

An employee applying for prior execution may not provide a security.

Article 45 An arbitral award shall be rendered according to the majority opinions of the arbitrators, and the dissenting opinion of a minority arbitrator shall be recorded in writing. Where an arbitral tribunal fails to form the opinions of a majority, the arbitral award shall be rendered according to the opinion of the chief arbitrator.

Article 46 An arbitral award shall expressly state the arbitral claims, disputed facts, reasons for rendering an award, result of rendering an award, and date of rendering an award. An arbitral award shall be signed by the arbitrators, on which the seal of the labor dispute arbitration commission shall be affixed. An arbitrator with a dissenting opinion on the award may or may not sign the award.

Article 47 Except as otherwise provided for by this Law, an arbitral award on any of the following labor disputes shall be final, and an arbitral award shall take effect at the date of rendering of the award:

(1) A dispute over the recovery of labor remunerations, medical expenses for a work-related injury, economic indemnity, or compensation, in an amount not exceeding the 12-month local monthly minimum wage level; and
(2) A dispute over the working hours, breaks and vacations, social insurance, etc., arising from the execution of state labor standards.

Article 48 An employee who disagrees with an arbitral award as provided for in Article 47 of this Law may bring an action in the people's court within 15 days after receiving an arbitral award.

Article 49 An employer that has evidence to prove that an arbitral award as provided for in Article 47 of this Law is rendered under any of the following circumstances may apply for revocation of the arbitral award to the intermediate people's court at the place of residence of the labor dispute arbitration commission within 30 days after receiving the arbitral award:

(1) An arbitral award is wrong in the application of a law or administrative regulation;
(2) The labor dispute arbitration commission has no jurisdiction;
(3) The legal procedure is violated;
(4) The evidence used to render the arbitral award is forged;
(5) The other party has concealed evidence that is enough to affect the rendering of a fair award; and
(6) An arbitrator in arbitrating the case asks for or accepts bribes, practices favoritism for personal gain, or renders an award by perverting law.

After a formed collegiate bench has examined and verified that an arbitral award is under any of the circumstances in the preceding paragraph, the people's court shall rule to revoke the arbitral award.

Where the people's court rules to revoke an arbitral award, a party may bring an action in the people's court for the labor dispute matters within 15 days after receiving a ruling paper.

Article 50 A party who disagrees with an arbitral award in any labor dispute case other than one as provided for in Article 47 of this Law may bring an action in the people's court within 15 days after receiving an arbitral award; and where an action is not brought upon the expiration of the above-prescribed period of time, an arbitral award shall take effect.

Article 51 A party shall execute an effective mediation record or arbitral award according to the prescribed period of time. Where one party fails to execute the same before the prescribed period of time, the other party may apply for execution to the people's court according to the relevant provisions of the Civil Procedure Law. The people's court accepting the application shall execute the same according to law.

Chapter IV   Supplementary Provisions

Article 52 This Law shall apply to a labor dispute arising between a public institution that adopts an employment system and a staffer thereof, except as otherwise provided for by a law or administrative regulation or the provisions of the State Council.

Article 53 No fees shall be charged for the labor dispute arbitration. The funds of a labor dispute arbitration commission shall be secured by the finance authority.

Article 54 This Law shall be effective as of May 1, 2008.

5. Employment Promotion Law of the People's Republic of China

Order of the President (No. 70)

The Employment Promotion Law of the People's Republic of China, which was adopted at the 29th session of the Standing Committee of the Tenth National People's Congress of the People's Republic of China on August 30, 2007, is hereby promulgated and shall come into force as of January 1, 2008.

President of the People's Republic of China, Hu Jintao

August 30, 2007

(Adopted at the 29th session of the Standing Committee of the Tenth National People's Congress on August 30, 2007)

Table of Contents

Chapter I   General Provisions

Article 1 This law is enacted to promote employment, promote positive interaction between economic development and increase of employment, and promote the harmony and stability of society.

Article 2 The state highlights the increase of employment in the development of the economy and society, implements active employment policies, upholds the guiding principles of workers choosing their own jobs and the market regulating employment and the government promoting employment, and increases employment through multiple channels.

Article 3 Workers shall have the right to equal employment and to choose jobs on their own initiative in accordance with the law.

Workers seeking employment shall not be subject to discrimination based on factors such as ethnicity, race, gender, religious belief, etc.

Article 4 The people's governments at and above the county level shall regard the increase of employment as an important goal for the development of the economy and social development, integrate it in the plan on development of the national economy and society, and work out medium- and long-term plans and annual work plans on promoting the increase of employment.

Article 5 The people's governments at and above the county level shall create employment conditions and increase employment by taking measures such as developing the economy, adjusting the industrial structure, regulating the market of human resources, improving employment services, strengthening vocational education and training, and providing employment aid, etc.

Article 6 The State Council shall establish a coordination mechanism for employment promotion work throughout the country, study the significant problems in employment work, and coordinate and push forward the employment promotion work throughout the country. The labor administrative department of State Council shall be responsible for the specific employment promotion work throughout the country.

The people's government of each province, autonomous region, or municipality directly under the Central Government shall, according to the needs of employment promotion work, establish a coordination mechanism for the employment promotion work and coordinate and solve the significant problems in the employment work in its own administrative area.

The relevant departments of the people's government at or above the county level shall, under their respective functions, make joint efforts to accomplish the employment promotion work.

Article 7 The state encourages workers to form a correct concept of job selection, to enhance their employment and business start-up capabilities, start up businesses independently, and employ themselves.

The people's governments at all levels and the pertinent departments shall simplify procedures and increase efficiency so as to make it easier for workers to start up businesses independently and employ themselves.

Article 8 An employer is entitled to enjoy the right to hire workers on its own initiative in pursuance of the law.

An employer shall guarantee the legitimate rights and interests of workers in accordance with this Law, other laws, and regulations.

Article 9 The labor unions, communist youth leagues, women's federations, the disabled persons' federations, and other social organizations shall assist the people's governments to carry out the employment promotion work and protect the workers' working rights.

Article 10 The people's governments at all levels and the pertinent departments shall commend and reward those entities and individuals who have made outstanding achievements in the employment promotion work.

Chapter II   Policy Support

Article 11 The people's governments at and above the county level shall regard the increase of employment as their important duty and uniformly coordinate the industrial policies and employment policies.

Article 12 The state encourages various enterprises to create more jobs by launching new enterprises or expanding businesses within the range as prescribed by laws and regulations.

The state encourages the development of labor-intensive industries and the service industry and supports medium and small enterprises so as to increase jobs through multiple channels and by diversified means.

The state encourages, supports, and directs the development of the nonpublic economy so as to increase employment and create more jobs.

Article 13 The state develops trade both home and abroad as well as international economic cooperation so as to increase more employment channels.

Article 14 When the people's government at or above the county level arranges a government investment or decides on an important construction project, it shall make the investment or the important construction project play the roles of driving up the employment and creating more jobs.

Article 15 The state implements fiscal policies that are helpful to the promotion of employment, allocates more funds, and improves the employment environment so as to increase employment.

The people's government at or above the county level shall, according to the employment situation and the goal of employment work, make its fiscal budget include an exclusive employment fund for employment promotion.

The exclusive employment fund shall be used as subsidies for job recommendation, vocational training, posts for the public good, assessment of occupational skills, special employment policies, social insurances, etc., as guaranty fund for small loans and discounted interests on small guaranty loans for minor-profit projects; and be used for supporting the public employment services. The administrative measures for uses of the exclusive employment fund shall be formulated by the finance department and the labor administrative department of the State Council.

Article 16 The state shall establish a sound unemployment insurance system so as to ensure the basic living of unemployed persons and promote their employment.

<u>Article 17</u> The state encourages enterprises to create more jobs and support unemployed persons and disabled persons to get jobs, and offers tax preferential treatments to the following enterprises and persons:

(1) Enterprises that meet the requirement for offering jobs to unemployed persons who satisfy the conditions as prescribed by the state;
(2) Medium and small enterprises set up by unemployed persons;
(3) Enterprises that meet the prescribed rate of offering jobs to disabled persons, or that use disabled persons in a centralized manner;
(4) Unemployed persons engaging in individual industrial and commercial households and meeting the conditions as prescribed by the state;
(5) Disabled persons engaging in individual industrial and commercial households; and
(6) Other enterprises and persons entitled to enjoy tax preferential treatments under provisions of the State Council.

<u>Article 18</u> For the persons as mentioned in Article 17 (4) and (5) of this Law, the relevant departments shall give favorable consideration in such aspects as business site, etc., and shall exempt them from administrative fees.

<u>Article 19</u> The state shall adopt financial policies helpful to the promotion of employment, increase financing channels for medium and small enterprises, encourage the financial institutions to improve financial services, give medium and small enterprises more loans, and provide, within a certain time limit, small loans to persons who start up businesses independently.

<u>Article 20</u> The state shall implement employment policies under an overall urban and rural plan, establish a sound system for equal employment of urban and rural workers, and direct the transfer of employment of the excessive labor force of rural areas in an orderly manner.

The local people's governments at and above the county level shall push forward the construction of small towns, accelerate the economic development of county areas, and direct the excessive labor force of rural areas to find jobs at their own localities or near their own localities. When creating plans for small towns, they should regard the transfer of employment of the excessive labor force of their respective areas as an important component.

The local people's governments at and above the county level shall direct the excessive labor force of rural areas to transfer to different urban places to get jobs in an orderly manner. The people's governments of the labor force moving-in areas and moving-out areas shall cooperate with each other so as to improve the environment and conditions for employment of rural workers entering into cities.

Article 21 The state supports the development of the regional economy, encourages regional cooperation, and coordinates the balanced increase of employment in different areas.

The state backs ethnic minority areas to develop economy and increase employment.

Article 22 The people's governments at all levels shall do a good job in the employment of the newly increasing urban and rural labor force, the transfer of employment of the excessive labor force of rural areas, as well as the employment of unemployed persons.

Article 23 The people's governments at all levels shall take measures to gradually improve and implement such flexible labor and social insurance policies as part-time employment so as to provide help and services to employees under flexible employment.

Article 24 The local people's governments and the pertinent departments at all levels shall intensify the guidance to unemployed persons in engaging in individual industrial and commercial households, and provide them with such services as policy consultation, vocational training, and instructions on starting business.

Chapter III   Fair Employment

Article 25 The people's governments at all levels shall create an environment for fair employment, eliminate employment discrimination, and formulate policies and take measures to support and aid the people who are finding it difficult to get a job.

Article 26 When an employer recruits employees, or when a job intermediary agency engages in job intermediary activities, it shall provide workers with equal employment opportunities and fair employment conditions and shall not have any employment discrimination.

Article 27 The state shall ensure that women enjoy labor rights equal to those of men.

When an employer recruits employees, it shall not refuse to recruit women or increase the thresholds for recruitment of women under the excuse of gender.

When an employer recruits female employees, it shall not stipulate in the employment contract any content that restricts female employees from getting married or bearing a child.

Article 28 Workers of all ethnic groups enjoy equal labor rights.

When an employer recruits employees, it shall give appropriate consideration to workers of ethnic minorities.

Article 29 The state shall guarantee the employment rights of disabled persons.

The people's governments at all levels shall make an overall plan on the employment of disabled persons so as to create employment conditions for disabled persons.

When an employer recruits employees, it shall not discriminate against disabled persons.

Article 30 When an employer recruits employees, it shall not refuse to recruit any person under the excuse that he is a carrier of an infectious disease. However, before a carrier of an infectious disease is confirmed upon medical test that he is cured or excluded from the possibility of spreading the disease, he shall not take up the jobs in which he is likely to spread the disease and which are prohibited in laws and administrative regulations and by the health administrative department of the State Council.

Article 31 Rural workers who go to cities in search of employment shall enjoy labor rights equal to those of urban workers. It is prohibited to set discriminatory restrictions against rural workers seeking employment in cities.

Chapter IV   Employment Services and Management

Article 32 The people's governments at and above the county level shall foster and improve uniform, open, competitive, and orderly human resource markets to provide employment services to workers.

Article 33 The people's governments at and above the county level shall encourage all walks of life to carry out employment service activities, strengthen the guidance and supervision over the public employment services and job intermediary services, and gradually improve an employment service system covering urban and rural areas.

Article 34 The people's governments at and above the county level shall intensify the construction of information networks and relevant facilities of human resource markets, establish a sound information service system for human resource markets, and improve the rules on announcing market information.

Article 35 The people's governments at and above the county level shall establish a sound public employment service system and set up public employment service agencies to provide the following gratuitous services to workers:

(1) Offering consultation on employment policies and regulations;
(2) Announcing information about supply and demand of jobs, guiding market wages, and vocational training;

(3) Offering vocational guides and job recommendations;
(4) Offering aid to persons who are having difficulty finding a job;
(5) Handling the register of employment and unemployment, as well as other affairs; and
(6) Other public employment services.

A public employment service institution shall incessantly improve the quality and efficiency of services. It shall not engage in any commercial activity.

The operating funds for public employment services shall be included in the fiscal budget at the same level.

Article 36 The people's governments at and above the county level shall, under the relevant provisions, give subsidies to job intermediary agencies, which provide public good employment services.

The state encourages all walks of life to provide donations and aid for non-profit employment services.

Article 37 No local people's government or pertinent department may set up any job intermediary agency for a commercial purpose or do so jointly with others.

No fee may be charged to workers at job fairs held by local people's governments at all levels and by public employment service agencies.

Article 38 The people's governments at and above the county level and pertinent departments shall strengthen the administration of job intermediary agencies and encourage them to improve their service quality and play their roles in the promotion of employment.

Article 39 The principles of lawfulness, good faith, fairness, and openness shall be observed when engaging in job intermediary activities.

When an employer recruits employees via a job intermediary agency, it shall faithfully furnish the job intermediary agency with the information about the posts it supplies. It is forbidden for any organization or individual to impair the legitimate rights and interests of workers by taking advantage of job intermediary activities.

Article 40 To establish a job intermediary agency, the following conditions shall be satisfied:

(1) Having express articles of association and management rules;
(2) Having a fixed business site, office facilities, and a certain sum of start-up capital, which are essential to carry out businesses;
(3) Having a particular number of full-time employees, who have corresponding occupational qualifications; and
(4) Other conditions as prescribed by laws and regulations.

To establish a job intermediary agency, an administrative license shall be applied for in pursuance of law. A licensed job intermediary agency shall go through the registration formalities in the industrial and commercial administrative department.

Any institution without a license and registration shall not engage in job intermediary activities.

If the state provides otherwise for foreign-funded job intermediary agencies and those job intermediary agencies offering overseas employment services, such provisions of the state shall prevail.

Article 41 No job intermediary agency may

(1) provide false employment information;
(2) offer job intermediary services to any employer without a lawful license;
(3) counterfeit, alter, or transfer to others its job intermediary agency license;
(4) detain workers' resident identity cards and other certificates, or charge a deposit against workers; or
(5) conduct other acts in violation of any law or regulation.

Article 42 The people's governments at and above the county level shall establish an unemployment pre-warning system so as to prevent, adjust, and control cases of larger-scale unemployment, which are likely to appear.

Article 43 The state shall establish a labor force investigation and statistical system and a register of employment and unemployment so as to investigate into and collect statistics of resources of the labor force, as well as the status of employment and unemployment, and announce the investigation and statistical results.

When statistical departments and labor administrative departments investigate and collect statistics of the labor force, and register the employment and unemployment, employers and individuals shall faithfully provide the information required for the investigation, statistics, and registration.

Chapter V   Vocational Education and Training

Article 44 The state shall develop vocational education in pursuance of the law, encourage vocational training, promote workers to improve their vocational skills, and enhance their employment capabilities and business start-up capabilities.

Article 45 The people's governments at and above the county level shall, according to the economic and social development and market demands, make and execute plans on the development of vocational capabilities.

Article 46 The people's governments at and above the county level shall intensify the coordination under a uniform plan; encourage and support various vocational colleges and schools, job skills training institutions, and employers to carry out pre-employment training, on-the-job training, re-employment training and business start-up training; and encourage workers to participate in various forms of training.

Article 47 The local people's governments at and above the county level and the pertinent departments shall, according to the market demands and the direction of industrial development, encourage and direct enterprises to strengthen the vocational education and training.

Vocational colleges and schools and vocational skills training institutions shall keep in close contact with enterprises, combine teaching with production, serve economic development, and foster practical talents and skillful workers.

An enterprise shall make a provision of the operating fund for education of employees so as to offer to workers vocational skills training and continuing education.

Article 48 The state shall take measures to establish a sound labor preparation system. The local people's governments at and above the county level shall offer a certain time period of vocational education and training to junior middle school and high school graduates so as to make them obtain corresponding vocational qualifications or grasp specific vocational skills.

Article 49 The local people's governments at all levels shall encourage and support employment training, help unemployed persons to improve their vocational skills, and improve their employment capabilities and business start-up capabilities. Where an unemployed person participates in an employment training, he is entitled to enjoy the government training subsidies.

Article 50 The local people's governments at all levels shall take effective measures to direct and guide the rural workers seeking jobs in cities to participate in skills training and encourage various training institutions to provide skills training to rural workers seeking jobs in cities so as to enhance their employment capabilities and business start-up capabilities.

Article 51 The states adopt a vocational qualification license system for workers engaging in special jobs such as those relating to the public safety, personal health, safety of life and property, etc. The concrete measures shall be formulated by the State Council.

Chapter VI   Employment Aids

Article 52 The people's governments at all levels shall establish a sound employment aid system and give priority to supporting and helping the persons who are having difficulty finding a job and by taking such measures as exemption and deduction of taxes and fees, discount interest loans, social insurance subsidies, post subsidies, and by offering them public good posts.

The term "persons having difficulty finding a job" refers to those persons who could not find a job for health, skill level, family factors, loss of land, or any other reason, or who still could not find a job after continuous unemployment for a certain time period. The specific range of persons having difficulty finding a job shall be prescribed by the people's government of each province, autonomous region, or municipality directly under the Central Government according to the actual situation of its respective administrative area.

Article 53 For the public good posts invested in and developed by the government, the persons having difficulty finding a job shall be given a priority to such posts if they meet the relevant requirements. Those who are offered public good posts shall be given post subsidies under the pertinent provisions of the state.

Article 54 The local people's governments at all levels shall strengthen the grassroots employment aiding services so as to lay an emphasis on the help to persons having difficulty finding a job and offer targeted employment services and public welfare positions.

The local people's governments encourage and support all walks of life to provide skills training, post related, information, and other services to persons having difficulty finding a job.

Article 55 The people's governments at all levels shall take special support measures to promote the employment of disabled persons.

An employer shall arrange the employment of disabled persons under provisions of the state. The concrete measures shall be formulated by the State Council.

Article 56 The local people's governments at and above the county level shall, by adopting diversified employment forms, expand the range of public good posts and develop posts so as to ensure that at least one member gets a job in each urban family that needs employment.

For a family of urban residents in which all family members within the statutory labor age are unemployed, it may apply for employment aid to the public employment service institution of the local subdistrict or community. If it is true upon verification, the public employment service institution of the local subdistrict or community shall provide a proper job to at least one member of this family.

Article 57 The state encourages resource exploitation in cities and independent industrial and mining areas to develop industries catering to the market demands and to direct workers to change jobs.

For an area in which there is a large cluster of persons who are having difficulty finding a job due to exhaustion of resources or economic structure adjustment, the people's government at the superior level shall give them appropriate support and help.

Chapter VII   Supervision and Inspection

Article 58 The people's governments at all levels and pertinent departments shall establish a target responsibility system for promotion of employment. The people's government at or above the county level shall, under the requirements of the target responsibility system, evaluate and supervise the performances of its subsidiaries and the people's governments at the next inferior level.

Article 59 The audit organs and finance departments shall supervise and inspect the management and use of special employment funds in accordance with law.

Article 60 The labor administrative department shall supervise and inspect the implementation of this Law, establish an exposure system and accept exposures of violations of this Law, and timely verify and handle such violations.

Chapter VIII   Legal Liabilities

Article 61 Where the labor administrative department or any other relevant department or any of its functionaries violates this Law by abusing his power, neglecting his duties, or seeking private interests, the directly liable person-in-charge and other directly liable persons shall be given a sanction according to law.

Article 62 For anyone who violates this Law due to employment discrimination, workers may lodge a lawsuit in the people's court.

Article 63 Where the people's government or relevant department or public employment service institution violates this Law by establishing any job intermediary agency for commercial purposes or engaging in job intermediary activities for commercial purposes or charging workers any fee, the superior administrative organ shall order it to make a correction within a time limit, refund to workers the fee illegally charged, and give a sanction to the directly liable person-in-charge and other directly liable persons.

Article 64 For anyone who violates this Law by illegally engaging in job intermediary activities without license or registration, the labor administrative department or other administrative departments shall shut it down. If it has any illegal gains, the illegal gains shall be confiscated and it shall be fined not less than 10,000 yuan but not more than 50,000 yuan.

Article 65 Where a job intermediary agency violates this Law by providing any false employment information, or providing employment intermediary services to any employer without a lawful license or certificate, or forging, altering, or transferring to others its intermediary agency license, the labor administrative department or other administrative departments shall order it to make a correction. If there are any illegal gains, it shall confiscate the illegal gains and fine the violator not less than 10,000 yuan but not more than 50,000 yuan. If the circumstance is severe, it shall revoke the job intermediary agency license.

Article 66 Where a job intermediary agency violates this Law by detaining the resident identity cards or other certificates of workers, the labor administrative department shall order it to return them to the workers and shall punish it in pursuance of relevant laws.

Where a job intermediary agency violates this Law by charging workers any deposit, the labor administrative department shall order it to make a refund to the workers and shall fine it at a rate of not less than 500 yuan but not more than 2,000 yuan per person.

Article 67 Where any enterprise violates this Law by failing to make a provision of the operating fund for education of employees or by misappropriating the operating fund for the education of employees, the labor administrative department shall order it to make a correction, and it shall be punished in accordance with law.

Article 68 For anyone who violates this Law by impairing the legitimate rights and interests of workers and causing property losses or other damage, he shall bear civil liabilities. If any crime is committed, he shall be subject to criminal liabilities.

Chapter IX   Supplementary Provisions

Article 69 This Law shall come into force as of January 1, 2008.

Index

arbitration of cases, 101–102
disability or health condition, based on (*See*
    Disability or health condition,
    discrimination based on)
enforcement of laws, 101–102
ethnicity, based on, 83–86
gender, based on. *See* Gender,
    discrimination based on
height, based on, 100–101
maternity, based on, 75, 78
migrant workers, against, 86–91
race, based on, 83–86
recruitment of employees, in, 67
religious belief, based on, 91–92
sexual harassment, 75, 81–83
social origin, based on, 87
unprotected categories, 99–101
Disparate economic impacts, 6–12
Disparities in wages. *See* Wages and hours
Dispatched employees
    hiring practices, 71
    illustrative cases, 196
    individual contracts, 39
    injury compensation, 117–118
Dispute resolution, 168–183
    arbitration. *See* Arbitration
    collective negotiations, in, 57, 61–62
      illustrative contracts, 248–250
    FIEs, involving, 170
    legal regulation, 168–171
    litigation, 180–183
    mediation, 5–6, 171–172, 178, 180
    regional disparities in, 170
    SOEs, involving, 170
    statistics, 169–170, 173, 180
    wages and hours, 132

Economic development
    labor reform, balancing with, 3–4
    migrant workers and, 6
    wage disparities and, 6–12
Eleventh Five-Year Plan, 17
E-mail, 73
Employing units, 25
Employment Promotion Law (EPL)
    administration of, 17
    disability or health condition,
      discrimination based on, 92, 96, 98
    discrimination, prohibition against, 76–77
    economic development, in context of, 5
    enforcement, 101

    injury compensation under, 117
    litigation under, 182
    migrant workers, discrimination against, 30,
      86, 89, 91
    promotion of employment under, 65–66,
      68–69
    race or ethnicity, discrimination based on,
      84
    text of, 310–321
Employment relationships, 23–35
    administrative employees, 33
    application of law, 24–25
    civil servants, 32
    contingent workers, 30
    de facto relationships, 25
    defining, 23–25
    employees, 29–31
    employers, 25–29
    employing units, 25
    enterprises, 25–26
    exclusions, 31–33
    executive employees, 33
    exemptions, 33–35
    illegal employers, 27
    illustrative cases, 196–198
    independent contractors, 30, 32
    individual economic organizations, 26
    managers, 34
    migrant workers, 30–32
    multiple employers, 156
    overseas workers, 33
    part-time workers, 30
    professional employees, 33
    public organizations, 26
    representative offices, 28
    state organs, 26
    statistics, 24
    students, 35
    workforce profile, 23–24
Enforcement of laws
    discrimination, 101–102
    injury compensation, 121–124
    minimum wages, 125
    safety and health protection, 18, 110–111, 113
    wages and hours, 132
Enterprise Bankruptcy Law, 158
Enterprises, 25–26
EPL. *See* Employment Promotion Law (EPL)
Ethnicity, discrimination based on, 83–86
Evidence in arbitration, 177
Executive employees, 33